Activist, historian, columnist and writer, widower and father of three, customs officer and teacher in his earlier life, left T&T in 1967 to pursue studies in history and political sciences at Sir George Williams University (now Concordia) in Montreal, Canada. In 1969, he was jailed and then expelled along with other Black Caribbean students and 49 white Canadian students. He has refused since to attend any university. He co-founded and edited UHURU, a Montreal Black Community newspaper. On his return to T&T, he co-founded and led the New Beginning Movement and edited its newspaper, New Beginning. From 1978 to 1983 he edited vanguard, the Organ of the OWTU. He continues to research and write.

This book *Mettle and Metal -The Birth of Steel Pan Music and the Story of Trinidad All Stars Steel Orchestra* is dedicated to Neville Jules and to the hope that never again in the history of T&T will any creative genius be ever treated with the disdain and utter disregard as has been done to this son of the soil who gave the world the melody-pan and the steel orchestra…

A. Bukka Rennie

Mettle and Metal

The Birth of Steel Pan Music and
the History of Trinidad All Stars
Steel Orchestra

Austin Macauley Publishers™
LONDON * CAMBRIDGE * NEW YORK * SHARJAH

Copyright © A. Bukka Rennie 2023

All rights reserved. No part of this publication may be reproduced, distributed, or transmitted in any form or by any means, including photocopying, recording, or other electronic or mechanical methods, without the prior written permission of the publisher, except in the case of brief quotations embodied in critical reviews and certain other non-commercial uses permitted by copyright law. For permission requests, write to the publisher.

Any person who commits any unauthorized act in relation to this publication may be liable to criminal prosecution and civil claims for damages.

All of the events in this memoir are true to the best of the author's memory. The views expressed in this memoir are solely those of the author.

Ordering Information
Quantity sales: Special discounts are available on quantity purchases by corporations, associations, and others. For details, contact the publisher at the address below.

Publisher's Cataloging-in-Publication data
Rennie, A. Bukka
Mettle and Metal

ISBN 9781685622718 (Paperback)
ISBN 9781685623845 (Hardback)
ISBN 9781685622732 (ePub e-book)

Library of Congress Control Number: 2023908417

www.austinmacauley.com/us

First Published 2023
Austin Macauley Publishers LLC
40 Wall Street, 33rd Floor, Suite 3302
New York, NY 10005
USA

mail-usa@austinmacauley.com
+1 (646) 5125767

The main interviewees: Neville Jules, Prince Batson, Hamilton Thomas, Elmo Alleyne, Oliver Joseph, Leroi Boldon, John Douglas, Noel Davidson, Winston Gordon, Courtney Charles, Beresford Hunte, Leon Edwards, Barbara Crichlow-Shaw, Hamilton Alexander, Nigel Williams, Noel Lorde. Recording technician: Computer-Aided Transcript (CAT). Reporter: Ms. Beulah Dalrymple. The Cover Concept Creator & Designer – Mr. Osei Kwabena Lumumba Rennie: A.R.C. Design Studio.

Table of Contents

Chapter One: The Day of the "Alguazils" — 13

Chapter Two: The Hour Now Come — 19

Chapter Three: TASPO (Trinidad All Stars Philharmonic Orchestra) and TASPO (Trinidad All Steel Percussion Orchestra) — 98

Chapter Four: Setting Standards 1954–1971 and Beyond… — 150

Chapter Five: Building the Physical Assets and Reforming the Administrative Structure — 346

Chapter Six: The Epilogue — 369

The Proposed "Neville Jules Centre for Social Change" — 385

End Notes — 427

Courtesy "The Guardian" (Saturday, 2 February 2008)

Basking in the tropical rays, glinting on the bleachers, the New Yorker, octogenarian Neville Jules, surveys the "Hell Yard" he's known since his boyhood days in Port-of-Spain. (Michelle Loubon)

He walked into the Yard of Hell in 1941 at the age of 14 and in the process of the following years developed the focus that gave the world the gift of the Steel Orchestra.

Neville Jules in Paramin—Courtesy Maria Nunes.

Chapter One
The Day of the "Alguazils"

The story of the birth of "Pan' as a crafted musical instrument is indistinguishable from the story of "Hell Yard". It was not only a question of the ex-enslaved after emancipation rejecting the concept of apprenticeship to former masters with their shouts of "Pas de six ans" and their settling in East Port-of-Spain and on the overlooking hills of Laventille but in addition, there was the fact of the estate owners, planters and government officials, with their political clout, doing everything possible to block the ex-enslaved from purchasing land that was available, while at the same time increasing the severity of the campaign dealing with squatters.[1]

The result of these deliberate actions was the overcrowding of Port-of-Spain as a steady flow of desperate human beings flowed into the city, giving rise to communities of barrack rooms, with the attendant squalor, disease, and deprivation, described by many as "dens of vice and crime."[2] "Hell Yard", or the yard of hell, was the most notorious of such urban settlements and when the cholera epidemic struck, in September of 1854[3] and beyond, over 2,000 fell to the disease in Port-of-Spain alone, and Hell Yard certainly paid its price in a fair share of the carnage.

Yet it was from this social milieu that would come not only primal nurturing of local indigenous cultural manifestations imbedded in the artforms of Carnival and Calypso but the most stoic defense of them. It seemed as if given the historical genesis of a community like Hell Yard, born initially out of bold defiance and resistance, the attitude and posture and stance of the people therein would always somehow reflect that history, even though at times it's all buried deep in their sub-consciousness, and only awaits explosive rekindling. All it requires is a spark.

As early as 1858, the then Governor, William Keate, attempted to stop the Carnival by force and the people paying notice to his actions then responded in 1859 with an even grander Carnival and the police was sent out in full force but were beaten back by the people in Port-of-Spain, and "compelled to retire" to barracks.[4] In 1868, an Ordinance was passed prohibiting "the carrying of lighted torches to the annoyance of any one",[5] again a measure geared to curtail a key practice of Carnival revelers at J'ouvert (i.e., day-break). In fact, this fusing of Canboulay (i.e., cannes brulee) celebrations with Carnival came after Emancipation in the 1840s, precisely because the masses were excluded from the Carnival of the elites for fear that the masses would use the cover of Carnival for acts of insurrection, so the masses integrated their celebration of emancipation with the spirited abandon of Carnival, and Canboulay could then be said to have been moved from August 1st annually to Carnival.[6] Thereafter there was growing condemnation of Carnival by the upper classes who viewed the people's Carnival as "obscene and an immoral outrage."

Subsequently, the attempts to stamp out certain practices at Carnival came to be viewed by the authorities as half-hearted and the person blamed was the then chief of police, Lionel Mordaunt Fraser who later wrote a history of Trinidad and seemed a person appreciative of the people's culture; not surprisingly therefore he was deemed weak and replaced after 1871 by the more strident Captain Arthur Wybrow Baker.[7]

In discussing the relationship between the police and the people, the R.G.C. Hamilton Reports advanced the viewpoint that in the early stages of British rule in Trinidad, the free colored's were forced to be policemen, they were called the "*ALGUAZILS*" (a Spanish word for an inferior officer of justice, a warrant officer, a constable or an inspector of weights and measures in the market place) but in Trinidad then their police work included hangings, floggings, and burnings; no enslaved person was allowed to become an *Alguazil*, and no white-man "degraded himself by occupying such office", and that estrangement between police and the people continued to the extent that in time no Trinidadian wanted to join the police, so Barbadians were brought in thereby exacerbating the hostility imbedded in the relationship.[8]

During the Carnival of 1880, the Hamilton Reports indicate that the "zealous officer Baker" made the masqueraders put out their torches and people of East Port-of-Spain quietly dispersed without any immediate reaction.[9] Baker must have thought then that he and his modern-day *alguazils* had done enough to sufficiently scare the people into uncharacteristic passiveness. But apparently it was conscious, deceptive tactics since one month before the 1881 Carnival, there appeared, all over East Port-of-Spain, posters which said:

"NEWS TO THE TRINIDADIAN"

"Captain Baker demanded from our just and noble Governor, Sir Stanford Freeling, his authority to prevent the Right of Canboulay, Excellency refused."[10]

The posters suggesting, whether fact or fiction, that the Governor was in support of the people's right to Canboulay, was geared obviously to prepare the minds of the people psychologically to openly defend their rights to an accepted tradition in Carnival; the lighting of torches and flambeaux symbolizing the burning of cane and their emancipation from slavery. One can just imagine how much the people's resolve was enhanced with the knowledge that the Governor was in support of their civil rights. So when Baker came in 1881 adamant to stamp out Carnival and Canboulay for good, he and his "*Alguazils*" met the sternest of defense ever put up then by the people at the corner of Duke and George, just outside Hell Yard.

Clearly, the Riot of 1881 was not spontaneous; it was well planned and the site of the confrontation strategically chosen precisely because Hell Yard was the most likely place where the salt of the earth could readily be found and where the defense of the creative arts of carnival would always find its most ardent activists and exponents, and as well Hell Yard offered easy means of escape via the Dry River if the situation demanded quick retreat.

Hell Yard encompassed that block on Duke Street, between Charlotte and George, bordered to the north by Park Street and to the east, north-east, by the banks of what was then called the St. Ann's River, today the Dry River. It was home and habitat for members of the working masses and the lumpen-proletariat, a central place of social gathering for pimps, prostitutes, hustlers, gamblers, stick-fighters, calypsonians, down and out artists, bad-johns and so on, providing thereby a natural resort for entertainment and a creative milieu for all activists and proponents of the "jamette" culture. As Big-Head Hamil, the fourth captain of All Stars, declared: "once you come in Hell Yard, any size, yuh had to fight."[11]

Everybody with even a remote interest in the culture, both from the eastern and western environs of Port-of-Spain, found their way to Hell Yard. People from all over Trinidad & Tobago, from as far off as Sangre Grande and Point Fortin, and visitors from other islands like Grenada and St. Vincent, all frequented the district in search "of one thing or another", according to Big Head Hamil.[12] Hell Yard was constantly "jamming" as they were wont to say. And there was enterprise as well; a slew of small businesses, e.g., coffee shops, parlors, bakeries, and pastry shops which lined the main streets of the area, and by the mid '30s, elements of the now awakening, politically conscious Black professional middle-class, people like Dr. McShine and the two Cyrils, Duprey and Monsanto, would establish the Penny Bank at the corner of Charlotte and Duke; the aim being to attract and encourage savings from the lower classes, hence the display of a huge Penny in each window of the Bank beneath which, in bold lettering, was the motto: "Sunshine Today, You Have To Prepare For A Rainy Day."[13]

And just as well to complement the Penny Bank, other enlightened folk established at the corner of Duke and George, the Eastern Unity Friendly Society, an early concept of mutual funds. Such was the high level of socialization and cross-fertilization effected in and around Hell Yard that the area in time began to assert itself as a vanguard location for the local art forms despite all its limitations and setbacks. One observer of the goings-on in Hell Yard described it this way: "The DRY RIVER, especially so in that part between Park Street, on the north, and Queen Street in the south, was always flooded with a flow of humanity representative of T&T's heterogeneous Heritage…"

"…It accommodated an overflow of ethnic plurality which contained elements as murky as the water which literally tumbled down from its St. Ann's source on the occasions of seasonal showers as there were those as clean and as purified as the river's bed in the aftermath of such showers and resulting floods. With the streams of so many cultures coming to a happy confluence here, it was only natural that there would be a current of unusual creativity that would synthesize into activity of profound depth and originality…"

"…The swirl of ethnic cross-currents manifested itself in no uncertain way in the Dry River with its motley assortment of Portuguese, Spaniards, Chinese, Baccra-Johnnies, Africans, East Indians, Jews, Germans and French Creoles. Of course the Africans dominated, but altogether it was a true Trini rainbow-colored admixture… When British Colonialism superseded Spanish hegemony in 1797, cultural and social freedom began to be unduly restricted. Trinidadians, brimming with Creativity, seethed with animosity since their original musical ethos was being frustrated at almost every turn…"[14]

Despite all that was being cemented in a manner positive to the process of the social development of a Nation, the attempts to curtail people's rights to free cultural and creative expression proceeded unabated as the *ALGUAZILS*, so to speak, continued to have their day. With the beating of skin-drums prohibited since slavery, their use was forced underground and became confined to the Orisha/Shango yards, however, the people by the 1890s had turned to the use of bamboo; in fact "bamboo-tamboo" or in patois "bamboo-tambour" meant "bamboo-drum" and the various cuttings of bamboo were done to assimilate specifically or duplicate the sound of the various skin-drums, i.e., cutter, fuller (foule), and boom which signified the three pillars of musical composition, i.e., melody, harmony and rhythm, the very pattern that would be carried over to the steel bands later on.

However, the vicious nonsense continued then with persistent attempts to suppress the use of bamboo particularly in the period 1932–1937 on the pretext that bamboo was used at times as weapons in open warfare between Carnival Bands. As a matter of fact, the proclamation for the 1938 Carnival that was gazetted further indicated that the following things were strictly prohibited: (a) the carrying of any lighted torch, any procession or assemblage or collection of persons armed with sticks or other weapons of offence and numbering ten or more; (b) the beating of any drum, the blowing of any horn and the use of any other noisy instrument except between the hours of 6 o'clock in the morning and 7 o'clock in the evening."[15]

But even more ridiculous were the Carnival Regulations of 1938 issued by Col. Mavrogordato, then Inspector-General of the Constabulary which prohibited "any person to sing or recite any lewd or offensive song", or indulge in behavior or gestures which could be deemed immoral, lewd or offensive. The inference being that some calypsos could be prohibited. The people did not take kindly to this and a mass demonstration was organized at the end of which a strong petition was sent to the Colonial-Secretary and the attempt to censor calypso was never enforced.[16]

The point was that the authorities and their *alguazils* had had their day from 1834 to 1938, over one hundred years, now the hour had come for the people to discover a way to put an end to their cultural deprivation, it was time to free up their creative self-manifestations.

Sagiator was the first captain of the SS Bad Behavior sailor band that emerged out of Hell Yard around 1935. He was described as a serious man who would instruct his masqueraders to get as black and dirty-looking as could be, to go up in the Savannah and "mess up all dem pretty mas since dey doesn't give we no prize!"

(Courtesy "Vincent De Souza's Story of The Earliest Beginnings of the Steelband" by Bernard Lange.)

Chapter Two
The Hour Now Come

There were always pieces of steel and iron lying around to be used creatively by percussionists on the island. Just as there was always "pan"—that varied assortment of soft metal containers which as discards and garbage-holders or dispensers could be found everywhere, emptied of their contents, then utilized percussively. From time immemorial, people in T&T were known to have utilized pieces of steel, iron and discarded bottles and pans, even dustbin covers and later hub-cabs to provide "back-up" rhythm to their "lavways", i.e., the chanting or singing of popular songs particularly on Carnival days or around stick-fight rings where each contestant had his own retinue of back-up "chantuelles" and rhythm-makers.

No particular attention was ever paid then to the use of pots and pans, just as no particular attention was paid to someone beating out rhythmic patterns on the back of a chair or someone doing the same with a glass-bottle and an aluminum spoon. The standard music accompaniment for the Carnival masquerade bands of the elites was the string band—and it is suggested that this was a Venezuelan-derived tradition of using "guitars, cuatros, mandolins, violins, clarinets and chac-chacs," however, after Emancipation, the masses, aroused by the great possibilities of their creative freedom, sought not only to indulge in Carnival with their own forms of masquerade but also with their own instruments, and therefore from as early as 1848 there are reports of Carnival that speak of the use of "inelegant instruments, of tin kettles, salt boxes, bangees and shack-shacks."[17]

In this context, there are a number of observations from certain professionals, e.g., one anthropologist, a playwright, and as well two Carnival activists that have been noted and must be taken into consideration: J. D. Elder indicates that the people of Congolese descent in Trinidad produced a percussion instrument made from an olive-oil container which they named a "marli-doundoun;" Errol Hill in his treatise on Carnival as national theatre described the implements used in the Carnivals of 1909, 1911 and 1912 as "old tins, graters and other discordant instruments," as well as "tamboo bamboo bands that included tin-pans;" and Alfred "Sack" Mayers of Red Army explained they would leave the yard on Carnival days with bamboo and return with metal containers because bamboo disintegrated after steady pounding; F.A. Crichlow is cited as describing J'ouvert in the early years of the century in which people utilized "the rattle of painted chac-chacs, tuneful pot-covers and kerosene tins;" and Prince Batson, one-time Captain of Trinidad All Stars, informed that metal containers were specifically used to accompany certain quite specific masquerades such as Jab Molassie, Knock-about Sailors and Cow-Mas'.[18]

The point is that "pan" was part of the Carnival and Mas' scenario from ever since the masses became involved. But the failure therefore to make the rigorous, technical distinction between such use of pans as discards to keep "rhythm" and "Pan" as the carefully and purposefully crafted musical instrument has resulted not only in a very unsophisticated, messy and unscientific assessment of our history but has caused us also to be left with a litany of contradictory stories and obvious misrepresentations which astonishingly are still in these modern times being foisted upon us as episodes in the adventure that is the story of the birth of steel-pan music.

A common thread in the stories that abound, is the element or suggestion of a supposed extraordinarily strong person, a "Mussel Rat" (Conrad Roache) in the Gonzales story, who after bursting his bamboo bass started beating out rhythms on an empty gas tank or "Thick Lip" (Wilson Bartholomew) in the Spree Simon/John-John story, who beat the daylights out of Spree's kettle pan; in other words, the implied suggestion being that these individuals were strong and powerful and dented ordinary utensils or pans to such an extent that talented ones like Spree and others were able afterwards to accidentally discover notes.[19]

As described by Prince Batson:
Knock-about suck-mih-nose Sailors by the Treasury—Carnival 1946
(Courtesy Mr. Roland Bynoe)

As described by Prince Batson:

Cow-Mas in Carnival 1946—(Courtesy Mr. Roland Bynoe)

It is important to note, as explained by Prince Batson, that there were certain popular forms of masquerade, such as Cow Mas, Jab Molassie, and Knock-about Sailors, which from inception utilized "pan" for rhythmic accompaniment to their specified dance movements and as a result of this

symbiosis these forms of masquerade contributed significantly to the Pan development process. The traditionalist string-musicians of the day could not comprehend this and therefore abhorred this fascination with "pan" but in reality the traditional instruments were not appropriate for expressing the rhythmic movements demanded by these specialized forms of masquerade. The people's mas nurtured the usage of "pan".

The Newtown individuals, i.e., Lord Humbugger (Carlton Forde) and cousins, Fredrick "Mando" Wilson and Victor "Totee" Wilson, presented many different, conflicting stories which though they did not imply any strong-man element yet emphasized the accidental discovery of "notes" on Carnival Days in 1936 when the Newtown Tamboo-Bamboo band was parading around the corner of Nelson and Prince Streets or after that Carnival at the corner of Woodford Street and Tragarete Road in a backyard where they began to burn pans and one of them found "the sound of the chimes of Queen's Royal College clock."[20]

And of course, there is Mando Wilson's claim that "the first man to beat pan… was a fella from Gonzales they called Little Drums"; apparently, Little Drums came to the Savannah on a day of Horse-Racing beating a dustbin and had the crowd jumping and then he, Mando, continued, in the same breath, to declare that at that time they, the Alexander Ragtime Band, were already beating pan.[21] So Little Drums from Gonzales was the *first* but anyhow they in Woodbrook were *already beating pan.*

There are also claims by one C.H. Yip Young writing in the Sunday Guardian in 1950 that the Gonzales Place Band was the first to play tunes on "ping-pongs" developed by one Fred Corbin who was followed by New Town Boys and then Hell Yard.[22] Of course, there is absolutely no evidence to support such claims. And even in recent times, the confusion is intensified when none other than Oscar Pile, the now deceased one-time leader of Casablanca, was heard on tape, posted on the web-site, "When Steel Talks", saying that "no one person could claim the invention" of the steel pan instrument, that it "was discovered by coincidence" and he repeats the story of the Gonzales Band and places none other than "Totee Wilson" as being present there on one fateful Boxing Day when pan was discovered.[23]

So, quite strangely, there is a Totee Wilson discovering pan in three different places at distinct moments (in Gonzales, at Nelson and Prince and in

Woodbrook). But what did this "Totee Wilson" do after having discovered "pan"; did he just stop having anything else to do with this great discovery of his? Where else does he appear in this great journey and perilous adventure of the crafting of this unique instrument? What is amazing is that this country has not only allowed such pronouncements to persist but has continued to nurture its persistence. Moreover there are gate-keepers whose sole task is to maintain and defend such unscientific conception. It is now time to say, enough, and no more, to this travesty.

The truth is that strong men and not-so-strong men were beating on and denting pots and pans for years and years, and nobody suddenly woke up one morning and in the course of the day found notes on dented pots and pans and started playing melodies. To lay any such claim is to deny history and to deny completely the existence of process. To move from **pan**, the old discarded container that provided back-up rhythms to our "lavways", to **Pan**, the crafted instrument, there had to come into being a particular focus which simply did not always exist. That focus, that consciousness, had first to be brought to the agenda. That certain focus has to become the litmus-test, if we are to ever unravel the true and only story of the birth of steel-pan music. The question is, from where was this focus derived, and who first brought such a consciousness to bear on the agenda of the development of an indigenous crafted musical instrument.

One thing is quite certain about this story, this adventure, and it is that it all starts with children. We are talking basically about twelve, thirteen and fourteen year old people. Roaring Lion, the calypsonian (formerly Raphael Charles, an outstanding sign-painter around East Port-of-Spain, according to Prince Batson, the sixth Captain of Trinidad All Stars[24]) is reported by George Goddard to have said: "…The steel band was not the dream of anyone nor was it the result of any mishap. The fact is that the STEELBAND (sic) has been with us for a period of at least one hundred and twenty-five years (sic)… But of course no one paid any attention to it… It was called the Bobolee Band… with the passage of time, about 1919 (sic) the music of the Bobolee Band CAUGHT ON WITH THE ADULTS (my emphasis) and the result was that it found its way into Carnival and became the main feature of a certain Carnival band at the time… The band in question was a Sailor Band USS Bad Behavior… The beating of the Bad Behavior pan was identical with that of the Bobolee Band."[25]

Despite the lack of rigor in his classification of phenomena (i.e., steelband) and his careless and incoherent time sequencing, Roaring Lion made the significant point that the beating on pans in the time when bamboo prevailed had become largely an expression of children which the adults later came to adopt. Prince Batson also reported that on Good Friday in 1927, the year that his family moved from Port-of-Spain to San Juan, he first observed children on Argyle Street, Belmont, using only pans to beat out rhythms to accompany their chants of "bobolee, bobolee, beat the bobolee!"[26]

The question arises: how prevalent was it at that time for children on Good Friday to engage themselves in such an activity utilizing particular rhythms on pans, the bottom and/or sides of containers, used to fetch water. One can certainly argue that, with the advent of both Spanish and French Colonialism to these shores, Roman Catholicism took deep roots here and with it the tradition of beating a "bobolee" had come to signify the Trinidadian expression of the universally-accepted Good Friday beating of a caricature of Judas, the betrayer of Christ and the epitome of human evil according to biblical history. When British Colonialism took control after 1797, Anglicanism or English Catholicism (EC), one thread of Protestantism that broke from the former universal Church, became the religion of officialdom for the State Administration, while Roman Catholicism remained for quite a while the religion of the majority of the masses causing ongoing tension between the two for pride of space and place.[27]

It is in this context that one must understand the historic significance of Roman Catholicism in T&T and the extent of the religious passion of the faithful that would obviously have had its effect on the children at their most impressionistic ages. Furthermore as the treatment to be meted out to Judas was an overall Christian manifestation one could envisage the two Christian communities competing on the ground to outdo each other in rallying the masses to participate in the beating of the Good Friday "bobolee". But again such a development would not be anything unusual as all the Christian Festivals and Celebrated Days were always duly recognized by the population; so for Christmas, the string bands as well as the bamboo, bugle and pan-percussion bands would serenade their neighborhoods just as the Venezuelan-derived Parang-string bands did; on Discovery Day as the Military Bands paraded and placed wreaths at Columbus Square, the pan bands also paraded; at Easter, the pan bands would go by bus on excursions to the various beaches;

on St. Peter's Day, they would parade down to Carenage; and for La Divina Pastora, the pan bands would go by train to Siparia for the celebrations; every single Christian celebration provided opportunity for the pan bands particularly after 1939 and in the early 1940s to perform, to exhibit their wares so to speak.[28]

What begs to be discerned and requires some examination by professional musicologists is whether, as suggested by Roaring Lion, the "bobolee beat" of the children was in any way really significantly different to the African-influenced beats of the Orisha yards that had been paramount for so long and had influenced the bamboo and pan bands from inception? And more so how widespread was this practice of children in East Port-of-Spain on Good Friday?

Another commentator discussing the internal ramblings within the USS Bad Behavior Band said: "Whereas Sagiator was hesitant to embrace metal instrumentation in the original Bamboo-Tamboo Band, two of his five brothers, Lennard and Cecil, in particular, joined with the Stowe Brothers to enlarge and enhance the innovation. The Bobolee Beat, which emanated from the Pan-beating with which they accompanied their childhood custom of beating Judases (Bobolees) on Good Fridays, was established as the main rhythm of their new musical pursuits."[29]

This comment supports the view that the Bobolee beat was made a distinct feature of the Bad Behavior Band. However it must be noted that, despite the claims of our two eye-witnesses, i.e., Roaring Lion and Prince Batson, and the assertion from Jerry Serrant quoted above, neither Big Head Hamil nor Neville Jules supported this assertion of a distinct "children's Good Friday bobolee" engagement with pan in East Port-of-Spain; both recall themselves as children beating a bobolee with sticks but couldn't recall ever witnessing the scenario outlined by both Roaring Lion and Prince Batson and reinforced by Serrant. "We used to come over the Hill, beating the bobolee, and come all the way down Tragarete Road, beating the bobolee, we didn't have pan," said Neville Jules.[30] Nevertheless, both Jules and Hamil agreed with the view that there was a natural attraction and affinity of children to pan in general and agreed with the view that children were particularly involved in the development of pan music.

Hamil, speaking from personal experience, said: "If you take a pan here and start beating you go see the house here full with little people, you will always see little children; they would dance. I hope you understand that. Music is a thing, it's a code; it travels very fast with the wind..."[31] The Invaders' historian, Andre McEachnie also made the point: "Probably, the most amazing feature of the development of the steelband movement was the extremely young age of the little boys who were involved in the creation and early development of the new musical instrument while constantly becoming innovators of the new artforms. Most of these boys were just eleven, twelve years or in their early teens when they first became involved in steelband related activities during the end of the 1930s and the start of the 1940s."[32]

There are salient variables to support the gist of the gradual move away from bamboo to pans. The African drums, comprised of wood, hollowed or dug out tree trunks, covered with stretched animal-skins, had been banned since the days of slavery and that ban, over the years after Emancipation, would have been enforced from time to time with varying degrees of severity depending on the particular leadership of the constabulary. As a result, African skin-drums as an integral part of ceremonial and religious ritual were virtually driven underground and confined to the sub-culture of the Orisha/Shango yards. To continue openly the pursuit of the development of their musical expression, the people turned to bamboo-tamboo, and as indicated above sought to duplicate the sound of the skin-drums, i.e., "fuller (foule), the cutter and the boom".

But interestingly, almost every bamboo-tamboo band and by extension, early metal pan bands, would come to emerge in close proximity to an Orisha yard or shared the very same space, forging thereby a symbiotic relationship between the two manifestations, so there would have been cross-fertilization involved. The point to note, obviously, is that, given the proscribing of the Orisha/Shango religion, it stands to reason that their yards, their space, would in turn provide sustenance to any manifestation of the people that could be deemed by the establishment as potentially subversive from a political or cultural perspective, hence the natural affinity between bamboo-tamboo yards, pan yards and palays. The resulting spiritual sustenance therein would have provided these social rebels with the energy required to persevere with their manifestation.

It is important to note, however, that the bamboo rhythm instruments were not readily available; they had to be carefully fashioned from varying sizes and lengths of bamboo dragged down from the hills and the river banks, but most of all they were fragile and therefore guarded jealously by adults. They were never left to be the playthings of children as the early pans were according to the story told by the Hell Yarders.[33] In most instances it was the fragility of bamboo that forced the integrated use of bamboo and pan particularly on Carnival Days, when as suggested before, players in the bamboo-tamboo bands would have to abandon their bamboo drums and pick up discarded utensils, dust-bins, pieces of steel, etc. to continue keeping rhythm to their "lavways" and later to the riffs from frontline bugle players. So from the very inception of bamboo, there had to be this integration by necessity.

The efforts to ban bamboo intensified after 1937 on the pretext that bamboo was being used at times as weapons in open warfare between bands— it was alleged that revelers sharpened one end of the bamboo and used them "like spears".[34] Not surprisingly the regulations proclaimed for the 1938 Carnival as shown before clearly prohibited "any procession, assemblage or collection of persons armed with sticks or other weapons of offence numbering ten or more" but at the same time allowed the beating of any drum or the blowing of horns between the hours of 6 am and 7 pm. If the bamboo could be used as a sharpened weapon it meant that in most circumstances the banning of it would be covered by the broad brush of this prohibition.

Given such an assumption, it logically followed that the then only alternative was the use of "pans". The suggestion is that after the banning of bamboo, particularly after 1938, the use of only metal pans to induce rhythm became more and more highly probable, at first competing with bamboo within the Carnival Bands and eventually superseding the use of bamboo altogether. One commentator summed it all up quite succinctly in this manner: "This form of folk music using "steel" instruments instead of bamboo, appealed to the tastes of the bamboo musicians: (a) because of its superior tonal qualities; (b) because of the durability of the instruments; (c) because of the inconvenience saved of felling bamboo on distant hills far away from the district... where it had to be again cut into suitable lengths... before 1937 however, instruments of steel were played but never was there any proper organization to warrant recognition."[35] There should therefore be no wonder or unusual level of amazement that in 1939 a band from Woodbrook, the Alexander Ragtime Band, came into Port-of-Spain with pan as the only percussive support to their chants.

But interestingly, much had begun to happen by then on the Eastern side of Port-of-Spain. The Hell Yarders had by this time fully merge themselves with the Mafumba George Street bamboo band into a new found amalgamation out of which evolved the USS Bad Behavior Sailor Band which for about twenty-odd years thereafter ruled the Carnival as "the largest masquerade band on the streets of Port-of-Spain."[36] Hamil was the one who informed that the name "Bad Behavior" was taken from a small US Destroyer that "used to blow up all other ships during the War" and that it was Sagiator's father who selected that name.[37]

There is also the story of Sagiator, himself, real name, Herbert Drayton, the much feared leader of the USS Bad Behavior Sailor Band, leading his band, on Carnival Tuesday in 1937, down to the Jetty where he ordered all masqueraders to jump into the sea, then to roll themselves in the mound of coal by the Railway station and when they were "totally black and dirty", he declared: "We goin' up in de Savannah and we go rub up we-self and mess up all dem pretty mas' since dey doh give we no prize." It was reported that the journey up to the Queen's Park Savannah was done at frenetic pace fueled by a hot lavway:

"Las' lap, look we big and we bad
Las' lap, we ain't 'fraid nobody
Las' lap, look we strong and we hard
Las' lap we go beat everybody!"

In the heat of the moment it is said that two girls, Vorvin of Queen Street, and Fitsy Banwright's sister "Long John" abandoned their bamboo and picked up dustbins and the sounds they created were so effective that by the time Bad Behavior reached the Memorial Park every single member was beating a dustbin. The disguised, pretty masqueraders waiting to compete all "scampered away for fear of being smeared" but the MC Alfonso De Lima and Colonel Mavrogordato saved the day by calling on "Mr. Sagiator" to come up and receive a prize for USS Bad Behavior: a case of Caroni White Rum, one case of Boors' Beer and $24 cash. Back downtown, Bad Behavior was also awarded a case of Rum, a case of Tennant's Beer and $24 cash.

At the end of the day, the writers of this report asked themselves rhetorically: why was such "soot-covered, dirty-looking masquerades honored in such a way" and they answered themselves: because in the history of Trinidad Carnival it was the first mas' band to be accompanied only by pan-beating revelers.[38] All the Hell-Yarders indicate that Bad Behavior's act of dirtying themselves was par for the course and standard procedure J'ouvert morning every year, but if Vincent De Souza's eye-witness account is true and there is no reason to doubt it, then it means that the use of pans in the Bad Behavior sailor band on Carnival Tuesday in 1937 proved to be a mere "flash in the pan" or it simply wasn't unusual enough to demand recognition, because come Carnival 1938, Bad Behavior proceeded to continue with bamboo as was customary and of course the usual mix of bamboo and pan later in the course of the day. Logically, it seems that the mindset still warranted a major shift. Maybe the news media did not cover this aspect of the 1937 incident or if not, they did not cover it sufficiently enough to make a difference.

However, the media certainly did so in the case of Alexander Ragtime Band probably because of the bit of theatre that Carlton Forde, Lord Humbugger, added to the picture with his symbolic music sheets, scissors-tail coat and top-hat. Obviously such drama would be fodder to voracious news media. Added to this is the consideration that Ragtime was neither dirty nor stink, nor seemly obnoxious to the elites.

One early pan-man, Sonny Jones, tells a story that implies that Sagiator the Captain of Bad Behavior/Hell Yard objected to the use of pans being advocated by the noted arising leader of the younger men, Big Head Hamil, on the pretext that the noise level of the pans made it difficult for the chanting of the lavways to be heard.[39] Sonny Jones contends that Sagiator's objection to pans provided Ragtime with the opportunity to be the first band parading utilizing only metal pans, and that it was only after one of the Stowe Brothers, Eric, whom Sagiator accused of "horning him with a woman named Lily", sliced up Sagiator with a razor and Sagiator left Hell Yard for good, that the younger men eventually turned fully to the engagement with metal pans.[40]

Elmo "Bully" Alleyne refuted the Sonny Jones story outright, as do Jules and many others, and Bully clarified that there was never any such pan dispute and that the altercation between Sagiator and Eric Stowe in 1937 was all about one woman who became involved with three Hell Yard men simultaneously and though it all seemed to work for a while, Eric in a rage of jealousy, knowing fully well that he could not fight with Sagiator, took a knife from a shoe-maker on Prince Street and cut up Sagiator; and the result was that all five Drayton Brothers left Hell Yard, never to return.[41]

The other point made by Sonny Jones that however needs to be fully noted and was not disputed by Bully and others was that Carlton "Lord Humbugger" Forde who lived in Newtown but was a messenger at the Co-operative Bank and others like Totee (Wilson), Police (i.e., Estein Small), fellahs from Belmont and Gonzales "all used to come in Hell Yard **to play because no other where had pan.**"[42] Jones's time sequence here is fuzzy and it is not clear whether "notes" were yet applied. However that view of Hell Yard as the first location of pan **being played** as a distinct instrument is supported by Boots Davidson's brother, Noel "Ginghee" Davidson when he asserted that Hell Yard was the single hub of early note-development pan activity.[43]

After Sagiator's departure, his assistant, Lennard "Waj B-Pump" Augustine took over Bad Behavior for a while; then it was Eric Stowe's and Hamil's turn in the years 1937 to 1945 to organize and lead the Bad Behavior Sailor Band as well as the Hell Yard "First Eleven" pan players.[44] Hamil was a noted disciplinarian, a much feared wrestler and fighter and noted bugle player who like Sagiator also taught the Hell Yard boys how to fight, to wrestle and how to defend themselves if attacked with a kind of militarist precision. Likewise under his leadership no one dared to confront the Hell Yard band: "I wasn't the baddest man, but I was then the No. 1 fighter in Port-of-Spain."[45]

Lennard "Waj B-Pump" Augustine, described as a close "confidante" of Sagiator took over the captaincy for a short while after Sagiator, savagely wounded by Eric Stowe over a woman, left Hell Yard for good. (Picture courtesy Jerry Serrant's "From Hell Yard and Back")

Traditionally, no band dared to confront Bad Behavior/Hell Yard since this band was well-known to be replete with famous boxers, stick-fighters and wrestlers from all over T&T, and this fear of the band further intensified under the leadership of Big Head Hamil who was considered to be a young man "whose imagination was alloyed to an incorrigible waywardness."[46] This probably explains why in the entire history of Hell Yard from early Bad Behavior under Sagiator to Trinidad All Stars under Jules, there were only two clashes with other bands that were quite quickly dispelled. There was a clash with certain individuals from George Street at the gambling club called the "Wang" which resulted in these individuals forming their own band, but it could have been deemed almost an internal squabble which was expressed in the following calypso:

"Riot in the Wang with Hell Yard and George Street
Once again they meet.
I say riot in the Wang with Hell Yard and George Street,
Once again they meet.
The only thing that made me feel bad
Knowing that they fought for a pack of card.
But the pelting of the bottle and the throwing of the stone
They made George Street a battle zone…"[47]

The other altercation involved a misunderstanding with Casablanca and Hamil indicated that Casablanca men were forced to go to the Police because they could not come down Charlotte Street to go to the Market without having to face the forces marshaled by him, ever ready and awaiting, arrayed in military-type formation.[48] Hamil would lead the band on impromptu parades over the Hill or up the Dry River where they would encounter and compete with other bands like Hill 60 and Bar 20, and later Casablanca and Dead End Kids (i.e., Desperadoes) and he described how on occasions the Police would "block" them and seize the pans which sometimes they threw into the River or took back to Barracks "to train horses."[49]

That was a strange concept that both Hamil and Jules explained: apparently, the mounted branch Police in order to get their horses acclimatized to the noises on Carnival Days would put on masks and dance and beat the pans they seized to train the horses not to shy away.[50]

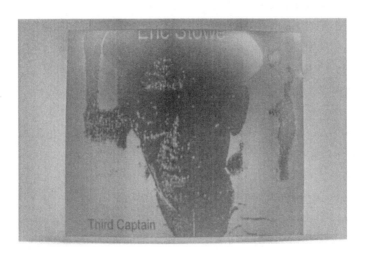

ERIC STOWE

Eric Stowe aided by his brothers, Errol and Carlton (Broko), held the captaincy and led the band to one of its earliest winnings in a 1941 competition held at the RAF Calypso tent on Nelson Street. It was said that Eric took the baton and was the first conductor to do so in the history of the early steelbands (Courtesy Jerry Serrant). He held the captaincy from 1937 to 1943.

As indicated above the Bad Behavior Sailor Band had grown since the early 1930s to be the biggest band on Carnival Days and Hamil opined that all other bands came to town to try to better Bad Behavior who were usually resplendent particularly on Carnival Tuesdays in their "blue dungarees and kaki shirts", enamored and constantly followed by the females even while chanting one of their favorite lavways: "Oye ya oye, aye ya aye, Bad Behavior coming down, Telma bloomers fall on de ground."[51]

At that point, the move from bamboo to pan seemed a most natural and quite logical development. It was only natural, given the prohibition of skin-drums and the regulations of 1938 Carnival that sought to reinforce the ban on bamboo, that the people, in their quest for the freedom of creative, musical expression, were left no alternative but to turn next to whatever lay before them in the greatest abundance. All the media reports on Alexander Ragtime Band, including the pictures thereof, suggest that they came into Port-of-Spain with nothing different to rudimentary percussive pan discards, used to provide rhythm to vocal chants, i.e., dustbins, motor-car hubs, the cuff-boom, the du-dup, etc. all of which to one extent or another had already shown up in the mix of pan and bamboo in the traditional bamboo-tamboo bands.

The basic distinction of the Alexander Ragtime Band was the total and complete absence of bamboo, and that salient fact alone served to bestow upon them the title of being the First All-Iron/All-Metal Percussion Band in our history. The contention here, given specific scientific terminology, is that the first steel-pan music band or steel orchestra was yet still to come, and it took about 6 years, i.e., 1945, for it to emerge. The cuff-boom was the big biscuit drum thumped with the open palm of the hand or fist to provide a steady "booming" or bass sound; the du-dup was a lighter pan, smaller in size, held under arm or strung around the neck or the hip and which provided a two-tone sound pattern by striking one extremity of the face of the drum and then the other with a stick. The "du-dup" was also called a "bass-kettle".

Later, there appeared the "tenor-kettle" which was strung around the shoulders and under the arm and was beaten with two sticks to provide the rapidity of three tone riffs, it was the smallest of the pans, usually a zinc or paint pan, that provided sounds of the highest pitch. There is no evidence of tenor-kettles in the Alexander Ragtime band. At that time, according to the Hell-Yarders, when someone was said to be "rattling" or "ramajaying" it was in reference to that person playing the tenor-kettle which as the very name suggests indicate a use similar to that of the kettle-drum in the military bands that would parade through Port-of-Spain on special festive occasions and had become quite popular with the people.

In fact, the Hell-Yarders argue that at that point on Carnival Days the use of tenor-kettles and bugles, cuff-booms, and also du-dups which were also called two-tone bass-kettles, particularly if played with two sticks, began to assimilate the sound of the military bands; so that whereas the early bamboo-tamboo players sought to duplicate the sound of the African skin-drums, the introduction of pans particularly after 1939–1940 triggered a diversion, i.e., the duplicating of the sounds of the military bands particularly given the social prominence then of the American military bases at Chaguaramas and Waller Field. Also there is the observation that this attraction to the military, to the military kettle-drum beats and eventually to a prevalence of military-type carnival masquerade may be traced back to the 1907 visit of the United States Atlantic Fleet to T&T or even to the pre-Emancipation proclamation that all free men had to join a militia in their community, in fact, the following quote establishes the full dimension of this view: "...*In pre-emancipation Trinidad, Christmas was the celebration that involved the greatest participation by the diverse segments of the population... Africans were given considerable freedom to enjoy themselves during the Christmas season, but it was also believed that this freedom sometimes led to insurrections... Thus every year at this time martial law was declared, business came to a halt, and all freemen were required to enlist in a militia... There were a variety of Corps with names like "Royal Trinidad Light Dragoons," "St. Anne's Hussars," "Diego Martin's Chasseurs and Infantry," "St. Joseph's Light Calvary," however, the slaves, excluded from affairs of the militia, but encouraged to celebrate, danced to fiddle and drum and shac-shacs...*"[52]

The point is that all forms of festivity throughout the country began to take on military-type influences. In this context, Neville Jules recalled that the USS Bad Behavior Band and others around town would rehearse before Carnival by going on imitated "route marches" to perfect their masquerade portrayals, he said it was called "drilling" and he recalled Bad Behavior going over Laventille Hill parading led by a "drill instructor", a volunteer by the name of "Blacks" from Hell Yard, who took charge of what eventually would be referred to as "road marches".

This picture displays an early all metal or iron-band with cuff-booms, hub-caps, flat du-dups, dust-bin covers, etc., very much like Alexander's Ragtime Band when parading in 1939–1940. Picture taken from the "History of Renegades." This is the most utilized picture of an all metal band of this period.

In fact, Jules even surmised that the modern concept of a "Road March", i.e., the most played calypso during Carnival, may possibly have emerged as a result of this "route march/road march" tradition.[53] Hamil conferred with this and further explained that the purpose of the route-march or road-march practice was to get the precision of the marching to military drumbeats (i.e., "drill") perfected for competition purposes but after leaving the competition point, Bad Behavior would usually revert to its noted carefree abandon and "lavways."[54]

After the departure of the First Eleven Hell Yarders such as Mark-Off, Schul, Tackray, the Brassey Bros., etc. the reins fell to Eric Stowe who renamed the band, "Second Fiddle" and he became the band's first conductor at a competition the band won that was organized by the RAF Calypso Tent on Nelson Street in the build-up to the 1941 Carnival; the first prize received was $25.00.[55] But that was the very year, when Neville Jules, then just fourteen, summoned up the guts and gumption to remove himself from being just another far-off observer of the goings-on down in the Yard of Hell and confidently entered the fray of life, living and creating. Neville's first, salient, historic act was to challenge for the supremacy on the tenor-kettle.

There is, however, quite a bit of confusion about the "tenor-kettle" which seems to have arisen as a result of people writing about pan craft not in the 1930s and 1940s when memories would have been quite fresh but in the '50s and '60s, decades later, and started referring to the "tenor-kettle" as the "ping-pong" when in terms of the developmental sequence the "ping-pong" did not appear until V-J Day whereas the "tenor kettle" appeared earlier, in fact one writer has placed it in the period 1880–1910,[56] but whereas there is no evidence to support this, information was unearthed recently to place the advent of the three-note tenor-kettle firmly in 1940; how this discovery came about will be dealt with later.

Hamilton "Big Head Hamil" Thomas. He was described as a fierce fighter and the one who trained the forces of the band in the ways and means of attack and defense. He held captaincy from 1943 until the end of the War. The folklore says that he on one occasion cuffed a man at the corner of Duke and Charlotte and the man fell at the corner of Park and Charlotte and did not regain consciousness until the following day (Picture courtesy the band files).

What however can clearly be certified from newspaper Carnival reports and such the like is that pans began to supersede bamboo after 1937–1938 and definitely dominated after 1939/1940. "But all dem pan dey playing then was flat," Hamil declared in reference to Alexander Ragtime Band of 1939/1940 and much of what occurred throughout the island shortly thereafter. And when questioned about what he meant by "flat", he said "no distinct raised notes!"[57] It has been well established from historical reports that members of the Ragtime Band jeered the Hell Yarders for not having turned fully to metal pans like they had done, and one member of Ragtime nicknamed "Police" who frequented Hell Yard explained to the Hell-Yarders, i.e., Hamil, Bully, Eddie Rab, Broko and Sonny Jones, how they had cleaned the pans of their chemical remnants by burning and by so doing had enhanced the rhythmic tonal quality of the pans.[58]

Ragtime's appearance, and more so the recognition that they got, accelerated the full change-over from bamboo to pan that had been happening gradually over time. However, the actual date of this change-over seems to be in dispute. George Goddard, in probably one of the more informative documents to date argues as follows: *While I agree that Victor "Benbow" Wilson is the person who introduced the Pan into the Tamboo Bamboo Band of New-Town, I am in total disagreement that this transition took place **prior** to late 1938 or sometime in 1939, at the time of preparation for the Carnival of 1940… My contention is supported by the dating of the Roaring Lion's calypso on "Alexander's Ragtime Band", sung he claims, during the Carnival Season of 1940… My contention is also supported by the Trinidad Guardian of Carnival Tuesday February 6, 1940 which reported that a band "Alexander's Ragtime Band", had made an appearance at the Carnival competition at the Besson Street Square the day before, that is, Carnival Monday, February 5, 1940.*[59]

Most people have agreed with the year 1939 as the cut-off point for the transformation and dispute any version that cites earlier dates such as the report cited above by Vincent De Souza and Bernard Lange about Bad Behavior and the use of Pans during the Carnival of 1937 which as described above may have merely been a mere, unheralded "flash in the pan" in the course of the transformation, nevertheless it underlines the fact that the process of pan usage had been gradual and had been an ongoing factor since the initial implementation of fragile bamboo instruments.

In the change-over, Hamil clarified that the bamboo-bass was replaced by the biscuit drum pan, the boom; the bamboo fuller (foule) by the bass kettle/dudup pan; the bamboo cutter by the tenor kettle pan, which he described as a smaller pan to which they applied upward dents of varying sizes or even "holes" of varying sizes[60]—and it was obvious from what he was attempting to describe that this pan was geared to provide distinct tonal qualities when struck at different spots; Ginghee Davidson in his story supports Hamil's view when he talked about his "silver pan" that he had beaten whole day with a stick without rubber, and at the end of the day he began to get "different tones" from different areas on the pan but the pan was not tuned, had no notes, and he called the pan "mellow-tone."[61]

(Pic. A1)

Oval Boys with Ellie Mannette, the youngster second from right, photo taken around 1940. There are no notes on the surfaces. The pans provided rhythm to the lavways sung by the players. Courtesy (Sunday Express, 29 October 2000, "Ellie Mannette—Journey to Roots.")

Big Head Hamil ended his discourse on the change-over from bamboo to pan indicating that, around that very moment in the course of the developing circumstances, the Iron (brake iron, etc.) became the favored choice, instead of the gin-bottle and spoon, for high-pitched, basic rhythm and timing.[62] He jokingly mentioned another Hell-Yarder named Lulie who turned up with a "broad piece ah iron" from the foundry that deafened everybody's ears,[63] and another goodly gentleman with a 40lb piece of iron on his shoulder which he beat for the entire Carnival Monday, jumping up and beating, refusing to lend it to anyone and at the end of the day his hand and shoulder were so swollen that he could not put down his hand or relax the muscles, everything froze; he had to be massaged with warm water, and yet that same individual came back on Carnival Tuesday to start all over again.[64]

It was to such "guts and gumption" that Jerry Serrant also paid homage as he described the mettle of the early Hell Yarders whose names he suggested signaled a "bevy of fascinating Humanity with a roll-call that was fascinating music to the ear" and he listed them as "Waj, Teckie, Big Sarge, Lawah, Coco-la, Tall and Short Blacks, Broko, Eddie Rab, Big Head Hamil, Bully, Johnny Wilkie, Tab, Taj Mahal, La Cour Harpe Donald, Cobo Lak, Schul, John Bruce (father of Renegades' Doctor Rat)… Tackray, Brassey, Orderly, Eric and Errol Stowe, the Fish-Eyes, Buck, Big Jeff, Granville, Jitterbug, Rugged Lloyd, Doo-Doo, Oliver, Shurland, Sonny Jones, Taffy, Joe Bell, Mano, Mark-Off, the fatmen (Vernon Allen and Zamore Bates), Prince Batson, Tattoo and the Dougla's, and there to back them up were an equally-fascinating Trinity of legendary Stick-Fighters in Joe Pringay (from far-off Sangre-Grande), Willie Sweet Water, and Hit-Man Dempsey (from down deep South, Chatham)… They, (the original Hell Yarders) had Hell Yard humming."[65]

In fact, Elmo "Bully" Alleyne also cites Lulie as the first "iron man": He said, "there was a fella in Hell Yard name Lulie, tall dark fella, he used to beat the gin bottle and one Christmas they serenading Sagiator's Family at 91 Henry Street and Lulie's gin bottle break. He run down by Percival Bain garage lower down Henry Street, pick up two pieces o' iron and start beating to the lavway. He never put down that iron at all after that and from then on every single person hear the band on the road, they would bawl "you want to bet that is Hell Yard?"

…Lulie used to put it (the iron) down in a corner and say "nobody touch that"… and they (the band members) would warn everybody not to touch that iron, that is Lulie iron. *Lulie is the first man bring iron in band…*[66] Oliver "OJ" Joseph also supports this view of the strength of the rhythm section of the Hell Yard Band. He said: "Rhythm moves people and is the basis of everything, and All Stars inherited that from Hell Yard…" and he cites in this regard the contribution also of one "Jeep-Mouth Ranney" in addition to Lulie.[67]

Goddard's description of the early pan aggregation put together by Ragtime more or less dove-tails with what Big-Head Hamil said the Hell Yarders did after seeing Ragtime. Goddard said: "In the original steelband the instruments were the ping-pong, the dudup, the biscuit drum bass, and pieces of iron or steel… The ping pong was made from a small zinc pan, the contents of which were used as a base in the manufacture of paints; the dudup which was larger than the ping-pong, was made from the containers of caustic soda;

the "boom" was a large biscuit drum and the iron or steel was usually discarded motor car brake hubs."⁶⁸

It is rather strange that there is no mention of the "tenor-kettle" in any of the reports of early pan development emanating from West Port-of-Spain whereas the "tenor-kettle" is featured prominently in what transpired in East Port-of-Spain and particularly in Hell Yard. All the reports on Alexander's Ragtime Band indicate that they possessed "ping-pongs (sic), du-dups and cuff-booms" but as a band they were only capable of providing rhythm, so it stands to reason that what they were describing as ping-pongs were not capable of carrying distinct melodic lines and most likely were, according to Hamil, "flat pans" or mere three-tone rattlers, i.e., an earlier version of the tenor-kettles. One gets the impression therefore that in the West their "ping-pongs", pans which they used to play rhythmic riffs, were three-note pans held in one hand and played with one stick much like the "chu-fac" or "chu-fak" that is noted in the East Port-of-Spain saga.⁶⁹

In the end, it may simply have been the result of people from different geographic areas using different names to allude to the same item as we shall see later in the history of pan development. However, in the story that emanates from East Port-of-Spain, the tenor-kettle, slung over the shoulder and played with two sticks, represents a major transition point in the process on the way to crafted musical instruments. It is a salient difference in the narrative of pan development presented by West Port-of-Spain as opposed to that presented by East Port-of-Spain.

Andre "Lulie" Abbott—the man who introduced "iron" in the steel orchestra. He was said to be the best or baddest iron man in the 1930s (Courtesy Dr. Fedo Blake's "The Trinidad & Tobago Steel Pan—History and Evolution."

Some old warriors of Hell Yard's Bad Behavior sailor band and tamboo-bamboo band described as having simply faded away.

Left, "South", Middle, "Big Mac Sandiford", Right, Herbert "Sagiator" Drayton, Captain of the Bad Behavior Hell Yard Band. (Courtesy Dr. Fedo Blake's the Trinidad & Tobago Steel Pan—History and Evolution.

The Tenor-Kettle: The Transition and Battle for Supremacy

The tenor-kettle development is a key stage in the chronological sequencing of the pan adventure. It was raised to prominence in the early 1940s, i.e., 1940–1942, in the course of World War 2 and the banning of Carnival. As described above, the tenor-kettle, a zinc/paint pan or sweet-oil pan, was slung around the shoulders and played with two sticks. By then the change-over from bamboo accompaniment to pan accompaniment had become fully complete. With the inducing of three raised dents on this pan, players began to play simple rhythmic riffs of a richer quality.[70]

In the early 1940s, there emerged a leading master of the tenor-kettle by the name of Zigilee, Carlton Barrow Constantine, then a member of the Bar 20 band of Bath Street, East Port-of-Spain. Zigilee was acclaimed by the people as the undisputed master player of speedy rhythmic riffs on the tenor kettle. Kitchener, the calypsonian, paid homage to Zigilee in his 1946 calypso titled "The Beat of the Steelband" in which he describes the Bar 20 band parading:

"Port-of-Spain nearly catch a-fire
When the bands were crossing the Dry River
Zigilee, master of the ping-pong
Had people jumping wild in the town…
"Black James, Fisheye and Barker
Bar 20 leading kettle beaters
Well they sure made us understand
The kettle is the foundation of the band…"[71]

What Kitchener was describing in reality was Zigilee on the tenor-kettle playing his noted rhythmic riffs while Black James and Barker on bass-kettles or du-dups provided the "foundation". Kitch therefore was incorrect on two counts; Zigilee at that point was master of the tenor-kettle, not the "ping-pong", and Fisheye was then a member and one-time Captain of the Hell Yard band. Norman Darway Adams cites Zigilee as an original Hell Yarder who, after his arrest at a tender age and charge in juvenile court for being in the panyard, was banned by his mother from Hell Yard, so he gravitated to Bar 20 in Bath Street; and Darway in addition also quotes Leon Noel, Sparrow's one time Manager, who alleged that Zigilee was too young to be a member of Bar 20 and at that time "played more of the kettle than anything else".[72]

Leon Noel in other words was suggesting that Zigilee at that time was not known as a ping-pong player but more a tenor kettle player and he, implicitly, may have been seeking thereby to make the distinction between the two pans particularly as Kitchener's song may have served to enhance the blurring of the difference between the ping-pong and the tenor-kettle. Zigilee himself acknowledged that he started in Hell Yard,[73] and during his last visit to T&T before he died, he was on a radio call-in show and an aged lady called in expressing amazement that he could be the person mentioned in Kitchener's calypso of the mid '40s and be still alive, and Zigilee replied, "Lady, in 1940 I was a youngster," and since he was born in 1926, it means that he was 18–19 years old when he had people "jumping wild in town" on V-E Day in 1945 which Kitchener sought to describe in the above 1946 calypso.

The point to note, and to note well, is that despite which of the pans anyone claimed to be playing, ping-pongs or tenor-kettles, on V-E Day, Tuesday May 8, 1945, and on the V-J Days August 15 and 16, 1945, it was still largely all about rhythmic patterns to accompany the singing of victory songs and simple lavways: e.g., "Five years, eight months we ent play no mas/Whole day, whole night we go play de arse" (sung to the melody of the calypso "Mary Anne")[74] Goddard quotes the following newspaper report on what occurred: "On both days the steelband boys kept up a deafening din with their improvised instruments which all but crushed recognized orchestras off the streets as revelers showed preference for music thumped out of old iron…"[75]

That "music" (sic) was merely rhythmic patterns "thumped out" of any discarded item that the people could put their hands on and which in turn provided some resonance when struck, but the riffs created were done so exquisitely that the panmen succeeded in "crushing" or minimizing the presence of the recognized string orchestras.

However, during the early years of World War 2, certain developments began to emerge at first quite unnoticed by all and sundry except for the regular participants and observers in and around Hell Yard, the Dry River and the hilly environs of East Port-of-Spain. A younger person had emerged and began to challenge Zigilee's claim to supremacy on the tenor-kettle. Some reports suggest Neville Jules walked down from Laventille Hill, i.e., No.3 Richardson Lane and into the famous "pit" of Hell Yard around 1941, which puts him at age 14, and henceforth immersed himself in the pan adventure; however Jules himself says that he first went there in 1939 which puts him at age 12, and that he met there early pan players such as Tackray, Brassey and Elmo "Bully" Alleyne, furthermore he said that his family had moved down to Mango Rose which is obliquely opposite Piccadilly and Duke and from that home he could hear the rhythm of the pans down in the river.[76]

But most importantly Jules indicated that while living on the Hill, he frequented an Orisha Yard where bamboo tamboo was played and after visiting the Yard he would go home and practice the Shango beats on the back or the bottom of a chair, perfecting thereby the beats of the Conga, the Omele (the second drum) and the Big Drum; furthermore, as a child, he would pick up any bamboo abandoned by older folk and likewise practiced all the various beats of the bamboo, i.e., cutter, foule, bass.[77] His earliest experiences down in Hell Yard, as he described it, involved childish play with Fisheye and others savoring rides down the slope of the river-bank on an old motor-bike with no engine.[78]

That sort of play engagement was quite typical of children at that age, but when Jules graduated from such childish play to involvement with pan in Hell Yard whether it was at 13 years old (1940) or 14 (1941), it could be deduced from the information available that he was proficient with all the popular rhythms and could play any of them with both hands. Jules contends that as the World War intensified the older Hell Yarders moved on leaving Hamil and Bully who were two of the youngest of the older brigade, and who together with Prince Batson, would serve to assist Fisheye and Jules to keep the pan-band going while others like Eric Stowe involved themselves in the mas' playing aspect.

However, just prior to all this, another early Hell Yarder, Oliver Joseph, who was born in 1929 and went down into Hell Yard around 1938 when Waj B-Pump was still the Captain, cites the following as the people he saw playing bamboo and beating iron and biscuit pan down in the pit of the river: Hamil, Eddie Rab, Bully, Shurl (also called Schul) who also played the iron and Brassey, in particular, he identified as the person who played a three-note "pan" that he described as a long pitch-oil pan, "about two feet long" which Brassey held with his left hand and played with the other.[79] Now, if Oliver Joseph was born in 1929, in 1938 he would have been nine years old, still a bit young to be visiting Hell Yard, leaving one to suggest that it would most probably have been 1940, when he was eleven or thereabouts.

Nevertheless, there are two other references to hand-held, convex, three-note kettles or "ping pongs" (sic) which were circular zinc paint pans and/or small caustic soda pans, much different to the elongated pitch-oil tins described above, and though both references claim this pan was given the name "chu-fac" or "chu-fak" by the person who first made one, nevertheless, they differ in regard to whom the maker was; one reference named the inventor as Zigilee, the other named Neville Jules.[80] John Slater also described how at that time they used the "costic (sic) soda drum" and how "Neville Jules started tuning three(3) notes on (those) same size steel-drums, but he used a better method in that he tuned the notes with a piece of broom-stick about six(6) inches long; in other words he would pound the three chosen parts at the bottom of the steel-drum with the broomstick in and out continuously until he got the desired sound. By using that method the notes looked smoother and sounded more distinctly."[81]

One Christmas, during the War, as the bands of the area were as usual parading Laventille Hill, Jules, while going over Gonzales with Second Fiddle, said he saw and heard Zigilee with Bar 20 playing a three-note tenor-kettle, strung around his shoulder and played with two sticks; the tonal quality was far superior to any that Jules had heard before.[82] Slung off the shoulder, this particular version of a three note-pan allowed for greater dexterity with the use of both hands facilitating the playing of more complicated and intricate riffs. What this suggests is that this version of the three-note tenor-kettle was an improvement on all the hand-held three-note "chu-facs/chu-faks" that were already in use. Jules asked Zigilee to allow him to play that special tenor kettle and Zigilee refused and that prompted Jules to make a similar tenor-kettle of his own, duplicating exactly the one he had seen and heard, using the same kind of pan and placing the upward or convex dents or notes in the same location as Zigilee's and from then on the rhythm rivalry began between them.[83]

"Joe Bell", i.e., Hugh Alexander, an old Hell Yarder of "Janet's Gang", according to Sparrow's calypso, spoke of the days when there were clashes between Jules and Zigilee down in the Dry River; Zigilee would come down leading Bar 20 and he would be out front ramajaying on his tenor kettle and similarly Jules would be coming up leading the Second Fiddle band of Hell Yard doing the same, i.e., the changing and reversing of riffs; hundreds of people would line all the pathways and roadway along either bank of the Dry

River to experience the clash between Zigilee and Jules and to cheer them on and, afterwards, the argument would continue for hours as to which of the two titans created greater excitement.[84]

Slater informs that shortly after the appearance of the three-note chu-fak or kettle, "Jules tuned four (4) notes at which point Jules' band was named Cross of Lorraine, situated in a place called Hell-Yard on the banks of the East-Dry River, and subsequently renamed Trinidad All Stars."[85]

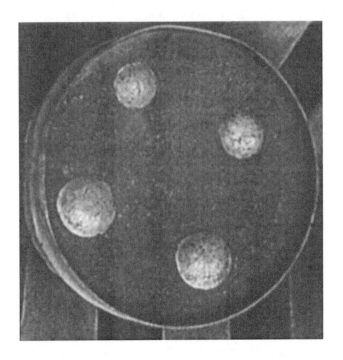

Neville Jules' 4-Note Ping Pong. This is what started the process of crafting musical instruments from metal containers.

In 1988, there appeared a piece in the newspaper written by a one-time member of Zigilee's band in England who recounted stories related by Zigilee and that person said: "Yes, it was the way Zigilee told a tale, the humor which can't be reproduced on paper except to say that it was razor sharp and had us in stitches and wishing the stories would never end; **how he created the second or third note, I'm not certain which,** on the first ever pan and even, I think, on some kind of tin, so that not long after, with the invention of one or two more notes, they could play "Mary had a Little Lamb" and what a triumph that was..."[86] What that piece clearly indicates is that Zigilee claimed the three-note pan and he could quite easily have sought to claim the four-note, given all the existing confusion that abounds, but he never did and so until he died in London at 68 on December 31, 1994, he remained truthful to himself and his contribution, i.e., the tenor kettle, to the pan movement.

Oliver "OJ" Joseph, speaking to Jerry Serrant at Point Fortin Borough Day in May 1997 told the story of how he first came to recognize Jules's genius: "…It was one of those days when the fellas were parading around the block. I was on Duke Street and the band was coming up George Street. In those days Zigilee was the top rhythm player; metal was taking over from Tamboo-Bamboo then. The rhythm was really sweet. But this wasn't Zigilee. For sure! This Pan was much sweeter. I found myself walking toward the sound. Lo an' behold, there was this little black boy revvin' up on this kettle: ah ticky, ticky, ticky, tack, tack, tack, ticky… Boy, if you hear rhythm! This was the same little black boy I used to see hustling bottles down Harbor Scheme with another tall guy. A veritable vagrant! I was surprised. I just couldn't believe my eyes! For sure, he would take over from Zigilee…

…What I did not know then was that the guy used to be around The River and the Yard for a while before that. Fisheye would point this out to me later. That was my introduction to Neville as a Panman. And what an intro…"[87] When asked if he had anything to add to what was quoted above, Oliver Joseph said: "I have never heard anybody as rhythmic as that fella (i.e., Jules). I am telling you. And Zigilee was good; there was another guy from Gonzales—Chandler, he was another very good kettle player, and Paulie from Edward Street, the brother of Popo the calypsonian, he was also very good. But Neville was the boss, he was pure magic."[88]

After that encounter with Neville Jules, OJ, who grew up on Sackville Street opposite the Police Headquarters and was already enamored of the sound of the military kettle-drums,[89] became one of the most gifted members of All Stars, trusted to play some of Jules's early prized inventions before leaving for England in 1954 where he was to become a professional master drummer performing with Tommy Flanagan and some internationally renowned jazz singers like Pearl Bailey and Dakota Staton.[90]

It was probably the intense competing between Zigilee and Jules that pushed the latter to begin to think out of the box, as one would say today, and led to the focused creation of crafted steel-pan musical instruments. It is essential to indicate that up to this point, given the ban on African skin drums and then bamboo-tamboo, the mindset remained basically the duplicating of rhythms, at first African rhythms, then military rhythms, until someone expanded the thinking and sought to duplicate the string and reed orchestras. Elmo "Bully" Alleyne said: "He (Jules) stopped Zigilee from beating... He was plenty faster, and he leave Zigilee with the three (note) and he went on to four (note) and five (note) and they come peeping below the pan. I doh hear nobody say nothing at all about that. Peeping below the note(s) of the pan, saying he put something below the pan. But he was improving all the time..."[91]

Jules could not be exact in regard to the day and time he crafted the first four note ping-pong or melody pan, and he suggests that it could have been Empire Day which would have been May 24, 1945 but certainly sometime between V-E Day (Victory in Europe—May 7 and 8, 1945) and V-J Day (Victory in Japan, August 15 and 16, 1945). Jules recalls that the entire Nation was in a celebratory mood in that period, there was anxiety in the atmosphere and people were anticipating excitement.

In fact, the mood must have been building since Empire Day 1943 when the Secretary of State for the Colonies signaled what was on hand when he sent the following message to the people of T&T and the Commonwealth: "...*I send you on this Empire Day a message of confidence and good cheer. This last year has had its hardships of which the people of the Colonial Empire have had their share. But it has also brought a steady improvement in our fortunes and prospects. We have just won a great battle in Africa. We have still to pass through many dangers and the end will not be yet, but we can now see more clearly the road to victory. Just as we have fought together, worked together and together made the sacrifices demanded of us, so we shall rejoice together when the day of victory comes—victory, which though it has still to be fought for, cannot in the end be denied us...*"[92]

When the people burst onto the streets on V-J Day 1945, the band from Hell Yard, according to Jules, was the only band playing songs, definite melodic lines, while on parade; Jules said that he showed Fisheye how to play the melodies of "You Want To Come Kill Me" by Lion, "Do-Re-Mi" (by Radio) and the melody from the movie "Alan Ladd, this Gun for Hire" on the ping-pong that he made while he played his tenor-kettle to accompany Fisheye.[93]

Jules describes the moment, i.e., the first public appearance of defined steel-pan music, in this way: "...When we came out on V-J Day and was the only steel-band playing a song, this guy by the name of Eric Stowe, a member from the old Hell Yard band, came in front of the band as the conductor. Every corner we came to, he stopped the band, then Fisheye would start the band with a rendition of "Do-Re-Mi." The other bands weren't playing any music, you know. It was only a "clackety-clack" that kept rhythm as they moved down the road. So, it was a big thing to be playing a tune and the talk spread, "Boy, you ent hear what that fella was playing? We played those songs for the victory over Japan..."[94]

Elsewhere Jules sought to make it abundantly clear that "*All Stars was the first band to play a song on pan. All before that people were only playing rhythm. If anyone challenges that, their credibility is at stake...*"[95] Now that is a clear-cut, fundamental historical claim that has to be corroborated or refuted in its entirety. The newspapers of the day carried comments on the spontaneous parades of the people on both August 15 and August 16 which were declared V-J (Victory in Japan) public holidays and there is a picture of the Red Army Band parading the streets with "scratchers" and rhythm instruments but there is no mention of Red Army playing any melody-pans.[96] In another report, the caption to a picture of revelers said: "All day, all night, they sang—this was one of the first steel-bands that claimed the streets last night after the BBC announcement... colored bulbs flashed on to light the way and steel-bandsmen pounded the rust off brake drums and dust bins..."[97]

However, the strongest comment on the steel-bands came from a certain columnist who wrote.: "Have you ever seen thousands of men, women and children moving like coordinated pistons in a devil-dance induced by rhythmic pulse-beats beaten out of scrap metal and other morsels lifted from the scrap-heap? The Orchestra of the motor-car junkyard... At first I thought that these odd musical instruments were hastily improvised for the occasion, that all they did was to descend upon some junk-depot and select all that they wanted... You would be surprised. Skill and effort are indispensable elements in this art of the "steel orchestra". The articles are carefully selected and tested, since each must produce its particular tonal flavor. Moreover, the instrumentalists who comprise the orchestra go through several rehearsals. Sections of the tin are soldered in order to produce nuances of sound and the whole affair is very skillfully coordinated..."[98]

And though he condemned the dirty song the panmen sang, "Spoat, Spoat", which he claimed originated in Donkey City, nevertheless, this columnist was the first to identify that there was a focused process involved in the preparation of a steel or iron band. Otherwise the newspapers of the day merely highlighted, for example, the parading of the local Chinese community on trucks while carrying the flags of the Big 4 Nations who allied to defeat the enemy, but particularly, in this case, to mark the surrender of the Japanese with whom the Chinese had fought for 10 years before Pearl Harbor.[99]

STEEL BAND PERMIT

Permits for steel bands to play on the streets of Port-of-Spain and Northwestern Divisional areas from 6 p.m. to 9 p.m. on Saturday, March 2, may be obtained up to 12.00 mid-day from the office of the Superintendent of Police, Port-of-Spain Division. Permits issued earlier in the week and not otherwise cancelled are valid for this occasion only.

Police patrols have instructions to check and examine permits of all bands found playing in the streets, and those not in possession of valid permits will be dealt with according to law.

No bands will be permitted to play in the streets on Sunday, March 3.

R. A. E. LINDOP,
Deputy Commissioner of Police.

An ad from the police in 1946 restricting panmen to three hours parading on the Saturday before Carnival (*Courtesy Trinidad Guardian*)

A 1946 cartoon ridiculing steel band as junkyard music
(Courtesy Trinidad Guardian)

What however seemed to have grabbed the general attention of most reporters and commentators alike was the "lewd behavior" of the revelers, the nakedness, the vulgarity, "the unrestrained display of undesirable features" and the conclusion that if nothing was done to stem such immorality, "society will degenerate."[100] But the people had been denied their annual Carnival since 1941, and they had been informed by the Colonial Administration to expect mammoth celebrations when victory became a reality, so their burst of overheated exuberance must be understood in that context. The people of T&T "played themselves" as the popular saying goes.

But shortly, after all the victory celebrations, by November of that very year, 1945, the very same perceptive columnist quoted above, recorded for posterity his observation of a new development. He wrote: "Once again the "Steel Orchestra" is in the lime light. The ears that are susceptible to noise are communicating with the mouths that are always eager to denounce in order to build up a case against the boys who enjoy beating the sensuous, primitive rhythms out of their bizarre orchestra of biscuit tins, bottles and the varied bric-a-brac of the junk heap.

It is an interesting situation seeing that one votary of the "steel orchestra" has succeeded already in producing the healthy blush of anger in the editorial countenance of the Trinidad Guardian... The "Steel Orchestra" has been dismissed as a mere noise-producing device that should be outlawed by any self-respecting, civilized society. It has been suggested that it is fantastic in the extreme to associate its noise with music. How many of the persons who pen these masterpieces of invective have listened to a well-organized band of the steel orchestra? *How many persons know that the "steel orchestra" has been developed **in recent times** into an interesting and original art? These "musicians" have succeeded to the extent of interpreting well-known American dance pieces through the medium of the "steel orchestra". **But how can we expect to understand what is happening "beyond the Bridge" if we refuse to venture beyond what we consider to be the accepted boundaries of our social estate?***

And surely we ought to ask ourselves why it is that the "steel orchestra" is so popular among the people... Sympathy for the other fellow's point of view is the hallmark of genuine civilization; and the tendency in Trinidad is much too often to condemn the pastime of the poor and at the same time tolerate the offences of the powerful..."[101] So whereas this columnist was talking in August 1945 merely about "the orchestra of the motor-car junk yard", and even then he had the acute perception that all was not random procedure, yet by November 1945, "in recent times," he said, steel-pan music was born, he was hearing then on the pans "well-known American dance pieces." *It is indeed the very first report of pan actually playing melodies. And this new sound is clearly located behind-the-bridge.*

The only person in the whole wide world to claim that he developed the capability to put melodies on pan between V-E and V-J Day and that his band was the only band capable of doing this on V-J day is Neville Jules. No one else has laid such precise claims. And it all dovetails with what our late world renowned anthropologist who lived in the neighborhood of Hell Yard, JD Elder, said about all the experimentation on pan in the Dry River coming to fruition at the end of the War. The columnist quoted above who used the pen-name "Ubiquitous" was none other than Albert Gomes. This was revealed in a secret dispatch from Governor Shaw to Arthur Creech-Jones, the then Secretary of State for the Colonies.[102]

However, not surprisingly, it was at that very moment when pan had begun to exhibit its new potentiality that the anti-pan attacks intensified severely. One letter to the editor called for the "reviving of string bands":

"On a recent night about 10 o'clock, a band of about 40 to 50 persons including children who were in front making gestures, came down from Belgrade Street into Duke Street and then to Piccadilly Street, sweeping everything before them, beating old dustbins and pieces of iron, with one chap blowing a bugle, to the great horror and annoyance of the law-abiding of the East Dry River locality… Sometime ago someone said in public that he liked this sort of music. I would like him to live in this district and see if he can stand it for a week. It is imperative that a ban be put on this music outside of Carnival days because, in my humble opinion, the authorities will be responsible if anything serious happens. These persons are getting bolder every day and it is the sort of thing which I think commenced the Red House riot. I say so because I was there. In the old days almost every young man played a stringed instrument, and every band on the streets was a string and reed instrument band…"[103]

The editor in response drew the letter-writer's attention to the fact that the Legislative Council had by then made it illegal to "beat any drum or play any noisy instrument in any street or public place without a license from a police officer."[104] So clearly the anti-pan legislation had been strengthened and there were letters commending the Attorney-General and the Government for the "most appropriate and progressive legislation" against the steel-band nuisance that is a "shame and disgrace to society," and for protecting the "cultured and peaceful from the retrograde step into the jungle and barbarism."[105] There was even a call for the re-introduction of flogging with the "Cat O' Nine tail" and a demand that the government be as fearless and as adamant with this legislation to bring back flogging as they were introducing anti-steelband legislation.[106]

And if that was not enough, there also came an appeal from a professional musician for the government to defend and save his capacity to earn a living. This is what he said: "It seems impossible to find strings for musical instruments on sale anywhere. Numbers of professional musicians would like to earn a living by their talent, but are unable to replace strings on their instruments. I look forward to a sad Christmas and Carnival… This will give more freedom to the "steelband" army in their offensive on our eardrums, with their **Lardpandolins**, **Dustbinolas**, and their **Paintpotnatros**. We want real strings to fill the streets with good music."[107] The traditionalists were dumbfounded by the people's preference for the rhythm of the pans. Think about it, could the string instruments do anything for the Jab-Molassie bands?

As the Hell Yarders all maintain, Pan and the Mas' fed each other. What however this letter and the earlier one titled "Revive String Bands" inform us is that by mid-December 1945, there were still pan-bands in Port-of-Spain without the capacity to play distinct melodies and were still at the stage of beating un-tuned pans and that some therefore were still using bugles/and or chanting lavways. It meant that the whole of town, Port-of-Spain in its entirety, was still to be swept away by Jules's invention and his introduction of melody-pans.

Jules also made it abundantly clear that on occasions he would change the fourth note to suit the melody he wished to play but of course that would only be for quite a short time as in the blink of an eye the process and the competition therein had forced Jules to push the movement to five and onto eight-note ping-pongs.[108] What do others who were then active in the movement have to say? It was already indicated that John Edward Slater, after discussing the emergence of the three-note kettle or "chu-fak", as he calls it, said that "soon after, Jules tuned four (4) notes," also that he, Slater, then lived Behind-the-Bridge between two steel-bands, Hill 60 led by Andrew "Pan" De-Labastide, and Tokyo led by Spree Simon, and he continued his story with these very telling words: "…One day while Neville Jules was visiting the area he started beating his four (4) note ping-pong that he brought with him. De-Labastide then asked him how he managed to tune four notes and he was shown the technique. At that time, all other steelbands were still beating three (3) note pans."[109]

Andrew "Pan" De-Labastide himself, coming home from Los Angeles in 1987 after some 26 years, found himself in the midst of the raging controversy concerning the gigantic hoax about Spree Simon being the inventor of the four (4) note melody pan, and he revealed that Spree was a "latecomer to the steelband scene", that he, De-Labastide, had sold a four-note pan to Spree for one shilling in 1946; then, much like Slater did, he uttered the very telling words: "I started out by looking at Neville Jules down in Hell Yard. I used to look at what Jules was doing and do the same thing. Finally, I started fooling around with steeldrums like Jules.

Although we were rivals as far as pan side was concerned we became good friends while working on pan tuning."[110] Norman Darway Adams, of course in typical "Darwayan" style, quotes the bit from the T&T Mirror article about Andrew Pan selling Spree the ping-pong for a shilling in his attempt, and quite rightly so, to debunk the Spree myth but at the same time he completely ignores the part of the story that cites Jules as the originator of the four-note ping-pong.[111] Jules said: "I take the pan (i.e., the four-note ping-pong) up the Hill to mih sister 'cause in those days it had a girl name Doreen who used to go around with Mayfield. I was with her... at the time I took the pan up there. And as I playing the pan, Andrew Pan hear me. He call me and I tune a pan for him..."[112]

And also with his typical cool aplomb, Jules, elsewhere, explained somewhat philosophically: "You may hear a lot of talk about who did different things. You may hear Spree Simon was the first person to put a song on a pan. That is not so. We had a lot of guys in our band that played before him. There was a gentleman who I tuned one for and he said that he did it. He came where I was and he saw the pan. To argue with that is petty stuff and it didn't make any sense; but it showed that he got the idea from me. He was the guy who tuned one for Spree. His name is Andrew "Pan" De Labastide from Hill 60. He went to England with Trinidad All Steel Percussion Orchestra (TASPO)."[113]

By the time Carnival was returned to the people in 1946, all the bands, according to Jules, were playing calypso melodies.[114] It turns out that that statement by Jules that "everyone else was playing a song" by Carnival 1946 was in fact an exaggeration which has been contradicted somewhat by newspaper reports. One report states that during J'ouvert 1946, the bands from Belmont came down "pounding away on improvised drums, biscuit pans and other pieces of iron **singing** (not playing) *Mary Anne* and *Lai Fook Lee*," while Tripoli from St. James "won good applause for the beating of their drums to martial strains."[115]

Obviously, it would seem from these reports that with the coming of J'ouvert 1946, bands of both Belmont and St. James were yet to catch up with what was happening in the City-Centre, but by mid-year, 1946, according to newspaper reports, the Nation had awoken to the melody-pan. However, it was quite logical that, once the melody-pan became a national reality and five-note, seven-note and eight-note ping-pongs emerged, the bugles disappeared.

While talking about "pan" in that nascent period and how much the elites in society were hostile to it, both Big-Head Hamil and Neville Jules indicated that panmen themselves, because of the given stigmatization and the association of "pan" with violence and hooliganism, were usually ashamed to be openly identified with the movement. As this discussion continued at All Stars panyard on that day, Jules said openly that in that period he would never have thought of putting his sticks in his back pockets if he was going out to play as would most youngsters do nowadays. "No one wanted to be known as a panman," Jules said, "and right where we are sitting now, was people who hated pan; the neighbors had a kitchen here, and if you didn't look out, they would throw garbage on your back... nobody thought then that pan would be sounding the way it is now or that pan would be accepted..."[116]

Big Head Hamil concurred with Jules and recalled the day when Eric Stowe came at his home and said that he had a job to make a record, and how they were so ashamed "to walk with pan in the road" that he put his pan "in a flour bag" and followed Stowe; and having said that, he went on to conclude that that was the day when *pan was first immortalized*. He explained: "six panmen played pan on a recording of Roaring Lion's "Leggo de lion", each man got $5.00 except Stowe. He took the lion's share..."[117] When he was asked to provide the year this recording was done, his memory failed him and after all the people who were present attempted to jolt his memory, he suggested that it might have been "around 1949."

However, if Eric Stowe was the man in charge as implied in Hamil's story, then it follows that the recording would have been done much earlier, maybe between 1937 and 1943, the period of Stowe's captaincy. In reality, the recording that Hamil referred to was done by Decca Recording on February 11, 1940 at the Sa Gomes Emporium located at Marine Square and the name of the calypso was "*Lion Oh*" the first two lines of which were "*Leggo me Lion, Lion Oh, Oh leggo me Lion, Lion Oh*" and the Decca recording card listed the performers as "the Lion with his West Indian Rhythm Band."[118] The Decca Record Sheet also asserts that this performance "is the earliest known recording of a steel-band" and list the instruments used as "boom (metal drum), tenor (two large cans or biscuit tins), du-dup, and the ubiquitous bottle and spoon."[119]

The "tenors" playing rhythmic riffs in this case were two 3-note hand-held tenor-kettles or "chu-faks" as they were labelled by John Slater quoted earlier. However, contrary to the popular belief that Decca Recording operated in T&T in the years 1945–1953,[120] the Decca officials first came to Trinidad during Carnival of 1938 and followed suit in 1939 and 1940 and were able to produce what is now acknowledged as "the greatest library of calypso music ever captured," but they also recorded "topical songs, dance bands, shango and shouter-Baptist hymns, Carnival chants, stick-fighter songs, Indian music, etc." however much of what was recorded was never released including "*Lion Oh*" featuring the first recording of a "nascent steelband."[121] And this was despite the fact that Mr. Louis L. Sebok, the Vice-President of the Decca Corporation said then that his aim was to select and record the best calypsos and take pictures to help give publicity throughout the US to the "magnitude of musical talent in Trinidad."[122]

The fact that the "*Lion Oh*" record was never released meant that this piece of information most relevant to steelband development remained hidden until a casual discussion in 2002 between Hamil, Jules and Robert Clarke of the Trinidad Guardian about the social ostracism of panmen and their resulting shame and reluctance to reveal their involvement with pan suddenly triggered this most salient bit of memory and led to a search for the evidence. "*That was the day pan was immortalized*," were the words of Big Head Hamil which triggered the search. Clearly this revelation lends credence to Roaring Lion's contention in the 1983 interview, quoted by George Goddard, that the year after the appearance of the first all-iron band, Alexander Ragtime of Woodbrook, "a band calling itself "All Stars" (sic) using empty steel paint pans caused a sensation…"[123]

First of all, this discovery of Lion Oh recorded in 1940, one year after the appearance of Ragtime, settles once and for all that they in fact emerged in 1939. Secondly, it calls to question the claim made in 2003 that the 1948 Casablanca recording was the first pan record made. What this 1940 revelation now establishes is that the very first record of the steelband phenomenon was the record of the Hell Yard Band on Roaring Lion's "*Lion Oh,*" eight years before Casablanca. And it is strong evidence to support all the people such as OJ, Bully, Noel "Ginghee" Davidson, Sonny Jones, etc. who maintain that notes were first placed on pans in Hell Yard. Also it is interesting to recall here that Zigilee, an early master of the three-note kettle was also a member of Hell Yard in 1940 until he was charged by the police, placed on a 3-year bond and was then banned from Hell Yard by his mother.[124] Zigilee, as already indicated, then fell in with Bar 20 which was located closer to his home.

Since the 4-note melody-pan first appeared on V-J Day in 1945, it now stands to reason that the 1948 Casablanca recording may very well be the first recording in which the large pans, the 45-gallon oil drum tenor, voiced melodies and that distinction ought to be acknowledged. Research reveals that the Casablanca recordings, done in Trinidad in 1947 and released in 1948, comprised two (2) 10 inch discs with twelve takes that included a medley, a calypso rhumba, a calypso called Bandy Legs sung by Ziegfield, as well as a Jive sung by Roaring Lion.[125] The players and instruments were as follows: Philip Dunbar on big ping-pong; Don Henry on big ping-pong; Wallace Reed, (a round disc of iron); a steel drum; and Sidney Corrington on an oblong piece of steel (he played the length of the steel, using his fingers to vary the tone) but most interestingly the author indicated that the ping-pongs are played at different pitch when more than one player is heard.[126]

The above is quite helpful in that it clearly indicates the full extent of what Casablanca had to showcase in 1947: Two ping-pongs tuned at varying pitch; a circular iron hub-cap; a drum—most likely a du-dup, and an oblong or longish piece of steel, the Indian-derived "dhantal." When one listens to that record there is clear evidence of rhythmic implements such as a tock-tock, a shac-shac, iron and the unique sound of the dhantal in the last tune, "Serenade."

Roaring Lion (*Pix courtesy the Roaring Lion Foundation*)

The cover of Casablanca's 1948 78 LP. It was recovered recently and projected as the first ever recording of steelband music. It was the first recording of big (45-gallon drum) melody-tenors or ping-pongs. There is now the evidence of a 1940 recording of the Hell Yard band, then led by Eric Stowe using three-note kettles. The latter recording is now lodged in the archives of Trinidad All Stars.

Neville Jules and His Family of Pans

After being attracted to the magic and genius of Jules, Oliver Joseph said that he began at first to hang around the band and to follow them as they paraded the streets of East Port-of-Spain and over the Laventille Hills, eventually resulting in him getting involved when Jules made the **Bele** and introduced him to playing it.[127] The Bele he described as being "hung around the shoulder; it was rhythmic, rather than melodic."[128] There are two known references to the Bele. Slater called it "Belleh" and described it as one of a particular set of pans, the others being the "grumbler" and the "grundig" of five to nine notes which "used to invoke some sort of spirit into pan lovers" and "gave off a pulsating vibration that (sent) revelers into a frenzy."[129]

The other reference came from a foreigner who some locals claim visited Trinidad sometime between 1946 and early 1948,[130] around Carnival time, and described in a travelogue what he saw down in the Dry River where he was taken to listen to the band then led by Fisheye. The foreigner referred to is Patrick Leigh Fermor and because of the details of what he recorded for posterity, the date of his visit to T&T is crucial to establishing certain relevant time-lines in regard to the history of steelband development.

Having researched Fermor's life and travels the following is now known: After the second World War, Leigh Fermor and his wife to be, Joan Eyres Monsell, remained in Greece "wandering the country and initially finding work in the British Council" but apparently his lust for travel soon overwhelmed him, so he resigned from the job and it is said that "in 1949 they caught a ship for the Caribbean, a trip that resulted in two books: a travelogue, The *Traveler's Tree*, and a fine novel, *The Violins of St. Jacques*."[131]

This is how Patrick Leigh Fermor, PLF, described his initial experience in Hell Yard: "We all four took a taxi to the street called Piccadilly, on the other side of the dry river, and our new acquaintance led us down an alley-way between heavily populated wooden houses, over a wall and into a large pit built in a bay of the embankment... The leader rose, shook hands, and gave us four little rum kegs to sit on, and went on playing. The leader or Captain was a Negro in his early twenties called Fish Eyes... when the din had stopped, he made some introductions. "This is Neville Jules, my second-in-command, and this is my managing Director, O. Rudder! Now I'll show you our yard..." It was a piece of waste land, a-flutter with clothes-lines, jammed between the embankment and the backs of houses, and the only way in and out was by climbing the six-foot wall we had just negotiated.

The band was a little group of young men from the neighborhood who had installed themselves here and turned it into a stronghold. A large blue banner, embroidered with the name of the group, was stuck in the ground, and, beyond the minstrels, half a dozen familiars were playing gin-rummy on a plank between two kegs... all of them were between sixteen and seventeen and the early twenties. The little enclosure was illuminated by flambeaux tied to the branches of a tree; Fish Eyes Olivier (sic) played the most complicated of them all, the Tock-Tock, which has a range of fourteen notes. The Tock-Tock is the sawn-off bottom of a cylindrical kerosene tin, and the different notes are made by striking with a spanner or with a metal bar the different-sized triangles enclosed between segments of the rim and the two radii that enclose them. Each radius is hammered into a groove to detach the resonance of the triangles from that of the ones on either side, and fourteen radii produced fourteen distinct notes varying in pitch according to the distance between the enclosing grooves. Fish Eyes struck them in turn with his iron bar and each one rang distinct and true; two notes short of two octaves, which **"is a pretty good range…"**

Rudolph "Fisheye" Olliverre was the fifth Captain of the band. He was given the 4-note ping-pong in 1945 and shown by Jules how to play popular calypso melodies, e.g., "Yuh want to come kill mih", "Doh Re Mi", and the melody from the movie "Alan Ladd, dis Gun fuh Hire." There were 5 Olliverre brothers in the band which at one time was located in their yard: Rudolph, Willie, Desmond, MacDonald (Man) and Bunny. Fisheye gave the band the name "Cross of Lorraine". During his captaincy of the band in 1949, he played by that time a 14-note tenor off the shoulder with one stick. His captaincy ended shortly thereafter.

The Tock-Tock is the dominating instrument. It is seconded by the Belly (sic) kerosene tin, divided into seven deeper notes. Then comes the Base (sic)-Kettle drum, which is made out of a large Vaseline drum, and the Base-Bum (sic) a vast biscuit container from a local factory.[132] An unremitting clash is furnished by the "steel"—a brake drum beaten with an iron rod—and by the Shack-Shack. Other lumps of machinery, manhandled into shapes that produce the correct notes, form the remainder of the orchestra…"[133]

Of course, the goodly gentleman had the names of the instruments all wrong; the "tock-tock" was a ping-pong now with as much as fourteen notes, the "Belly" was the "Bele", pronounced as "belleh", providing rhythmic accompaniment, the "base-kettle" was the bass-kettle or du-dup and the "base-bum" was a bass-boom.[134] (See end-note!) Now clearly this is an eye-witness account from an objective or dispassionate observer that indicates exactly what existed in Hell Yard before the Carnival of 1949, and which in fact reflected what developments had taken place in Hell Yard between 1945 and 1949. This is neither the emotional bias of fanatics nor the typical idle "picong" of bragging rights.

The Neville Jules' seven-note Bele has therefore been clearly placed in context of time and place of origin as supported by Oliver Joseph and Slater as well as the foreigner Patrick Leigh Fermor. Furthermore, Oliver Joseph, who, as mentioned before, went on to become an internationally acclaimed drummer, and who was then a "mechanic's apprentice", (at the time he was "learning trade") contends that Jules had by then also introduced a drum-set to the steelband; he said that Jules attached a pedal to the biscuit-drum, used another lighter pan as the snare-drum and added cymbals and a hi-hat which had to be played not with sticks but with brushes,[135] all of which dovetails with what Jules said on November 12, 2009 that the tune-boom was different to this bass-boom which was to be played like the kick-bass of the conventional drum-set.

The foreigner, Patrick Fermor, an Irish-born, British National War Hero, also attested to the musical capability of the aggregation before him when he referred in his account to the music they played for his group of four. He said that Fisheyes, the Captain, announced that the band will play "Ave Maria" to please the lady amongst them, then "the sound that burst on the ear was hallucinating. From a mile, it might be almost agreeable; but it was BACH alright and without a single false note."[136]

Clearly, it can be deduced from what is now before us at this point that Jules in the period 1945–1949 had already moved pan significantly away from the military-type constructs which had pigeon-holed the visionaries of the movement for quite a while particularly after the 1907 visit of the United States Atlantic Fleet and the regular military drills performed by American navy-men which in turn led to the growing prevalence of military mas'.[137] It indicates that in so doing Jules had moved pan development onto assimilation with the instruments of the modern conventional orchestras. That was Jules' single-mindedly focus, i.e., to make pans that assimilated the sounds of the traditional instruments of the string bands.

However, once it is established that the year 1949 was the year in which Patrick Leigh Fermor visited the Caribbean islands (T&T, Grenada, St. Lucia, Antigua, St. Kitts) it means that the ambiguity and uncertainty of positing that this visit was "sometime between 1946 and 1948" has to be disregarded totally. Secondly, it serves to pinpoint exactly when Fisheye left the band, Second Fiddle. Some say that Fisheye was lambasted after the Carnival of 1946 largely because of his refusal to equitably disburse funds earned by the members of Second Fiddle for providing music for the Belmont masquerade band led by one Martin Sampson.[138] But Fermor who visited in 1949 indicated in his piece that the Hell Yard band was at the time practicing for the Carnival and that Fisheye was the Captain.

It therefore stands to reason that Fisheye was removed or more so removed himself after the 1949 Carnival when interestingly Second Fiddle had divided its forces, ten players each, and played for both Martin Sampson's *Aztecs* and Jason Griffith's launch of his first fancy sailor band, *USS Sullivan*,[139] and when therefore the financial expectations of the members would have been much greater and much more widespread given the double engagements playing on the road that Carnival.

However, the reasons outlined for Fisheye's departure, much unlike the date it occurred, have remained quite consistent over the years. This is Jules' explanation: "Fisheye really didn't know how to be a captain and so on. He was for himself. I think it was the Carnival of 1946 (sic) when we played for a sailor band in Belmont and he charged the band thirty dollars. Come Ash Wednesday, Thursday and Friday, he had the money but he didn't pay. Eventually, he started to pay players twelve cents here and there and so on. At that time, I was tuning and arranging and also playing on the streets. I said to myself, "let me see how long it is going to take this guy before he gives me something." I followed him like his shadow.

There was a parlor on the corner with a long counter. Fisheye went (in) and ordered an orange juice and he paid with a two-dollar bill. The change that he got had a sixty cents piece. I was at one end of the counter and he at the other end and he skated the sixty cents to me. That was my pay for arranging and playing. We had... problems and the guys said "no more!"[140]

Interestingly, the band, sometimes registered by the then Captain as "Fish Eyes Band", had won the 1946 Carnival Improvement Committee's Silver Cup in the competition organized by E. Mortimer Mitchell for Steelbands in the City, beating Casablanca and Stalingrad into second and third place respectively and in the overall competition for all mas' bands came second to Tribal Warriors.[141] So it was said that on account of the band's successes, Fisheye went on an "ego-tripping" scene and held on to "monies he had collected on behalf of the band" eventually "skating 60 cents to the Maestro" while "remarking dis is all ah could afford."[142] Prince Batson who took over the Captaincy remarked: "If Rudolph had a half, only a quarter, for that matter, of Jules's talent, he (Fisheye) would have long been atop some high mountain peak. He was always aggressive. Jules, in direct contrast, was too reluctant in grabbing the limelight."[143]

Jules admits that Fisheye had some talent, was never a great pan player, but was a mighty show-off and he cites the example of how Fisheye, whom he taught to play the three melodies the band performed on V-J day, placed a small towel on the head of a little boy and on top of that towel he placed the 4-note ping-pong and continued to play as they paraded drawing attention to himself much to the amusement of the crowds,[144] or the fact that after his departure from the captaincy of the band, he gravitated to Invaders, playing mas' with them and when a certain international magazine did a story on Invaders around that time no one's photo but Fisheye's turned up in the Magazine, not even Ellie Mannette's, and Jules laughed as he recalled that apparent absurdity which served indeed to assert how "pushy" Fisheye was.[145]

With the departure of Fisheye and the official change of name from sometimes simply Hell Yard or Second Fiddle or Cross of Lorraine or even Fish Ryes Band to the affirmed Trinidad All Stars Philharmonic Orchestra (TASPO), according to the new leader, Prince Batson, Jules's creativity really blossomed. Ellie Mannette by 1947 with his skill as a machinist and metal turner (Darway informs that Ellie worked then at East-End Foundry) had improved the sound of Neville Jules' original styled ping-pongs by moving from convex uplifting of the notes to concave sinking of the pan with the demarcated notes then elevated upwards,[146] and Jules explained that by the time he had heard what Ellie did, he was already going in that direction, discovering the method and recognizing the difference in tonal quality achieved but at the same time he made it abundantly clear that in no way was he attempting to detract from Ellie's prowess as a tuner or dispute that Ellie was the first man to go both ways.[147]

Ellie's style of tuning that combined both concave and convex working and grooving of the metal of the pans became then the standard norm. However, between 1947 and 1949 Jules had begun to put the modern steel orchestra together and he explains how he came to conceptualize the instruments starting with what he called the "cuatro-pan" and "tune-boom": "I was on Duke Street, it was around Christmas time. A Parang band was practicing and I stood up and listened to the guy strumming the Cuatro. I decided I was going to make a pan to sound like that, which I did. I had it playing and the other bands saw it. One gentleman, Philmore "Boots" Davidson, heard it and he tuned one identically. He played it the same way but he called it the guitar pan and that name stuck…"[148]

"We had another instrument called the "tune-boom". It was made from the biscuit drum. I got the idea from the (box-bass) used by young men going around with guitars, singing and doing their stuff. They had a box with a hole in it like you would see in a bass (i.e., double bass). They had three pieces of steel or metal cut at different lengths that they bolted onto the box in front of the hole and they would pluck at it (i.e., the pieces of metal) imitating a bass. It wasn't musical but it sounded like a bass while they were singing and playing their guitars. I made a "tune-boom" that would make at least some of the chords. You can say that the tune-boom was the real predecessor of the bass."[149]

Prince Batson was described as an excellent administrator and an "ideas man". He was the first to advise that rubber be placed on the sticks. He was a highly spiritual Orisha person who gave All Stars the bell that is still today used to call the band members to order and to start their performances. He was an archivist by nature and because of this specific characteristic of his, he was able to lend pan artifacts from the All Stars journey to the then Director of Culture for exhibiting during the Carifesta V exposition. Prince took over after the departure of Fisheye. The band used the name Trinidad All Stars Philharmonic Orchestra (TASPO) under his leadership.

Prince Batson's Artifacts

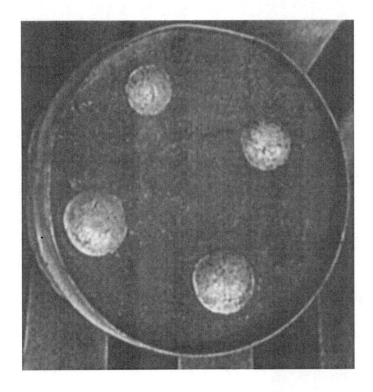

This four-note ping-pong made by Neville Jules was given to Fisheye to play melodies during the 1945 Carnival. Slater indicated that Jules used a "broom stick" to fashion the smooth upraised notes. Prince Batson the archivist kept this and other artefacts listed below in his safe-keeping for decades and lent them to the Ministry of Culture for display during Carifesta V. This four-note ping-pong has been deemed to be missing when last All Stars officials enquired about it. However, it mysteriously turned up, freshly painted, at another exhibition organized by the Ministry of Culture where no mention is made of the archivist who provided it nor the pioneer who invented it. Every other known pioneer was duly acknowledged at that pan exhibition.

*Early four-note bass pan (top, left), 8-note tenor pan (top, right)
Bottom left, soap box, bottom right, bucket.*

*Early sweet-oil pan (top, left), early convex pan (top, right)
Early Du-dup (two-note) (bottom, left), bass-pan (bottom, right)*

Again, controversy reigns about the "tune-boom".[150] And Jules explains: "Some people say that Fisheye made the first tune-boom, but that is not true. If you asked Fisheye, he would tell you that I, in fact, made the tune-boom. Believe it or not, he (Fisheye) was once captain of Second Fiddle... not because of what he could do in Pan but because the band was in his yard on Charlotte Street... We went down Christmas time to Invaders yard with the tune-boom and played. When we were leaving, they all stood up and watched us as we were walking back up Tragarete Road. That may have been the first time some people saw the tune-boom and came to conclude that Fisheye made it. Fisheye didn't make anything... He was just there at the time the thing was happening..."[151]

Elsewhere, Neville Jules was more precise in terms of the time the tune-boom was presented: "I remember the first time I made a tune-boom; we went down to Tragarete Road by Invaders. That year one of the popular Calypsos was "Georgie Porgie Pudding and Pie, Kiss the Girls and Make Them Cry". When we went down there they were astonished to see and hear what we did. The Carnival, after that Christmas, a band named "Katzenjammers" came up from down there with more tune-booms than us..."[152] So according to the above statement the tune-boom first appeared in the Christmas season of 1948 and on the road for Carnival 1949 since that was the year that Melody's "Georgie Porgie" was the popular calypso.

In fact, at the very first Carnival Sunday Pan Competition held that year at the Savannah, Invaders came first playing *It's Magic*, Sun Valley of St. James came second playing *George Porgie* and Trinidad All Stars came third also playing *George Porgie*.[153] It was reported that Sonny Roach of Sun Valley was so annoyed that Invaders was given first despite having played a rumba and not a calypso, he never competed again.[154]

Oliver Joseph however supports Jules' contention that the first time the members of Invaders saw a tune-boom was that Christmas when Jules and his band went down to their yard and played, however the one difference in Oliver's story is that he claims that it was Invaders, not Katzenjammers, who came into town the Carnival following that Christmas with plenty tune-booms playing "Hide Yuh Daughters Inside!"[155] Prince Batson in his take on this issue also indicates that "it was no big thing when Ellie took to reproducing Jules's Tune Boom" since they enjoyed a ready rapport and were good friends."[156]

The point to note, however, is that after Jules took the **first tune-boom** to Tragarete Road during the Christmas of 1948, within mere weeks, i.e., Carnival 1949, another band would produce on the road "more tune-booms" than Jules' band. It indicates the speed, virtually in the blink of an eye, with which any pan development in those days took root and became widespread in scope.

So having already contributed the tenor (the melody ping-pong), the (cuatro) guitar and the tune-boom, Jules contends that he "continued to make pans and was the first to bring out the caustic soda drum—the first single bass pan—and later two caustic soda drums that set the groundwork for the multi-bass section we have today... I also made the grundig to play the rhythm with chords—that was a background pan, now called the cello."[157] Jules also indicated that he "...made a pan called the trombone pan, a single pan—but they didn't play it the way I wanted it to play and so I discarded it, as I did the grundig; that's the complete list of the pans I experimented with—the trombone pan, the tune-boom, the grundig, the caustic soda bass drums (*i.e., from two-bass on the caustic soda drums, to the three-bass, and then to five-bass and six-bass after the introduction of the 45-gallon oil drum—BR's elucidation*) and the guitar or cuatro..."[158]

Jules waxed philosophically when he summed up what his mindset was back then: "...In those days, time didn't really matter to us. We were just doing all these things. I was concentrating on building *a family of pans*, even though then I wasn't consciously doing that. What I mean is that I didn't start out saying to myself I was building *a family of pans*. I was just imitating sounds I heard..."[159]

So up to this point, given the information provided sequencing the emergence of different pans, we can add to the above list, the 4-note ping-pong and ping-pongs up to as much as 8, 10 and even 14 notes; we can also give special credence to the existing folklore of the mid-forties that said that if anyone, anywhere in T&T wanted a ping-pong one only had to go into Port-of-Spain to Hell Yard and buy one from Neville Jules for a "bob" (i.e., one shilling). Also to the list of *a family of pans* we must add the "bele" which was witnessed by Patrick Leigh Fermor during his visit to Hell Yard and which as we have recorded above was at one time played by Oliver Joseph.

Leroi Boldon, born in 1936, and presently a practicing Veterinary Surgeon in California, USA, said he joined All Stars shortly after he entered St. Mary's

College, 1948, at the age of twelve, and he indicated that by the early 1950s the instruments being used were as follows: 1st Pans (i.e., Tenors or ping-pongs), alto pans, single second pans, the cuatro pans, the tune-boom and then the basses, i.e., five-note bass, called the high-bass, 4-note bass and 3-note bass.[160] He also indicated that in his second or third year in All Stars, i.e., 1950–51, Jules introduced the Grundig and a "made a special pan for Audra that was not named" at that time.[161]

Audra Preddie confirms that that special pan was called the Trombone Pan and it was not so much that it was made for him but it turned out that he was the one who handled it most effectively; he also informed that he played completely "by air", he could play all the various pans because he practiced "night and day" even by himself and could at that time play both melody and harmony simultaneously.[162] Audra much to Jules' lament did not stay with the pans as he chose to move on playing traditional instruments and touring with Aubrey Adam's Trinidad Folk Performers.[163] "If he had stayed, he would have been known as one of the great virtuoso pannists," said Jules.

Leroi Boldon however, played almost exclusively the cuatro pan, though he could play both the single second and the grundig, and was fascinated with the basses which were too heavy for him to carry.[164] He said: "I was a staunch supporter of Invaders until the family moved from Woodbrook to Nelson Steet and I heard All Stars playing a Country and Western tune called *Whispering Ho*, and there was a guy called Shurland, a very animated bass player, playing a three-note bass. He had really good moves and he had a way of corking the note, damping, he would hit the note, then touch it with his palm, so it sounded just like a string bass… I got hooked."[165]

That was a known technique of All Stars, i.e., to play the basses with short sticks and so be able to dampen the notes with the palm in order to affect sharper tonal quality and to minimize the resonance of one note against another. "The 3-note bass," Boldon declared, "was the power-bass; Neville never burned those, he would just sink and tune, and they were powerful, you could hear them from a block away; Shurland played one and Man, that's Fisheye's brother, who became a policeman afterwards, played one."[166]

When he spoke about the "power basses", Boldon was unaware that he had just verified another bit of the general folklore that surrounds All Stars, i.e., the famed Neville Jules's power-basses that you could hear for miles, the basses which were all that the people in the Black Melton Section at the rear of the band could have heard and all they needed to hear to play their mas' during carnival, and much later, so the folklore goes, the power basses of the 1960s that almost "blow down Salvatori building one J'ouvert morning, when All Stars dropped the bomb, "Marriage of Figaro," that famed J'ouvert morning when All Stars strangely did not follow its normal route, did not turn into Keate Street on the way to St. Vincent Street, but instead chose to push on straight down Frederick Street and as the band found itself jammed up at the location of Frederick and Independence Square, the Mouche-Man stopped the band, effecting the strict attention he desired and then dropped Bomb "No.1— *The Marriage of Figaro or The Day of Madness.*" Today, it is year 2020, and the old folks after all those years still talk about that moment. *Dey say dem basses almost throw down Salvatori building.*

Oliver Joseph reaffirms that Neville Jules was the person who first moved away from the military band mindset of the very early steel-pan pioneers; he moved it away from the strict rhythmic mood and mode, and in seeking to assimilate the sounds of the string bands, the wind instruments and the parang bands, he made the whole thing more musical in the sense that you now had melodies and as a result you now had harmonies to complement the melodies and a whole new sense of orchestration in steel-pan music developed as a result.[167] ***Jules never stuck to any one instrument; he made them, played them and he passed them on, showing other persons how he wished them to be played.***[168]

When the band moved from Charlotte Street to George Street, i.e., at the back of the coal shop, Neville, according to OJ, made the "alto pan" to harmonize with the tenor; whereas the tenor then was comprised of 18-notes, 4-notes in the center and the other 14-notes lined around the circumference of the pan, the alto had 14-notes, only two notes in the center and twelve notes around; "I was the first guy," says Oliver Joseph, "whom Jules gave an alto to play, then he made three others and gave one each to Desmond, Fisheye's brother, Joe Bell (Hugh Alexander) and to one other person."[169]

Jules's 18-note big tenor in the late '40s early 1950s—4 notes in the center and 14 notes around the circumference of the pan.

FATMAN BATES

Fatman Zamore Bates—It has been verified by three people, Martin Albino, Winston Gordon and Sonny Blacks, that Zamore Bates was the key person who assisted Jules sinking and tuning pans in the '40s and '50s. in Hell Yard.

Oliver Joseph also insists that Jules in addition also made single-second pans which he, Oliver, never played opting instead from time to time to play the cuatro or guitar pans which were quite deeper than the seconds.[170] Oliver Joseph, who could not identify Jules as the inventor of the single-second pan, maintains that he was an eye-witness to Jules experimenting and developing his '*family of pans*'; and verifies that the only pans he did not personally see being created by Neville Jules were the grundig and the trombone."[171]

Oliver Joseph also had a rather interesting story to relate. "I'll tell you something," Oliver said. "I sit here and I'm watching the television and they were presenting Ellie Mannette, and I am sitting and listening to him. And he said in 1955 he invented the tenor basses. I'm saying, but how could he invent tenor bass in '55 and I played tenor bass in '54 before I left for England. The day Jules made the basses I was playing cricket in the river on the concrete. By that time I had said to Jules, well, I finish with pan, because of the stigma attached, and I had loved cricket and football and you go to practice and guys turning up dey nose at yuh because some of them are civil servants, and I am a pan man. It was getting ridiculous. Your own brother and sister would pass you in the road, that sort of thing."

"So I say I am finished with pan. So I am playing cricket and he (Jules) is sitting on the bank swinging his feet—like ah seeing him now—and as I finish, I jump on the wall to go and wash up to go home. And he said to me: 'is you I waiting on Ah say, me, what for? He said, 'listen, I just made some pans and I think you is the only person I can get to play them.' I said which pans you make? He said, 'come, come.' Now, the next day is the festival, and this evening is when I play mih cricket and he challenged me. Anyhow, we went to Royal Club and these three pans were there, not painted, just tuned and they dirty. So he say to me, you know a tune called La Mer? Ah say, yes. He say, all right, I want you to sing it for me in this key. So he play a few notes. He give me the key. So I start singing La Mer. La Mer is a tune of just 16 bars, but you keep repeating and you changing the key."

"As you play one chorus you change the key; there are about three changes. So by the time he played the first change, I say to mihself, oh gawd, he have mih. You talk about music! So he said, what yuh think? Here you are and he hand me the sticks with a big grin on his face. And he start singing and I start playing, and in no time I had it. Because I was like that. He could rely on me; call on me any instant and get results. He say, all right, I will get these pans painted in the morning. And we did La Mer in that 1954 festival; with me playing that tenor-bass. That is the sort of relationship that I and Jules had. One day we sat in the Coal Shop, those days I used to play alto pan and he is sitting playing a tenor."

"Now, he isn't playing any tune, he is just making music. And I am playing and I'm following him, I'm playing the chords to match. And this went on for about ten minutes, and one guy turned to us and said, all yuh is some criminal boy, allyuh learning tune and nobody ain't know it and all yuh ain't passing it on. And Jules just look at me and laugh. The guy didn't know that it was straight free improvisation. Jules was something else, boy. You know, my years I spend in England, no matter who I play with, I always say, there is one born musician that I know, a guy by the name of Neville Jules. And I played with some good musicians. People like Tommy Flanagan, a piano player, Pearl Bailey, Dakota Staton, great jazz singers, Jon Hendricks of Lambert, Hendricks and Ross fame and so on. I played drums and sang. And all that ability came from All Stars..."[172]

John Edward Slater, on the other hand, in his testimony cites Neville Jules as the sole inventor of the single Second Pan and supports his claim with a diagram of what he identified as having been created by Jules (See pic. 1). But Jules in fact has never claimed the single Second Pan, in fact Jules indicated that Sonny Roach of Sun Valley was the first person he saw with a single-second.[173]

However, Slater also declared that "Neville Jules was the first to tune a whole costic(sic) drum as the bass, while other bands were still cutting the steeldrum 2/3 length. He was the first tuner to tune and beat the two (2) costic(sic) drums together as bass. He was the first to tune the Grundig as a background pan, or Cello as it is now called. He was the first to introduce a new beat to the do-doop (sic), a small pan... used for timing. He was always willing to share his talent with those who were interested. Neville Jules as Captain of All Stars demanded and got respect from all his members, even to this day Trinidad All Stars is a well-disciplined band and is still sticking to tradition... **I hope the day would come when we would all recognize Neville Jules for what he's worth** (my emphasis)..."[174]

One other steelband activist, Albert Jones, of the '40s and '50s, said: "Zigilee lived up on the Hill and Jules lived close to (the) Dry River. Jules was the one who added the fourth note. Then he started tuning pan with a broomstick. He was getting a lighter sound and was more interested in being artistic. He made four notes right in that Dry River. His band was Cross of Lorraine..."[175] Jones also indicated that Neville Jules shared his work with Andrew De Labastide who in turned shared with Spree Simon, and in discussing the inherent politics of steelband development then as compared with the steelband politics of today, Jones had this to say about Jules: "I happen to know that Neville Jules is still trying to help out the best he can, but others are only trying to take advantage. He's still the kind of person who will give more than he'll get. Always did a lot. Always tried to give a true picture of the way things were and not give any false impressions of himself because he always had a bigger picture in mind for Pan. That included helping others. Then, when with his help people got so big that they forgot who helped to get them where they are, they overlooked him. Some of these boys here in the States behave so badly, I really don't know what to say. **But not Jules. His story gives a good picture of how Pan evolved."**[176]

There is a lot of support for this view of Neville both from the point of view of existing folklore and as well as actual testimonies from people who were involved then in the movement from its inception. For example, this is what Rudy King said: "I first got into Pan in 1939 as a kid and was about nine or ten years old when I began experimenting with making my own pan. I can't remember the specific year... I can recall that when I started tuning I was attending Calvary Hill School, before I even attended Rosary RC School. As soon as school let out, I'd run down the hill and go by Hell Yard by the Piccadilly Street bridge and lean over the bridge and listen to what new song Hell Yard had. As soon as I heard what they were doing, I'd run back up the hill and do the same thing..."[177]

Similarly Vincent Hernandez of Arima, said: "I was born in 1929 in Success Village, Laventille in POS, Trinidad. I went to Western Boys RC School on Richmond Street. For a while I lived in Arima... what we had before the war you couldn't really call a steel-band. It was people using sticks and pans and so on to keep rhythm... *I taught myself to tune and to play by copying from Neville Jules*. I knew him but only from a distance and he didn't know me. To teach myself to play, I used to run away from Arima to his group, which was a big size. Whatever his group was playing, I would race back to Arima and try to do. I, being the big boss in my band, used to puzzle my boys who wondered where I got that from. This is probably the first time Jules will know that I used to fudge (cheat or steal) all the time from him..."[178]

Hernandez continued: "I remember when Jules used to use the caustic soda drum and he was the only one with a whole lot of those drums, and it was years I wanted to do that, too, but never did. I couldn't get my hand on one of them. There were some good bass drums he made back then..."[179] Another steel-band activist, Leroy Williams, while lamenting about the treatment meted out to all the great pan pioneers talked about the "disrespect" to *Neville Jules,* *"who is the father of all panmen…"*[180]

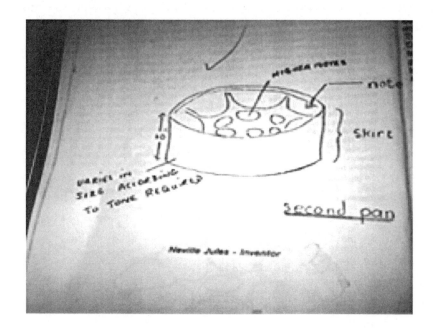

(Pic. 1)

Slater's drawing of Jules' second-pan (sic). This is taken from "The Advent of the Steel Band and My Life and Times with It" by John E. Slater. N.B. Jules himself has never claimed to be the inventor of the "single-second" and is quoted to have said that the first "single-second" he saw and copied was one made and played by Sonny Roach of Sun Valley.

In addition, when the Trinidad Guardian newspaper column, "Lies and Distortions of Pan" appeared on November 01, 1999, one unnamed person responded by e-mail to the then raging controversy in this manner: "In that time, 1954–1959, Invaders was one of the top bands and Ellie was the captain and was recognized as one of the top tuners in the business. The tuner at North Stars from Upper Bournes Road, St. James, was also one of the best. *However, growing up, Neville Jules was always recognized as the founder of pan (Canada)…*"[181]

The point is that "town" always knew where it all started and by whom, and the folklore evolved accordingly; it is only in modern times that the conspiracy of silence and misinformation seemed to have become almost insurmountable as certain noted gatekeepers adamantly strive to maintain the misrepresentations. However, as a result of Neville's work and the explosion he triggered, it is said that steelbandsmen began to play simple melodies and the "Sankee songs that the Baptists used to sing,"[182] and Albert Jones added that "**...Ellie came in later with his change, the concave with pushed up notes...**"[183]

What is amazing is that, despite all this wealth of information that is readily available, Jules and Hell-Yard is still to be given official recognition as the innovator and place of innovation of steel-pan music and the steel-pan orchestra. Neville Jules was the one person who was focused on crafting instruments of pans with a major point of departure from what obtained before; he moved the process away from the mindset of assimilating first the sounds of the African goat-skin drums and secondly the sounds of the military bands. Yet there continues to exist in this country a mental lethargy and a kind of recklessness and a-don't-give-a-damn about truth and integrity, "a kind of everything goes once you are bold enough to claim anything."

For example, Norman Darway Adams contends that Sonny Roach made the first "second pan" in 1946 and Jules acknowledges this though not in 1946. Darway went on to draw reference to a 1946 Trinidad Guardian report that indicates Sonny Roach's Band, Sun Valley, creating "*a sensation with its first and second ping pong (single second), drawing rounds of applause from the crowd.*" When the actual report was sought, the following is what was actually described in an article titled: "Steel Bands Play Brahms, Tchaikovsky in Contest; Island-wide Competition organized by Mr. Ranee Phillips: "*Sun Valley created a sensation with their first and second ping-pong which coordinated to give full expression, drawing rounds of applause from the mammoth gathering.*[184]

Darway simply added his own words "single second" in brackets after the words "second ping-pong" to give the impression that the reporter was describing a modern single second pan. But the reality is best explained by Vincent Hernandez one of the early pan-tuners who said: "In 1945 when I first started tuning pan, I had no method. I started when we had two or three notes on the pan and used pan more for timing, rhythm. Whatever spot on the pan I placed the note and tuned it and it sounded right, I left the note there. Then, we advanced to six to seven notes on the pan. *We used to call those pans ping-*

pong and had two of them to play a song. I would play on one ping-pong and another player would answer on his ping-pong."[185]

Neville Jules himself confirmed that at this point because of the limited size of the popular paint-pans most bands utilized the ping-pongs in this way especially when attempting the more complicated melodic lines of classical music, and, he intimated that the call and answer effect could be quite dynamic especially when the two ping-pongs used were each tuned at a different pitch.[186] In fact this practice of using tenors tuned at varied pitches must have been the key factor that led to the mindset, to the logic and to the emergence of the Alto Pan, forerunner to the High Tenor, very early in Jules' Family of Pans as indicated by both Leroi Boldon and Oliver Joseph. And this had to be shortly after the appearance of the 45-Gallon Big Tenor in 1947, certainly not before.

However, on the contrary, there is a claim by Sonny Roach that he invented the "alto pan—forerunner to the modern second pan—on instructions from Cecil Ward, Sun-Valley's arranger" when they desired to enter the "first Island-wide Steelband Competition" playing an arrangement of "Home Sweet Home".[187] Darway claims Sun Valley went into that competition with "single-seconds" invented by Sonny Roach who himself claims that it was an "alto pan—forerunner to the modern second", the question is: which was it? However, when the first island-wide competition, won by Sun Valley, was held at Mucurapo on 17 September 1946 at Mucurapo Stadium, the instruments used were small ping-pongs, kettles and du-dups; as already indicated there were first and second ping-pongs (i.e., ping-pongs tuned at different pitches); finally the alto-pan cannot be deemed a forerunner of the single-second for the "alto" is higher than the normal "tenor" whereas the second-pan is "lower" than what we term the normal tenor, and carries a deeper skirt. Interestingly, Neville Jules has always maintained that what we call "second-pan" is really a "tenor" in classical terms and what we call "tenor" is really "soprano".

The point is that the constant negative and unscientific approach to Pan History must be dumped once and for all. We must cease to support in anyway claims that are espoused without any supportive evidence, more so claims that are made in hindsight with complete disregard for historic chronology. We must debunk the unscientific and crass nonsense that makes it somehow honorable not to credit any one individual for the development of pan as a specific crafted musical instrument, especially after having credited the wrong individual with great pomp, passion and pageantry.

As a nation, we now attempt to hide the shame of that wrong-doing behind the creative nonsense about no one person should be credited for the birth of the steelband. The point is that certain individuals along the way accomplished very specific things and each one of them must be credited for their specificity. Imagine, after the lionizing of Spree Simon in 1974 for the birth of the melody-pan and in the immediate aftermath the casting of doubt on this accreditation from numerous sources, yet one historian in 1985 had the gall to declare that "...the knowledge that men such as Simon, Olliverre and Jules were acquainted, spent time together in at least one pan yard and may have shared their ideas suggests to me that none of them, or indeed any individual, could or should be given sole credit for early pan innovations."[188]

Imagine that, when a simple visit to the Hell Yard area and an interview with any of the people who were involved in the then goings-on around East Dry River, many of whom were then still alive in 1985, would have served to correct the history. Then that particular historian would have been able to indicate that Neville Jules built the first melody pan for V-J Day 1945 celebrations and showed Fisheye (Olliverre) the tunes to play; that Spree Simon bought a Jules-styled melody pan from Andrew Pan De Labastide who learnt from Jules; and that Jules subsequently built the supportive family of pans; he put the steel orchestra together.

The point is that in regard to the birth of the melody pan there is quite a body of evidence and citations by both people who were directly involved in the pan movement as well as by people who were far removed from the goings-on in the world of pan but were citizens nevertheless who happened to witness certain developments that made an impression on their minds and who spoke without any particular "axe to grind".

Noel "Ginghee" Davidson, the elder brother of Philmore "Boots" Davidson, in talking about the birth of the melody-pan, states without any fear of contradiction that "East Dry River was the hub of everything, in East Dry River you had fellas like Elmo "Bully" Alleyne, Eddy Rab who was Eddy Mitchell, Sonny Jones, Hamil, the Copper-Head, even Zigilee was a Hell-yard boy but he got arrested and left, and Brassey, who went to Tokyo, and the Stowe Brothers, those were the fellahs featuring in Hell Yard, where they start tuning pan—three notes, four notes, five notes—I even saw women playing pan in Hell Yard: Bubulups, No-Teeth Jean, Ruby Rab and others..."[189]

Furthermore, both Hamil and Bully, who were eye-witnesses to the appearance of Alexander's Ragtime Band, have confirmed that Ragtime "had no notes," therefore undoubtedly Ragtime was a transition to, but not the creators of, the melody pans. Ragtime's emergence in 1939 signaled the complete abandonment of bamboo-tamboo for good and for all time. And they identified themselves using quite apt, relevant and historically precise terminology: they called themselves the "First Iron Band" and that is exactly what they were, the first all-metal band.

Interestingly, actual music or recognizable melodies emanating from Pan had to have startled the uninitiated and uninvolved folks back then; it is something that they would not have easily forgotten; where they first heard it and what was being played must have registered. JD Elder the famous, world renowned anthropologist who lived not far from Hell Yard said the Hell Yard boys referred to their orchestra as an "Iron Band" and he claims they began experimenting with discarded implements and that it took the duration of the War for the experiments to come "to a head", to fruition.[190]

Christy Eversley, the son of deceased artist and sculptor, RUL (Randolph Ural Lionel) Eversley, recalled that his father ran a business on Jackson Hill, the fourth house from the Piccadilly Street corner, making marble, stone and granite tombstones for the merchant navy and for all the Churches and Funeral Agencies as well as brass plaques for offices,[191] and furthermore that his father hired young men from Hell Yard, sometimes as much as 10–15 of them to mix the cement to make the molds that would fashion the monuments. Christy Eversley was born in 1937 and he cites that the first time he heard music on pan was one day as he walked across the Duke Street bridge on the way to Rosary Boys Primary School as he usually did every day; that he had grown accustomed to hearing them beat out their rhythms but then on that particular day he suddenly heard the distinct melody of popular Calypsos being played by the band down in the pit of the river.[192]

Some of the band members worked for his father and Christy recalled seeing them on many occasions running from the police; seeing them jump over the bridge to escape and on a few occasions the results were broken limbs.[193] Christy said at times he would sit and listen to them talk as they worked in his father's business-place and that he was always enthralled with their colorful anecdotes that in each case reflected their sterling commitment to this wonder called Pan.[194] The point to note from these citations from two neighbors of Hell Yard is that they both imply that somebody or somebodies down in that pit of the Dry River, a definite location, had engaged himself or themselves in a relationship with playing rhythms on pan and pan development that eventually brought forth, melodic pan music.

Christy Eversley lived at Jackson Hill and first heard the melody of calypsos on Pan emanating from down in Hell Yard while on his way to school crossing the Piccadilly Bridge. Christy Eversley died in London in mid-2013.

The point is that everything that went before V-J Day, including Alexander's Ragtime Band was about merely utilizing pan, discards without notes, to "keep timing" and to assimilate the sounds first of the goat-skin drums and later the kettle-drums of the military. The birthplace of "Pan" as crafted musical instrument is Hell Yard. Norman Darway Adams argues that all reports that do not cite St. James as the birthplace and Ragtime as the originators are lies and all the people who have been quoted in historical accounts that indicate otherwise are liars; he is emphatic in his view that "Pan never started in Laventille, John-John, Gonzales, Belmont or in the South... These beliefs are all lies fabricated by people in search of a quick dollar... The original birthplace (of Pan) is Tragarete Road, St. James (sic), next to the place called Big Yard..."[195] And the public is informed that Darway, "this legend", this guru "has too much knowledge to let it waste like that."[196]

The underlying distinction between "pan" as the mere imitation of skin-drums or discards used to provide rhythm and keep timing, and "pan" as crafted, controlled, scientific musical device or instrument is either beyond Darway's comprehension or deliberately disregarded in his account as well as in most other accounts of the early history of Pan. But the story does not end here. In the aftermath of the 1946 Carnival, the new trend in pan-craft development, initiated by Neville Jules, really took off and anyone who today reads the newspapers of the mid-1940s will see that this fundamental difference was duly noted by commentators. Aged pan aficionados also testify to this from their own involvement with the instrument.

Julien Darius, then 88 years old in 2011, was a member of Red Army after they changed their name to Merry Makers. He was able to provide for us names of some of the Red Army members in the picture No.2. He resided in Florida and visited his children in T&T periodically. He died in January 2015.

Julien "JD" Darius before he left T&T.

One such person is Julien Darius, known in the then pan fraternity as "JD", who tells a rather interesting story. He was born in 1923 in Fyzabad and came into Port-of-Spain as a young man in the early 1940s and became heavily involved in the steelband movement when he joined Merry Makers. He informed that Merry Makers concentrated a lot on touring the Caribbean, Venezuela, Florida ("the first band to play at Cocoa Beach"), Canada, etc. during the early 1950s and up until 1967. He spoke of a close relationship between Merry Makers and the Dutchy Brothers as a result of which on their tours of Surinam they usually visited the "relatives of the Dutchy Brothers who lived there."

He also informed that he and other members of Merry Makers, including the captain, Lennard Morris, were helpful in 1955 in establishing the Katzenjammers Steelband in Black Rock, Tobago and recalls that he gave them the tune "Be Still My Soul" which became one of Katzenjammers' major musical pieces. His recent visit to the Tobago band after some 60 years, he said, "brought tears to the eyes of many" amongst whom was Ethelbert Williams, the father of the present captain of the band. JD played Pan all his life and most of all he was adamant in his confirmation that when he came into Port-of-Spain after the War, the person widely considered then as the leading pan-pioneer and pan-manufacturer was the one and only Neville Jules of Hell-Yard.[197] His is just another affirmation of the many underscoring the contribution of Jules to the development of the steel-orchestra.

However, in the course of time, there came to emerge a most salient pan development outside of Port-of-Spain. And once again today's pan historians in T&T were initially provided with a signal cue from enduring folklore. From time to time in the late 1960s, '70s and '80s, a particular story kept making the rounds of all the rum-shops, snackettes and favorite watering-holes in the East particularly those located in that area between Tunapuna and Arouca; it is a story that was usually brought up the moment any group of imbibers got involved in argument relative to pan and the pros and cons of panorama competitions.

All the youths of the area would be enthralled and be fascinated by the story related by elders about "...*the biggest f***ing pan that they ever saw in their lives which a certain fellah played in a competition in Monarch theatre, everybody laughing at the man with he cap turned "round, the peak at the back, and the pan so big that a man on either side was holding it up and he was in the middle playing it; is the biggest f***ing pan it ever had...*" So went the folklore. Now, while having discussions with Jules one day he suddenly turns to the issue of the first to tune a 45-gallon drum which is the norm today, and Jules said that he and Ellie went to Tunapuna with small 8-note ping-pongs to compete in a pan soloist competition at the Monarch Cinema in which Ellie came first and Jules, second, and there they were confronted with this guy "with the cap turned round" playing the first ever 45-gallon tenor pan, with a man on either side holding the pan, and all the while being laughed at and heckled by the crowd.[198]

It was then that the realization hit home; to anyone who was born in 1946 and after and grew up knowing the tenor pan and all pans being crafted from the 45-gallon oil drum, that bit of folklore would certainly have deceived such a person's sense of pan dimension. And my response to Neville's words were, "wait a minute, back up there one second, you mean to say that that was the first 45-gallon tenor pan; my gosh, that story of the player, with the cap turned around, and a man holding it on either side, has made the rounds in Tunapuna for years and the impression left always was that that Pan was so unbelievably huge that it might have been crafted from sheet metal." What is suggested by the folklore is that the variant or the departure from what was then considered the norm, the difference in size between the small paint-pan ping-pongs and the 45 gallon tenor-pan, seemed then to be so immense that, in the story-telling, the actual bigness of that 45 gallon tenor came to be vastly exaggerated.

It appeared to be so big precisely because its opposite, the norm then, was so small. Given the perspective of such response to this particular 45 gallon pan, i.e., the player was virtually jeered off the stage, there can be no other **first** 45 gallon tenor pan save and except that one which appeared at Monarch Cinema in Tunapuna sometime in 1947.[199] "Within a few months, two to three," said Jules, "Ellie, I and everyone else, began using the big pan, the 45-gallon drum."[200] With all this before us, it is time to debunk all the various claims and to pay homage to the first creators of a 45-gallon tenor pan.

Who were they? That historic event, the first appearance of the 45-gallon tenor pan, has been recorded for posterity in the following manner: "In 1948 (sic), when steel-bands were still made up of ping-pongs made from small Vaseline and paint pans, with just a few notes, Boom Town Steel-band (of Tacarigua) entered its first competition at the Monarch Cinema, Tunapuna. It was at that competition that Cyril "Snatcher" Guy featured in a historic event when he went on the stage and played his "big pan," a ping-pong, made from a "fifty-five"(sic) gallon oil drum, for the first time in the history of the steel-band. The pan was tuned by Mr. Randolph Phill "Ladd" Wiltshire and Mr. Andrew Beddoe. Snatcher appeared on that stage with what was considered his trade mark style of attire, wearing his bebop cap with the peak to the back."[201]

"Ladd" Wiltshire indicated that he and Snatcher Guy were employed at the construction site of the Caura Sanatorium and they got that drum, which was used to store water, at the cost of $3.00.[202] Cyril "Snatcher" Guy said they stole the drum from the Caura Hospital site.[203] Andrew "Run-In" Beddoe, a noted Orisha drummer and member of the John-John steel-band, was the confidante and paramour of Mother Gerald, the Orisha High-Priestess, whose palay was next to Boom Town's pan yard. It was said by author Kenrick Thomas, also a Boom Town member, that "Ladd" Wiltshire learnt a lot about tuning pans from Beddoe who with a cold-chisel made clear indentations to demarcate each note providing thereby a clearer sound on the concave "55(sic)-gallon" oil drum.[204] In his book, PANRIGA, Kenrick Thomas places the date of the appearance of the big pan as 1948 (sic) but he recalls in a discussion later that the Boom-Town band took a cultural exposition, "a whole troop of performers, singers, dancers" on tour of Tobago in 1947 and that the band went with big tenor pans on that tour and therefore may also have been the first band to introduce the big tenor to Tobago.[205]

In 1947, Cyril "Snatcher" Guy (above) played the first big tenor (45 (metric)gallon drum or 55(imperial) gallon drum) at a competition in Monarch Cinema, Tunapuna. This picture is courtesy Kenrick Thomas.

In addition, Cyril Scanterbury, better known as "Crapaud", a person knowledgeable of Tunapuna's history, recollected, in an unrelated discussion, that one of the earliest pan-men of Tunapuna, "Satan", i.e., Rufus Moses, bought 2 big pan tenors from Neville Jules in 1947 and he said that he recalls the incident precisely because the two tenors were "tuned in different keys" and Jules had to correct this subsequently.[206] Both recollections supports the view that the first appearance of the 45-gallon tenor pan was in 1947 which has also been acknowledged by none other than Neville Jules himself in discussion with Kim Johnson.[207]

Ken Duval of the well-known Duval Family of Port-of-Spain who was born in 1936 indicated that at the age of twelve (i.e., 1948) he was taken to All Stars Yard by one Cecil Edinborough (relative of Walton and Felix) and they bought a 45-gallon drum "first pan" from Neville Jules for $3.00 which they had gotten from Ken's father Edwin Duval then the owner of a hardware store and the developer of Diego Martin lands.[208] Ken Duval also informed us that himself and Cecil invited their CIC schoolmates home to show them the Pan and the idea to form a band was discussed; subsequently they acquired a "bass-kettle" and a "second pan" and they began, he said, to "jam music" in a sort of "entertainment and recreation area" of the Duvals' property, and eventually Ernest Ferreira of Corbeau Town was made Captain of the band and the band was moved to the Ferreiras' yard and from those humble beginnings the great Dixieland Steelband emerged.[209]

This information is corroborated by John Ernesto Ferreira himself who was honored and inducted into the 2008 Sunshine Awards Hall of Fame in New York and who talked about that tenor pan, "purchased from Neville Jules, painted in All Stars colors" and which was transported in "Mr. Duval's car to his Petit Valley home."[210] Ferreira also detailed the transformation of this band from being a CIC-Boys band to *Boys from Iwo Jima* to *Melody-Makers* and eventually *Dixieland*.[211] The point of all this: further evidence that the big tenor was widely in use by 1948, and secondly that this Ken Duval/John Ferreira story implies that even those middle-class boys of Port-of-Spain West, just as most people of Tunapuna, Arouca, Arima, and as well people from South Trinidad knew where they had to go to get Pans in the early period just after the War. Roy Regis, a personal friend of Theo Stephens, informs that Emile "Zola" Williams, captain of Free French, was so impressed on hearing Theo play that Zola brought Theo into POS to get Neville Jules to make a pan for Theo.[212]

This fact is supported by the direct words of Theo Stephens himself and it indicates how early in the process Jules had become the go-to person... *Port-of-Spain was it and at that time Jules was it, so my godfather say he got to take this boy to town and see if he could get him a good pan... So myself, Zola and my godfather and a friend went up for the day. So we went to him and after a little bit of style he decide to make it and he did. It was an eight-note pan and we brought the pan back in the night.*[213]

There is certainly enough here to once and for all remove the "picaroon" approach to the important affairs of pan development; certainly there is enough information now to defy the Port-of-Spain or town-centric outlook, "the-everything-happened-in-town" myopia, and in this context, the even narrower view that seeks to remove altogether "the birth and struggle for pan" away from Hell Yard and Laventille, and center it foremostly in Woodbrook and its immediate environs (i.e., St. James). Steelband development took place over the length and breadth of the entire country.

Proper documentation will have to examine the contributions that came from all the major community areas and establish the essential linkages before the total picture can be revealed to us. However, with the emergence of the 45-gallon oil drum as the most durable and appropriate drum for the crafting of the musical instrument, pan development made a quantum leap, and so Neville Jules in the years 1948–1951 could then have utilized the 45 Gallon drum to conceptualize and further build his *family of pans* as described above…

The Seventh Captain

Neville "Cap" or "Big Moustache" Jules was the 7th Captain of All Stars (1950–1971) and the creator of the family of melody-pans. He has been regarded by the pan cognoscenti as the father of the modern steel orchestra. Both Fisheye Olliverre

and Prince Batson were bestowed with the Captaincy of All Stars by Jules who desired to spend his time crafting pans into musical instruments rather than in the administration of the band. He died in 2020 at the age of 93.

March 1946: An overhead view of panmen parading along a street in Port-of-Spain, during Trinidad Carnival celebrations.

(Photo by Earl Leaf/Michael Ochs Archives/Getty Images)

By 1946, as this picture indicates the bugles were still carrying melodic riffs or bits of melody backed by cuff-booms, du-dups (bass-kettles) and the instruments in the middle were "beles" which were four or seven note pans played with two sticks; one held downwards and the other upwards...
(Courtesy Earl Leaf and Michael Ochs/Getty Images)

(Pic 1)

Courtesy Patrick Raymond. Waterloo Steelband of East Duke Street, 1946. Instruments: biscuit drum, bass kettle (du-dup), three-note kettles, and one handheld tenor(ping-pong) with 13-14 notes. N.B. No Bugles.

(Pic 2)

A picture of Red Army around 1947. Note well, two eight-note Ping-Pongs and probably 3 Beles. Note also how the Bele players in the middle hold the sticks, the stick in the left hand is held downwards like the military kettle players did, and the stick in the right hand is held upwards. On these three Beles there seems to be a range of 4 to 7 notes. This band went to BG in the Christmas of 1946. Picture is taken from Darway's Stories in Steel. Julien Darius, JD, identified Lennard Morris "Aga" (far left) as the leader; "Choie" (Atkins), far right, with small tenor, and the man standing in the middle with the Bele, JD identifies as Ulric "Chick" Springer.

After all these years, JD born in 1923 and then 88 years old could not identify anyone else in the above picture, but he did reveal that other key members of Red Army, a band whose red flag carried the symbolic "hammer and sickle" were Alfred "Sack" Mayers, Teddy and Mack Kinsale, Alfred Cooper, the drummer, Kenrick Drayton, brother of "Maifan" Drayton of Invaders, Lucas and "Nancy" whom he said was the brother of the famous boat-builder on Sackville Street. Note well, there are no bugles.

(Pic. 3)

Band in South with 45-gallon tenors in 1948. Courtesy the Trinidad Guardian, Wednesday February 11, 1948. The Big Tenors are not strapped and are played with one stick. The Cuff-Booms however are strapped. Mr. Roy Regis has identified the above band as Southern Marines of Marabella that was led by the Lyons Brothers, one of whom, namely Fitzroy, was a well-recognized pan soloist and a national cyclist. Regis also identified the teenage conductor in the photo as Billy Green. Kim Johnson in his Series titled "Pan Pioneers" informs that Southern Marines was founded by five Lyons Brothers and five Green Brothers and indicates that Milton Lyons was the recognized soloist (see "If Yuh Iron Good You is King" by Kim Johnson, pp. 152–154).

(Pic. 4)

Picture of Band in Port of Spain in 1947 with big pans strapped around their necks and using two sticks. Courtesy the Trinidad Guardian, Tuesday Feb 18, 1947. The name of the band is not mentioned but the width of the skirt of the pans suggests that they were middle-background pans (i.e., second's or most likely alto's as the picture is dated 1947). Whoever they were, they were some of the early ones to strap the pans in this manner. TASPO in 1951, four years after, did not have such straps. Obviously the straps were essential for playing on the road on Carnival days.

(Pic. 5)

This is a picture of Invaders in 1949. Note well, big tenor, du-dup (bass kettle), an alto-pan, and two 5-note tune booms. Courtesy Trinidad Guardian Saturday February 19, 1949. Melody lead pans are also strapped. How come TASPO in 1951 did not go to England with straps? Jules showed Ellie the Tune-Boom during the Christmas of 1948. The time lines are quite clear.

Chapter Three
TASPO (Trinidad All Stars Philharmonic Orchestra) and TASPO (Trinidad All Steel Percussion Orchestra)

Another name change was visited on the Hell-Yard Band sometime in 1949. After "Second Fiddle", during which time the band was sometimes registered as "Fish Eyes' Band", the next name chosen was "Cross of Lorraine" but even that had to be quickly dropped when it was realized that Casablanca had already adopted the Cross of Lorraine itself as their band's quite identifiable insignia. Of course, all of that had come about through the steelbandsmen's long-standing attraction to War memorabilia and Casablanca's particular penchant for portraying French Sailors on Carnival Days.

After some deliberation and on cue from Odgrell "Vats" Rudder, the ex-Casablanca mas-player, who on hearing the band play a few of Jules' in-depth arrangements, shouted out, "you are all, Stars," the new name was declared: All Stars.[214] Bully's version is that Vats said "boy, all I see around me is a setta stars."[215]

Odgrell Rudder nicknamed "Vats", a shortened version of "Vatican" which implied in local parlance "a pretty masquerader," was born in St. Vincent in 1919, was brought to T&T at the tender age of two and grew up first in San Fernando, then Port-of-Spain and as a young man was gainfully employed at the US Chaguaramas Base as a boiler-man.[216] Vats Rudder was the person whom Fisheye in 1949 had introduced to Patrick Leigh Fermor as "my Managing-Director." It was Samuel "Jitterbug" Peters, the master flag-waver, who added the prefix "Trinidad" to the "All Stars" name implied by Rudder's acclamation.[217] Jules in his usual brutally honest way suggested that Vats Rudder's assessment then that the band was a collective of "Stars" did not necessarily stand up as in his (Jules's) own opinion, Invaders, Casablanca, Sun Valley and some other bands had at that time stronger virtuoso players.[218]

Mr. Odgrell "Vats" Rudder (1919–2010) when he was around 35 years of age. He was a "big mas-player" who left Casablanca to join All Stars.
(Pix courtesy Ms. Akende Rudder, his daughter).

Mr. Odgrell "Vats" Rudder when he was 91.
(Pix courtesy Ms. Akende Rudder, his daughter).

Nevertheless, whatever the members of All Stars may have lacked in terms of individual ability, Jules knew he could surmount with tight discipline and well-rehearsed orchestration;[219] and in this context, Prince Batson and himself were the band's rigid enforcers.

It seemed that the toughness for which the Hell Yarders were noted from since the days of Sagiator and Big Head Hamil had simply passed from generation to generation. Hamil kept order with a "bull pestle", and so, in similar fashion, when Prince Batson's directive one night that all "coasting" be stopped while the band rehearsed was ignored by Fisheye, the former Captain, Prince threw a flambeau at Fisheye and the kerosene from the flambeau fell on Fisheye and set his whole head on fire.[220] That most likely was the final incident that led to Fisheye's complete separation from the band, though the other Olliverre brothers, Willie, Desmond, MacDonald (Man) and Bunny stayed on.

The band was divided into "committees" with specific functions and there were clear-cut rules and regulations to which all members had to adhere: internal friction over women was taboo; personal conflicts were to be kept out of the band; each member was warned from the moment of joining that for the first year of involvement there would be no pay; there was to be no argument or confrontation with other panmen; and on no accord should any member visit any other panyard.[221]

In discussing these rules and regulations of All Stars, one commentator said: "The more important of these (rules) are attendance at practice sessions on specified days, voluntary obedience to the leader in matters concerning the organization, loyalty to the group, and good behavior in public; minor deviations from the rules are subject to small fines which are invariably paid without coercion, as the members themselves experience great pride in membership of the organization..."[222]

In regard to Jules's style of leadership, this is what the commentator said: "From my observations and conversations with members of the group, it appears that the single abiding virtue which endears Jules to his fellow members is an overall sense of simplicity and sincerity. He can be firm without bullying, and regards himself with a peculiar lack of arrogance as being *primus inter pares* (first among equals) in the group..."[223] But even more telling is the fact that given earlier negative experiences with money, All Stars under Jules adopted the strict policy that all proceeds from engagements would be shared equally among members "after depositing a fixed proportion in the central fund of the organization..."[224]

The full and proper name of the Band, according to Prince, during the period under his watch, was Trinidad All Stars Philharmonic Orchestra (TASPO), though the "philharmonic" was seldom used, and the flag, still ever present today with the map of Trinidad draped with stars, was designed by Kenny Waldron, a tailor by profession,[225] who was one of the original single second pan players in the band.[226] Even that distinctive bell which is still used today to start performances was the special property of the deceased Orisha man, Prince Batson, strong then both in his spiritual as well as his secular discipline.

When on that fateful Carnival Tuesday, the All Stars Sailor Band passed through Belmont and some mas players "raided parlors and vendors on Jerningham Avenue," it was Prince and Jules who, the next day, went the rounds and compensated the victims for the damages received.[227] That was an indication of the kind of organization these two were attempting to build and the nature of the internal system of relationship they desired to foster.

Prince said in no uncertain terms that All Stars had to be a "brotherhood" which, with an open democratic spirit, was supposed to share everything possible whether it was food, i.e., the roasted breadfruit that kept them from hunger many a day, clothes, cigarettes, whatever, and to cement all this, the catalyst was the music.[228] Prince indicated that the band at that time could not participate in the early competitions outside of the Carnival because some members did **not have proper shoes**.

One regular visitor to Hell Yard in those days described the hardship the panmen endured then in this manner: "It was not only a matter of Jules living on coffee and cigarettes while making and tuning pan; those fellahs suffered. I remember men in their drawers while their one and only pants on a line drying. There was a breadfruit tree in Hell Yard that sometimes would save the day— because mankind hungry, so it was roast' breadfruit and roast' saltfish. And don't talk about de women! **Without the women dem fellahs and Pan would not have survived**. Women like "Orka-Dork", she used to live with Fire Kong, she would cook and bring food fuh dem fellahs in Hell Yard. Those women, many of dem unemployed, they were not rich, but with the little change they could afford, they would bring food fuh dem panmen in Hell Yard. **That is how Jules and dem survive. Without dem women panmen and Pan would**

not have developed. I talking about women like Mayfield, Ruby Rab, Janet, and even Barbara Pan-Cup who does still be in this yard, she would come here, sit down and quietly have a beer and most people don't know she and how long she in dis Yard..."[229]

Sonny Blacks who grew up in the Hell Yard area and now lives in England where he has contributed significantly to the development of the Trinidad-style Carnival, also testified to Neville Jules' contribution when he posted the following: "Jules is one of the humblest humans you will ever meet... I knew him from my schooldays, holding the tuning fork while he and Bates were tuning in Hell Yard. People do not know the hard work and dedication Jules, Bates, Jitterbug, Hamil and other unsung heroes spent each and every other day to create and innovate and develop the steel pan."[230]

Jules referred to Prince as the "ideas man", whatever the problem, Prince would pose a solution, for example when the wooden mallets with which they struck the notes began to fray at the edges, Prince suggested that the ends be wrapped with strips of rubber and the end result was enhanced tonal quality and smoothness. Now there are many who claim to be the first to place rubber on the sticks supposedly in order to obtain better tonal quality but Prince and Jules are the only persons who say that they were addressing a practical problem, i.e., the fraying of the sticks and they found a practical solution that by pure chance provided tonal quality. That difference signifies a great deal about the process and sociology of invention.

Jerry Serrant also indicated that Prince Batson was "the main provider of meals many a day and night"; and what meals—"broken biscuits, salt and sweet, eaten with relish with or without pieces of saltfish tail; mauby and rock cake from Tom Keen's parlor, orange and lime squash, belly-full made from stale cakes, and accra and float" and as most of them were unemployed, Prince became a "veritable Savior" probably because Prince himself had known hard times earlier in his life after he was forced out of the family home because of his association with the band and had "lived in trees and under houses to escape the wrath and big-stick beatings from his father."[231]

Jules himself tells that when his mother moved to St. Joseph, he stayed in town to be near the band, and had to hustle and gamble to stay alive, sleeping sometimes "by Fisheye and them or in Royal Theatre",[232] all this probably explains why the bonds between Jules and Prince were so strong. Eventually, it was Prince who would prove able to even house the band for a short while at No.15 Bath Street opposite to Bar 20 in a place for which he was the caretaker, before the band ended up in their **first garret** location upstairs the Royal Club on George Street, through Bully's connections.

Much later in the late '60s and '70s, Prince would turn up with his personal lorry or truck whenever transport became an overwhelming issue for the band. Indeed, he was a savior to the band, as was Bully Alleyne, and according to many, these two had great influence on Neville Jules and Neville's way of thinking.

The years 1948–1950 were marked by serious violent clashes between steelbands in Port-of-Spain; Invaders, Tokyo, Casablanca, Red Army, Sun Valley and Cairo of St. James, etc.[233] The one quite notable Band, absent and totally removed from the spate of violence caused largely by friction over women and other petty jealousies, was Trinidad All Stars. One commentator was moved to say the following: "To be a steelbandsman in those days was synonymous with being a hooligan, a social outcast. We see a change from this pattern of development with the emergence of a new leader of the Hell Yard group in the person of Neville Jules, whom they regarded as their most skillful exponent of the steel drums. Unlike the previous leaders, Jules foresaw the great potential of this new type of musical expression and proceeded to develop it into a respected local art form. He embarked on this venture with great assiduity and at the same time sought to remove the social stigma attached to the steel-band by striving to eliminate violence and anti-social behavior within its ranks…"[234]

It is interesting also that whereas most of the bands took their names from War Movies which denoted "violence"; All Stars chose not to do so. It was testimony to the management of Prince and Jules who steered All Stars away from the typical tendency to embrace internecine warfare while readying the forces only for all musical confrontations.

In fact, in all the years of the Hell Yard aggregation, there were only two violent episodes; the one in 1937 at the Wang already mentioned, which was more or less an internal dispute, and the other during the War, in the mid-1940s, with Casablanca at the corner of Pembroke and Duke while on the famous allotted 3 hours parade from 6pm to 9pm;[235] it is said by some people that Casablanca personnel were rattled by the defection to All Stars of Vats Rudder who previously had been their main benefactor, and this resulted in their attack on All Stars, "just where the Hall of Justice is today" and led to the killing of a Hell Yarder, named "Dog-Twenty" who was struck in the head with a biscuit drum and died from the blows he received.[236] According to this source, the altercation went on for about two weeks; Big Jeff, Big Sarge and Jitterbug were the front-line fighters in the name of All Stars backed up by Big Head Hamil who, although he no longer frequented Hell Yard as before, returned to organize a bull-pestle posse that prevented Casablanca's personnel from utilizing Charlotte Street under any circumstances, and finally Jules and Oscar Pyle held peace talks and thereby settled the matter by way of negotiation.[237]

Other sources to the contrary, indicate Casablanca went to the police-station to have this fracas stopped, but confirmed that there were only about three supporters of All Stars who were doing all the fighting, i.e., Big Sarge (Hugo Peschier), Big Jeff (Henry Patterson), and Mark-Off (Cuthbert Parsons).[238] There is the view that although the pan-playing members of All Stars were not themselves "bad-johns", nevertheless the presence of people like the three mentioned above, together with others such as Granville Roberts, guaranteed that "Trinidad All Stars remained free of fear of hooligan rivals."[239] And of course, there were always other Hell-Yard "limers" present such as Joe Pringay and even Eugene De La Rosa (Mastife) to daunt the spirits of any would-be opponents.

Nevertheless, at the end of it all, it would be the respect with which Neville Jules was held as a pioneering musical giant within the steelband movement nationally at the time that guaranteed All Stars the space Jules required to enhance his in-depth orchestration and his professional musical techniques quite unmolested, while others persisted with the wanton, useless violence.

Jules tells an interesting story of how on one occasion he quelled a budding clash of the titans, i.e., Big Sarge and Big Jeff: apparently Big Sarge had had a series of altercations with certain individuals who were members of the infamous Boysie Singh Gang and in a particular incident an attempt by one of the latter to attack Big Sarge with a hand-grenade led to the pin being pulled and the individual lost both hands; as a result of this and other such engagements, Big Sarge was always in and out of jail and on one of these occasions, while Sarge was in jail, Big Jeff befriended Sarge's woman and this led to a confrontation between these two while All Stars was on the road during the Carnival. When Jules was informed of the building conflagration between the two, Jules went to them handed them each a piece of iron and said "let the three of us play the iron together" and they did as instructed, kept the timing and thereafter ignored their hostilities.[240]

And it was not as if in the early years Hell Yarders, and later All Stars players, did not have to absorb much of the brunt of the attack from police officers. John Slater in his document cites one occasion in 1942 when a band was parading over the Hill and the Police came to arrest the pan players and a "certain fellow we used to call Jitterbug performed a heroic role when he grabbed a revolver from one Policeman and threw it into a cesspit", and Slater concluded that such was the extent to which panmen defended their rights to beat their pans; "there were instances where (sic) panmen and their supporters were beaten by policemen unmercifully... some panmen were even jailed for disturbing the peace... but despite (sic) all the harassment and all the trials and tribulation we continue (sic) to beat our pans..." [241]

This is how an eyewitness described one scenario after the suspension of Carnival in 1941: "The escape valve of Grassroots frustrations was caulked yet again and, as in the past, the exuberance of the populace would explode. Revelers would defy Headquarters and Besson Street Police patrols. Raid followed raid, night after night. Loads of Pans and People were whisked away in the Black (or Blue) Marias, as the Police vans were known then. But, night after night, more Pans and People would appear. It was a mixture of terror and excitement as our Steelband Baby was exposed to the rigors of our own local social war. Up and down Nelson Street and George Street, along Charlotte and Park, on Observatory Street and Behind-the-Bridge. In and out of gateways and through the Dry River. Everywhere terror and excitement! Hell Yard and its pan People did not—could not—escape the turmoil and turbulence...

...Jules, the Maestro himself, was among those arrested (many times), only to elude the Police in a hilarious situation on one occasion. But like the rest of his Pan confreres, he refused to allow the Police crackdown to curb his experimentations in developing the Steelband-instruments and movement."[242] There are a few descriptions of that said "hilarious situation" mentioned above. Guy Boldon, the father of the international athletic star, Ato Boldon, described it best: "It was approaching dusk when members of the Trinidad All Stars Steelband took it upon themselves to come out of the yard and "make a block..."

"...In a short space of time, there was the "black maria" approaching from the rear of the crowd. It was noticeable, however, that there was no mad scramble to escape; there must have been something worth celebrating that day. The policemen alighted and enquired, "who is de Captain of dis band?" and meekly Neville Jules stepped forward and accepted the mantle of captaincy. "You are under arres' fuh disturbin' de peace!" The officer held on to Jules' right hand as they proceeded toward the black maria. As they arrived at the back of the van, Jules bent his head downwards and removed the instrument from about his shoulders laying it gently on the ground, perhaps strategically, between himself and the officer. He placed both his hands on one side of the bass and with a nod of his head invited the officer to assist him in gently lifting the instrument into the vehicle.

By the time the officer had completed pushing the pan further into the vehicle and turned to complete the arrest, there was no Jules. I will never forget those Dunlop shoes. In the winkle of a red ants twinkle, there was a blaze of flashing white soles in the now fading evening light, heading east along Duke Street, leaving behind the hapless police officer, the Black Maria and a solitary bass without a player."[243] From what in reality had Jules escape? Probably a fine, a few days in jail and /or six (6) lashings with the tambran whip, and the charge would have been recorded as disturbing the peace and a breach of the Habitual Idlers' Ordinance, usually enforced at that time by a Bajan senior police officer.[244] Not unlike the "alguazils" of an earlier time.

Guy Boldon suggested that the stoicism he witnessed on that occasion implied that there must have been something worth celebrating that day. Jules indicated elsewhere that that incident took place at a Christmas time, that the band had gone over Laventille Hill parading and that they had made up their minds beforehand that they would not scamper if confronted by the police, in fact Jules's direct words were: "that Christmas, a particular friend of mine said, "let's go on the road, man, if police come, me ent running at all."[245] Jules did not name that person, but one can hazard a guess that it could well have been someone such as Hamil, Jitterbug or Bully.

Furthermore, Jules indicated that they may have been deceived by a Casablanca member who used to serve warrants and who had entered the band on their return from the Hill and he had begun to "direct the band and the traffic" so they felt comfortable that they would not be arrested.[246]

On another occasion, Jules would explain his philosophy that whenever he made a new instrument, or recrafted an old one, the only way to test it, to measure it's suitability, he had to go on the road with it; so he used to take the opportunity of parading at any time they felt in order to test instruments. There is also the view that Christmas-time, given the parang or parandero concept, had become an accepted traditional time to parade. The panmen, according to Jules, were very stoic about their stance that if parang people could parade, then so could steelbands, and since Christmas time was the ideal time to prepare and rehearse for the coming Carnival season, panmen seized that time to parade with their pans, defying any attempt by the state functionaries to discriminate in favor of the paranderos. Later as the War progressed, cultural activists such as Albert Gomes, negotiated from government, the 6pm-9pm, allotted hours on specific days for parading which all pan people grasped enthusiastically.[247]

Jules' view that the suitability of a pan was best measured by the people's response to it while parading, is taken to further depths by another pan activist who explained the affinity between calypso and pan development in this manner: "…The beauty of Pan is that it can play all music. However, it's best suited for Calypso. You see, it originated from calypso music, with the people who were developing an instrument to go with the calypso tradition. So, Pan evolved in the Calypso tradition… A culture is something, eh! Our culture is Calypso and Steelpan. The piano was made for the European classics, and that is their culture. Drums and jumping and dancing go together, as you can see among some Africans and Native Americans. That is how culture evolves, with one activity complementing another. For us, it's Steelpan and Calypso. That's our culture…"[248]

So Jules and others had no way to measure the perfection of their craft other than playing for the masses and judging their psychic connection to the instrument; for when the music hit them way down in their bellies, they would usually respond with deep, guttural sounds and frenetic movement of their bodies, their inner emotions exploding in mad exuberance. Slater's account of the effect pan had on the people has already been quoted, he said that revelers used to get into a frenzy… they used to jump like crazy people."[249] Whenever pioneer panmen like Jules saw such passionate response from the people, it was only then that they would acknowledge and accept that "de pan good."

1951: The Tour to Britain

While the violence between steelbands raged and All Stars remained aloof to these petulant goings-on as Jules continued to focus on building his family of pans, a group of concerned citizens, "progressives" and social and cultural activists, came together to devise means to curb the wanton violence and at the same time pay homage and honor to the culture of the pans for which the grassroots had shown such great preference even at the expense of all other forms of music. Despite all the ferocious attempts by the colonial state to stamp out physically the practice of "beating on pans", despite all the disparaging adjectives and contemptuous language used to describe the activity, including the stated desire that such devilish creation should not be used to play Christmas Carols; the reality was that no form of repression or suppression could curtail the love of the masses for this growing phenomenon.

Leroi Boldon reports that the priest who was in charge of the choir and the symphony orchestra at St. Mary's College tried everything possible to get him to be involved in the so-called respected musical art forms and when that priest could make no headway with this personal project, he found his way to Boldon's mother to protest Leroi's preference to "beating ends of dustbins."[250] On the other hand, Boldon emphasized the fact that when they lived in Woodbrook, John Buddy William's son, Noble, a good friend of Leroi's, used to be "tapped up" by the guys around because he attended violin lessons.[251] So the movement toward pan had become a groundswell, almost a tsunami, to use today's vocabulary.

As it is noted throughout the history of mankind, anytime the elite prove unable to stem the tide of any grassroot development, elements among them, usually the more liberal of their kind, join the movement from below with the aim to guide and channel it into "acceptability", and in that way they come to earn citations and social rewards and recognition for being citizens of substance who had the vision to embrace the doings of lesser beings who at the time supposedly "couldn't speak for themselves." It was therefore no historic accident that at this point, the government, taking cue from outspoken political activists, foremost of whom was Albert Gomes, set up a committee in November of 1949 under the chairmanship of noted cleric, Canon Farquhar and comprised of people like George Mose, the Chief Probation Officer, Lennox Pierre (radical lawyer), CR Ottley, historian, Beryl McBurnie, folk artist/dancer, etc. to investigate the cause of the steelband violence and to recommend solutions.[252]

As a result of the deliberations of the first meeting of the "Government Steelbands Committee", as it came to be known, the suggestion was posed that a Steelband Association be established as "a means of preventing misunderstandings that lead to violence."[253] At early meetings in 1950 called to discuss the formation of the Association, they found themselves having to deal with a number of very pressing issues such as pending indictments against certain steelbands; members of bands who were incarcerated at the time and the individual matter of a charge against Ellie Mannette for stabbing.[254] George Goddard indicated that after a few meetings in 1950, the Association was formed with Sydney Gollop of Crusaders as President; Nattie Crichlow of City Syncopators as vice-President; Sonny Harewood of Crusaders as Secretary; George Goddard of Invaders as vice-Secretary and Carlton Bidhi of Rising Sun as Treasurer.[255]

Furthermore, Goddard reported that the first assignments of the elected officers were (1) to call a halt to all steelband competitions organized by individuals at which the standard of judging was poor and contributed to clashes between rival steelbands and their supporters; (2) the establishment of a Southern Branch of the Association which in his view was accomplished rather quickly and smoothly given the positive response from the people of San Fernando.[256]

All Stars stayed far away from the efforts to form the Association, and in hindsight many of those people involved then would probably confer now that not to have joined the Association was a grave mistake. But at the time the members and leadership of All Stars were tremendously mistrustful and suspicious of the middle-class citizens who were suddenly jumping on the steelband band-wagon. The newspapers had had a field day disparaging steelbandsmen whom they described as "undesirable elements who have no inclination or aptitude for work and are by nature, indolent, feckless and unruly..."[257]

One person that All Stars particularly held in disdain was a certain "white Probation Officer" who at one time advocated that a Steelbands' Register be set up so that authorities would have a line on everybody around the pan movement and know exactly where to reach them and how.[258] This may have been the reason why Jules at one time, under constant threat from the police that Hell-Yard would be raided and pans seized, chose to use a number of fictitious names geared to protect his identity and hide his place of location; names such as "Carlton Manuel", "Joseph Atkins" and so on, as a result of which, Batson maintained, people would be playing his own inventions and be none the wiser whom he was.[259]

(Pic. 6)

1951 TASPO in Britain. Note well a three-bass, played by Boots. Also note no strapping of tenor pans and the single alto pans (i.e., those with wider skirts). Given evidence of strapped pans in 1947, 1948 and 1949 in Trinidad, one is left to wonder whether TASPO frontliners chose to go to Britain in 1951 without straps because they were then more comfortable using one-stick.

(Pic. 7)

Lieutenant Griffith conducting TASPO in London during the 1951 tour. This picture is courtesy.
www.nohumK12.ca.us/mhs/ebridge/images/uploads/.../TASPO 0001pdf.

This picture tells us exactly what instruments TASPO used. The text carried with the above picture indicated that there was a three-bass, it's at the back played by Boots Davidson; two double-cellos, one played by Tony Williams,(Big Muff) on the left, and Dudley Smith, on the right; two alto pans (wider skirts) played by Belgrave Bonaparte and Sterling Betancourt, they are to the right in the picture; and five tenors (i.e., Pan de laBastide, Spree, Ellie, Theo Stephens and Patsy Haynes (the smallest). It was supposed to be six tenors but Granville Sealey of Tripoli was replaced by Sonny Roach of Sun Valley who in turn fell ill in Martinique and returned to T&T.

The position of his tenor at an angle between his legs suggests that Ellie had his tenor strapped and there appears to be a strap around his neck which would have allowed him to play with two sticks. See also the picture on pg.76 of George Goddard's book which also shows that Ellie's tenor is strapped around his neck unlike the others. Was Ellie the only tenor player in TASPO who strapped his pan and was he playing with two sticks?

(Pic. 8)

Boscoe and Shelia in Britain in 1950. Note, the tenors are strapped. Courtesy Sunday Guardian, August 10, 2003. Sheila's pan is strapped yet she is using one-stick. Boscoe, based on how his body is positioned, suggest that he is using two sticks, not surprising as the Holder Brothers were all competent musicians.

The fact that the early sessions called to form the Association were held at the office of the Chief Probation Officer, a Mr. George E. Mose, i.e., Probation Department Headquarters, an annex to the Red House,[260] must have caused All Stars great concern given their distrust of a particular "white Probation Officer".

Jules explained his position then in this manner: "…Though Pan was my life, I didn't become too involved with TASPO (i.e., Trinidad All Steel Percussion Orchestra). My band wasn't a part of it because All Stars was not a member of the steelband association. After hearing all the negative things about Pan, as a steelbandsman, of course I was a little suspicious of certain middle class people like Lennox Pierre who were suddenly interested in Pan. I decided then to stay back and look and see what was going on first. I was wary of the whole thing. That's the only reason I didn't get involved with the association…"[261] "Little suspicious" was indeed a great understatement.

In fact, back then as indicated above, the leadership of All Stars, i.e., Jules and Prince Batson were very "wary" of the sudden embrace by people who generally tended to view steelbandsmen as "wharf rats", "low country, small-islanders"—a term borrowed from the Yankees who referred to all Caribbean people as "small-islanders" and middle-class elements here picked it up and applied the terms to all migrants from the smaller islands, north of us [262]—and yet when Butler marched his people into Port-of-Spain in 1947 and he gained support from the Waterfront workers who were already on strike, it was the very steelbandsmen in Port-of-Spain whom the employer-class sought to suddenly befriend and use as strike-breakers.[263] Such developments played a great part in the decision of the All Stars leadership to stay away from this elite-led effort.

Interestingly, Prince Batson contended that if the internecine violence between the bands was the underlying and motivating factor that triggered the resolve to form the Steelbands Association, then All Stars, who were not party to the aimless violence, could exempt themselves by the very underlying logic of the exercise.[264] A similar view was also expressed by some steelbandsmen in the South, in fact members of the Southern Marines said that they did not join the Association because "we had no badjohns and we all decided to stay out."[265]

Furthermore, the very idea, promoted by the Association, that privately sponsored competitions for steelbands contributed to the warfare and should be curtailed immediately, was one that the leadership of All Stars rejected outright; in their view there was absolutely no evidence of any clash that resulted directly or indirectly from the judging of any of these competitions. That was a red-herring in their view particularly as the very opposite was the case; the competitions fostered development and to some extent even camaraderie among the bands. In fact, the promotion of this idea about privately sponsored competitions being a negative factor and the major reason for the violence may have served only to work in the favor of the self-interests of a few people.

Invaders and Casablanca fought each other on sight from 1948 to 1950 and were the main ones regularly appearing before the Courts for rioting, as the reports indicated "with cutlasses and corrosive fluids."[266] And not surprisingly these two bands, and others of similar mindset, were the main members of the Association and apparently from the very onset projected the pretext that their violence somehow had to do with jealousy and envy over who possessed better pans and better players hence the reason why one of the first acts of the Association was to stop competitions organized by individual promoters which they deemed were poorly organized and poorly judged.

Nothing could be further from the truth say the old members of All Stars; the war between Invaders and Casablanca began with a dispute between Zigilee of Casablanca and one of the Blackhead Brothers of Invaders, i.e., Carlton, over a woman whom they called "Little One."[267] And it is even suggested that the Invaders/Tokyo war really had nothing to do with Ellie's nine-note ping-pong, his "barracuda" as he called it, though it may have ended up a spoil of war, but rather may have had to do with some silly argument that occurred down on the "Gaza Strip", i.e., a string of nightclubs down on Wrightson Road, or it could have been over Norma Callender of St. Paul Street, East Port-of-Spain, who was then Ellie's main heartthrob.

Ellie himself at one time said: "…The rivalry and the clashes between the bands were for no particular reason. We were all beating the same rhythms. Sometimes, one guy would have a girl-friend and that might have caused some jealousy. But how the fights really started, I don't know. I was a part of it, and I have no regrets…"[268] However when he came home in October 2000 to receive an Honorary Doctorate from the University of the West Indies, he then lamented about the "senseless and reckless violence" of his time as a youth which served to stigmatize the instrument and he pleaded with the present authorities to "do the things" necessary today to promote and honor this "instrument of integrity" as the present generation are not reckless but are serious about their musical involvement.[269]

The point is that the leadership of All Stars always recognized that much, if not all, of the violence of the past had to do with conflict over women, hence the reason why, as mentioned before, there were clear-cut rules and regulations laid out for prospective members wishing to join All Stars and foremost amongst these rules were (1) avoid all friction over women, and (2) never bring personal conflicts within the band. The Sagiator/Eric Stowe debacle that occurred early in Hell-Yard's history obviously would have informed All Stars' rules and regulations in this regard.

The Trinidad & Tobago Steelbands Association became fully active after the 1950 inaugural meeting with a Southern Branch comprised of Free French, Destroyers, Tropical Harmony, Southern Symphony, etc. but this overall national effort continued without the input of a key Port-of-Spain Band, the Trinidad All Stars Philharmonic Orchestra. When the Festival of Britain was brought to the notice of the Association, the decision was taken to take a representative steelband to the Festival in 1951 and ten of the top panmen of that era were chosen to make the trip. Actually, it was eleven but one (Sonny Roach) fell sick and returned home from Martinique. Jules said that it was reported to him that when his name was mentioned as one to be selected, "Speaker" (i.e., Talkative), Wilfred Harrison, of Desperadoes objected on the grounds that All Stars was not a member-band of the Association.[270]

From a technical standpoint, no one could fault Speaker of Despers for the position that he advanced, nevertheless people were quite prepared to disregard that technicality to get Neville Jules on board, but Jules himself would not budge. Lennox Pierre, who helped Lieutenant Griffith to prepare the representative steelband to tour Britain, confirmed that numerous overtures were made to get Jules on that TASPO tour but all the approaches were rebutted.[271] Yet one historian, in probably the most hurtful of unkind cuts, informed the world that "Neville Jules was selected but failed to make the trip because of insufficient practice,"[272] thereby reducing the maestro, the musical genius, a most disciplined human being, to the most common level of ordinariness. And Darway, the Champion of the West, had to ask: "…When TASPO was formed, great panmen like Ellie Mannette, Spree Simon, Dudley Smith, Patsy Haynes and Sterling Betancourt were members, where was Neville Jules?"[273]

The reality is that Darway questioned the absence of Jules as if to suggest that one's absence from TASPO indicates one's lack of importance to pan history, and given such a level of thinking, Darway could not help but miss completely the salient distinction of the fact that all the persons he mentioned, were, at that time, all noted virtuoso players as opposed to being both notable pan pioneers/inventors as well as virtuoso players like Jules and Ellie.[274]

But what was the reality? Leroi Boldon, in response to the comment that Lennox Pierre and others had made numerous overtures to get Jules on board for the Tour of Britain, said: "…If you study the make-up of TASPO, you have to remember they were all frontline guys. Everybody in that band was a tenor player except Boots. Ellie was a tenor player. *But they couldn't solo*. Jules now, he could play tenor, but his strength was in the background pans.

However, ***Jules could solo***. But Ellie and the other guys, (at that time) couldn't solo.

I was talking to Hugh Borde the other day (*i.e., at the usual after Carnival lime that Hugh holds for panmen every year, this was in year 2009*) and Hugh was telling me that when Griffith pointed to guys they couldn't solo. So there was a big gap in that make-up. Jules would have filled that gap…"[275] "Solo" in this particular context refers to the ability of an instrumentalist to use his/her instrument to improvise or to perform extemporaneously, without preparation beforehand, to play counter-melodies on the chords, and what Hugh Borde in fact was saying is at that time none of the front-liners in TASPO could have done that competently. Of course they all could play the melodies of pieces they had memorized but were not adept at soloing on the chords extemporaneously. Boldon's argument is that Jules would have filled that "gap".

There is, however, some contention in regard to this question of the ability of TASPO players to solo on the chords. First of all it was reported that Boots Davidson played "solos" on his "three-bass boom" during the recital which the band undertook before leaving for Britain.[276] So if the front-liners could not, at least there was this accomplished musician on the bass, Boots Davidson, who could "solo". Furthermore, one Pan enthusiast, Roy Regis, argues that he witnessed Lieutenant Griffith positioning the microphone under the tenors of different people such as Theo Stephens and Ormond "Patsy" Haynes to allow them to "solo" at a cinema in San Fernando before they left for Britain in 1951 and he described all the TASPO front-liners as "crack-shots".

In addition, Regis is adamant that Theo Stephens then of "Free French" band was noted for bringing the house down with his ability to "solo" at a competition in Port-of-Spain also prior to TASPO.[277] What however is yet to be ascertained is whether these "solos" were in fact rehearsed, memorized solos or impromptu improvisations on the chords. Certainly Theo Stephens' soloing on the tune "Anna" that brought the house down at the 1954 Festival was pre-determined and learnt and that event was not prior to, but in fact three years after, the 1951 TASPO trip.

Ellie Mannette himself was reported to have said that Lieutenant Griffith not only expanded the horizons of the TASPO players in terms of their repertoire but also thought them the rudiments of improvisation.[278] Ellie said: "He showed us that steel drums could play other types of music and we didn't have to play the calypso rhythm all the time; so he started showing us the Blue Danube Waltz and other light classical pieces."[279] But as early as 1946 at the Mucurapo Stadium competition steelbands were already playing Brahms' "Lullaby" and Tchaikovsky's "Concerto" (cf Darway) and Ellie himself in relating elsewhere the story of his nine-note "baracuda" pan and the conflict with Tokyo reported that he made a "big-pan" (i.e., 45 gallon drum) and won a competition in Skinner Park playing Brahms' "Lullaby" and "Goodnight" as a result of which he was invited the next day to Radio Trinidad to play on Auntie Kay's program where he did Schubert's "Ave Maria".[280]

However, in regard to improvisation, this is what Ellie said about Griffith: "The third thing that was important was he showed us we could do improvisation. So when we were playing he would stop the band and have one of the guys get up and do a solo. He would point to Andrew DeLabastide or myself or Theodore Stephens and we would do a little solo. So that again was something different from what we did before…"[281] The impression one gets here from Ellie is that the players were not yet proficient in this regard but there are reports that indicate that Boots Davidson, the then TASPO three-bass player, a formally trained musician, was quite a proficient soloist. However "Chick McGroo" (Ulric Springer), and Neville Jules were by 1951 exceptional virtuoso tenor-players and competent soloists but sadly neither of the two were members of TASPO.

Interestingly, as Oliver Joseph indicated above in his recollections, Jules was quite proficient at soloing on the chords and this view is avidly supported by Leroi Boldon. But in describing Jules's proficiency as a tenor soloist in general (i.e., playing memorized as well as improvised harmonies), Boldon revealed a rather amazing fact: "…Jules would rest the tenor in his lap and play with two sticks. I remember Neville will be playing, again with the pan on his lap, and he's smoking those days, and we were playing a tune called *Brazil*, which is a samba, which is a reasonably fast tune, and he's playing; and he held the sticks very uniquely. I don't know if you ever saw him play. Neville holds the sticks like a drummer (*and Boldon demonstrates with the rubber-covered end of the sticks pointing downwards, rather than upright as is the norm*). Yes, and he was lighting a cigarette, and we played *Brazil* fast, and he put his cigarette in his mouth, lit the cigarette, but didn't miss a note. I was standing right behind him…"[282]

Jules in a recent conversation acknowledged that he held the sticks downward at one time, and when asked if that was possible because of the great skill he had developed as a youngster playing the tenor-kettle with two sticks off the shoulder, Jules in response, chuckled and said "Bukka, yuh really doing yuh wuk," meaning that the assessment was spot on...[283]

Furthermore, Dr. Leroi Boldon also quoted Ray Holman, now himself a renown pan soloist, on the question of Neville Jules' proficiency as a soloist. Boldon said: "Ray Holman did a lot of concerts with my band in San Francisco, and once told me that the best individual pan performance he ever heard about was Neville playing and although Neville only played half of the tune because the pan slipped off his lap and he stopped playing, nevertheless Neville was still placed second in that soloist competition..."[284]

Interestingly, the reference here is to the 1952 Music Festival when Jules placed second to Dudley Smith in the soloist competition. But Ray Holman, born in 1944, would have been only 8 years old when that Festival occurred which suggests that he most likely got that story when he became engaged with Invaders in his early teens. However, the following is what Jules himself had to say about that particular incident that *has been so deeply retained in steelband folklore*: "As a matter of fact, there is still talk going around about me at the first Festival we had when I performed as a soloist. All the top soloists at that time were there...

...During the test piece, when I started to play, the audience thought I didn't know what I was doing, because everyone else went up and began playing the test piece right away. They had no introduction, nothing at all. When I went up, I had an introduction that I played, and you could hear all their murmuring. Then suddenly they heard the test piece starting to be played. They started to talk even louder, and that threw me off. Now, a lot of betting had passed: Jules will beat this one, that one cannot beat that one, and what not. In the middle of the tune, I stopped playing and stood up and walked off the stage. Northcote, Pat Castagne, and all the other judges left and came backstage to encourage me to return to the stage and complete my performance. I refused. They continued for about five minutes or so, insisting for me to return and play. Eventually, I said okay...

...Then, Northcote went on stage to talk to the audience about how they must behave. He told them that when artists were performing, there must be total silence. He continued (saying) that when Jules returns to play, all who had placed bets had to take off their money. I returned and played and came second. I couldn't come first. Dudley Smith won that solo competition. That was in 1952. A lot of guys still remember that: Ah, you walked off the stage..."[285]

Oliver Joseph, who was in the audience then and from that vantage-point witnessed the incident, described it this way: "Jules was playing the introduction, and the introduction blew everybody away, and a guy just jumped up and bawl, "oh Gawd!" and that put Neville off, the pan didn't fall from him or anything like that..."[286] Jerry Serrant described the incident this way: "The trill with which the Maestro introduced his solo so thrilled the fans that they could not help but burst into applause, completely upsetting his concentration. Jules was in the process of walking off stage when Adjudicator Northcote recalled him..."[287]

So that was the performance which prompted Ray Holman to reminisce while in Boldon's company that it was the best individual pan playing he had heard about up to that point. Clearly, one could now comprehend why John Slater, after commenting on the fact that Jules did not participate in the tour to Britain by TASPO, "the greatest steel orchestra ever put together" because All Stars was not a member of the Association, lamented: "…What a pity, because as far as I am concerned **the world was deprived of seeing and hearing one of the greatest pannist of all times.** I knew he was a very reserved person, and that might have been the reason why he avoided publicity throughout his pan career..."[288]

A similar view was expressed by Prince Batson who said: "Jules is one of the greatest players of the tenor pan that I have known but he was and remains shy and always stays in the back-ground..."[289] Courtney Vincent Charles, the flag-man, also lent credence to Jules' pan-playing prowess when he said the following: "When Mano Charles died in 1959, All Stars accompanied the funeral to the cemetery… the pans covered with black cloth, boy, Jules crying, Mano was his best friend, the man crying long tears, and he playing tenor-pan like mad, people say they never hear pan play so…"[290]

Another commentator addressing that funeral described it this way: "In 1959, one of the most versatile members of this steel-band collapsed and died on his job at the Port of Port-of-Spain. The group decided to relieve his widow of all funeral arrangements and undertook the full cost of his burial expenses.

The general procession was solemnly attended by all the members, with their steel-pans draped with black cloth. At the graveside, amid the muffled cries of the relatives of the deceased, the band rendered a slow and mournful version of the well-known hymn, *Abide With Me*, and it is said that Jules' riffs were out of this world..."[291] OJ also confirmed that that funeral of Pascal "Mano" Charles on Boxing Day 1959 was the very first funeral accompanied by Pan; they walked from Simpsons to Sacred Heart Church and then to Lapeyrouse Cemetery; at certain moments the coffin was lifted above the heads of the pan-players, and he also described how Jules ramajayed, blowing people's minds, amidst all his tears.[292]

Many who were then close to Jules have concurred that his self-restraint, his introverted characteristics, probably even shyness, was a major factor that served to deter his involvement with the Steelbands Association and denied him the world recognition that would have come with the tour of Britain. One member of All Stars said that Jules "never went to the front, that was his only limitation, if Fisheye was the Captain then, things would have been different; ***Jules was concerned only with making his pans, tuning them and then arranging music for them, it was his only concern...***"[293]

There is another account that indicates that Jules was advocating that All Stars' much celebrated bassman, Eddie Shurland, be selected to make the tour while Boots Davidson was insisting on the selection of Jules himself.[294] But in his assessment of Shurland's ability, Roy Gibbs, a long surviving member of All Stars, identified Shurland's shortcomings: "*Shurland had flair. Great showmanship. But he couldn't create the chords to accompany a Tenor Pan Player carrying a melody on his own. Jules had to give him the music. All the time! Jules made him what he was...*"[295]

It is essential, however, to keep in mind that these assessments of pan-playing capabilities were done in the period 1950–1957 and are not to be misconstrued in terms of today's possibilities. The point is, however, that given the assessment from various persons noted above, Jules was exceptional and probably one of the leading virtuoso players.

This recording was done in 1957 by Kay Records on Nelson Street. Rhythm ah la Oil Drum displays Jules' dexterity as a master soloist. On the flip side is the calypso, "Doris Oh". This recording is available on YouTube.

The 78 RPM, LP, titled ***Rhythm a la oil Drum*** showcases Jules' soloing capabilities over the background pans on Side One; the flip side is the then popular calypso ***Doris Oh,*** which likewise reveals what Jules and a couple back-up All Stars players could have done back in 1957.[296] All Stars also has in its audio archives recordings of Jules' effective solos on "Ping-Pong Serenade" and "Maracas Bay" also done in this very period. Praise must be given to Aubrey "Bolo" Christopher who was co-owner of Dial Records and later owner and main technician at Kay Recordings at No. 7 Nelson Street.

At Dial Records, noted for the map of Trinidad in the middle of the disc, "several steelbands recorded. They were the Funland Steelband, the Johannesburg Fascinators, the All Stars, including Neville Jules and his **hot ping pong**..." The word **hot** was obviously used here to indicate the excitement generated by Jules' solos. "Bolo" Christopher also identified Jules "as a true pan innovator and one of the creators of the *kittle, ping-pong* and the *tune bomb*" and he credited Jules with "having had the foresight to record at his small studio on Nelson Street small sections of All Stars backing up Neville Jules"[297]. Moreover, these recordings were done outside, behind the studio, because of the limited space inside of the establishment.

This building was once the home of Aubrey "Bolo" Christopher's Kay Records at No. 7 Nelson Street POS, a stone's throw away from Hell Yard.

"Bolo" Christopher operated with limited space on the inside of his studio. Pictures taken from When Steel Talks © Donald Hill.

According to Wikipedia, EMI Records Ltd of Middlesex, England, a legal entity, was created in 1956 as the record manufacturing and distribution arm of EMI recordings in the UK. It oversaw EMI's various labels, including the

Gramophone Co. Ltd, Columbia Graphophone Company and the Parlophone Co. Ltd. Wikipedia reports that EMI Records was "one of the most culturally significant labels in popular music" and was at "the forefront of every seminal musical movement." (Cf. *https://en.wikipedia.org/wiki/EMI-Records*).

Apparently, Mr. Bolo Christopher established official relations with EMI Records UK where pressings were manufactured of his recordings done at his humble studio on Nelson Street. According to Jerry Serrant on pg. 66 of his periodical titled: "The Maestro Neville Jules—When De Bomb Explode—The Trinidad All Stars Steelband Saga—From Hell Yard an' Back," EMI recorded four very popular pieces of music by the Trinidad All Stars Steel Band and these are available today on YouTube; the tenor solos are indeed quite awesome, indeed "hot" and captivating.

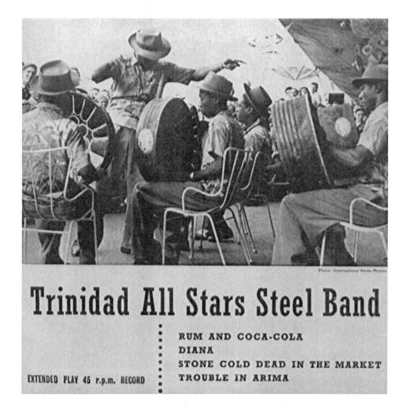

E.M.I. Records Ltd used a picture of the TASPO aggregation of 1951 on the record cover, one hopes that they had permission so to do.

The four very popular pieces of music by Trinidad All Stars which were recorded by EMI, according to Jerry Serrant, are as follows: *Rum and Coca-*

Cola sung by Lord Invader and popularized internationally by the Andrew Sisters; *Stone Cold Dead in the Market* which was composed by Wilmout Houdini and later became an international hit after Ella Fitzgerald did a cover version; *Diana* which was Paul Anka's first pop hit in 1957; *Trouble in Arima* which was a hit calypso Lord Kitchener sent back home and became the Road March for a number of years. Due to the availability anyone can go to YouTube and listen to the "hot" captivating solos a la Neville Jules.

Speaking about the hostilities, with which panmen had to come to terms in this **early** period of their development, Professor Donald Hill had this to say: "There were eight steelband clashes and several hundred people were injured, one person was killed, having gotten out of his car in the middle of a steelband fight. He was beaten to death when he was hit with a baseball bat. The riots erupted when there were high levels of post War unemployment and rivalries between grassroots and middle-class bands were intense. For several years the Trinidad Guardian, defender of middle class value, railed against the bands…"

Professor Hill also alleged: "…On the one hand, there were… tourist venues that glorified traditional arts and packaged them for foreigners and the middle class. On the other hand, there were the negative prejudices, some middle class people had toward the bands, the steelband clashes and the struggle for identity for the grass-roots folk…" (cf—Dr. Donald R. Hill, Professor of Africana/Latina Studies and Anthropology—A paper delivered at the annual meetings of the American Folklore Society, Pittsburg, Pennsylvania on October 17, 1956—When Steel Talks Exclusive@2013.)

The folks of Hell Yard have over the years rejected all such attempts to suggest as did Prof Donald Hill that steelband clashes were the results of conflict or tension between "grassroots and middle-class bands" or as a result of the buildup of frustration to survive in times of economic depression and the resulting intense competition that arose between steelbands within the depressed communities. The history as enunciated by the people who were involved clearly indicates that the supporters of the various bands clashed over rivalry for the amorous attention of women. It was the "man-thing"/ the macho-complex more than any other factor.

A woman from one community was off-limits to a pan man from another community. Any breach of this unwritten law led to open warfare as the men involved rallied their forces against each other. Invaders and Casablanca; Invaders and Tokyo, waged war for months with each other over exceptional women. The very same issue almost destroyed All Stars in its early formations (i.e., Eric Stowe vs Sagiator).

Otherwise, the main issue for the steelbands was the issue of outright State Repression by colonial authorities who utilized the police force in numerous ways hoping to curb the spirit and exuberance of the lower classes in their efforts to test their instruments parading the streets at Xmas time, Carnival time or on Discovery Day; a habit that came from their copying of the Military Bands who did their "route-marches" with their "kettle" drums whenever it was so required or desired or as did the traditional "parang" bands in announcing the birth of the Christ-Child with their mandolins, guitars and cuatros. Parading on Discovery Day in particular was promptly banned after the tourist was struck with a baseball bat and died after attempting to drive through a parading band.

However, on the other hand, when the lower middle-class college boys joined the process on Carnival days they were protected by older grassroots bands. There was one occasion when the college-boys of Dixie Land were threatened by one grassroot band but the then two foremost, outstanding grassroots bands (Invaders and All Stars) rallied to their cause and dispelled that apparent threat. Finally, the further development of Local Government structures; the establishment of the Steelband Association and with this the national recognition bestowed on the Steelband Music Festivals, coupled with the gift of TASPO to the world, together served to smoothen over the rough edges.

Moreover, it was Trinidad All Stars, led by Neville Jules, which instilled once and for all the understanding within the Nation that music competition, rather than fueling intense violence as so erroneously proclaimed by some, in reality generated further development of the skilled crafting of pan instrument and the deepening of a local culture.

So when the San Mateo on Friday, 6 July 1951, sailed for Britain to reveal T&T's great gift to the world, Pan, the then greatest living pan pioneer, the father of the steelband movement and probably its greatest virtuoso player was absent. Trinidad All Steel Percussion Orchestra (TASPO) was indeed made much poorer by the absence of the de-facto leader of the Trinidad All Steel Philharmonic Orchestra (TASPO). There were no hard feelings and All Stars was very much involved in the fund-raising process; playing at a concert held in the North in support of the effort to raise the 15,000 pounds needed to fund the trip, particularly after the Government of the day was unable to contribute the 6,000 pounds the Association requested, forcing everybody "...from Port-of-Spain to Sangre Grande, from San Fernando to Princes Town, Carenage to La Lune, St. Mary's, Mandingo Road, and New Grant, Old St. Joseph Road to "Puna—everywhere, everybody of count (led by the Governor, Sir Hubert Rance and Aide-de-Camp, Lt. Brian Gething) chipped in to send TASPO to Britain."[298]

All Stars played at the Old St. Joseph Road concert, and Roy Gibbs, after expressing the joy the band felt in helping the tour of TASPO, said: "The band headed back to camp, up George Street, playing 'After Johnny Done Drink Mih Rum'."[299] And as usual the people reacted passionately; rejoicing in the All Stars' music and at the same time honoring the fact that finally the world would be made to experience our gift. Roy Regis recalls that Bully Alleyne nevertheless always expressed the view that "TASPO's loss was All Stars' gain" because the year 1951 triggered the period in which Jules rose to his creative best and was able to build the foundation that has sustained All Stars to be the institution that it is today, and conversely Bully pointed out the number of bands that went into demise when their leading lights joined TASPO and left the country, e.g., Crossfire, Chicago (Hill 60), Rising Sun, Southern Symphony, City Syncopators.[300]

In the course of discussing the TASPO tour of Britain in 1951, there have been a few revelations that shed light on certain aspects of pan development:

Lennox Pierre's Information

Lennox Pierre, who is now deceased and was involved with the late Lt. Joseph Griffith in preparing the panmen for the tour of Britain, said: "Just before the band left for Britain, a fellow came and showed us how the frontline pans could be strapped around the neck and allow for greater dexterity, playing with two sticks but it was too late to make the change-over."[301] When he was asked to name that person, Lennox Pierre, thought for a while, then replied: "His name was "something Villaroel" from either Tunapuna or Tacarigua, somewhere up in the East, but it was too late for us to change anything."[302]

While on the tour of Britain, all the front-liners of TASPO, except for Ellie probably, had the pans seated on their laps, held the pans at the top or side with one hand and played with the other using one stick. Yet just before they left someone from the East had brought them a revelation. Lennox Pierre's information later resulted in a frantic searched beginning at Tunapuna with the intention to move to Tacarigua afterward. But, after some blanks as the name "Villaroel" did not seem to ring any bells, it was the late Hugh Clarke of Green Street, a well-known drummer, jazz aficionado and music-hound, who blurted out: "yuh mean, Sneggs, from Tacarigua; boy, he was the baddest improviser and soloist on a tenor pan we had up here in those days, he even play with Mexitones from Fairley Street, Tunapuna for a while, ah think he went away long time, playing pan on a cruise ship and never come back."[303]

Interestingly, "Sneggs" is Venice Villaruel who was born in Princes Town, came at the tender age of three with his family to live in Tacarigua, and from youth, "demonstrated his God-given musical talent" by way of a "fanatical love for the steelband" and was "always there practicing and experimenting" being consumed with the potential of the tenor pan and this "romance with the pans diminished his desire to attend school."[304]

Venice Villaruel was a star player in the "Boom Town" band which in 1947 at the Monarch Cinema competition had given the world the very first tenor pan made from the 45 gallon oil-drum. If that very band gave us the first 45-gallon drum tenor, it should be no coincidence that someone from that same band would come up with straps around the neck to solve the attendant problem that arose with the introduction of the "first big pan" that was held by a man on either side as Cyril "Snatcher" Guy played it.

According to the foremost pan-historian of Tacarigua, Venice "Sneggs" Villaruel in the period 1949–1955 had "…developed into a real master on the tenor pan; his dexterity with his hands and ability to extemporize in any tune, (an art that was then called "revving" but is now labeled "ramajay") was remarkable, and during that period in the band's history the repertoire was vast; whenever we were playing a tune, there was always a part reserved for him to display his artistry in "revving"… and he would gleefully go off rambling all over the pan, within the melody of the song, because he really loved to "beat pan." To Sneggs, pan came first, second, and third on his order of priority. He was really a consummate pannist…"[305]

One cultural activist and vintage music curator who lived in Tunapuna in the late 1940s also informed that he witnessed Sneggs at the home of music teacher, Marie Humphrey, on Fairley Street playing "Ave Maria" with one hand while simultaneously playing counter-melody with the other hand, which he regarded as an amazing accomplishment by someone so early in the history of pan development.[306] Sneggs Villaruel left T&T in 1957 and toured "the length and breadth of the continent of Europe as well as Northeast Africa" and was known to have sojourned in Istanbul, Turkey and Israel. He died in London in 1991 at the age of 55.[307]

The point to note is that the "someone" whom Lennox Pierre said brought the revelation of ***strapping the tenor-pan around the neck and playing with two sticks*** to TASPO in 1951 before they left for Britain was in fact a 15 year old boy from Tacarigua: **Venice "Sneggs" Villaruel**. Interestingly, there needs to be recollection of the fact that Boscoe Holder and his wife Sheila while on tour of Britain in 1950 with their dance troop took along with them two tenor pans made by Ellie Mannette, and this husband and wife team played the big tenor pans strapped around their necks, as the relevant picture of them performing *Bal Creole* for BBC television reveals.[308] Boscoe and Sheila therefore were the first to introduce Pan to Britain (see Pic. 8). However, one commentator who witnessed performances by TASPO before they left assures that none of the tenors or altos were strapped and were all played with one stick.[309]

Jules' tenor pan in 1958.

Ginghee's Story

Noel "Ginghee" Davidson courtesy Akende Rudder

"Ginghee" is Noel Davidson, the elder brother of deceased Philmore "Boots" Davidson, and probably because of his small physique as compared with that of his younger and famous brother, it is reported that, in places like Tunapuna, which they both frequented at one time, he was fondly referred to as "Little Boots." Ginghee provided a diagram of their Family Tree that started with the name of African ancestors from Dahomey, Nigeria and Sierra Leone, and at the very top was the name of Hunga Keesa, followed lower down by the name John Bonaparte Archibald Gordon and from there sprung names like the Davidson's, Grant's, Gordon's, Arnold's, Melville's, Christmas's, Price's, Murray's and so on stretching from Scarborough to Speyside to Roxborough; the length and breadth of Tobago.[310]

They inherited land passed on from old Colonial Masters and could be deemed to have become part of a new landed gentry in Tobago. "There were people in this big, integrated family," said Ginghee, "who shopped by catalogue from England; they ordered clothes from Bristol and other such places."[311] "And music," he concluded, "there was always music on both sides; the Gordon's as well as the Davidson's, there was always a piano in our house.

My mother played the piano as well as my sister Ira Davidson-Arnold, they were both accomplished and gave music lessons."[312]

As they grew up on Quarry Street, "Boots", not Ginghee, developed the ability to read and score music. "Boots" reflected the musical tradition of this family that originated in Tobago. In 1940, Ginghee at the age of 14 and Boots, then aged 12, got involved in the pan movement starting with a little band in the Tamarind Yard in Quarry Street, which they named "Buccaneers", eventually the Quarry Street band merged with Casablanca of Oxford Street that was only "300 yards" away, according to Ginghee, who, however, claimed that they, the "Buccaneers" had the better players in the likes of "Boots", "Patsy" Orman Haynes and Kelvin Pierre.[313] Ginghee confirmed that following on the developments in Hell Yard where "notes" were first placed on Pan, Boots and a fella named Calsie became two of the tuners in Casablanca.

Venice "Sneggs" Villaruel, one of the earliest virtuoso tenor players. This picture is courtesy Kenrick Thomas.

Then there is a rather interesting turn to Ginghee's story. He said: "…around 1943, my mother took Boots and me down to Point Fortin. *We met no band in Point.* Boots opened a band after the War and he named the band

Casablanca too. Boots was an apprentice in the machine shop in Point and started tuning pan down by the market and all about the place; he was also a good footballer and if he had remained down there he would have become known in this regard but he came back to Port-of-Spain in 1946 and stayed. I started working in UBOT and kept moving backward and forward from POS to Point because we owned property down there."[314]

This is supported in general terms by the following statement: "In another version by one Franklyn Roberts… (published in the Trinidad Express on May 4, 1996)"… it was said that "the steelband started on Adventure Road, in Point Fortin, at the end of the war… this was due in part to Philmore "Boots" Davidson whose mother lived on Caanan Road and allowed the Point Fortin youths to form a steelband and call their band "Casablanca."[315] When Ginghee was asked to provide names of persons who were initial members and supporters of the steelband that Boots started in Point Fortin, the following six names were the ones he readily recalled: Carlton Mollineau, Carl Assing, a Fireman then, the Hamilton Brothers, Iron Monger, Carlton Rondon and Sonny Mary."[316]

There was a comment in a newspaper by one Humphrey Reefer who claimed that Pan was invented in Point Fortin, so Ginghee was asked if he had encountered any such person during their sojourn in Point Fortin and he replied: "Reefer was ah ice-cream man, he used to sell ice cream from ah cart… Reefer knows there was no steelband in Point when we got there…"[317] Truthfully, it may have been the very first steelband that Mr. Reefer heard but he may not have been aware that the initiators of that particular band were two youngsters from Port-of-Spain.

In 1950, Ginghee said, they separated from Casablanca and formed City Syncopators and it was as leader and tuner of Syncopators in the years 1950–1955 that Boots really became widely known as a tuner and was responsible for the emergence of a number of steelbands on the East-West Corridor, i.e., Ebonites of Morvant; Zone Stars, the Chinese Association band; Syncopators of Tunapuna and St. Joseph; Joy Land Syncopators from which emerged "Tash/Ash" of Desperadoes fame; Dem Boys of Belmont.[318] Confirmation of Boots tuning pan in the Tunapuna area was provided by Carlyle McIntosh, brother of the late Ms. Louise McIntosh, famous music teacher and founder of the Pan Pipers Music Academy in the Tunapuna/St. Augustine area.

He indicated that both "Boots" and "Little Boots" actually "lived" in the area for short periods.[319] The reference to Noel "Ginghee" Davidson, the elder brother, as "Little Boots" is indeed quite interesting because though small in physical stature he was noted to be the defender of his younger but gentle giant of a brother; Oliver "OJ" Joseph indicates that on one occasion after a football game Fisheye beat Boots in a fight and Boots went for his elder brother, Ginghee, and Fisheye had to run for his life, "Ginghee, wasn't easy!" OJ declared with a laugh as he concluded the anecdote.[320]

When the members of TASPO were being interviewed before they left for Britain, the following was said of Philmore "Boots" Davidson: "We shall show the King how to beat pan," Davidson, aged 22, declared... ***Davidson is the only member of the band who can actually read music. He plays the piano...***"[321] What was not said is that he also had been an apprentice machinist and a skilled tuner much like Ellie Mannette and Jules. At this point, it is crucial to allow Ginghee's revelations to be provided in his own direct words:

"Boots was like a leader musically. When they came back from England in 1951, most of the guys used to congregate by Boots. They all use to come to our home in Quarry Street. Spree used to come, the Bonapartes, incidentally they were the only others who could read music besides Boots, and Andrew Pan as well used to come. The only man I didn't see come to Boots is Ellie Mannette. Tony Williams and Boots became good friends while on tour. Tony Williams, Muff-man, used to come every day in Quarry Street; ***they decided about the fourths and fifths pan, and Boots tuned one***. That happened somewhere around 1953–1955. I remember Boots drawing out the pattern on paper. The boys in Syncopators didn't want to play the pan that Boots tuned so he took that pan and put it away quite up under the house in Quarry Street. That is how Boots managed not to be around, because he leave in 1955, and this boy, Tony Williams, Muff-Man, he went along with it (i.e., the fourths and fifths pan), but the two of them consulted one another. Boots came back to visit once in 1982 and he died in England of an asthma attack on October 23, 1994 at the age of 65."[322] When questioned directly about whom he would credit for the invention of the Fourths and Fifths Tenor Pan, Ginghee replied: ***It was the result of collaboration between Boots and Muff-Man.***

In his book, *The Story of Pan Am North Stars*, Cyril S. Matthew indicates that Anthony Williams was a carpenter by trade, who possessed an interest in astrology, numerology, science and religion and used the Bible as his inspiration to develop his pan skills, began in 1953 to work on "his Spider Web designed pan." Mr. Matthew also informs us that Tony Williams got the idea "after buying a tenor pan from Lennox Pierre which was based on a circle of fourths and fifths." Mr. Matthew further indicates the following: "To accommodate as many notes as possible Tony looked at the spider's web and decided to place the notes on the pan in a Spider Web design… He then arranged the notes in the circle of fourths and fifths… each note was a fourth from its neighbor in a clockwise direction (a fifth from its neighbor anti-clockwise…)"[323]

Although Lennox Pierre, a lawyer, was neither a pan pioneer nor pan manufacturer, there is no indication of the source of this "fourths and fifths tenor" which he sold to Anthony Williams. Nevertheless, Ginghee's story puts Anthony Williams in close collaboration with a professional musician who could read and score music and was a pan pioneer and pan manufacturer devoted to pan development.

This is how Philmore "Boots" Davidson was described by one British reporter who covered his funeral: "Mourners yesterday remembered him as a gentle giant who carried his head "held up high". They talked about his shy manner, his soft speech. He was a maestro, one said, a 'teacher extraordinaire'."[324] Another report indicated that the Police were of the belief that the excitement of a proposed trip to New York "to receive an award in recognition of his services to pan" may have triggered the asthma attack.[325]

What is indeed quite salient is the similarities between Davidson and Neville Jules; they have both been described as shy but at the same time selfless in their capacity to share with others; Jules was always willing to share his knowledge of the building of the family of pans just as Davidson would help initiate steel-bands all over the East-West Corridor and help extend people's musical capacity; they were both described as extraordinary "teachers". **The other feature which they also share is that they both can be described as the two most forgotten men in the history of Pan Development.** They are truly the unsung heroes of the history of Pan.

Interestingly, this is what Ginghee had to say about the Pan Competition that was held during Carnival 1950: "…When Boots became the (leading) player in Casablanca, he passed and he heard All Stars playing *Bless This House* and he came and told Oscar Pile, "Oscar, boy we ain't stand a chance in that competition. " That was the 1950 competition. So Oscar asked, "what we go do?" And Boots say, "Well, I go do something for the band!" And Boots came home and he asked mih sister to play *Nocturne in E-Flat* every morning and (after some time) he went to the yard with the tune and the band start playing it… When Devlan Comma from Woodbrook heard what Casablanca playing he came up the hill to hear them play the tune and after he hear them play it, he gave them the end. And so said, so done. We played *Nocturne in E Flat*, we played *My Love Loves Me*; we came on stage with that, and the other tune was *Bells of St. Marys*. We won the competition outright…"[326]

In fact, Boots' advice to Oscar Pile turned out to be quite favorable as All Stars did play *Bless This House* and *My Wild Irish Rose* on that Carnival Sunday and placed third, while Southern Symphony of La Brea led by the "musically-gifted Bonaparte Brothers placed second playing *Samba Cumana*."[327]

However, Ginghee advanced the view that Casablanca's playing of Chopin's *Nocturne in E Flat* at that competition in 1950 was, as he put it, "how classics began to be played by steelbands."[328] But to the contrary, there is evidence that All Stars, then the Hell Yard Band led by Fisheye, played Bach's version of *Ave Maria*, for Leigh Fermor and friends while rehearsing for the 1949 Carnival,[329] and even as early as September 1946, steelbands, such as Sun Valley of St. James, Red Army and even Casablanca themselves, at a competition at the Mucurapo Stadium, some four years before that 1950 competition, were reported to have presented European classics such as Brahms' *Lullaby* and Tchaikovsky's *Concerto*.[330]

It stands to reason therefore that the introduction of European classics to the Pan instrument coincided with the very early moments of the development of Pan in the late '40s. However as Prince Batson pointed out, prior to the 1952 Festival, All Stars did not participate in competitions outside of the Carnival because the members did not have **proper shoes**. There are other bands who would have experienced the very same predicament.

Philmore "Boots" Davidson and Anthony "Muffman" Williams.

Ellie Mannette

Inappropriate Dedication and American Intervention

In summation, it can be concluded, based on all that has been described so far, that there is solid evidence by way of eye-witnesses' accounts and reports from early Pan pioneers and enthusiasts that Jules in Hell Yard invented and in the period 1945–1954 built a family of melody pans which today can be listed as follows: the *ping-pong* or melody tenor pan, the *bele* pan, the *alto* pan, the *cuatro* or *guitar* pan, the *grundig* (fore-runner to the cello pan), the *trombone* pan, and the bass-pans, starting with the *tune-boom* and moving on to *two-bass, three-bass, five-bass, six-bass, and lastly the tenor-bass*.

Moreover, the pictures (See Nos. 2–5) presented before, though not pictures of All Stars but of other bands, nevertheless, help provide evidence of, or corroborate, the time-lines of the various inventions as provided by Neville Jules and eye-witnesses. The significance of these Neville Jules' claims is that they establish a clear-cut historic chronology of the various pan inventions. With such chronology as defining measure, it can be considered anachronistic for anyone to lay claim to having invented and played music on Pan or claim to have seen someone do so previous to V-J Day. The picture of Invaders (pic. 5) in 1949, with a big tenor, a du-dup, an alto-pan and two 5-note tune-booms, fits perfectly the time-lines presented by Jules. The question to be asked is how come there is such a mountain of evidence in regard to the invention and inventor of the initial steel-pan family of musical instruments and yet there continues to be this widespread conspiracy that serves deliberately to obscure, obfuscate and dumb-down the history of pan development?

How come, in the 1940s, 1950s and even up to the mid-1960s, it was common knowledge at the grassroots level and amongst panmen themselves that Neville Jules was the founder of the melody pans and creator of the family of crafted melody-pans, and then suddenly by the 1970s and onwards collective amnesia steps in and an entire Nation goes blank on the history of its own peculiar creation and manifestation? Could this be purely accidental?

A lot of the deliberate obfuscation has to do with the fact that pan development coincided with the development of the nationalist political agenda and the promotion of "local culture". Just as it became fashionable and opportune for the middle-class strata leading the anti-colonial struggle to seize hold of popular grass-roots symbols, such as local flowers, e.g., the balisier, to signify the aspirations of the masses of people, so too they began to seize hold of the Pan as a most significant art-form being developed before the eyes of the world. Not surprisingly, therefore, the elements of the very middle-class who had previously condemned the pan movement and did everything possible to obliterate it, suddenly in the years 1950–1960 sought to embrace it and fashion it in their own "respectable" likeness with "commercialization" as the key motivational factor. And true to form, while they have contributed a lot to pan development, they also have to date remained the **stoic gatekeepers** of the butchery that has been done to our cultural history.

There developed a tendency to disregard developments initiated by the people who inhabit the down-trodden and impoverished areas and sectors of the city and of the country. So whereas the roles played by recognized elements like Beryl McBurnie, Norman Tang, Lennox Pierre and others in assisting development of pan people in Port-of-Spain West were well publicized, and moreover, *Girl Pat*, the all-female steelband of Woodbrook, was lionized to the hilt, no such recognition was duly given to activities on the opposite side of the City. The roles played by the likes of people such as Sonny Denner, a leading local music tutor, and Kenneth Layne ("Guns"), a leading member of the Police Band who also brought along the famous Frankie Francis to assist All Stars and how, as a result, this generated a great improvement in Jules' "techniques of instrumentation and orchestration,"[331] were never publicized.

However, what the intense promotion of the "Woodbrookians" meant eventually is that Neville Jules and All Stars of Hell Yard and all those behind-the-bridge pan people and early pan women like Bubulups, Ruby Rab, No-Teeth Jean, etc. were eventually confined to obscurity. It was a natural, objective result of the rise to supremacy of the middle-class agenda after the working-classes lost command of the nationalist movement in the mid-1950s.[332]

So no one paid any attention to what was happening within All Stars, when for instance, Jules, after listening attentively to the comments of the foreign 1952 Music Festival Adjudicators, in particular Dr. Sydney Northcote, on the problematic of pan instruments, changed around his methodology, according to Roy Gibbs, and began sinking the 45-gallon drum first before cutting and was able then not only to procure more depth to enrich tonal quality of his tenors but also to produce more notes allowing ***the playing of tunes in three keys*** while at the same time enhancing the sound of the 8-Note Cuatro Pan and the 5-Note Basses.[333] And Jerry Serrant would indicate that in this regard, Jules was "heeding the advice of Dr. Northcote who suggested that it would ***take patience to build up the technique and the purity of the steel band to make it really effective…***"[334]

Prince Batson, who was then a confidant of Jules and a witness of these developments, pointed out tirelessly that "All Stars did not enter pan festivals until 1952 because we played **barefoot** right through the '40s and we couldn't afford uniforms either… As a result we didn't put a single player in TASPO because we didn't enter festivals…"[335] Prince further added that in the 1952 festival, All Stars' tune of choice was *Dream of Olwen*, and "after listening to the recording of the piece Jules detected the sound of an instrument that the band could not duplicate, so Jules went back to the Dry River and spent days upon days down there trying to develop a pan that would emulate the tone of that particular instrument… we needed a high bass for *Dream* and he stayed down there on the river bed to invent one. That was his genius…."[336]

Oliver Joseph countered this on the grounds that the tenor bass was developed by Jules not for the 1952 Festival but for the 1954 Festival when the band played *La Mer*. In regard to the outcome of the 1952 Festival, Prince Baston also recalled Adjudicator Northcote's advice to pan musicians in 1952: "My advice to you, on account of your limitation with your instruments, is that you must stay with Latin American music or calypso… mixed in with all that were things about counterpoint, etc. leading Jules to say then that the judge himself didn't have a proper guide…"[337]

Jules followed Northcote's advice to the letter but it certainly worked against All Stars in the 1954 Festival prompting Jules thereafter to stay away from all pan competitions until 1965 Panorama and 1968 Festival. Of course, Jules' version of all this is told later, however the point that is being made here was the tenacity of Jules to follow to the letter the "advice" of the musicologists particularly in context of the quality and potential capability of the pan-instruments and which reinforced Jules's commitment to improve constantly his instruments.

In 1954–1955, Errol Hill, the popular playwright, was motivated to write and publish a play titled "The Ping-Pong" supposedly about a steelband based in a "low-class" area of Port-of-Spain and in the foreword of that publication, written by none other than Dr. Eric Williams, who would shortly thereafter become Premier and then Prime Minister of T&T, it is said that the play is "appropriately dedicated to Ellie Mannette."[338] However in the story line of the

Play there are two quite salient references: (1) the steelband, named the Canary Steelband, seemed adverse to joining the proposed Steelband Association and implied distrust for certain "big-shots", certain elite elements, who were spearheading the move, and (2) while discussing preparation for an upcoming steelband competition, allusion is made to a pan being dropped by the band's lead player at the previous competition which resulted in Canary losing "de first prize."[339]

Interestingly, Invaders, was very much involved in the effort to form the Steelband Association in 1949 and in fact the first assistant-secretary of the Association was George Goddard representing Invaders, whereas Neville Jules and All Stars refused to participate and openly expressed distrust of the intentions of certain elite proponents of the Association. In addition, there was a popular rumor, which became folklore around Port-of-Spain, that Neville Jules' tenor pan fell off his lap while playing the test-piece in the 1952 competition and as a result caused him to be placed second to Dudley Smith of Sun Valley in the soloist segment of that competition.

The logical question arises: to whom therefore should it really be said that this play was "appropriately dedicated?" It is a case of the salient facets of a Hell Yard story being attached to someone from elsewhere. Given all that was taking place at the time and given Ellie's prominence, Dr. Eric Williams, in his innocence could not have done otherwise.

Another factor that influenced the direction of Pan History came as a result of Admiral Dan V. Gallery of the US Navy having decided to set up a Navy Steelband in Puerto Rico where he was based after he had experienced in T&T the sound of steelbands during the Carnival of 1956.[340] Ellie Mannette of Woodbrook was the person who built the pans for the Navy-men who came from Puerto Rico and virtually lived in Ellie's yard while they learnt the rudiments of pan-playing.[341] Then in 1957 Ellie was flown to Puerto Rico to continue his work there and he stayed for three to four months.[342] Once again the question of Ellie's accessibility had to be a motivating factor for besides his then quite known pan-tuning competence, one could not expect navy-men from the Chaguaramas Base to be frequenting Hell Yard or East Dry River for obviously, as is the case today, "advisories" would have been provided by the military administration to set parameters to the movement of US Militiamen on the island.

In addition, the gas and oil required for servicing the aircraft and other equipment at the base was shipped utilizing 45-gallon barrels, so there was always a large stock of empties readily available to all panmen and more so to Ellie Mannette as he prepared pans for the Navy Steelband. Needless to say, at the end of the project, Ellie's work was greatly admired by the Navy-men who came to regard him as the "father of the Navy Steelband."

One unnamed person of West Port-of-Spain e-mailed to inform that when Ellie went to Puerto Rico to tune pans for the US Navy, he was unfortunately called a "Judas" of the steelband movement and accused of "selling out his birthright" by, of all people, the Public Relations Officer of the Steelband Association.[343] The facts of this matter are as follows. The Evening News in a report entitled "Ellie takes the Pan to US School" outlined that Ellie was leaving to go to St. Stephen High School in Charleston, South Carolina to teach students there to play and tune pans.[344]

Subsequently, Mr. Lisle F. Lashley, the then Pro of the T&T Steelbands Association, sent a response to the Trinidad Guardian in which he raised the following salient issues: that the Steelbands Association was not paid the courtesy of being informed of this development; that the Association was forced to express its "deep indignation that such an eminent son of the soil should have to sell his birthright and cultural pride for some pieces of silver," whereas Ellie was not offered a similar job to teach locals by the Government; that the redeeming factor of this whole matter was that the public would now be quite conscious of the need to honor our own; that whereas US Trade Union laws prevent Pan musicians from working in the USA, the doors of T&T were wide open to the "pilferage of our cultural talent and musical skills;" and lastly that all our panmen get from locals is "lip service support."[345]

The T&T Steelbands Association claimed that Lashley's letter carried by the Trinidad Guardian under the headline "Steelbands see Ellie as Judas of the Pans" was "distorted and published in such a manner" that a totally different meaning, to what was originally intended, was conveyed, and as a result the Association sent both Lashley's letter and the Trinidad Guardian report to the Nation, newspaper of the People's National Movement (PNM), in an attempt to get the Nation to convey the true intent of the Association's lament which in fact was done in the Friday May 27th, 1960 issue of the Nation.[346]

It is significant to note that the emailed comment from the person from Port-of-Spain sought to imply that the then PRO of the Association called Ellie "a Judas" and that the Nation, the newspaper of the PNM, was supportive of this most unfair analogy. The facts indeed were quite to the contrary. The Nation newspaper sought to dispel the "Judas" label and to note that it was in fact a vicious creation of the Guardian newspaper. At that time everyone was very much aware of the Guardian's anti PNM advocacy.

However, in order to counteract any groundswell of sentiment that somehow T&T's birthright was being subverted by the emergence and promotion of a US Navy Steelband, the leading lights of the project while touring all over South America, the Caribbean (i.e., Antigua, Guyana, Barbados, Bahamas, Cuba, etc.), Europe, the USA, etc., said that they took pains to inform the world that the steelband was originated in Trinidad and that they "featured the evolution of the pan, giving full credit to Trinidad and to Ellie Mannette."[347] Ellie's prowess as a tuner was as a result rated above all competing contenders in T&T and he was invited to move to the USA, which he eventually did in 1967.

However, once again there is controversy in regard to what really motivated him to take up this option at that point given that it was an option readily available to him before. It is said that a young tuner, Alan Gervais, emerged from the South and placed octaves on Invaders' styled pans that blew everybody's mind and that this may have prompted Ellie's departure.[348]

"Cliff" Alexis noted musicologist and pan instructor operating out of Northern Illinois University also made note of the emergence and recognition of the tuners from South when he said: "...I can talk about Alan Gervais, Earl Rodney, the Bonaparte brothers—those guys from Southern Symphony who were doing their thing down South... They were tuning their pan, adding notes, octaves, etc. In fact, I can tell you that Alan Gervais made some improvement to the tenor pan and double-second... But it was Alan who changed Ellie's double second by moving the low E up to F-sharp. I remember what event lit our eyes up... There was a jamboree in the Oval, I think it was Christmas of "64, and the National Steel Band played. The Guinness Cavaliers—I know Bobby Mohammed very well—performed after the National Steel Band. When all of a sudden Guinness Cavaliers started playing, everybody ran over to them. "You hear dem pan?" and was asking them, "Who made dem pan?" Everyone wanted to know this new thing, this new sound. They answered, "Alan Gervais, a guy from Point..." **Ellie couldn't come close...** Once, Ellie wasn't getting as much work in Trinidad, if he was getting any work at all, because all the tuning was going to guys who could put octaves on the notes. I'm not lying… It's a whole lot of people who started the new type of sound, which Ellie wasn't doing. Ellie's pans weren't ringing like some other pans. We'd go to the Savannah knowing that our Invaders band wasn't going to ring like some of the other bands. I'm not betraying anyone because I'm still an Ellie fanatic. Ellie came to America with the help of Murray Narell… **and learned some of the new things about tuning…**"[349]

There is another view expressed by some that Ellie, having contested George Goddard for the Presidency of the Steelbandsmen Association in the July 18th 1965 elections, lost heavily to Goddard[350] and as a result of the threats and counter threats that occurred during the elections, he may have been prompted to leave the country. George Goddard contends in his book that during the elections, he received a "telephone threat" forcing him to arrange "police escort to the convention" and "police security" during the proceedings.[351] However Cecil Paul, a member of the Leadership Council of the then NATTS (National Association of Trinidad & Tobago Steelbandsmen), expressed the view that it was Goddard who employed intimidatory tactics to stymie the efforts of a Rebel Group of steelbandsmen who, fed up of Goddard's dictatorial tendencies, sought to organize to remove him at that 1965 Convention, and were confident of success, given their count of the delegates.

Paul said: "There were several panmen, mostly from San Juan, who were not delegates but were at the door preventing legitimate delegates from entering and therefore voting. As a result Goddard was re-elected. Ellie Mannette congratulated Goddard and left. Shortly thereafter Ellie Mannette left T&T for the USA. Later a group of steelbands formed Pan Trinbago and left NATTS with very few bands to represent…"[352] The prominent active bands that supported the Rebels and Ellie Mannette were *Finland* of San Juan, now *Pamberi*, represented by Paul; *Invaders* represented by Kenny Turner who later became President of the PSA; *Silver Stars* and *City Symphony*.[353] Interestingly, Goddard in his book clearly indicated that at that time he resided in San Juan, ***in San Juan All Stars territory***, to use his own words.[354]

At that time, it is important to note that Neville Jules, having kept All Stars away from all competitions for the decade 1954–1964, was forced by the demands of the younger members of All Stars to re-enter Pan competitions in 1965 (i.e., Panorama, which began in 1963) and Festivals in 1968 but by then Jules had to acknowledge to himself that just like Ellie he had been surpassed by the new tuners, i.e., Marshall, Wallace, Bassman from San Juan, Gervais, etc. **who were adding more notes and doubling the pans**, and so eventually with a few All Stars stalwarts he journeyed to the Southland to find first Alan Gervais, then Leo Coker who respectively took the sound of All Stars into the modern era.[355]

In fact, from that moment onward, Neville Jules ceased to tune pans and consigned himself to arranging music for All Stars. Of course his arrangements continued to mesmerize people; who can forget how All Stars supporters used to be motivated by his arrangements to hold their female partners and virtually "ball-room" dance in the midst of the madness of the Carnival days.

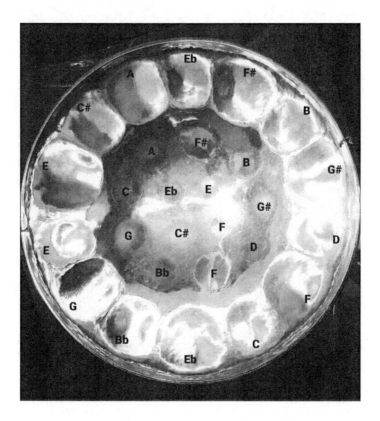

This is a picture of a present-day All Stars 27-note tenor (14 notes around and 13 in the center). This came as a result of the initial collaboration of Jules with Alan Gervais and later with Band officials and Leo Coker. This picture was taken, and notes identified, by Sule Sampson, leader of All Stars tenor section.

However by the 1980s the Band Officials of Trinidad All Stars also began to utilize 4th and 5ths tenors. Following is a sketch of a 4ths and 5ths tenor used by All Stars today:

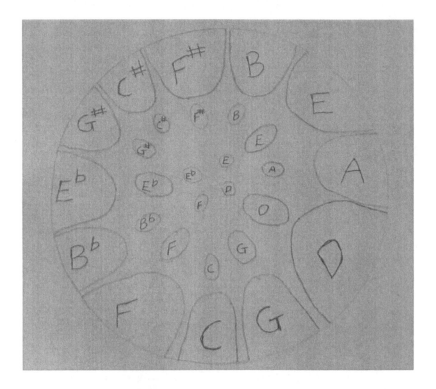

This tenor has 28 notes; 12 around and 16 on the inside. The notes run clockwise according to Fourths and anti-clockwise according to Fifths. Sketch by Akeem.

So, while other pioneers are lionized, Neville Jules, although he lived to the age of 93, he still remained, at the time of his death in 2020, brutally unrecognized. Even as this history was being researched and written in the period of our 48th to our 54th year of Independence, newspapers in tribute to pan pioneers highlighted only Mannette, Bertie Marshall and Rudolph Charles, without even a passing mention of Neville Jules. In 2011, our 49th year of Independence, the Guardian published a tribute to Pan titled "The Story of the Steelpan" and once again Ellie Mannette and other notable contributors such as Spree, Bertie Marshall and Tony Williams were duly recognized. We are adamant that this must not be repeated in the years to come. Over and over again in the past it has happened.

In the NOTES of a 2005 Schools' Broadcast which is declared to be "the intellectual property of the Ministry of Education," the children of the Nation were told succinctly in that lesson titled "Musical Moments" that "...*1939— The Alexander Rag Time Band poured joyfully into Port-of-Spain making a tremendous sound and an infectious rhythm. All sorts of improvised percussion instruments were used in this band such as buckets, dust-bins, pitch-oil pans, paint pans, soap boxes, motor-car hubs and other noise making devices. At first, the sounds and rhythms were exciting but soon the musicians felt that that was no melody and the first panmen wanted melodies... 1945—World War 2 was in progress. The Carnival was banned for security reasons. In the panyards of Port-of-Spain, discovery and experimentation were taking place. Men like Winston Spree Simon, Fisheye Olliverre and Neville Jules were making new discoveries. However, Spree Simon has been credited for producing the first melody on a pan. The tune was Mary Had A Little Lamb...*"
356

The view expressed in the later part of the above quote was denounced vehemently by early panmen in the years 1974–1987 and yet by 2005, it still remained acceptable for reputable institutions like the Schools' Broadcasting Unit to disseminate such misinformation to our Nation's children. When will we come to desist with this sole proclivity of the nursery rhyme, "Mary Had A Little Lamb" being the first melody played? The first tunes played on Pan were calypsos such as "Yuh Want to Come Kill Me", "Doh Re Mi", "Georgie-Porgie" as well as a theme from a 1942 movie, "Alan Ladd, this Gun for Hire", Baptist/ "Ira Sankey" melodies, and Christmas Carols.

There was recently an exhibition of the Evolution of Pan organized by the then Director of Culture in which artifacts, lent to her Ministry by the now deceased Prince Batson for display at Mille Fleurs for Carifesta V and which her Ministry in the ensuing years claimed to have lost, have now suddenly reappeared but yet there is not one single reference or mention in that exhibition of Prince Batson or Neville Jules or All Stars. That very said exhibition is now being targeted to be taken abroad for international exposure. It means that once again not only this Nation but the World would be robbed of valued information about the history of Pan on account of careless, shoddy, superficial work by many locals.

Anthony Mark Jones attempted to correct Pan History when he wrote in 1974 the following: "Overnight we have recognized the phenomenal rise of the steelband. Within the last twenty years acceptance and proliferation of this new-found art form has mushroomed. However, we are now seeing a mad rush by many persons to lay claim as inventor, creator… (which) is extremely unfortunate… History lives and can easily verify or nullify claims… One can say that steelband belongs to Trinidad & Tobago and give all credit to the people of Trinidad & Tobago. This is for the tourist. We in Trinidad must try to verify facts in order to leave a true account for posterity, for the children of steelbandsmen…"[357] How can a historian start off with such clearly stated noble intentions and yet end up crediting the birth of the melody-pan to Winston "Spree" Simon because Spree said that he accidentally discovered 4-notes on his pan, sometime in 1939, after lending it to a "strong friend, Wilson "Thick Lip" Bartholomew."[358]

Insult was added to injury when Spree Simon himself returned to T&T after an absence of many years and in an interview claimed that he went to Nigeria as a Pan instructor and had been playing as a soloist throughout Europe and Britain and most of all boasted of being "the first man to put notes on a pan… to make pan talk music, playing a version of "Ave Maria" and "I am a Warrior" in 1946…[359] In reality, Spree was playing for the Governor and his wife using a Neville Jules invention to which he, Spree, was introduced by Andrew "Pan" de Labastide. Andrew Pan sold Spree a Neville Jules styled "ping-pong" for 24cents, a "bob," in those days.

In the meantime, misconceptions and blatant untruths continued unabated just as the duplicity of the American intervention in the story of Pan and their coloring of the story reigned unfettered. And if today there is still this undying fire in the bellies and in the souls of the members of All Stars that energizes them to endure as a **premier steel-orchestra** and to persevere after 85 years of existence from Hell Yard/Bad Behavior in 1935 to present time, still defying all odds, still winning competitions, in fact the only band that have won all the major existing competitions (i.e., panorama, bomb, festivals, best-beating on the road as well as Monday and Tuesday Mas in specific categories) at least six (6) times (festival), ten (10) times (panorama) and too numerous to count in other contests (e.g. bomb, best beating on the road, people's choice, etc., etc.), it is because of the pain of that skewed history and the deliberate, unkind treatment that has been meted out for so long to the founding fathers of this Band and more so to the creative genius that fashioned steel-pan music.

It is because of their mettle and Jules's engagement, his mettle, with which he crafted metal to produce a peculiar music that affords that this band, All Stars, can still stand unfazed and undaunted. Today, the time has come for the story to be told for the emotional and spiritual fulfillment of the generations to come.

Genius to Genius: Neville receives token of appreciation from Boogsie in 2007 at his 80th birthday celebrations.

Chapter Four
Setting Standards 1954-1971 and Beyond...

In 1952, the Steelband Association was successful in getting the Trinidad Music Association to permit the involvement of steelbands in the Music Festival. There was some initial objection from the traditional Music Association on the grounds that most steelbandsmen were professionals (i.e., performed for payment) while the Festivals were deemed solely for amateurs, but this argument did not gain popular traction and Pan-bands were allowed to participate.[360] At that competition steelbands were limited to 12 members and each band had to select two out of four categories of music: mambos, rhumbas, calypsos and classics, each band according to the rules had to play a tune of choice as did the soloists but the latter in addition had to do a Folksong Test Piece, so All Stars did *Dream of Olwen* and Jules as a soloist did *Bless This House* and the Test Piece.[361]

Even as recent as 2010, fifty-eight years after, some people still feel compelled to recall for us the power of Jules' presentation when he did his creative introduction to the Test Piece that triggered an uproar that caused him to stop playing and walk off the stage only to be recalled by the adjudicators and yet still was placed second to Dudley Smith, 173 points to 171.[362]

People remember such feats that leave them holding their breaths for long moments only to release their emotions in screams for "more" in praise of the sheer power of the creative engagement. One noted local columnist even recently wrote in wonderment about a "band that played *Dream of Olwen* in a Festival many years ago", he couldn't recall the specific band but he could never forget the power of that creative moment. In similar vein, a Professor of Literature writing about All Stars performing on the road said: "In 1952, when All Stars under Neville Jules, with their combination of "strum-swing", came down Park Street playing *Back Bay Shuffle*, I remember a White American tourist standing in utter astonishment in the middle of the street: "Jesus Christ! It's Duke Ellington!"[363]

But earlier, in the same piece, the Professor sought to clarify the distinctiveness of the All Stars sound which he suggested was derived from their particular genesis: "…All Stars had a combination of "strum" and "swing", with the emphasis on "strum", because the nucleus of their band, musically, was formed around Fish-Eye and Neville Jules. Jules was as adept at First (Pan) as at Second Pan, so that his strumming on Second often created the perfect cushion for Fish-Eye's first Pan. In fact, All Stars "strum-swing" style resulted from the personal aesthetic of Neville Jules…" Jules was such a gifted genius, that when he played first pan, he played a combination of first and second.

"He would often play a melody line for you in two-note arpeggio chords— all the way through; and not only that, his arpeggios would be in harmonics. He could put aside his first pan and play a complete melody for you on his second pan. Sometimes when the band left the Dry River for a jump-up at nights up the Hill, up Richardson Lane and Constitution Hill, Jules would be ripping off these delicate arpeggios in the dark, while looking over his shoulders to make sure that the police were not following the band. I have witnessed this myself as a young boy of about 9 or 10… I was attending primary school in the city at the time, and unknown to my parents, who had forbidden me to ever mix with Desperadoes, I used to visit All Stars in the Dry River on afternoons. Jules often sent me and my companions on small errands for him, to buy sweet drinks or cigarettes, which we gladly did, just to be near the great musician and watch him at work tuning pans or arranging tunes on his first or second pan… What is fascinating is that these steelbands were playing calypso music, deeply-rooted Afro-Caribbean Trinidad & Tobago music, yet there was an underlying stream of pure Afro-American jazz flowing like a crystal stream from the inside of the Pan music…"[364] No greater accolade has ever been paid to Neville Jules' genius as pan pioneer and virtuoso player.

The above quotation indicates that the affinity with Black-American jazz was noted from the very early beginnings of the steelband movement, in fact this view is supported by Leroi Boldon's statement that when Jules was asked by Rupert "Shadow" Nathaniel, Boogsie's uncle, how he came to approach the arrangement of *Back Bay Shuffle* in that manner, Jules's reply was that he had gained much from listening carefully to Earl Bostic the Black-American saxophone player,[365] which would suggest that the jazz influence was instinctive as suggested by Professor Lennox Brown but as well, it was learnt as implied by Leroi Boldon. But most of all, Jules possessed such great super "musical hearing" that it was said by aficionados of All Stars that even while the entire band was rehearsing Jules could pick out the one single person who struck an incorrect note though he was "not formally trained."[366]

Winston Rennie, senior economist and consultant, also a guitarist in his earlier life, was formally trained by Sonny Denner and he reports that Denner was never tired of speaking to the class about Neville Jules's super-human musical hearing; in fact it was described as uncanny.[367] Austin, a long-time All Stars six-bass player, talking about Jules' sharpness of musical hearing, said: *"One Carnival, we on the road and Jules, way down behind among the iron men, send someone up front to tell Innapo that he playing shit, and Inna, tight, and he know he make some mistakes, but he amazed that Jules way down behind could hear that, and Inna, laughing, reply, "tell Jules I say he have to be mad..."*[368] In this case, it was not only a matter of "hearing" but a positioning of Innapo's hands and body would tell Jules whether Innapo was "off" or "on."

What all his musical prowess brought for Jules at that juncture was great admiration and respect from all who dared to enter the world of Pan and for this reason people came from far and wide to hear Jules play or to play for him and get his attention and nod of approval. Many of us alive today can recall the days when Desperadoes, particularly after All Stars moved in 1957 to the Garrett of the Maple Leaf Club,[369] would come down Charlotte Street, early on J'ouvert mornings, their pans then painted black, to play for Neville who by popular acclaim had become a kind of barometer against which all panmen measured themselves.

Jules himself indicated that All Stars twerked the competitive spirit of panmen: *"After a certain time, all the bands were looking for All Stars... It ended up where a lot of bands were coming to contest All Stars on Monday morning... I remember seeing a lot of bands coming down Charlotte Street because we were in the Garret. That is the way it was..."*[370]

The point is that it was in those very years 1954–1964, during which the leadership of All Stars refrained from participating in all competitions, that the band came to be recognized for its superiority of arrangement and its depth of musical orchestration. Jules's reasons for quitting competitions were as follows: "...In 1952 and 1954, I went to the first two festivals then quit. I said no more festivals for me because I didn't like what was going on. The first festival we played and they gave us eighty-seven points... In those days, they were using the indelible lead—what you wrote with those lead could not be erased. They gave us eighty-seven, then tried to turn that seven into a three. That placed us third. The second year we went back.

Judging from what Northcote said in '52 about what the steelbands should and should not do, we followed those instructions. There were six bands and we played number five. Southern All Stars played number six. When band number six went up to play, we were at the back of the stage. That competition was held at Roxy Theatre. When we heard what was going on with them, we said that couldn't win. Dr. Wiseman was the adjudicator that year, 1954. In '52, it was Dr. Northcote who said what we shouldn't do and we followed his instructions. While listening to band six, we knew they couldn't beat us...

After they were finished playing, the time came for them to announce the scores. Band number one was called and they announced what they did and what they shouldn't have done, and so on. When they announced our band, number five, he gave us a lot of credit, because a lot of what we did none of the other bands did; in fact, no other band ever did... Other bands never had a conductor or used the bongos. When we arrived on stage, we first set up then waited for the conductor. When he arrived, we stood up and bowed. We started all that. All Stars was, and is, the trendsetter. When the adjudicator began his comments, he announced, "Band number Five, here came Sir Thomas Beecham,' referring to our conductor... He continued talking about all the good things the band did. When he called out the points the band made, they were the highest points for the night and the crowd cheered.

So, we were sure that band number six... couldn't score higher than us... in that band a guy... alone played, and the band accompanied him. He soloed a lot, and Northcote had said that we shouldn't be doing that. We were sure that band couldn't win... Then the adjudicator said, "Wait, more runs are to come after lunch," using that cricket term. When I heard that, I knew we had lost... when he commented on their performance; he talked about how amazed he was that the members' hands moved so quickly, and gave them first place. We came second. I said, "No more Festival for me." We did not return until 1968..."[371]

In fact, Jules indicated elsewhere that Band Number Six played *Anna* and was led by Theo Stephens whom he described as "a very good player."[372] Interestingly, there was an incident outside the theatre that night whereby Theo Stephens' mother was being prevented from entering and Theo was threatening not to play if his mother was kept out and Jules supported Theo and insisted that All Stars likewise would not play if Theo's mother was refused entrance, at that point the organizers relented.[373]

Another interesting story has been revealed about that final night of the 1954 music festival by Dawad Philip. Dawad informed the Facebook Blogger, Glenroy Joseph, that Theo "Black James" Stephens told him one day (after he, Theo, had resettled in the US after leaving London) that "…on the night of the competition, a contingent of supporters from San Fernando including some heavy roller gamblers made the journey to support Southern All Stars. Big money passed in the betting that night. When the results were announced and Southern All Stars declared the winner, some big name jefes from Port-of-Spain decided that the band was not going back San Fernando with their winnings from both on and off the stage. Rivals from POS blocked the truck loaded with Southern All Stars pans and declared that nobody was leaving town with their money. Supporters of Tokyo, Blanca et al lined up for battle and things were tense. But just then Trinidad All Stars members formed a circle around their "sister band", Southern All Stars, thus ensuring safe passage South…"[374]

Over the years, there have been varying positions from stalwarts of All Stars on the question of those two festivals, 1952 and 1954, which do raise concerns. It was reported above that Prince Batson credited Boys Town's victory in the 1952 Festival to a "young All Stars prodigy who conveyed All Stars" musical techniques to Boys Town and "we were stabbed in the back…"[375] One other person reported that a member of All Stars who played double-seconds and lived in Point Cumana, named Desmond Collette, alias "Crazy", did in fact carry "Mambo Ocho" to Boys Town and was known at times to "give Boys Town Jules' top-class arrangements, and when Jules found out, Jules wanted to kill him…"[376]

However, it has been clearly established that the 1952 adjudicator, Northcote, was of the opinion that steelbands were not yet equipped or ready to handle the classics and therefore should stick to lighter forms of music, calypsos and Latin American melodies, so with that obvious bias he scored pieces like Boys Town's "You are My Heart's Delight" higher than All Stars' "Dream of Olwen" and Free French's "Largo". Most of the old folks, including Courtney Vincent Charles, hold pleasant memories of Boys Town's "You are My Heart's Delight." Courtney Vincent Charles, however, is adamant in his contention that no explanation was ever given for the Steelband Association's unilateral and highly suspicious decision after acknowledging the results of the 1952 Festival in which Boys Town came first, Southern Symphony, second, All Stars, third and Chicago, fourth, to leave All Stars out and select three bands, i.e., Boys Town, Southern Symphony and Chicago for automatic qualification to the 1954 Festival.[377]

Furthermore, it is also the considered view of Courtney Vincent Charles that it was because of the inconsistency of the adjudicators; the early bias against steelbands attempting European classics; compounded by the suspicious machinations of the administration of the Steelband Association why Jules felt compelled in the 1954 Festival to change the tune of choice to *La Mer* and even to invent the **tenor-bass** to capture a different sound that he desired to exploit in his presentation of *La Mer*, which means that he, Courtney Vincent Charles, agrees with OJ and not Prince Batson.[378] Was all this a targeting of All Stars because the band was not a member unit of the Steelband Association?

At the time, no one in the administration of the Association felt it necessary to clarify or explain the reason or reasons for any of the preposterous decisions. In addition, no one questioned the inconsistency of the adjudication; precisely because as colonials we swore then by the validation bestowed on us by foreigners. Needless to say, Jules, as a result became even more wary of the whole set-up and after considering the lack of consistency exhibited openly by both the 1952 and 1954 adjudicators, Jules felt that he had to walk away.

In the decade 1954–1964, All Stars, despite having stopped competing, stood apart, set its own standards and precisely because of the popularity of the band those standards became the benchmarks against which all other bands were measured. As a consequence, whatever All Stars did, wherever All Stars went, wherever All Stars positioned itself, the others followed with one salient objective: *"to cut All Stars' ass*!" and, in the course of this, measure themselves. Indeed, most of the engagement came in that early period from the bands of West Port-of-Spain, i.e., Invaders, Crossfire, North Stars, Tripoli, and later Symphonettes and Starlift.

At that time, All Stars from East Port-of-Spain virtually would stand alone facing the onslaught from the West; the days when it was said that "Bands from the West were the Best," according to the calypso, and which had become a reality for a short spell given the fact that bands like Casablanca and Syncopators of East Port-of-Spain had seen their best days prior to the departure of Boots Davidson, while others like Ebonites, Desperadoes, City Symphony, Highlanders, Tokyo, Renegades and Savoys were not yet the musical giants that they were to become in the glorious '60s.

So it was left to All Stars to defend on behalf of the Behind-the-Bridge Bands and All Stars could only have done so successfully because of its capacity for creative innovation. People around in those days recall, for instance, the first and only Carnival Sunday Night fete ever held at the then newly-built Town Hall when Shadow's Symphonettes dropped the dynamic presentation of the calypso, "*Tattle-Tale*" and All Stars in response had to dig deep and put them to rest with the bomb, *Cara Nome*.

In terms of creative innovations, Neville Jules himself advanced the view that no other band in T&T's history can claim to have had "more firsts" than All Stars; meaning that All Stars was the leading light. In addition, Neville himself was one of the first persons to play the melody-pan with two sticks, while All Stars as a collective unit was the first band to do likewise.

There are however some aspects of this issue to be clarified: *First of all, Zigilee as well as Jules and Paulie (the brother of Calypsonian Popo and a leading light of the early steelband, Commandoes of Edward Street),*[379] *and a man from Gonzales named Chandler were the noted masters of the "tenor kettle", a three-note pan strapped around the shoulder and played with* **two sticks***; secondly, the* **Bele-Pan** *invented by Jules was strapped around the neck and also played with two sticks, one stick held upright and the other downwards; the four-note or* **ping-pong**—*the first melody pan invented by Jules, was at first held on the shoulder with one hand and played with* **one stick***; thirdly, when Jules invented the five-note* **tune-boom** *shortly thereafter, he strapped this pan around the neck and played it with* **two sticks***; fourthly, two-stick playing came to prevail particularly after the emergence of the big tenor, the 45-gallon drum in 1947 and the resulting elimination of the small paint pans but in reality the two-sticks phenomenon was already second-nature to the likes of people like Jules; finally, the incident of Ulric "Chick McGroo" Springer, winning a 1946 soloist competition playing with two-sticks "on a* *large ping-pong he'd tuned from a CGA pan"*[380] *has to be viewed as part of the transition to the 45 gallon drum pans, although two-stick playing would not have been much of a revelation to persons who were already masters of the tenor-kettle, the bele, and the tune-boom.*

But for being the first publicly to play a melody ping-pong with two sticks in a competition, that honor has been given to Chick Springer of Hellzapoppin according to available reports, however it is interesting to note that Ulric "Chick" Springer has been identified by Julius Darius as the man in the foreground of the picture of Red Army with a Bele-Pan around his neck and two-sticks; one held upright, and one held downwards; in other words Chick Springer, since the days of the Bele-pan, used two sticks.

As already indicated All Stars was the first steel orchestra to wrap rubber on the sticks and the first to introduce a number of innovations, i.e., single alto-pans, single guitar pans, and basses, that were quickly adopted by the others, and Neville listed just a few of the other "firsts"—the first to introduce the tenor bass in 1954; the first to use "skins" in the rhythm section, i.e., "bongos" (for Festivals) and "congas" (for Road Performances during Carnival) which were played mostly by "Eddy Rab" Mitchell; also the first band to introduce in the 1954 Music Festival a conductor on stage, i.e., Joe-Bell (Hugh Alexander) who walked on stage, knocked the side of a pan and the entire 12-member band bowed to the audience, (he was the person Dr. Wiseman dubbed Sir Edward Beecham after a famous British conductor); Jules indicated that Joe-Bell was trained to be the conductor by Kenneth "Guns" Layne a member of the T&T Police Band.[381]

And to this list of "firsts" could also be added the first band to play an "own tune", i.e., *East Dry River Drive* composed by Jules in 1947.[382] Jerry Serrant named this 1947 "own tune" as *River Vine Cavalli*.[383] Finally, it is now recognized that an early version of the Hell Yard band under the then captaincy of Eric Stowe was the very first steelband to be recorded.[384]

The Bomb Creation

One eventful J'ouvert morning, All Stars had an altercation with supporters of Crossfire and the result of this feud led once again to another example of Jules's creative imagination and musical prowess. The story indicates that during J'ouvert Morning of 1957, Crossfire of St. James came into the City looking for All Stars. Crossfire led by Eamon Thorpe had Port-of-Spain "rocking with a pulsating rendition" of *Another Night Like This*" and then at the corner of Prince and Charlotte Streets they met All Stars whose "piece de resistance" that year was "*El Meringue"* with a "wicked, mesmerizing Latin beat" replete with the sound of "congas" on the road.[385]

That Monday morning, 4 March 1957, the famous policewoman, Jessica Smith, on duty, directing the flow of people and bands, ordered All Stars to "back-track" on Prince Street to ease the pressure that was building up at the inter-section, so All Stars stopped playing and complied with the directives of Jessica Smith. That incident triggered enough bad-mouthing and bragging by Crossfire's supporters, i.e., Big-Belly Bouncanz, Jazzy Pantin et al, that Crossfire demolished All Stars and put All Stars on the run.[386]

Courtney Vincent Charles, "Charlo", the flag-waver who was anointed by Jitterbug to be his successor, insist that when Crossfire caught up with All Stars that morning most of All Stars players, being close to home-base, had already lifted their pans in the air while only a few were still "coasting", and *"Bouncanz and Jazzy start de talk that Crossfire mash up All Stars, well, boy, that open up Jules, so the next year we went looking for Crossfire, dey couldn't come close!"*[387]

Jules himself painted the following scenario: *I remember a Carnival Monday morning we were coming up Henry Street and about five or six bands were coming down Charlotte Street: Invaders, Crossfire and some others. When we swung onto Prince Street going toward Charlotte Street, toward the Market, so many bands were coming down Charlotte Street that we had to wait till all these bands passed. All the bands from the West plus other bands. I think that was the very first year we had women police and there was one standing at the corner. So, we stood there playing and jamming while the bands passed by. Crossfire came by while we were on Prince Street but we didn't give them a second thought. We stayed there so long at the corner of Charlotte and Prince Streets that Crossfire had time to go up Henry into Duke Street. Finally when the time came for us to go through, the crowd was so thick, and I decided to follow the policewoman's direction to go straight ahead on Prince Street. Because of the thickness of the crowd, we had to raise our pans over our heads and walk through the throngs of people. Some of them... when they saw us walking with our pans over our heads, they said: "Dem other bands beat better than All Stars, so All Stars put dey pans up in the air and surrender." Anyhow after getting through, we played an old piece, not our special piece, and when* we reached the corner of Nelson and Prince Streets, Crossfire was there again playing their best piece… with the crowd bawling "Crossfire today beat All Stars!"[388]

Nevertheless, the "picong" from the Crossfire supporters was as vicious as it was ferocious and Jules swore to teach them all a lesson and so the "BOMB" was conceptualized; Jules the following year began to "calypsorise the European classics"[389] and come J'ouvert Morning 1958, the very first BOMB was dropped: Ludwig Van Beethoven's *Minuet in G Major*. They say: All Stars swept the City clean and left no one untouched. Jules said: *When the time came in 1958, I was looking for one band—Crossfire. We were coming up Henry Street by the telephone company—we had scouts on the road, you know, looking to find out where the bands were…The scouts reported that Crossfire was coming down Frederick Street. We went and waited for them at the corner of Duke and Frederick Streets while we were jamming "Minuet in G." After that, there was no more talk of Crossfire. No more. That talk was finished.*[390]

The BOMB practiced secretly by All Stars up in the garret of Maple Leaf Club became from then on a major fixture in Carnival proceedings. Prince Batson's take on the genesis of the "Bomb" was as follows: "*…Other Bands used to come to the yard and either copy or improvise on the work Jules was doing. A decision was then taken to learn tunes secretly… Tunes were learnt with the fingers so that members did not hear the tunes (in full) until J'ouvert Morning…*"[391] But there was more to it; the Garret could not accommodate the entire band at one time, so small groups of the band comprising one person from each section, i.e., tenor, seconds, guitar, grundig, bass, rhythm, practiced at different times with their fingers and they only heard the full sound of the band when they assembled in Nagib Elias' Yard on J'ouvert Morning.

Come 1959, Jules further intensified the hurt with the dropping of not one but three BOMBS: *Intermezzo, Leiberstraum and Baccarolle,*[392] From then on every year All Stars dropped **No.1, No. 2** and **No.3** Bombs. Some of the most devastating were, e.g., **Musetta's Waltz** and **Caro Nome** by Puccini; **Anniversary Waltz** by Franklin-Dubin; **In a Persian Market** by Ketelby; **Turkish March** and **Hall's Concerto** by Mozart; **The Swan** by Tchaikovsky; **Marche Militaire** by Schubert; **Tales from Vienna Woods** by Strauss and **The Marriage of Figaro or The Day Of Madness** by Mozart, the latter of which is probably the most difficult piece of music ever to have been played by any band on the streets of Port-of-Spain according to Neville Jules. In his tribute to Neville Jules, Winston Gordon described Jules as "a master of the upright string-bass" and also said that in those days Jules was *shy and quiet but musically crazy and ahead of his time.*

Winston Gordon kindly provided the following bomb tunes missing from the above list: **Celeste Aida** (opera AIDA); **M'appari** (from the Opera **Martha**); **None But The Lonely Heart** (Tchaikovsky); **Air On a G-String** (Bach); **Meditation** (Thais—Itzhak Perlman—Violinist); **Symphony #40 in G Minor** (Mozart); **Jesu Joy of Man's Desiring** (Bach); **Blue Moon** (Rogers and Hart); **La Mer** (Debussy); **Humoresque** (Dvorak).[393]

Courtney "Charlo' Charles remains adamant that *the greatest impact ever of a bomb tune on J'ouvert morning was Anniversary Waltz* and he describes the following scenario: *That was 1960 and Jules had three bombs; from the Garret to the Market, Jules tried No.1 and for some reason, being a perfectionist, he was not satisfied; it just wasn't coming together then as he wanted, it didn't get off, so he stop it... clang, clang clang, (iron knocks), then he drop No.2 from the Market to the corner of Queen and Frederick and he stop. People start to talk saying Jules better watch it now because Invaders coming down Frederick playing "With a Song in my Heart" but Jules already knew that because he used to have "spies" moving around and reporting so he knew where Invaders was and what they were playing, and in that kinda atmosphere, Jules drop No.3—"Anniversary Waltz", boy, people went crazy. Is the first time people hear the basses at intervals carrying the whole melody; yuh know man does normally have their women in front o'dem, well, dat morning, man spin around dey woman and start to dance ballroom style in the road. Tuesday night at Police Headquarters when All Stars drop "Anniversary Waltz", the impact was the same, people ballroom dancing on the grounds of the Red House. As we reached back home after last lap, we sitting down on the pavement on Charlotte Street, cooling off, and a police vehicle come up the street and off-load drinks and cigarettes for Jules and the band members. When they left, then Jules tell we that the Doc send the stuff and that the Doc does come to the Headquarters to listen to All Stars. Just imagine, the Prime Minister used to be in the Headquarters to hear All Stars and that was never made public...*[394]

Jules himself talking to a group of All Stars people in 1997 claimed that *Anniversary Waltz* was "my most loved and most unforgettable Bomb ever... You recall the Bass line in that tune, Fellas? Especially when we played it in our concert on the Red House grounds, serenading the Police... I'll never forget it... I believe I finally found what I sought from the very beginning. That tune really made me feel great..."³⁹⁵

But it was not only All Stars supporters who praised Jules's work in the arrangement of *Anniversary Waltz*. This is what an avid supporter of the Starlift Steelband said: "The Bomb, as the panmen used to regard it, was started by All Stars somewhere around 1957(sic) when they played *Minuet in G*. All other bands started gunning for All Stars on a J'ouvert Morning after that... In 1960, I was having my first play with Starlift, feeling proud this little Maraval country boy was playing with a town band. Up Park Street we came playing *Ave Maria*... and the entire city bowed... That is until we met All Stars at the corner of Queen and Charlotte Streets. The Stars stopped and allowed us to pass and the pride rose in my heart for surely we had conquered the great All Stars. We turned up Henry Street and All Stars followed playing nothing under the slight drizzle. We stopped under the Telephone Company to return the courtesy to the Stars... All Stars shocked us right there with *Musetta's Waltz (Don't You Know)*, and after playing it for about three minutes, changed easily and instantly—as in one motion—to *The Anniversary Waltz*... **and that's when I cried...**"³⁹⁶

Significantly, the leadership of All Stars in those years never dropped the proverbial ball in terms of consistently providing positive guidance and direction to the rest of the steelband movement which others had come to expect of them. Whereas from time to time other bands persisted with their wanton violence against each other, this was never the case with the band led by Neville Jules. Jerry Serrant quotes Birdie Mannette as having acknowledged the commitment of Jules and his big brother Ellie to the development of Pan, and "to the Freedom of Steelbandsmen, to the establishment of Joy and Togetherness in the hearts of all Humanity, and they were never given to boasting. In Jules and Trinidad All Stars, Ellie, as all of us, was sure that we (Invaders) had an ally that would eventually help us rid the Steelband Movement of all violence and negative communal rivalry, through our Pan talent, producing great instruments and even greater music."³⁹⁷

Courtney Vincent Charles in telling the story of how he came to be the flagman establishes rather sterling characteristics about the modus operandi of this band from Hell Yard: *From small, I wanted to wave flag and growing up in Belmont I used to watch Arthur Tramcar wave for the Belmont band. I used* to practice at home with the broom and my mother used to say "you want to be a criminal, waving flag." When at the age of 13–14, I followed my Duke Street cousins and came into All Stars, I used to follow Jitterbug during the Carnival. One J'ouvert morning, All Stars left Marine Square and came up Henry Street, Jitterbug was bareback and the rain began to fall. At the corner of Queen and Henry, Jitterbug was going in Black Cat Bar for a straight puncheon and he turned to me and said: "Young boy, hold dis flag fuh me, doh drop it!"

When he came back he met me dancing the flag and Mayfield, Irma Payne and Ermintrude tell him, "leave de young boy, let him wave!" And Jitterbug said to me: "I go let yuh wave, but anytime yuh reach a corner, stop, and I will take over; if yuh see a band coming down, I will take over, other than dat you go ahead" and he was monitoring me all the time. He explained to me the significance of the flag. He said if it is a band like Casablanca, Tokyo or Invaders coming down, he would go forward and negotiate with their flagman: "you take the right; I'll take the left and so on." In those days if you are a small band without name, Blanca, Tokyo or Invaders would push you up on the pavement. Jitterbug show me that. In those days, you had to be a bad-john to be in front of a band. So I wave in 1958.

Then in 1959, J'ouvert morning, the year with the three Bombs, I liming downstairs Maple Leaf, me ain't studying flag and Jitterbug came downstairs and said to me: "This is yours!" and hand me the flag. I take pride in carrying the flag, from 1958 to 1968 when I left for England. The flag in those days wasn't light, the pole was solid pitch pine and heavy. Yuh had to fly dat flag, it couldn't touch ground. To handle dat flag, I used to train to get fit, running every morning from Champ Fleurs to Eddie Hart Savannah in Tacarigua…"[398]

With such an understanding, the flag, apart from the ordinary use of keeping tempo, also had its purpose as a tool of guidance with which to gain a favored positioning of your band and with which you negotiated space and place on Carnival Days. It was no surprise that All Stars with such an understanding of a symbolic flag, displaying stars positioned around a map of Trinidad, proved over the years capable of using this tool to steer the band away from internecine and puerile warfare.

In other instances, flagmen were known to be initiators of riots during Carnival. A case in point was the 1959 San Juan All Stars/Desperadoes riot on Carnival Tuesday, an incident that Trinidad All Stars was able to position itself to observe from a distance. This is how "Charlo", Trinidad All Stars' flagman, described the unfortunate disturbance: *That year there was talk that San Juan All Stars was coming to tackle Trinidad All Stars. But that was just rumor.[399] We were going up Henry Street when Jules sent a message to me by Desmond Fisheye to stop the band at the corner of Henry and Park, so I stopped the band in the middle of that intersection. When I looked across at Charlotte Street, there was San Juan All Stars, "Battle Cry", Blakie with the flag, moving at about 60 miles per hour: they had come from the train station, moved up Henry, turn on Queen to George Street, and swing onto Duke and across to the Penny Bank and up Charlotte Street moving at a pace. I held our band at Henry and Park until another message came from Jules by walkie-talkie to "carry the band up to Progressive High School and stop!" That signaled to me that something was wrong because we were supposed to be going to the Savannah: a riot between San Juan All Stars and Desperadoes was taking place by the Hospital. From where we were, I could see sections of people from Cito's Fruits and Flowers running away from Charlotte Street; some heading down Henry, others across to Frederick Street.*

After the riot was over, we began to move up to the Savannah but we were not allowed to get there. That year, Renegades was banned from parading; so half of their people played with Trinidad All Stars and half with City Syncopators. Goldteeth, Stephen Nicholson, played with Synco and they came up behind us. Then the Renegades people in our band and those in Synco began play-acting out a fight. Goldteeth drew a line across the road and they began pulling and tugging each other across the line. One resident, in the upstairs house at the corner, opposite the Hospital, a woman, saw that and called the Police, insisting that the riot was about to explode again. The police, in two Black Marias, came up the street and turned back the two bands from going into the Savannah...[400]

Prince Batson confirmed that All Stars, at that stage in its development, "was never involved in any fights" for "Jules was a disciplinarian who held his men sternly together" and "members were constantly disciplined and "fined" for misconduct, (even) for coming late to practice, etc."[401] It was as a positive in this context that Jules chose to honor the police-officers, who worked hard to keep the peace and were confined to headquarters during the Carnival Days, by providing for them a concert on Carnival Tuesday night outside the

Headquarters during which the police were treated to key bits of the repertoire of the band for that year.

And, as expected, all the other bands began to turn up at the St. Vincent Street Police Headquarters on Tuesday night, not to honor the police as was the original intent of the initiators, but to serenade the huge crowds that gathered and of course to "**cut All Stars' ass**" and in so doing "big-up" themselves. In the ensuing years, referred to today by Pan enthusiasts as the "glorious '60s", as a result of this Tuesday Night Police Headquarters Concert, the citizens of T&T and in particular the burgesses of the City of Port-of-Spain were indeed treated to the "last-lap" musical excellence of not only the initiators but other bands such as **Ebonites** (*Slaughter on Tenth Ave., Roses from the South, March of the Toreadors*); **City Symphony** (*Agnus Dei, Night and Day, Tunes of Glory*); **Casablanca** (*Unto to us a Lamb is Born, Filandia*); **Syncopators** (*Marche Militaire, Malagaenia*); **Desperadoes** (*Flight of the Bumble Bee, Czardas*); **Invaders** (*In a Monastery Garden, With a Song in my Heart*); **Tokyo** (*Beethoven 9th Symphony, Caterpillar*); **Silver Stars** (*Salut d'Armor, Ghost Riders In the Sky*); **Highlanders** (*Let Every Valley Be Exalted, Italiana Girl in Algiers, Gyspy Rondo*) and so on.

In addition to encouraging and enhancing such competitive engagement and camaraderie among steelbands, All Stars was also the first band that took the initiative in the late 1950s to formally invite other bands to a social engagement at their panyard without the promptings and involvement of State Officials much as happens today in the regular Panyard Jams and "Blockoramas" throughout the country. Leroi Boldon, then the youthful administrative secretary, whose idea it was, said that "they all came and communicated well", and it was then that he mentioned Shadow's (i.e., Rupert Nathaniel's) questioning of Jules on the approach to arranging "Back Bay Shuffle", also Boldon did intimate that Ellie, in true panman spirit, threw down the gauntlet to Jules at that first social occasion, saying: "if it's classics yuh want, then is classics yuh go get!" in context of the J'ouvert morning "bombs".[402]

Courtney "Charlo" Charles confirmed that other bands in those early days were indeed invited to the Maple Leaf Club; he explained: "After Carnival, Jules used to invite four (4) persons from each band and he would place the names of the bands on the tables, which were covered with white cloth; Invaders, Tokyo, Crossfire, Blanca, etc., Charlo recalls that this socialization initiated by All Stars was done at least on two occasions, and that similarly Jules after Carnival would fete players and "close members" at his home in Malick, people such as the Fisheye Brothers, Bully, Prince, also Alex Mitchell whom Charlo said helped Jules a lot with the music and was a second-line leader of the band, but moreover, Charlo indicated how much these people felt honored to be invited by Jules to these events at his home or at Maple Leaf Club."[403]

Clearly, Jules possessed a bigger vision for the Pan fraternity than most of the other steelband pioneers, yet strange as it may seem Jules himself would at one point question himself and eventually have cause to lament that he himself may have to take some blame for engendering this intense competitive spirit among pan players from the very beginning to the extent that all they think about today is winning titles, as if they suffer from tunnel vision, and have lost sight of the bigger picture.[404] However, though there is some truth to that lament, one must recognize that the rapid development which Pan underwent in the '40s, '50s, and early '60s had a lot to do with that very competitive energy in an environment of camaraderie that people like Jules, Ellie, Boots Davidson, Tony Williams, Eamon Thorpe, Shadow Nathaniel, etc. generated and for which they, particularly Jules, must be commended. Nevertheless, the internecine warfare among certain bands would continue well into the mid-1960s forcing Kitchener after his return from England to introduce one of his calypsos with the following lines:

Well, ah hear de talk again/Carnival, dey say war in Port-of-Spain.

Mas' and Pan

However, it is important to note that in those days the competitive spirit wasn't limited only to the music product; it was also about Mas' production since Carnival, Pan and Calypso were three handmaidens that were never separated when Carnival really belonged to the people. Who can forget the competition on Carnival Mondays between the steelbands portraying different versions of "fancy CB's (i.e., Construction Battalions that were notable after the War years), or the pretty mas' of the "saga-boy" bands such as Dem Fortunates of Belmont and Sputniks of the inner City. Then come Tuesday, the fancy-sailor bands with sections of choreographed dancing firemen, with their stokers, and king sailors with their "crook sticks", creating new dance-steps as they moved along.

The competition was indeed quite intense between USS Fleets-In (All Stars), USS Detroit (Synco), USS Corncob (Desperadoes), USS Nautilus (Crossfire), USS SkipJack (Tokyo), USS Ohio (Invaders) and USS Tripoli. In addition, portrayals of the Red Indian culture of the plains of North, Central and South America popularized through the Movies gripped the imaginations of steelbands for many years. Jerry Serrant recalls that Invaders played *Samba Dancers* in 1953 and *Aztecs* in 1954, while All Stars did *Mexican Fiesta* in 1952 and *The Great Teton Council* in 1955.[405]

Today, however, in this time when bikini and beads and feminine narcissism prevail in the middle-class, commercialized version of carnival that has taken over, there is a disconnect between the triad of pan, calypso and mas', and as a result once the Panorama competition is over, many steelbands virtually disappear until the new year when it's time to prepare once again for Panorama competition which has become the "be-all-and-end-all" of Pan involvement in carnival. Some silly people seem to believe that Panorama is killing Pan. In reality, the *over-emphasis on Panorama is not the logical cause of the demise of steelbands in Carnival, it is the effect…*[406]

In this regard, Jules' lament about the tunnel vision of steelbands and the society's over-emphasis on competitions takes on wider dimension and is worthy of serious in-depth consideration. Today there is even talk about taking "steelbands" out of "Carnival" altogether because steelbands, it is said, contribute the most to the congestion on the streets which in turn is being viewed as the eventual death-knell to Carnival itself. Gone are the days of the glorious '60s when steelbands also sought to compete for the title of masquerade band of the year such as *Gulliver Travels* (this was Russel Carter's band in collaboration with Silver Stars, and the band actually won the title), Desperadoes—*Cult of the Crocodile, Snow Kingdom* and *Noah's Ark*; Renegades-*Legends of Valhalla* and All Stars-*Fiesta in Mexico*(1965) and *Modern Africa (1969)*.

However, at present, 2010–2020, All Stars has remained the only one of those steelbands that still maintains a significant masquerade presence in Carnival on both days. It is a tradition that the institution that is All Stars has no intention of giving up. Beresford Hunte summed it up nicely during the celebrations of the 2002 "Firestorm" Panorama victory that came after 16 years: "It sweet, it sweet!" he said about the band's long awaited Panorama victory, "but we don't complain… we were prepared to accept the judges' decision... we are not a Panorama band; All Stars is a mas' band, a J'ouvert band, a Bomb competition band, anything but a mere Panorama side..."[407]

From Sagiator's USS Bad Behavior (with their kaki and/or "chambre" shirts and blue dungarees as described by Big-Head Hamil) to USS Fleets-In (noted for their mass of Admirals, Generals, Off-Duty Officers and Black Melton sections), All Stars, from the 1930s, '40s, '50s and onto the '60s, '70s, '80s and '90s have remained consistently not merely the largest sailor band on Carnival Tuesdays in the City of Port-of-Spain but the largest masquerade steelband in Carnival bar none, save the few years that Desperadoes, Synco and Tokyo excelled.

In 1959, the band experienced its biggest turn-out ever according to Leroi Boldon who left that very year to pursue his studies abroad: it is said that the then flagman (by that time Charlo had taken over from Samuel Peters alias "Jitterbug") took the band from its muster point at Nagib's Yard down Charlotte Street, across Prince, up George and then turned west on Duke Street only to meet the back of the band at the corner of Duke and Charlotte. Charlo himself confirmed Boldon's assessment of the vast numbers; it seemed that All Stars on that day, like a giant snake, did in fact wrap itself around that entire city-block.

Fleets" In 1958. Usually the largest steelband mas' portrayal on the road Carnival Tuesday. (Courtesy Trinidad Guardian)

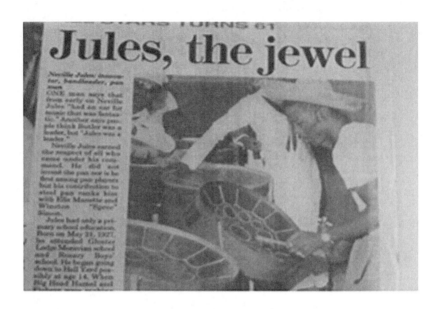

Neville Jules in 1958 touching up a tenor pan before taking All Stars back on the road. (Courtesy Trinidad Guardian). This Jules tenor pan has more notes than his earlier tenor of 18 notes (14 around and 4 notes in the center).

The pan-players had to be strategically divided up in three separate sections, according to Joe-Bell, to be able to provide music equitably. Winston Gordon supports the view that given the 4000 plus sailors on Carnival Tuesdays the steelband had to be divided "to satisfy persons in the back and in the front."[408] The power-basses that Jules tuned without burning and which could be heard from afar really made the difference that Carnival according to both Leroi Boldon and Roy Gibbs.

The point to note, however, is that Trinidad All Stars remains to date the one steelband that has consistently maintained a full commitment to the Carnival tradition, to Pan and Mas, parading on both days, even from its earliest or previous configurations whether as Bad Behavior or Second Fiddle or Cross of Lorraine. The band in 1941 Carnival won the steelband competition organized by Reynold Wilkinson at the RAF Calypso Tent on Nelson Street, taking home $25.00,[409] as well as the E. Mortimer Mitchell 1946 "premier competition for Steelbands in the City, beating Casablanca and Stalingrad into second and third place" for which they got a Silver Cup donated by the

Carnival Improvement Committee,[410] and from thence to the present time winning $1 million for Panorama in 2007; $2 million for Panorama 2011 and $1 million again in 2012.

Some people like Courtney Vincent Charles (now deceased) advanced the view that All Stars despite staying away from competitions from 1954 to 1965, yet has won the most competitions, more than any other steelband, in the history of Trinidad & Tobago: they calculate that All Stars has won some 50 plus competitions inclusive then of 9 Panoramas,(it is now 10 Panoramas), 6 Festivals, 7 People's Choice competitions, numerous Pan on the Move competitions, many Best Beating on De Road competitions and Bomb competitions—these are the different competitions held throughout the city at 3 or sometime 4 judging points, when most times All Stars would have done a clean sweep, e.g., "The Good, the Bad and the Ugly" won 4 such competitions; as did "Mood Indigo"; as did "Precious Lord"; and in 2011 "You Are My Special Angel" won 4 such competitions, giving All Stars a grand total over the years of some 26 Bomb victories competing as always with the best of the bands of the day.[411]

The salient point however is that people can justify such bragging rights only because of Trinidad All Stars' fervent commitment to the handmaidens of Pan and Mas for 85 years. The only competition in which All Stars does not hold the most "wins" is Panorama. At present, 2019, All Stars (10 wins) stand second behind both Renegades (11) and Desperadoes with (12) wins. Only recently a pan enthusiast posted on the Internet, the following: "All Stars with Smooth (as panorama arranger) established eight (8) records from 2007 to 2013: won the First Final Panorama in South (2007); won the first One Million prize (2007); the first to defeat another arranger with his own composition (2008—Silver Stars—Thunder Coming); first to defeat and win performing another arranger's composition (2011—Silver Stars—Showtime); win the only Two Million first Prize; the only band to place in the top three from 2007 to 2013; won $6,000,000 from 2007 to 2013; broke the record with 23 top-three panorama placings to date."[412]

Actually, it is now 26 such placings to date, (10 Firsts, 10 Seconds, 6 Thirds) the most outstanding record in 54 years of Panorama history given that there was no Panorama in 1979.

It was, however, in April 1960 that All Stars as an institution of the people came to gain considerable mileage, social leverage and added public acclaim, this time from the vanguard of the Political Mass Movement of the people, i.e., the PNM who had triggered confrontation with the Americans over the return of the Chaguaramas Peninsula. There developed as a result a tumultuous groundswell among the masses demanding that the American Base be removed and there was a call to march on Chaguaramas. In fact, Chaguaramas had become a salient symbol of national aspirations and political independence precisely because the PNM, led by their two most outstanding leaders, Dr. Eric Williams and CLR James, had argued the case in 1958 that T&T "… be given the site for the Federal Capital of the West Indies as the Chaguaramas Peninsula was seen as ideal given its aesthetics and the fact that the Treaty with the Americans for their naval and military presence there was up for renewal." The general consensus in light of national aspirations was that there should be no renewal.

CLR James had this to say: "Williams, in the drive for the return of Chaguaramas, made what I believe to be his finest speech: From Slavery to Chaguaramas… what created him (Williams) and sent him along a dangerous road was the response of the people of T&T… It is the people of T&T who pushed Williams out on a limb, to the furthest end of it. He got into the habit of saying things, making proposals, that astonished and, I confess, at times frankly frightened me…"[413] CLR also indicated that there was a lack of support and help from the other West Indian politicians (whose duplicity in regard to a strong Federation and West Indian Independence was a major hindrance).

Williams, on the other hand, addressing a Party Convention said: "…Here, then, is the ammunition of the PNM in the war of West Indian Independence— a fundamentally sound party machine which needs complete overhaul, a stable and buoyant economy, a revolutionary inter-racial philosophy, a mass movement for political education which constitutes the best in modern West Indian democracy, and a vigorous, hard hitting party weekly newspaper which may not be first with the news of murders and pictures of sex orgies and striptease episodes, but which is certainly first with the analysis and interpretation of the news on Independence, self-government, overseas bases, federal system of government, cultural achievements and aspirations, and the challenge to the Old World in every sphere… The Nation today, under the able leadership of CLR James, has become the textbook of Independence…"[414]

Undoubtedly, CLR and Williams both helped to develop the case for the return of Chaguaramas, encouraged and pushed by the people from below.[415]

On that fateful day, April 22, 1960, the people marched in the rain singing *"Listen Uncle Sam, we want back we land/take yuh rotten grapefruit and go!"* and were prepared to march on Chaguaramas to confront the Americans but instead they were marched around the Queen's Park Savannah and back to Woodford Square.[416] It was reported by the PNM that over 50,000 people participated, despite the pouring rain, in what was billed the "April 22 Independence Demonstration"; that the entire Trade Union Movement and all the other progressive Parties and social organizations, e.g., Butler Party, West Indian Independence Party, League of Women Voters, Caribbean Women's League, etc., etc. were involved but "…the momentous and perhaps most solemn part of the ceremony was the Declaration of Independence and the hoisting of the flags of the West Indies and Trinidad & Tobago by the Political Leader… This was accompanied by the playing of **Handel's Largo** by the **All Stars Steel Orchestra**. It has been reported that persons among the mammoth crowd were seen shedding tears…" [417]

Simply put, Jules had chosen and arranged a most moving and haunting piece of music, befitting such an august occasion when the Mass Movement of T&T had cause to express its demand for self-actualization and self-determination. ***Largo*** is a solo song from the opera *"Ombra Mai Fu"* which translates from Italian to mean *"Never Has There Been A Shade"* in praise of a tree's shade as the soloist sits beneath it. It was first heard on Pan when Free French of San Fernando played it at the 1952 Music Festival. One wonders whether it would be far-fetched to assume that Jules was compelled to choose ***Handel's Largo*** because he intuitively recognized the 1960 political mass movement as a symbolic "shade", protective of the dreams and aspirations of the whole people? Whatever, Trinidad All Stars, true to form, once again rose to the occasion and enhanced the atmosphere that stirred people to "tears".

When the Panorama competition was first introduced in 1963, the year after Independence, All Stars began to come under further social pressure from its younger members, its staunch supporters, and the general public to re-enter competitions. The band was hard-pressed in the mid-60s to maintain its supremacy of numbers on Carnival Days given the then growing attraction of other bands such as Desperadoes, Silver Stars and Highlanders, then in their glorious years of ascendancy, yet still All Stars was forced to move slowly on the congested streets of Port-of-Spain moreover because of the tendency of its masqueraders to opt for ball-room style dancing, now part of the band's tradition, as they inched their way along Duke or around Piccadilly to the strains of Jules' phenomenal arrangements of tunes such as **Musetta's Waltz**, **Tammy**, or Melody's *Iceman*. It would take a full decade (1954–1964) for the band to finally concede to the pressure that had been building up all along.

In 1965, All Stars entered its first Panorama competition. This was the very year that Guinness Cavaliers under the leadership of Bobby Mohammed came into Port-of-Spain and swept everybody away with their arrangement of Melody's Mas and more so with their "ringing" tenors tuned by Alan Gervais. **It was the first and only time that a band came to a Panorama and was compelled by the demands of the masses to deliver a concert**. In fact, it was the signal of the coming to the fore of a set of younger and more exacting tuners (e.g. Gervais, Coker, Marshall, Wallace, Bassman, etc.) that would take bands like Cavaliers, Desperadoes, Harmonites and Highlanders to the top.

As outlined before, both Ellie and Jules had to concede; Ellie, after a short sojourn in the US, left T&T eventually in 1967 choosing to be domiciled in the USA, whereas Jules chose to head down to the South of Trinidad to find Alan Gervais. Jules said: *At the time, we had no sponsor and a lot of the guys were not working, but I was working. There was a tuner called Alan who was in Point (Fortin) and I told him I didn't have a sponsor. I said to him (Gervais), "I want you to ease me up and tune some pans for me," and he agreed. I bought some drums and I took them down there. He tuned them for me and I paid him…*[418] Beresford Hunte maintains that some of the tenors made by Alan Gervais back then are still in use and are some of the "sweetest" tenors around.[419]

From 1965 to 1967, Jules continued to mesmerize the public with his arrangements, e.g., Sparrow's **Patsy** in 1965 with which All Stars placed fourth, but the band's re-introduction of its old style of bass-playing in which the players "dampened" notes with the palm of the hands to curtail the flow of vibrations from one note to another, something they could readily do because of the short bass-sticks for which they were noted, had town "talking" and signaled All Stars' return to competition after an absence of 11 years. In 1966 it was another Sparrow selection, **Sir Garfield Sobers**—who is the greatest cricketer on Earth or Mars—and the folklore has it that when Prime Minister, Dr. Eric Williams, heard All Stars playing this Jules arrangement, "he get up in the stands and wine down the place…" A switch to Lord Kitchener came in 1967, as **"Sixty-Seven"** was the choice for Panorama. That was the very year that Clive Alexander, noted architect and jazz pianist returned from England, and when he was asked by Neville Jules for an opinion on the arrangement of "**Sixty-Seven**", Clive Alexander was moved to say, "change nothing!"

Mr. Alexander himself arranged for All Stars a calypso by the Merrymen of Barbados based on the TV series "The Fugitive", the song was popularly known in T&T as "**Nimble, Nimble like Kimble**" and Zanda's bass-lines that he inserted in that arrangement remains still a popular topic in Hell Yard for the frenzy it generated that J'ouvert morning. And there were other second-line road tunes that Neville Jules arranged for the band in that 65–71 period that were indeed just as outstanding: Sparrow's "A Fool and his Money", who could forget the use of the double-second pans in that arrangement; "Valarina" by the Lord Laro before he opted to live in Jamaica; the theme from the movie "Is Paris Burning" (a compulsory piece in that Panorama, and though this component part of the competition was won by Solo Harmonites nobody recalls their arrangement of the tune; nevertheless, there are many today who can still whistle or hum the counter-harmonization to the melodic lines that Jules placed on the inside pans); the Mighty Duke's "Productivity" and last but by no means least, "Cloak And Dagger" by the Lord Shorty; the tune that really launched Lord Shorty's journey toward becoming a calypso icon.

That J'ouvert Morning, most people, on hearing Jules' arrangement of "Cloak And Dagger", wondered loudly whether it was another one of Jules' classical Bombs, only to discover that it was the song of a yet unknown calypsonian from South by the name of Garfield Blackman, the Lord Shorty. Whenever Jules was asked how he came to have selected any of those calypso musical pieces mentioned above he would always answer in the same manner: it was simply, "the most **OPEN** tune", in other words, the tune that most readily lent itself to the imagination and machination of an in-depth arranger.

All Stars 1965 presentation—"Fiesta in Mexico". Third from right is Kenrick Rennie, later Dr. Kenrick Rennie and President of the PSA.

1965 Fiesta in Mexico. Bukka Rennie, middle, Pinky Grant with sombrero over face.

From left, Pierre, Pinky Grant, Vinnie Barrow and Bukka Rennie. Missing: Gideon Harris.

The All Stars Mt. Hope Posse, stooping, left, Carlton Grant (dec) and the famous Ringo (dec)—"the fastest gun in POS." Carl "Jacko" Jackson, standing on the left. 1965 Fiesta in Mexico. Pix courtesy Debbie Jackson.

Ronnie Jackson flanked by the Gabriel Brothers, Ruthven (dec), left and Terry. 1965 Fiesta in Mexico. Pix courtesy Debbie Jackson.

"Stars Pitch, Dey Never Fall!"

(…an old Trinidad All Stars maxim)

In 1967, the band encountered its first major split. The issue of sponsorship was at the center of the problem that arose. Some members of All Stars held an ongoing job playing music for the tourists around the swimming pool at the Hilton Hotel; they utilized All Stars instruments, used Hilton colors and overtime came to be regarded, and to be referred to, as the Hilton All Stars. An LP titled *"Neville Jules gives you Classic in Steel"* by Trinidad Hilton All Stars Steel Orchestra, comprising music arranged by Jules, was even put on sale to the public during this period (see cover of album, below). So initially, no one anticipated any problem developing since this loose arrangement guaranteed those particular members their jobs as musicians at this popular hotel and tourist resort.

Winston Gordon indicated that in August 1962, the year that T&T was granted political Independence from Britain, the Hilton Hotel was opened with great pomp and ceremony; Sammy Davis Jr. was the featured international guest artiste and Trinidad All Stars was recommended to the Hotel and the band was invited to play at the pool-side and at Sammy Davis's suite later that night. Gordon said that Sammy Davis fell in love with All Stars' music and so did the Hotel's management. As a result All Stars was contracted to play every night for the following three weeks at the pool-side at dinner time and this contract continued for the next six years.

The band's engagement at the hotel was extended to three nights per week, i.e., Mondays, Wednesdays and Saturdays from 7-pm to 10pm and on Sundays at lunch time, 12pm-3pm. Engagements were also extended whenever cruise ships were in Port.[420] He indicated that he was charged with the responsibility to manage the band members employed at the Hotel and pointed out that after a while ill-disciplined crept in owing to the fact that the rigorous schedules became burdensome to some players who opted to be absent without notice leading eventually to termination of the arrangement.[421]

Jules explained the difficulty that arose in another manner:... *Some people think that the first sponsor we had was Hilton Hotel, but that wasn't really so. Some members of the band used to go up there and play, especially when tourist boats came in. To keep the job for them, we began merely calling ourselves Hilton All Stars... but then I realized (that) that was hampering the band. If a Company was looking for a band to sponsor, it wouldn't consider (Hilton) All Stars. And as I said I was the one spending money to buy the instruments and have them tuned. After the band played for Carnival and for dances all the money we made was counted and I would be reimbursed any money I used...*

...The Green Giant Company then came along and considered sponsoring us. The guys who played in Hilton who were calling themselves Hilton All Stars wanted to use some of the pans I had made. I told them no, that since they were working throughout the year they could tune their own pans. To audition for Green Giant, so to speak, I then took some of the pans, used the Panorama uniform we had, and with some extra men went to play for the Green Giant people who came to the Hilton to hear us.

It so happened that the manager of the Hilton heard the band and didn't know it was All Stars. He asked the guy who was in charge of the band, what band that was, and then learned it was All Stars. The manager responded that he was seeing different people in a different uniform, and the pans were painted in a different color. So the Hilton guys blamed me and said I, as the captain, didn't want them to use the other pans... The manager said to the guys, "Okay, you have a band, then get your own pans..."

...Somebody or somebodies then went to the newspaper and accused me of stealing all the money. They used this line as an excuse to leave, when I wasn't even involved with the band's money. At the time I was in the city and was merely asked to hold the money for them, which I did. But to say I stole it: they merely used that story to break away and form their own band and call their new, little band, Boston Something or the other, I can't remember. But it didn't last long...[422]

In terms of legal contracts, ongoing practice and precedent are as binding to parties as any signed agreement. The fact that members of All Stars, in fact the cream of the crop, were playing professionally at the Hilton under the name "All Stars" on an ongoing basis would be construed in any court of law to be an air-tight contract. "We began merely calling ourselves Hilton All Stars," says Jules, which therefore meant that those few members of the band were in fact presenting themselves to the public as "Hilton All Stars" without any objection from the Trinidad All Stars per se or from Hilton Hotel resulting therefore in a mutual acceptance of a de facto contractual arrangement. Luckily neither side sought legal determination of any aspect of this matter, and all concerned simply went their way terminating what had becoming ongoing practice.

At the end of March 1967, the following report appeared in one of the newspapers:...*The assurance was given yesterday that Trinidad All Stars Steelband "will continue to function as always and that everything will be done to maintain a high standard of performance." The band's leader Mr. Neville Jules issued a Press release following rumors that several members of the band had resigned because of a split in the ranks of the steel orchestra.*

Pix of All Stars on upper Henry Street, Carnival Tuesday 1967, courtesy Dalton Narine. In 1967 due to the conflict with members of the stage side who played at the Hilton, Neville Jules repainted the pans. The Hilton colors of "Tangerine & Black" were replaced by "White" with a "Red" band. In the middle of this picture, the tall player with big pom-pom on hat and no letter on shirt is Grant Boland, brother of Clyde "Neck" Boland who played a major role in keeping the band together.

He pointed out that no section of the band was ever sponsored by the Trinidad Hilton and that monies received from the Hilton management went to the members of the band and not to the organization... Miss Georgiana Masson, Public Relations Director of Trinidad Hilton, said yesterday that 15 members of the band were employed at regular periods at the hotel and so carried the name of Hilton All Stars, but Hilton had no other obligation of sponsorship... Recent disagreement among members of the band led to the Hilton curtailing the regular employment of the 15 members in the interest of the band and the hotel..."[423] Apparently, the 15 members assumed that the Hilton would continue to employ them so their decision to break completely from All Stars was predicated on the view that their jobs at the hotel would be safe;[424] that was the first rude awakening which they were forced to face.

The split would have been extremely painful to Neville Jules in particular for the group that left after Carnival 1967 to form **Boston Symphony** represented the best of the playing membership, i.e., people like Winston Gordon and Rupert Alexander—the dynamic duo or the "terrible-twins" of the Six-Bass section, as well as Britto (Brother Hog)) and virtually most of the then stage-side." To Neville Jules, Gordon, who had emerged the most likely leader of **Boston Symphony**, was quite a special person, he was the one that Jules had earmarked to be his successor, the next captain, and already Jules besides simply regarding Gordon as his protégé had begun to allow Gordon the space to arrange tunes of his own choice and to provide the band with his own voicing, and to tell from the public reaction on J'ouvert Morning in 1966 to Gordon's arrangement of *Stella by Starlight*, it seemed that Gordon was well on his way to fulfilling Jules' wishes. Sadly, it was not to be.

But there was another aspect to Gordon's specialty or specialness that needs to be told. Gordon grew up "behind-the-bridge", was a product of the environment on Clifton Street, the first of five children, could not recall what is father did for a living but his mother was always there taking care of their needs. He attended Piccadilly Government School and then Tranquility Boys but due to financial difficulties he had to walk away from taking final exams and began job hunting. In 1957, he got a messenger/porter job at Scotia Bank. He said that whenever he did not have to be on the road, instead of sitting back until his next run, he would volunteer to help the banking staff with any filing that needed to be done.[425] He indicated that his enthusiasm and willingness to learn did not go unnoticed so much so that in 1963 he eventually was offered a clerical position in the forex department.[426]

The Scotia Bank, as all other banks in T&T, was under pressure from the building social and political consciousness of the times to recruit young Afro-Trinidadians, so when the split in All Stars came in 1967, Gordon was already on his way up the Corporate Banking structure at Scotia, eventually becoming a Manager.[427] Probably it was because of the then demands of his job why he could not give Boston Symphony his undivided attention, however by late 1969/early 1970 they were on the wane and, then, some of the leading lights, faced with the rigors of unemployment, migrated, and so by 1971 the band disappeared completely from the world of Pan. However, Gordon indicates that the bank experience taught him "care and caution" for in banking without those guides "you are dead."

He also reinforced the view that in life "there are opportunities for everyone, you have to see it, grab it and run with it", and he was emphatic that "there is always a better way to do things well and if you do things well, the results will follow."[428] But it was the music within the All Stars experience up in the Garret that served to instill the discipline that made him the man that he is. "The music," he said, "it is the thing that revives me."[429] Indeed, the bond between Jules and Winston Gordon would be reignited in New York when they collaborated on musical arrangements for the Sonatas steelband there.

Neville, despite his great disappointment in people whose development he had personally guided, was adamant that "new members will come to All Stars and the institution will make them as good as or even better than those who left, and he, moreover, proved likewise to be quite prophetic as he also predicted that the breakaway band would not last."[430] The acid test for the young players, the new recruits, Noel "Cin-Cin" Lorde outlined, came on Carnival Monday night in 1968 when All Stars was coming down Charlotte Street and news came that Boston Symphony was coming up; that information according to Cin-Cin brought some tension and nervousness among the new players but the older folk kept saying to them "keep calm, just keep focused and concentrate on the music you are playing and everything would be alright, do not bother with what Boston Symphony is doing!"

Cin-Cin said it worked because they were able to maintain tempo and play without missing a note as they drove past Boston Symphony without flinching.[431] As an afterthought Cin-Cin pointed out that it was quite symbolic that that musical "confrontation" took place on Charlotte Street, outside of the Crown Bakery and the original entrance to Hell-Yard, the birth place of Trinidad All Stars.[432] It was a sterling signal to Boston Symphony on that Carnival Monday Night, a signal which indicated that All Stars was still All Stars rising at all times to meet the required occasion despite the departure of any of the top membership. Psychologically, the wane of Boston Symphony may have begun that very night. According to Courtney Vincent Charles, the return to triumph after this heart-rending split served to validate the maxim, often mouthed by stalwarts of Hell Yard and All Stars: ***Stars pitch, they never fall!***[433]

In all respects, 1968 was truly a benchmark year in the history of Trinidad All Stars. Jules said: "When they (i.e., the 15 guys who formed Boston Symphony) left, **it was a blessing for the band** because we had a group of guys from Jackson Place…"[434] Prince Batson elsewhere further described this "blessing" when he said: *After Carnival 1967… Jules was left with a handful of young, green men who had now joined the band. These members were from the Jackson Place, Jackson Hill area. They were called Jacksonville and among them were members who had experience in club life and parliamentary procedure. In these men Jules placed his confidence and the future of the band. 1968 came and the band was successful on the road, contrary to what some people thought would have been the case…*"[435]

Web Alexander indicated that Jules firmly believed that All Stars, the institution, would "make the new members as good or even better" that those who went before.[436] Indeed, the names of these "young, green men" would ring out loud in the pantheon of individual contributors that today must underscore the history of All Stars: Hamilton "Web" Alexander, destined to become Captain of All Stars; Noel "Cin-Cin" Lorde; Errol "Reds" Collins who also was to hold the Captaincy for two distinct periods; Clyde "Neck" Boland and his brother Grant Boland. In fact, at that point in their lives they were basically "secondary school-boys" who in the mid '60s had formed the Jacksonville Youth Group and had gained some political, organizational and administrative experience from their affiliation to the St. George West Congress of Youth, and it is said that this Jacksonville Youth Group led by their President, Noel "Cin-Cin" Lorde, did become "a driving force behind the revitalization of Trinidad All Stars."[437]

What is clear is that Jules saw these young members as a "blessing", a matter that Prince Batson clarified when he insisted that Jules placed "his confidence and the future of All Stars in these men," whom he described as having experience in "club life and parliamentary procedure." Did these members of the Jacksonville Youth Group go into All Stars as a collective unit with a clear-cut agenda or were they merely a group of starry-eyed individuals anxiously desirous of developing pan-playing skills?

Noel "Cin-Cin" Lorde answers: *Sometime around August—September 1966, Neville Jules began to discard the old pans that All Stars had and began to get new pans from a tuner down South. Clyde "Neck" Boland, then a tenor player with All Stars and a member of the Jacksonville Youth Group brought some of the old pans to Jackson Place and stored them under building No. 9. Then "Neck" began to teach the Jacksonville members All Stars music. The first tune I remember we learnt was "Brazil".*

That went on until December of 1966. Then in January 1967 our group went over and joined All Stars; it was around that time that the band moved from the Charlotte Street Garret to Henry St. and later the St. Vincent Street pan-yard. After Carnival 1967 the split came and the Jacksonville group found itself from then on being the core of the new All Stars stage-side... next thing we know, we in the 1968 Music Festival...[438]

"Web" Alexander, on the other hand, recalled that "a meeting was called by "Neck" Boland," after the split and the formation of Boston Symphony, "for us to trash out what we will be doing; will we be going to Boston Symphony or staying with Trinidad All Stars?" and he recalls "Neck" saying: "I is a so and so Jules man, I staying with All Stars... and in the end the vast majority stayed with All Stars..." [439] And according to Prince Batson, these youths proved their mettle.

But there were other variables that would have contributed to the band rising above what was generally expected of them that Carnival. Neville Jules said that a member of All Stars "placed an ad in the papers" indicating the need of sponsorship for the band.[440] Lincoln "Abbos" Aberdeen, then a much respected bright-boy, tenor-player and an ex-pupil of Trinity College, repeatedly claims today that he was the one who took the initiative to place that request in the newspapers.[441] Apparently that plea for assistance must have touched the hearts and awoken a long-standing interest of a number of people who had been supporters of the band for quite a while.

Jules said: "Peter Pitts, deceased, was a strong supporter of the band. He and some other guys, from since back in 1948, used to come right there on George Street and sit with us at the side of the canal and 'ole talk'..."[442] Jules also mentioned on another occasion that Pitts and "about four or five white guys, Mr. Hale and their friends from Catelli..." and Jules included in that group, Pat Castagne, the Guyanese who composed T&T's national anthem, all of whom Jules described as "regular guys" who on Carnival Days "came out with our band..."[443]

OJ indicated that the connection with these individuals began even earlier, he said: "All Stars got their first public relations boost while the band was still in the coal shop yard on George Street. They were invited to bring a small group for a live performance in Radio Trinidad and happened to be at the studio the same time that Pat Castagne and his friend, Peter Pitts, were there. On hearing the band perform, the two men immediately offered them a contract to play at Perseverance Hall and Casual's Club—two elite clubs for society's upper class. This contract lasted for two years but providing music in such an environment did not sit well with their grassroots' supporters..."[444]

Clearly, the emotional attachment of these "white, upper-class" gentlemen to All Stars was indeed quite powerful. What, however, is described thereafter is most amazing. It was the semi-final night of the 1968 Panorama competition and All Stars had just come down the "bull-track" and was awaiting to go on stage when a message came to the band that Neville Jules was wanted on the phone. Jules recalls: *A call came for me from Peter Pitts while we were in the Savannah... he asked whether I would consider being sponsored by Catelli... I said yes... he said, "what about if you go on stage right now and introduce your band as Catelli All Stars," I said, "sure..."*[445]

There is another dimension to this story. Apparently, Peter Pitts had been taking Ossie Hale and others of the Hand Arnold Group to listen to All Stars since the days of the Garret, and over time Ossie Hale and family had become like Pitts "staunch supporters" of the band.[446] On the night of the Panorama semi-finals on February 23, 1968, there was a party at the Mr. and Mrs. Hale's residence in Maraval celebrating their daughter's 21st birthday but the pan fans at the party were listening to the Panorama on the radio and while doing so Peter Pitts related to them the situation in which All Stars had found itself: that Neville Jules had carried the financial burden of the band out of pocket for quite a while, that he was no longer in a position to continue to do so and as a result the band was "suffering severe financial strain to meet expenses and was facing a serious threat of total collapse."[447]

The end result was that Ossie Hale, there and then, convened a meeting of Hand Arnold directors, "a few telephone calls completed the quorum of directors and the sponsorship decision was taken."[448]

"Catelli, then the newest wing of the business according to the report and, probably, the branch that needed promoting most crucially, was given the honor of assigning its brand name to All Stars, a steelband with a long and an illustrious history. It was the indomitable Peter Pitts, then General Manager of Radio 610, who organized the hook-up to the Savannah that night and got Neville Jules on the phone, and the report confirms that immediately after the Panorama, the sponsors and band officials met from 2am to 4am and by J'ouvert morning of Carnival 1968 All Stars hit the road in Catelli colors—yellow, black and gold."[449] In fact the colors were "yellow" and "blue" as indicated by Web Alexander.

From that moment, the band became formally the Catelli Trinidad All Stars. Jules reported that full negotiations with Catelli (i.e., Hand Arnold) took place after Carnival and being mindful of the band's commitment since 1965 to re-enter competitions, including the Music Festivals, a salient aspect of those negotiations became the taking on of a full-fledged Musical Director who in this case was Mr. Fitzgerald "Gerry" Jemmott.[450] Thus began a most fruitful association between All Stars and Uncle Jem that was to last a full twenty years, 1968–1988, and which shall be described as the "Jemmott Years".

So, for All Stars, 1968 was indeed a benchmark year that brought the emergence and the solidifying of the engagement of the young "turks" of Jacksonville; the full sponsorship of Catelli and more so the directorship of a formally trained musician and musicologist.

The Jemmott Years

The man, Uncle Jem, had a profound impact on the membership of the band and on its modus operandi; he was a transformational catalyst. According to Roy Gibbs: "Rudolph Wells introduced Uncle Jem to us. I could remember the night Jules, Wells and I went down to Carlton Avenue, St. James to ask Uncle Jem to arrange for the band and he accepted… he was a sergeant in the police band."[451] In response to a question about Jemmott's influence on the band's performances, this is what Neville Jules said: *The first thing he*

(Jemmott) did when he came was make us change the way how we were doing things. In the early days (of tuning), the lowest note on the pan we would call "C". Jemmott now came with his flute and... he would say "eh, eh, that ain't C," and he would (call) the note that was played instead. He went around and he got the full range of the complete band and then he started to do his thing. He didn't just teach them sounds, he also gave them exercises which they had to follow. He was very good...[452]

Ossie Hale concurred with that view and maintained that the Catelli/Hand Arnold people, i.e., himself, Mike Hackshaw, Peter Hale, Frank Kirkley, etc. and the All Stars Executive planned the development process of the band with the aim to utilize classical music under the guidance of Jemmott as a means to "improve both in equipment and performance" and he explained that All Stars deliberately refused to take on the "massive things (i.e., 12-bass, etc.) that are produced by Despers and other bands" because "our philosophy was to develop an instrument that can be easily transportable... and to work to make the pans sound good. They do sound good, there is no question about that..."[453]

Roy Gibbs also indicated that Uncle Jem brought to the band "a form of reading music; instead of symbols on the reading board, yuh getting the notes like A, B-flat, B, so we got the letters that corresponded with markings on the Pans; we had though **to read the pauses and spaces** and that was good, good experience."[454] Noel "Cin-Cin" Lorde also described the "hand and eye co-ordination exercises" which Uncle Jem introduced to the band and how he insisted on mental and physical fitness as a prerequisite to excellent performances and as a result would take the entire band up to Memorial Park for physical work-out sessions as a component part of routine, daily music practice.[455]

Smooth Edwards indicated Jemmott "was a smart guy, he never played a pan in his life, but he was able to watch those who played pan well as opposed to those who did not, and, by compare and contrast, he came up with or found out the theories on how to play pan efficiently, you know, how to cover your pan, how to position your legs or open your legs, and so on and these things helped the weaker players."[456] John "Poison" Douglas, ex-Captain, concurs with these views indicating that Uncle Jem's approach to a rudimentary teaching of musical notation to the members was in fact "visionary" and that furthermore Uncle Jem "recognized what the steelband was truly capable of and he used classical music both to develop technique while exploring and expanding this potential of the steelband," and he suggested that the "exercises that Uncle Jem fine-tuned, i.e., wrist movement, deep-breathing, the smooth rolling of notes without staccato effect, the massaging of the pan and how to "go into the note", all of which Uncle Jem had made a detailed study, placed All Stars above the rest to the extent that people began to refer to All Stars as the classical band as if the band could not and did not play calypso.[457]

John Douglas dismissed such a preposterous conclusion and declared that from its inception, All Stars, from the days of Jules to the time of both Jules and Jemmott, remained always focused on its overall musical product; and there was always a close affinity between the two in regard to their disciplined and professional approach to music, to them each piece of music was "a story" and to clarify this Douglas said that when Jules arranged a tune such as Sparrow's Lizard, the arrangement would tell you "how the Lizard lived and how it died" in the very same way that Uncle Jem would lecture the band about the story behind any classical piece of music the band was about to attempt; he would explain what the composer had in mind, what he wanted to depict so that "when All Stars played we had in mind how this piece should sound and what were the details surrounding the music which in turn helped to enhance our performance."[458]

Douglas lamented that the involvement and contribution of both Jules and Jemmott have yet to be fully ventilated; *these two meshed and under their guidance the development of All Stars skyrocketed, and after Jules left, Jemmott continued the process of developing the talents of everybody, he could spot latent talent and work to develop that inner talent of every single member of the band; he used the Classical Jewels concerts to do exactly that and as a result people like Clive "Cokey" Telemaque and Claude "Boof" Williams(dec) became virtuoso star-players and today the likes of Deryck Nurse, Yohan Popwell and Dane Gulston have become quite prominent and are highly regarded within the Pan Fraternity.*

In those days, the All Stars stage-side was probably one of the strongest stage-sides ever in the history of Trinidad & Tobago and I could say that without fear of contradiction... Uncle Jem made players over time, and any player who left All Stars under Jemmott and joined any other band automatically was given star billing.[459]

John Douglas indicated also that Jemmott's conceptualization of the **Oboe Pan** is a contribution of his to the Pan Family that seems to have been forgotten even by All Stars; "It was a Pan that Jemmott wanted to utilize in the 1982 Music Festival in the performance of *Carnival Romain* (composed by Hector Berlioz); it was to express a certain sound, between the tenors and double-tenors, and was made specifically to be played by Cokey Telemaque; the concept was taken to Leo Coker who built this special pan, and when this **Oboe Pan** was played in the festival, the sound blew people out of the water..."[460] When Douglas was informed that the **Oboe Pan** was indeed mentioned by the then leader, Beresford Hunte, who could not locate it, Douglas confirmed that the **Oboe Pan** is today still in his (Douglas') possession.[461]

The original Oboe Pan was a single pan that was the result of collaboration between Uncle Jem and Leo Coker. Since then it has been in the possession of John Poison Douglas who, in collaboration with Ronald Matthews, designed and extended the range of the Oboe Pan by way of an additional pan. See the following picture:

To put all Jemmott's ideas and approach to steelband music into proper context, it is necessary to convey Jemmott's direct words:... *In attempting classical music, steelband arrangers should bear in mind the following—(a) the range or compass (lowest to highest note) of the steelband, also the range of the various sections bearing in mind the possible range and the practical range; (b) a working knowledge of the instruments is also desirable. In this way, many awkward, if not impossible passages would be avoided or perhaps simplified without destroying the composer's intentions; (c) the fact that the instruments of the conventional orchestra, most of which the composer obviously had in mind when writing, are not as difficult to master as their counterparts in the steelband.*

Many passages which could be termed under the fingers in the conventional orchestra is not at all easy-pickings for the steelband; (d) the ability and experience of the players should also be taken into account, especially when it comes to the adaptation of the so-called serious music; (e) Key Signatures may be changed to ensure easier execution and a better sound as far as the Steelband is concerned, however this is not permissible in Music Festivals; (f) to ensure pinpoint precision and a good visual impact, there should be **unanimity in stick-work**, *not to mention the* **foot-work** *in the bass and tenor bass sections and the* (**dance**) *body movement generally (my emphasis); (g) there are composers whose music are more easily adaptable than others. To name a few: Mozart, Handel, Schubert and Franz Von Suppe...*[462]

But that was only one-half of the package according to Uncle Jem. In order to create the complete musical product, he opined that the conductor had to whip the aggregation, comprising individuals of varying levels of consciousness and talents, into a seeming or actual oneness. This is how he expressed the viewpoint: "...In many music ensembles there is always the outstanding performer or performers, the not so outstanding ones and perhaps the not so hot ones, in other words, at first they are a group of individuals each having their own idea of how fast is allegro, how soft is piano, etc. In other words how quick is quick and how soft is soft. This is where the conductor rules supreme; his task is to change this group of individuals into a unit, **one gigantic musical instrument** emanating from this unit played by the conductor. As it were, **interpretation** being his main task..."[463]

And Uncle Jem went on to pinpoint that interpretation comprised four (4) basic elements: (1) Rhythm, which he described as "the arrangement of successive tones usually in bars or measures according to relative accentuation"; (2) Dynamics, i.e., intensity of sound, varying from very soft to very loud; (3) Rubato, i.e., deviations from strict tempo; and (4) Phrasing; and here Uncle Jem indicated that like "phrases in sentences, musical phrases must remain distinct and must flow along" in other words must be coherent.[464]

At the end of his discourse, Jemmott painted a picture that inadvertently or not remains to date a pluperfect description and image of himself on the rostrum before the classical music war-machine into which he fashioned Catelli Trinidad All Stars: Listen to this amazing self-portrait: "There are also other factors which the composer can hardly put on paper which however should be captured by the conductor. In his attempt to accomplish these tasks, the conductor becomes oblivious to everything living or dead except his present environment. It is only when this is done that the most rewarding task of bringing out all the beauty in the music which the composer intended is accomplished. What is achieved is achieved through the gestures of his eyes, lips, facial expressions and movements of the body. However, his hands are the most used part of the body when communicating to his men..."[465]

The proof of the pudding had to be in the "eating", i.e., in the results that were gained from the application of those principles outlined above by Jemmott.

So having been aboard the All Stars ship for just a few months in 1968, Uncle Jem was able to take the band gloriously into winner's row in the Music Festival with a dynamic performance of Schubert's "Unfinished Symphony". One commentator said that Jemmott proved his talent to the Nation "by taking a bunch of inexperienced pan men and winning the 1968 Music Festival."[466] The test piece was "Sunday Morning" by Benjamin Britton; "that was one of the hardest pieces of music I ever played," said Roy Gibbs, "yuh hearing bells, yuh seeing people going to church Sunday Morning, yuh had to read the board (which Jemmott had put up in the yard) and get the pauses right, to get the right interpretation."[467]

The report carried by one newspaper read as follows: "...Catelli Trinidad All Stars has finally made it into the permanent Hall of Fame... All Stars' win was no surprise. From the word "Go" at the preliminaries, the band had established itself a firm favorite."[468] The report indicated that the tunes of choice performed by All Stars throughout the entire competition (i.e., preliminaries, semi-finals, finals) were *Mozart's Minuet in E Flat; Schubert's Unfinished Symphony; C. Chaplin's This is My Song* and the calypso *Kitchener's Marsicans*; that the adjudicators were particularly impressed with the Minuet as they felt that All Stars really captured the mood of the piece, i.e., the aristocratic way of life, the right moment of History, the right style, etc. also that Sgt. Jemmott was highly praised by the judges for his conducting of the band.[469]

In regard to the test piece—Sunday Morning by Benjamin Britten from the opera Peter Grimes—the judges were critical, felt that it was not the best choice, not suitable for steelbands and Sydney Harrison in particular expressed the view that it was "too big a leap in the dark" and called for a firm, lifetime intellectual commitment to the development of Pan wherein local composers would write specifically for Pan, and to this end he confessed to dreaming of steelbands "playing something that nobody else can play."[470] Amidst that report there was this single statement that simply said that Cordell Barbour of Catelli Trinidad All Stars won the ping-pong soloist competition at the Music Festival.[471] All Stars in fact had made a clean sweep.

Uncle Jem in a quiet and pensive moment listening to the band's rehearsal.

All Stars at the 1968 Music Festival

Cordell Barbour of All Stars—Soloist winner (Courtesy Trinidad Guardian—Wednesday, 2 October 1968)

That 1968 festival victory prodded all concerned to push even further to extend the musical capacity of the band. That period coincided with the relocation from the Henry and Duke Car-Park (1967, 1968, and 1969) to the Old Bus Terminus at the bottom of St. Vincent Street and Independence Square (1970–1980) where today the Twin Towers Financial Complex stands. It was there that Jemmott, Jules, Reds, Web, Cokey Telemaque, Smooth, Guy, Guerra, the Wells Brothers (Rudy and Bunny), etc. really got down to working assiduously under Jemmott's guidance to develop for the future the musical competence and technical proficiency of the band.

It was said that it was Rudy Wells's confidence in the musical prowess of Jemmott that led him to recommend Jemmott to the band and surely that confidence in retrospect was well placed. There are two pictures (See Pics 9 and 10) that depict a normal day at work in the panyard clearly showing the complex musical notations placed on the blackboard by Jemmott as he and others worked out theory in the practice on the various pans. It involved hard work and enormous sweat that eventually paid off.

Jules, confident that the band was well on its way to a glorious future, chose only then to hand over the Captaincy and took up the option to migrate to New York in 1971, thus bringing an era to an end; an era that lasted some twenty-five plus years of total, selfless commitment to the overall development of Pan and the specific nurturing of All Stars. Up to the time of his death in 2020, Jules was still addressed as, and referred to, as "Cap", regardless of whomsoever may have in fact been holding that august position. To the All Stars family, Jules will forever be "Cap".

(Pic. 9)

From left to right: Neville Jules, Prince Batson (partly hidden), Reds Collins and Cokey Telemaque, all hard at work under the guidance of Uncle Jem (foreground)

(Pic. 10)

Uncle Jem conducting a class at the Old Bus Terminus on St. Vincent Street, then the All Stars pan yard. The complex notations on the blackboard behind Jemmott suggest the intensity of his program uniquely designed for the young pan players of All Stars.

1970: Dr. Eric Williams Visits the Pan Yard

Noel "Cin-Cin" Lorde, in his youthful exuberance (center), as the band performs for the Prime Minister on his 1970 visit to All Stars' pan yard. Behind Cin-Cin, Neville Jules and PM Dr. Eric Williams converse. Pix courtesy Pan Trinbago's 1972 Music Festival Souvenir Brochure. Cin-Cin was the President of the Jacksonville Youth Group that proved to be key to the rebuilding of Trinidad All Stars after the 1967 split.

Hamilton "Web" Alexander described his rise to the Captaincy of All Stars in this manner: *My rise to (being) captain of the band happened through succession. In 1968, I became a committee member. Incidentally, that was also the year we got Catelli as a sponsor. The band's association with Catelli gave us opportunity to have Kelvin Scoon as our Public Relations Officer. It also gave me the pleasure of knowing people like Ossie Hale, Frank Kirkley, Peter Hale, Peter Pitts and many others. They were strong All Stars supporters. In 1969, I was voted in as vice-captain. Roy Gibbs, who was the departing Vice-Capt., offered me his full support. He was a great help in my understanding how to go about doing my duties.*

In 1971, Neville Jules migrated to the USA and I was voted into the prestigious position, Captain of Trinidad All Stars. The train of events that led me to the position of captain can be described as dedication to and love for Trinidad All Stars, and the leadership potential that I displayed. Some years later, Prince Batson, a former All Stars Captain shared with me that he had told Jules: "one day Web will become the leader of this band."

Taking a look-back, I now realize why Captain Jules would take me along with him to choose drums and carry them to the tuner for tuning. In a sense, he started showing me the ropes, so to speak. There were times I would travel to Point Fortin with him to see Allan Gervais... I also moved around a lot with Prince Batson... at that time he was the truck driver for the band. My travels on the long trips with these two knowledgeable gentlemen helped me to acquire a wealth of knowledge about not only the running of the steelband but also about the history of pan.

This mentorship for the position of Captain meant that I did not have to campaign nor organize any strategy to become captain. I served as a committee member and vice-captain before assuming captaincy of the band which I held for seven years. One of the processes that Jacksonville Youth Group brought into All Stars was the idea of electing the leadership of the band. I was elected using this system...[472]

Web, then only 23 years old, the youngest captain in the band's history, indicates that he enjoyed solid support from Kelvin Scoon, the PRO, and Jemmott, the musical director, as well as the young executive members who served with him and he listed Sonny "Tool" Alleyne, Errol "Reds" Collins, Noel "Cin-Cin" Lorde, John "Poison" Douglas, Anthony Guy, Cecil Lynch and Garth Roberts.[473]

Hamilton "Web" Alexander, well-respected by his peers, held the captaincy from 1971 after Jules migrated and held office until he, likewise migrated to Canada in 1977. As part of the Jacksonville Youth Group who came into All Stars in 1967, Web, though a stern disciplinarian, played a significant role in establishing modern democratic processes as part of the band's culture.

If, by the last quarter of 1968, All Stars, absent from Music Festivals since 1954, was back to its glorious self on the classical stage, certainly by 1969, 1970 and 1971 the carnival road band was likewise once again piping hot. Many can recall the viciously effective bass-lines that Jules inserted for the J'ouvert morning bombshells of soft pop: *Reach in, reach in, and see what you been missing!* by the Jackson Five and *Something in the way, she moves, begets me like no other lover, something in the way she grooves, ah don't want to lose her now...* by the Beatles.

They say that Jules, probably because he knew his migration was imminent, outdid himself; that the power of his arrangements of calypsos such as *Marsicans*, *Lizard* and *Margie* blasted the memory of the Boston Symphony split into the far recesses of forgotten history, and surely signaled that, in regard to all aspects of the music product, classics as well as calypso, the boss-band was back to full glory.

But with Jules having moved on, Leon "Smooth" Edwards, a neighbor of Web (Web lived at No. 2 Jackson Hill and Smooth, No.4) who was encouraged to join All Stars by Web for Carnival 68 and 69 while still in school at QRC, said: "Jules left Lancelot Lane to arrange music but Lancelot's rapso styling and bass lines were too different to All Stars' style and it had everybody grumbling, so Jemmott who had done the Bomb in 1969, *Fingal's Cave*, also had to do the Panorama tune, Kitch's *PP-99* in 1971 but he also was not successful because the music was too classical and people couldn't jump up to it."[474]

It was then, according to the new Captain, "Web" Alexander, that "Rudy Wells", as if by destiny, returned home and gave the band four Panorama arrangements: 1972, "Mrs. Harriman"; 1973, "Rainorama"; 1974, "Tourist Takeover" and 1975, "Trinidad Oil".[475] From the moment Rudy Wells stepped in, he significantly raised the tempo of Panorama performances by All Stars. It was a well-accepted fact that since 1965 Guinness Cavaliers with their winning number, Melody's Mas, had raised the bar in terms of the quickness and tempo of Panorama presentations; it was something that disturbed Jules who preferred the slower tempo to allow for the full sounding of the inside pans on which he placed so much of the salient parts of his voicing; with the quickening of the speed and the resulting increased loudness of the frontline, Jules felt that his arrangements on the inside pans will be lost to the listening public. Probably sensing that he could not stand in the way of what had become crystallized for the future, Jules may have taken this factor into consideration when he chose to move on. Rudy Wells had no such problem, and he took the bull by the horns and swung into full force switching to a strict musical diet out of Kitchener's repertoire which naturally lent itself readily to what he desired to do with the Panorama interpretations.

One can follow the development of Rudy's approach from "Mrs. Harriman" in 1972 for which All Stars won the vote for People's Choice in that Panorama, then on to the thunderous explosion of *Rainorama* that brought for All Stars its first Panorama win in 1973.

It was indeed a pleasing way to cap off the five-year period of rebuilding from 1968 to 1973 for the band's accomplishments then read as follows: 1st Place in the 1968 Music Festival; 2nd in the 1969 Bomb Competition; 1st Place in the 1970 Carnival Bomb Competition for which All Stars was awarded a trip to perform at Madison Square Garden; 1st again in the 1971 Bomb Competition winning both at the Savannah (Uptown) and Independence Square (Downtown); then as if to indicate that the music festival win in 1968 with novice players was no fluke, All Stars took 1st Place again in the 1972 Independence Music Festival performing Antonin Dvorak's "New World Symphony, Opus #9" for which the band was awarded the Prime Minister's Trophy for keeps as well as the announcement that All Stars would represent T&T both at Carifesta in Guyana that year and at the Black Arts Festival in Lagos, Nigeria, carded to be held in 1974–1975; and this winning streak continued with All Stars capturing the 1972 Carnival Bomb Competition (i.e., hat-trick 1970, 71 and 72) and finally the big plum of Panorama 1973 which brought an eventful two-month tour of Paris and the French Riviera with Aubrey Adam's Ambakaila Show.[476]

It was said that All Stars created "havoc" on stage with Kitch's *Rainorama* that night in 1973; that some supporters, "All Stars girls", fell off the stage in the heat of the moment but that these girls "did not mind" so eager were they to get back into the sheer excitement.[477] On the road that Carnival, All Stars also won the "Pan On The Move" competition followed by Blue Diamonds, 2nd; Carib Tokyo, 3rd; and WITCO Desperadoes 4th.[478]

After the 1973 Carnival, Trinidad All Stars went into the recording studio and the result was the LP titled "Inside Out". On Side A the tunes were *Café Regio*—a theme from the Movie, Shaft; *Rain-O-Rama*; *Como Tu*, arranged by Jules; and the two Road Bombs of that year—*Song of Songs* and *Che Che Coule*. On Side B were the following: *Summertime*; *Soul Makossa*; *You are the Sunshine of my Life*; *Folk Medley* (arranged by Jerry Jemmott) and *Woman*. The Tunes *Woman* and *Soul Makossa* were listed in the liner notes as having been arranged by "younger members of the band", "good friends who worked as a team", according to Web, and the names mentioned were Leon Edwards, Anthony Guy, Anthony Cox (now known as Anthony Guerra) and Earl Wells. However, players who were around then indicate that Smooth Edwards was key to the arrangements of *Woman* and *Soul Makossa* as well as the arrangement of Stevie Wonder's *You are the Sunshine of my Life.*

"In them days," Straker recalls, "the repertoire of the band was extensive, and we used to perform all over the country, in all the block-o-ramas, we was bad, only Tokyo coulda stand up to we."[479]

The author of the liner notes at the back of the album, "Inside Out", introduced an interesting concept when he wrote the following: "They have two kinds of steelband music," a pan man once said to me. "The kind that makes you get up and dance, and the kind that makes you sit down because it so hypnotizes you." If you accept that, it follows that there are two kinds of steelbands: The Mover and the Mesmerizer. I find that Catelli Trinidad All Stars is both of these, and able to throw in a third dimension: the **Musicators**. In my dictionary, a Musicator is a musician who sets the standards for the adjudicator. That's what Catelli All Stars have always been about...

They became that standards-setters for one commentator who said: "All Stars are not just winners tonight, they made it impossible for anyone else to win."[480] The cover design shown above was done by Noel Norton and the producer of the album was Mr. Kelvin Scoon who worked with All Stars consistently in this period and served as PRO in the then executive led by Web Alexander.

In 1974, playing *Tourist Takeover*, All Stars only managed to reach the semi-finals of Panorama. According to Smooth Edwards, "All Stars was the only band to win a Panorama one year, then get disqualified in the semis the next year on the grounds that *Tourist Takeover* was too long… it was from then on that Pan Trinbago say, look, that shouldn't happen again, and made it so that each winner had to defend their crown…"[481] However the band did not sit around lamenting that fiasco. Later that year, 1974, the band turned its attention to the first of its Classical Jewels Concert series held at Queen's Hall on November 6th and 8th.

The band treated the audiences to a wide-ranging repertoire that included Mozart's *Minuet from Symphony in E Flat* and *Serenade—Eine Kleine Nachtmusik*; Rossini's *Barber of Seville*; Dvorak's *New World Symphony No.5, Op 95 in E minor*, and ended with a rousing performance of Tchaikovsky's *1812 Overture*.

An Evening News report headlined "All Stars Boys Create their Jewels—Standing Ovation for Sweet Pan" described the presentation as follows: *All was quiet. A sea of faces raised with the arms of the conductor. The flood lights changed dramatically. And then a shadow came in at the side of the stage. Frankly I thought it was Peter Ilyich Tchaikovsky himself who had returned to grace our stage. For it was this very date in 1893 that the musical master passed away, and here we were about to listen to a great performance of his greatest work, the 1812 Overture. If indeed, the great Tchaikovsky was there to hear the sweet sound of the Catelli Trinidad All Stars as the steelband played his masterpiece, he would have walked on stage to congratulate the boys. Their performance last night was a remarkable feat for Mr. Jerry Jemmott's excellent and patient training.*[482]

Despite the widespread public accolades for All Stars, there were two commentators—Jeremy Taylor and Brian Dockray—who questioned the superlatives expressed by the citizenry who crave such musical expositions. Dockray in particular took pains to point out that Tchaikovsky himself had said that the 1812 Overture was *written in a great hurry… that it was very noisy, written without much enthusiasm and probably of no great artistic value*. And so, using the composer's own words as a springboard, Dockray launched his attempt at discrediting the band's performance and was even bold to suggest that *the roar of the cannons was most unconvincing (was it a thunder sheet?), although better than a performance I heard by the police band many years ago, when rifles and revolvers fired blank shots (I hope) behind the stage.*[483]

But Mr. Dockray surely would not have hesitated to wonder about Tchaikovsky's frame of mind when he described the overture in that manner since it is well known that the composer was regarded as "excessively sensitive" and noted for his "morbid tendencies". Furthermore, it was disingenuous to suggest that the music was "noisy" when the very Overture was written with the intention to capture the atmosphere of raging battle between Napoleon's army and the defenders of Moscow who had to resort to burning the city and its food supply as a defensive measure.

The 1812 Overture was done to celebrate and commemorate the gallantry of that occasion and in his work, the composer used Russian folklore, Russian hymns, the French anthem and the Russian National Song with the sound of canons and the bells of the city ringing out triumphantly as backdrop. Yes, indeed, quite noisy! And if Mr. Dockray had done a little research or even spoken for one minute with any of the organizers of this first in line of All Stars' Classical Jewels Concerts, he would have been told that what he heard was the actual roar of canons that was taped at the Tetron Military Base specifically for the occasion.

The Managing Director of Hand, Arnold (Trinidad) Ltd that markets the Catelli brand had this to say about this first Classical Jewel Concert: "As Sponsors… we see ourselves as advisors, assisting in providing the climate in which the members of the band could individually develop to the fullest their talents as musicians and as citizens of our country… This concert is the result of hard work by every member of the band… I am proud and delighted to be associated with Catelli Trinidad All Stars," and he went on to highlight the "progressive outlook" of the band as exemplified by its engagement in a number of its own business activities.[484]

The then-President of Pan Trinbago also indicated that the entire steelband movement "is watching All Stars Classical Jewels with hopeful anxiety", and complimented the band for its professionalism, its novel approach to sight reading, its democratic traditions, the social development of its membership and for its mutual respect for others.[485]

Uncle Jem conducts the performance of the 1812 Overture.

Mr. and Mrs. Ossie Hale congratulates Mr. Jerry Jemmott Musical Director of All Stars. On the right is Prince Batson, the sixth Captain of All Stars from 1949 to 1950. Prince did the historic review of the band that was carried in the brochure prepared for the Classical Jewels No.1—titled "The Band which grew from Hell Yard."

San Fernando Chorale and Rangers during their performance. Courtesy Evening News.

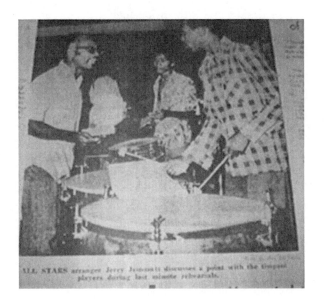

Jerry Jemmott rehearses the timpani players.

From the 1974 Classical Jewels Concert, it was a smooth transition into the 1975 Carnival season. And once again the band came face to face with yet another one of these unfortunate incidents that would seem to be prearranged machinations of external forces geared deliberately to stymie the band's trajectory of glorious successes; a situation which by then, given the experiences of the '40s and '50s, had become for this band a regularly repeated historic burden. In 1975, the band's hopes were dashed by the indecency of one Panorama judge, who, in the remarks column, stated that "Oil and Sugar" by Johnny Calypso was the "wrong choice" of tune for Panorama.[486] This supposedly upright, socially well-placed gentleman had chosen not to recuse himself from the judging process despite his attachment to one of the competing bands.

Johnny Calypso, who had just been released from the St. Anns' Mental Hospital, had the audacity to sing: *Dey looking fuh energy but is oil dey want/but dey ent getting, we ent giving, all o' dem got to scrunt/drunk or sober/dis year is we takeover/Oil and Sugar… so everything spoil and we must make dey belly boil/If we cetch dem tourists thiefing Trinidad Oil*. And Rudy Wells struck by a sudden revelation, abandoned Kitchener, and returned to Jules' noted affirmation which said go with "the most open tune."

Eliminated in the prelims, All Stars, never a band to protest, walked away with their heads held high and their pride intact. In fact, the 1975 Panorama finals will go down in history as the most boring as seven of the eight finalist bands played the same tune "Tribute to Spree Simon" by Kitchener. It would have been the utmost sacrilege for All Stars to have participated in the abomination that suggest Spree Simon to be the inventor of the steel orchestra and which serves to deny what is rightfully due to Neville Jules and Neville Jules alone; he being the father of the Steel Orchestra, the creator of the first "Ping-Pong" and the family of melody pans.

Instinctively extolling the beauty of the melody-pans, which Neville Jules initiated, Johnny Calypso the following year, 1976, sang… *Gone are de days of cutlasses and guns/No more steelband fighting, people on de run/And yuh could hear de rhythm and the sweetness of the pan… and no more bacchanal in de land…* then this artiste disappeared from the calypso world as suddenly and abruptly as he had come. What a pity!

Moreover, no band chose to honor Johnny Calypso by doing his music. However, when Rudy Wells informed "Web" Alexander that he had been accepted to the Berkeley School of Music in Boston to commence his pursuit of a Doctorate and would no longer be available to arrange for the 1976 Panorama, Web opted to allow the young arrangers within the band to take up the challenge.[487] The young arrangers who had been working under Uncle

Jem's and Rudy Wells' guidance were Anthony Guy, Anthony "Shortman" Guerra, Bunny "Fancy Face" Wells and Leon "Smooth" Edwards. It is said that there was a fifth person, Michael Andrews who migrated to America and became a pastor.[488] Web admits that when he made the decision to stick with these youngsters and not seek an arranger from outside of the band, *all hell broke loose; senior members and supporters of the band shouted, get Bradley, ask Ray Holman, dem little fellahs cyar win no Panorama, dem young fellahs cyar arrange no Panorama tune for All Stars.*[489]

Web's resolve to go with the youngsters remained firm against the rising groundswell and much credit must be given to him for having done so. The then Executive which included: Lennox "Sonny Tool" Alleyne, vice-Captain; "Reds" Collins, Sec/Treasurer; "Cin-Cin" Lorde, Asst. Sec/Treasurer; Kelvin Scoon, PRO; as well as the Committee Members, John "Poison" Douglas, Cecil Lynch, Anthony Guy and Garth Roberts, all stood solidly behind Web as did the musical director, Uncle Jem, and key members of the stage-side, and Web says: *I stood my ground under all the pressure from those particular individuals, even at the risk of having to tell some of them, if they don't like the decision, they can take a hike… Today, All Stars is still reaping the rewards of that decision. I consider this my most significant achievement as the Captain of All Stars…*[490]

Having left school in 1970 with only two passes and unable to get employment, Smooth said that he really began to involve himself deeper in the music, playing his pan all day, every day, developing his skills, running the scales, playing along with the radio, so much so that music and All Stars became "his solace".[491] Smooth added that Web, who lived next door, used to hear him practicing and insisted that what he was hearing was "panorama material" and suggested that he, Smooth, should try arranging for the band.[492]

Special attention should be paid to what Smooth indicates was his reply to the Captain's request back then: "I tell Web, you must be mad. How you mean I have to do the tune. Wells just win a Panorama, I can't follow in he footstep and go up against Ray, Rodney, Bradley and dem fellahs. Ah could help do it, but other people have to do it with me. So that year I did about five-sixth of the tune and I insisted that somebody else do a solo. They say go ahead, man, you doing good. Ah say, well, the tune go stop here because I ain't doing any more. I alone ain't doing a Panorama tune. **That is how much respect I had**

for All Stars… So then Tony Guy carry home a tenor pan and he work out a solo for *Pan in Harmony*."[493]

When All Stars appeared in the following Panoramas, 1976, 1977, 1978, and 1979, the banners indicated that the various presentations were arranged by the four youngsters—Guy, Guerra, Wells and Edwards, i.e., Kitchener's *"Pan in Harmony"* (8 bands in that 1976 final and All Stars placed 8th). Kitchener's *"Republic Dance"*, was done in 1977 when the stage-side eventually went to FESTAC in Nigeria as promised since 1972 and Captain Web stayed at home to run the Carnival activities,[494] but the band reached only as far as the semi-final). Smooth contends that All Stars would have made the finals with *Republic Dance* if Web had disregarded the judges' comments and had continued to play the music as it was meant to be played, as the 17-man stage-side played it in Nigeria where the tune was kicking up dust but the changes made upset the flow, you could have felt the drop and this cause one of the judges to say the tune "was disjointed, too many arrangers."[495]

Then in 1978 it was Kitchener's *Dog* when All Stars placed sixth (6th) in the finals; and finally in 1979, Kitchener's *Symphony in G* when the Panorama was discontinued after the preliminaries. At that time, the criticisms of All Stars music from the other big bands flew fast and thick; and town had this to say, "too many cooks does spoil the broth…" Now we knew that that sentiment originated from one of the judges in 1977. Yet, confidently, Uncle Jem, at least so the All Stars folklore goes, assured all and sundry that the band was in an experimental mode and that "out of that group of young arrangers, one shall soon emerge triumphantly." We certainly did not have to wait long.

At this point, a number of coincidences happened which served to enhance the story behind the story. Smooth points out that in January 1980, All Stars moved from St. Vincent Street back to Hell Yard; "so we left the industrial area and gone back to a residential area, and immediately a set of schoolboys came into the band: from South East Sec, Belmont Immediate, the yard "sick" with youths…"[496] Also, Smooth points out that 1980 was the year that the trend to bring back steelbands in Carnival fetes really took root and All Stars had "about eight to ten fetes lined up" which necessitated the band having to develop a repertoire for fetes.

And as fate would have it, Smooth had had his appendix removed in December 1979 and was recuperating at home at the start of the 1980 Carnival season, listening to the radio for likely party-tunes with his tape recorder at hand. He said that the day he first heard *Woman on the Bass*, he recorded it and played it over and over, convinced that it was a great party-tune, but not a panorama tune. After his recuperation, Smooth said that he went to the yard, gave the band *Woman on the Bass* as well as some nine other tunes and indicated to them that it was imperative that they all learn the ten songs because the Panorama tune will be chosen from that lot.

He said from the get go, whenever the band played *Woman on the Bass*, the youths would begin to behave "crazy, sweating and they carrying on," so much so that he recalls having on two occasions to stop the band and say to them: "Listen, *Woman on the Bass* is for party. We did this song for parties. Nobody ever won a Panorama outside of playing a Kitchener or a Sparrow calypso. The Panorama tune will either be a Kitch or a Sparrow selection…"[497]

The youths disregarded Smooth's admonitions and when the elimination process began, every round brought the discarding of other tunes, while the youths guaranteed that *Woman on the Bass* stayed in contention. Finally Smooth says that when it boiled down to three tunes, he repeated the same admonition and then instructed them that on the count of four each person would start his or her personal choice for Panorama and he gave the count and "after the second bar, only *Woman on the Bass* could be heard playing much to the grumblings of the older folk who were in the minority."[498]

Cecil Lynch, then considered one of the older members, indicates that when Smooth gave the count for each and every one to start their Panorama tune of choice, he was one who started "Tobago Girl" by Sparrow.[499] The rest is now history. Yet, according to Smooth, (who is still convinced that *Woman on the Bass* is a party tune to the extent that even after 40 years it is still demanded in parties throughout), had the band stayed down St. Vincent Street, the influx of youths would not have happened and the choice for Panorama would certainly have been either a Kitch or Sparrow.

And one can respond and say, yes, it's true that *Woman on the Bass* is a party tune, but it is also regarded as probably the greatest ever Panorama winning tune, the one that broke the Kitchener/Sparrow dichotomy simply because of the magic of the conversation between the various sections of instruments that he, Smooth, utilized in his coherent, flowing, very musical arrangement. Furthermore, it was never a tradition of All Stars to be constrained by the Kitchener/Sparrow dichotomy for Jules went for whichever tune lent itself most readily to his creative manipulation hence the reason why today we can still boast about Shorty's *Cloak and Dagger* and Laro's *Valerina*. Smooth has to acknowledge the social power of the precedent he, himself, set in the selection process of *Woman on the Bass*, a precedent that the youths of All Stars shall never let him forget.

As the saying goes, there has to be a synergy between arranger and band, and nothing less would be allowed to take root. Once Smooth's choice for Panorama resonates with the players and there is that synergy, he can then do whatever his creative juices mandate.

This is how one social commentator, Carl Simon, described the rise of this explosive phenomenon in 1980… *Coming on stage at the Queen's Park Savannah that year (1980) with a tune that had so far gone unnoticed "Woman On The Bass" arranger Leon Smooth Edwards staged one of the most remarkable feats ever in pan history. "Yuh ent hear that tune, boy" was the comment of the day as panatics awaited for the dust to clear 15 minutes after All Stars had kicked up their storm. At every stage in the Competition that year they won and even up to today "Woman on the Bass" lives on as one of the best tunes in Panorama's 24 year history. Even WITCO Desperadoes with a scintillating Clive Bradley arrangement of Kitch's "No Pan" had to play second fiddle to the Duke Street boys. By then, too, everybody had taken notice of the young, new arranger, the "Smooth" man of pan, Leon Edwards…*[500]

Not many people are aware that All Stars went onto the middle of the stage that night **with only 86 players**, pulled tightly together, to effect that bombshell. Today, 2020, some 40 years after, a Party or fete in T&T is seldom considered over unless a recording, usually the slow version, of *Woman On The Bass* by Catelli Trinidad All Stars is played. DJs and Party organizers dare not have it readily available to satisfy the demand of all publics. It has also been declared by many to be the most played piece of Pan music throughout the entire world, from Japan, Australia and New Zealand in the Eastern Hemisphere to Los Angeles, Columbia and Panama in the Western Hemisphere; and everywhere, throughout the world, says Beresford Hunte, past Captain/Manager, the reaction of people to that piece of music is the same even on first hearing it.

Just as Uncle Jem had prophesied, the "Smooth" phenomenon had arisen; Leon Edwards had emerged out of the group of 4. But the other three persons certainly were not obfuscating assistant chefs as the popular feeling among other bands around town would seem to suggest, in fact they all had their area of competency; Anthony Guy now lives and works as a professional pannist/percussionist in Japan; Earl Wells lives in the USA and Anthony "Shortman" Guerra, now deceased, lived in Santa Cruz, was a master parandero, noted in the past to be the major person assisting in chord-selection and voicing the bass-lines to Smooth's front line and middle arrangements.

However, it is not common knowledge that Smooth Edwards left T&T shortly after the phenomenal success of his arrangement of *Woman on the Bass* to take up residence in Gainesville, Florida.[501] There were two reasons provided for this move: (1) his wife had a US visa and for quite some time desired to migrate to Florida where her relatives resided; (2) in the early part of the 1980 Carnival season, the band via the new Captain (i.e., Reds Collins, Web migrated in 1977) informed Smooth that the executive had decided to bring back Rudy Wells to arrange the Panorama tune, so as a result, arrangements for Smooth's immediate family to migrate were firmed up.

However, when Wells informed the band that he was not available, Smooth did the tune and as he puts it "unfortunately" won the Panorama, at which point he chose to leave because as he said: "If Wells could have come, he would have arranged the 1980 tune, so because the band had their plans, I made my plans..." and he stuck to it.[502] So for 1981 (*Unknown Band*), 1982 (*Heat*) and 1983 (*Rebecca*), Smooth was brought back to T&T for two-weeks to arrange the Panorama tunes until he finally returned fully in July 1983 because his wife's mother who still lived in T&T, fell ill.[503]

"In those days," Smooth said, "I used to leave America and ain't know what I getting. Whatever they give me I used to take; that was the love I had for the band. That is how it was even when I was living here. Even when I was doing road tunes and stage-side tunes, because of the love for the band, I was just doing it."[504] When the then Captain, Reds Collins, was asked to outline the arrangements that were made with Smooth in that period, he said that the sponsor, Catelli, handled all the financial requirements, i.e., payments for the return tickets; payment for arranging; however, daily expenses were minimal as Smooth stayed at his mother's house on Jackson Hill.[505]

In regard to the overall period 1980–1987, the following extract from the Trinidad All Stars Newsletter vividly portrays the events that occurred: *On the night of Saturday 16th February 1980, Trinidad All Stars, bringing out all the skill and artistry it was capable of, confounded and mesmerized the Pan World with an electrifying, exciting, hair-raising, never-to-be-forgotten performance* on the Smooth Man's classic arrangement of Scrunter's **Woman on the Bass** to capture the Panorama championship. In 1981, the standard was extremely high, with some of the bands reaching dizzy heights of brilliance, but Trinidad All Stars, playing a superb arrangement of Blue Boy's **Unknown Band**, and with unbelievable skill and artistry, triumphed over its eleven rivals. In 1982, Trinidad All Stars playing **Heat** by Lord Kitchener in a manner of speaking turned on the heat, and in an excellent performance brought the Savannah crowd to an unbelievable pitch of excitement.[506] In the end, All Stars was placed second to Renegades playing Kitchener's Pan Explosion.

Some people maintain that in the history of Panorama to date the decision to place All Stars' performance of *Heat* second to Renegades was unfair. It was said afterwards by some that the aim was to prevent All Stars "winning three straight Panoramas", a feat that up to then had not yet been accomplished. Some say that All Stars' "surprise" on final night may have turned off the judges, i.e., at the last few bars of the piece a fire-extinguisher was shot off, clouding the stage in smoke, adding drama, color and atmosphere to the band's interpretation of *Heat*.

Indeed, it may have been seen as a silly idea by many people but to use that as an excuse to deny the band of a "triple-feat" is not acceptable; the pan players, according to Reds Collins, were expecting the gush of smoke in short spurts and though it came in one huge gush they did not miss a beat or a note so well-rehearsed they were, however at the end of it all the players ran off the stage, some gasping for breath.[507] The TV station, TTT, has a video-tape of it which they still play as a slot-filler and anyone viewing that tape can verify that it was a most masterful performance from the introduction down to the very last note; it was **heat** through and through and on that night, in that year, All Stars stood unbeatable.

Smooth's take on that Panorama final is as follows: "In 1982 when we were going for the three-peat, the very Carnival Saturday, I flew out of Trinidad. I got news that my wife was sick and in hospital (abroad), so I did not start the band (on stage). That made a big difference…"[508] Smooth seemed to be suggesting, as some people claimed, that the performance may have been a bit too quick. In the view of many people, on the contrary, the speed was appropriate for the interpretation of a "kettle building up to a boiling pitch" which was Smooth's view of the story he was attempting to tell in his arrangement.

Others have tried to justify the 1982 results on the grounds that previously bands hoping to seal three straight Panorama wins were likewise frustrated so who is Trinidad All Stars to complain. But what are the facts of the matter: the first band to win two straight Panoramas and was hoping to do it a third time was Pan-Am North Stars in 1963 (*Dan is the Man*) and 1964 (*Mama Dis is Mas*) but they were blown away by Guinness Cavaliers in 1965 with Bobby Mohammed's transformational arrangement of Melody's *Mas* that was widely acclaimed by the listening public who made Cavaliers stay put in the Savannah to deliver a concert; in addition the tenors tuned by Alan Gervais were a revelation, as already mentioned; and today Cavaliers' performance of Melody's *Mas* remains one of the few, great Panorama classics.

The second band that found itself in such a situation was Solo Harmonites (1971 tied in 1st place with Starlift—*Play Mas* and *Queen of the Bands* and 1972—*St. Thomas Girl*) but in 1973, the following year, all and sundry were blown away by *Rainorama* played by All Stars and Harmonites even placed a distant third. The next such dilemma was faced by Witco Desperadoes (1976—their master-piece, *Pan in Harmony*, and in 1977 they played *Hasely Crawford*, but quite unfortunately for Desperadoes in 1978, Starlift turned up with another one of the few Panorama classics—*Du Du Yemi* popularly referred to as *Natasha*. The point is that whereas in the above three instances which occurred in the period 1963 to 1978, the bands heading for three straight wins were beaten by outstanding classical performances and the decisions were widely accepted by public demand, it was not so with the decision of 1982.

The only conclusion to be drawn is that given the fact that All Stars had already won the Music Festivals of 1968, 1972 and 1980, it would have been too much for certain citizens of substance to countenance in addition Panorama wins in 1980, 1981 and 1982, facilitating thereby the very first three-peat. That certainly in their imaginations would have thrown All Stars unto the realm of another cosmos entirely. And such ought not to be facilitated.

The Trinidad All Stars Newsletter indicates that with the coming of 1983, "we were back desperately determined to regain the Panorama Crown."[509] However, this time it was All Stars' turn to be blown away with another one of the few Panorama classics: *Rebecca* by Desperadoes. Though All Stars eventually placed third, many are not conscious of the fact that Smooth's version of *Rebecca* was ahead of Bradley's on points until Bradley came up with that now inspired introduction that was used to frame the theme of the entire piece.

This is what Smooth had to say about the 1983 Panorama contest: "We whipped them (Despers) from preliminaries to semi-finals. On the final night, Despers turned their back to the North Stand and put everything up front to the Grand Stand. They had a dynamite intro which they brought back for the ending and slowed the tune a bit. The rest is history…"[510] Truly, Despers came up with a stellar performance on that night.

Sparrow waving the flag during All Stars' 1984 performance of "Doh Back-Back". The crowd roared their approval, it was reported.

Then, it was on to 1984 and the TAS report states that in 1984 "the atmosphere at Panorama became electric only when Trinidad All Stars ascended the stage and gave such a performance of Sparrow's **Doh Back Back** that the Savannah crowd shrieked and cheered and remained buzzing for minutes afterwards."[511] In the end, with a margin of 17.5 points, All Stars was placed second to Renegades playing *Sweet Pan* by Kitchener.

One newspaper report stated: "This Duke Street band was hoping to win another title but in the end won the admiration of the large crowd… the boys dressed in sailor outfits really made an impact during their performance…" and that report also indicated that when Sparrow made an appearance on stage with the flag, the crowd roared its approval.[512] In 1985, the All Stars Newsletter says "All Stars took the tune of Calypso Crazy, **Suck Me Soucouyant** and made of it such a wonderful pattern and tapestry of music that the self-same drowning roar of the Savannah went up again..."[513] But the classic interpretations of Kitchener's *Pan Night And Day* by both Desperadoes and Renegades could not be separated at the top; they were tied at first place with All Stars relegated to third place.

One newspaper report said: "the Duke Street band played Cazy's *Suck Mih Soucouyant* and what a reception they received from the large crowd at the Queen's Park Savannah; the Panatics were angry on Saturday Night. Reason? They felt that Catelli All Stars did not gain a fair berth at the 1985 Panorama finals... One angry Panatic, after hearing the result blurted: "Oh Gawd! Pan really in danger..."[514] All Stars did not complain, they took the decision with a smile but back then in Hell Yard there were many like Sandy, Sadist, Straker, Big L, Tallist, etc. who with sheer joy can hum for you the stunning musical introduction to *Suck Mih Soucouyant, suck/ suck/suck, suck mih all over*; it is what is known in Hell Yard as 'mouth-pan'."

1986, on the other hand, brought for All Stars another crowning glory. The Newsletter described it this way: "...Taking the stage at three in the morning, when a glimmer peeped from a lightly overcast sky, Trinidad All Stars, beating **The Hammer**, sent the crowd into ecstasies, their performance was a fusion of... flawless panmanship, excellently tuned pans, and a wonderful, sensitive arrangement, which earned the highest average to date in Panorama history— **97.7%**..."[515] Phase 11 performed their *Pan Rising* and afterwards "the chant was Phase 11, Phase 11, ringing out from the savannah"[516] but the folklore says that All Stars did not freeze coming on stage to play last knowing quite well "that they had their work cut out and how well they rose to the occasion as they always do on any final night... it was a night of All Stars who improved a massive 42 points from Prelim to finals..."[517]

The next year brought some deliberate experimentation; Smooth Edwards had the audacity to choose a tune with which no one believed he could do anything. But how wrong he proved them to be, since this arrangement, his "first positive effort at inter-weaving our multi-ethnic mix, via *Curry Tabanca*, seemed to be a clear winner."[518] In the end, the Phase with the classic masterpiece *This Feeling Nice*, followed by Renegades and Desperadoes with their special treatment of Kitchener's *Pan in A Minor* rose to steal Smooth's thunder. All Stars placed fourth but had served to announce to the world that *Chutney-Soca*, that ethnic musical mix peculiar only to T&T had come to fruition.

However, there are some who feel that All Stars' *Curry Tabanca* is "a tabanca that Pan Lovers will live with forever."[519] Today in terms of popular demand *Curry Tabanca* is "bested" only by *Woman on the Bass* and Smooth Edwards concluded that "many people, forgetting the outcome, assume that *Curry Tabanca* won the 1987 Panorama, and when I tell them, no, that tune was placed fourth, people still do not believe…" [520]

In 1985, a theme song for the International Youth Year was composed jointly by Mrs. Jean Sui Young of the Ministry of Sport, Culture and Youth Affairs and Mr. Gerry Jemmott of the Community Development Department. The youths of Trinidad All Stars performed the theme at a function at the National Stadium in Port-of-Spain on the night of Friday, June 14, 1985. Uncle Jem conducted the band. It was indeed an honor for All Stars to perform at the formal release of this special THEME SONG dedicated to the youths of the Nation. (Courtesy Trinidad Guardian, Monday, 17 June 1985.)

However, in reflection, it was a much rewarding period (1980–1987) for All Stars despite the trials and tribulations. One dispassionate commentator said: "There is no doubt that the Hell Yard boys is the band of the decade. It is from the pulse beat of panatics and the records that we can safely say, after this successful run; never placing lower than third in the last seven years and five triumphs (i.e., 3 Panoramas and 2 Music Festivals) in that era, that All Stars is certainly the best, ever…"[521] But that is by far not the total picture of All Stars' accomplishments in the decade of the '80s. Yes, All Stars won in that decade 3 Panoramas (1980, 1981, and 1986), 3 Bomb Competitions (1981, 1983, and

1984), won 2 Music Festivals (1980, 1984) and placed second in 1982 and 1986.

In the 1980 Music Festival—Pan Is Beautiful 2, All Stars performed *Von Suppe's Morning, Noon and Night in Vienna* for Tune of Choice; the calypso was *Woman on the Bass* together with the compulsory Test-piece *SINFONIA* Handel's *Arrival of the Queen of Sheba*...

The following describes the performance of All Stars and underscored the victory: "...All Stars A-Twinkle—In the end Catelli All Stars' *Morning, Noon and Night in Vienna* proved too much for even this level of competition and there were not many who doubted even before the decisions were announced that theirs would be the best tune of choice. Or doubted for that matter that All Stars would take the entire festival; "Big horse is big horse", "they just play and they win", "Class is Class!" Such were the comments of the night..."[522]

"Drunk with the Joy of Victory"—Members of Catelli Trinidad All Stars, 1980 Festival winners, celebrating. Courtesy Trinidad Express.

Errol "Reds" Collins, Captain of Catelli Trinidad All Stars, left, Mr. Hans of AHP Promotions, center and Arnim Smith of Pan Trinbago, right. Pix courtesy the Trinidad Express. All Stars won the 1980 Music Festival on August 17th and nine days after, the Managing Director of AHP Promotions offered the band a contract for a tour of the United Kingdom with billing to play at the famous Royal Festival Hall in London. According to Reds Collins, this tour proposal, though touted by Pan Trinbago to be a "big deal", turned out to be nothing but "ole talk" and "mamaguyism".

The 1980 Six-Week World Tour

Brothers Deryck Nurse, 16, and Leon Nurse, 15, bid goodbye to Angela Martin of the Trinidad Express. (Trinidad Express: Monday 6 October 1980—"All Stars Bids Goodbye" by Angela Martin)

Shortly after the AHP Promotions disappointment, a tour of the USA, Canada, China and India was sponsored by the Government of Trinidad & Tobago. Errol "Reds" Collins, the Captain, said then: "We are all looking forward to this trip simply because we would be visiting China and India, countries that are not at all familiar with our steelband and I am anxious to see the reaction... We would be leaving New York on October 15, spending five days in Canada, nine days in China and five in India."

Catelli Trinidad All Stars returned from the 1980 tour on November 10th. On November 23rd, a report from the Public Relations Division of the Prime Minister's Office was published under the Headline: "Shock For Catelli All Stars in China" and alongside the report was a picture of members of the band standing before a section of the Great Wall. That official report indicated that the tour was meant to be "a reciprocal one to cultural visits made here by the Chinese over the past couple years." The government took pride in stating that the National Airline took the band to Toronto, New York and Washington where "they performed from October 6th to October 18th," and from there on to the Far East.⁵²³

The SHOCK, of course, was the fact that All Stars was entertained in China by "two steelbands comprising mainly Chinese boys and girls playing simple tunes like, Mangoes", that well-known Olive Walke Trinidadian folk standard.⁵²⁴ The report went on to establish the following salient point: "Everywhere, All Stars performed—New York, Washington, Toronto, Peking, Bombay, New Delhi—they were fully applauded by overflowing theatres, and given much praise for their classical performances particularly their Music Festival winning piece—*Morning, Noon and Night in Vienna by Von Suppe*."⁵²⁵ The following pictures from magazines published in India and China during the tour indicate the response to the steel orchestra.

Indian dignitaries listen to the sound of the bass.

From the files of Edric Straker who was on that 1980 World Tour.

All Stars player, Deryck Nurse, explains the tenor pan instrument to Indian dignitaries.

All Stars at the Great Wall of China

1982: The Humming Bird Gold Medal

Dr. Cuthbert Joseph, then Minister of Local Government, pins the Humming Bird Gold Medal on Errol "Reds" Collins, the 9th captain of Trinidad All Stars then sponsored by Catelli. At right is John Donaldson, Minister of National Security. Reds in this his first period of captaincy (1977–1983) said that All Stars then was "on a roll".

It was indeed a defining moment in the history of Trinidad All Stars when the State, acknowledging the achievements and worth of this musical phenomenon, bestowed a national award to the band during the Independence celebrations in August 1982. Today that medal cannot be located. The fact that there was then no secured place in the panyard wherein the **Humming Bird Gold Medal** could be lodged obviously contributed to this loss. Hopefully, at some point in the future a replica could be had.

Reds Collins, left, Ossie Hale, Uncle Jem and Lennox "Sonny Tool" Alleyne at a reception at the home of Ossie Hale in Maraval, examining the medals which Catelli bestowed on each member of the band in honor of the string of successes. The picture is courtesy the Sunday Guardian, November 28, 1982 and the caption reads: "Catelli honors Steelband Stars."

Festival supporters of All Stars at Jean Pierre Complex.

Earl Bunny "Fancy Face" Wells receives trophy from Mrs. Marilyn Gordon, Minister of Culture, Sport and Youth Affairs, on behalf of Catelli Trinidad All Stars winners of the 1984 Music Festival.

1984 Festival Winners: In the frontline, on the left Yohan Popwell, and Jason "Stumps" Lewis to his right, between them is Donny Andrews—they were then all children of Trinidad All Stars.

Sticks in the air! 1984 Music Festival Victory! Forefront: Edric Straker and behind him, Barnabas "Tallist" Grant—stalwarts of the double-seconds.

In the 1984 Festival, Pan Is Beautiful 3, All Stars' Tune of Choice was Tchaikovsky's *Symphony No.4 in F Minor Opus 36*; the Test-piece was Mozart's *Cosi Fan Tutte* and *Doh Back Back* by Sparrow was the Calypso choice. Reporting on that 1984 Festival, Dalton Narine quoted Martin Bookspan, described as the most popular syndicated commentator of classical music in North America, as having said the following about All Stars' performance... *Pan is Beautiful 3 was an incredible experience. There has been talk about writing music for a combined symphony and steelband orchestra. But what you have here can certainly stand on its own merit. What can I say about All Stars? They simply knocked me out with their virtuosity, ensemble brilliance and showmanship. They are sensational. From the moment they walked out on the court their discipline possessed a certain elegance and grandeur. Even before they played a note, they had already seized your attention...*[526]

And certainly, the "elegance and grandeur" of All Stars' discipline showed, when in the midst of performing, the conductor's baton flew from his hands. This is how Dalton Narine, in a piece in which he describes All Stars as "our very own symphony orchestra by virtue of its long standing achievements," dealt with the baton mishap... *But it was Jerry Jemmott, who was the toast of the victorious band. In addition to astutely steering All Stars through crisp, clear and precise routines, he avoided a potentially embarrassing moment when his baton flew from his grasp and fell about twenty feet from where the judges sat. Jemmott simply stepped off the podium, fetched a replacement from Clive Telemaque's tenor stand and returned to business—all in one fell swoop. Of course, the beat went on.*[527]

***Sir Paul Hill rehearsing the band for Classical Jewels Concert.
Pic taken from All Stars' file.***

It is quite notable too that, in the very decade of the '80s, All Stars also organized and performed in 5 Classical Jewels Concerts to the wide acclaim by the public, i.e., Jewels No. III in 1981, Jewels IV in 1983, Jewels V in 1985, Jewels VI in 1987 and Jewels VII in 1989. No wonder according to one source, "Catelli Trinidad All Stars has the reputation of being one of the few steelbands considered an all-year band."[528] It was that total involvement, every day, every night that brought for All Stars such glory.

In similar light, All Stars also toured Toronto in July of 1984; had the honor of performing at the Toronto International Music Festival and to that end the band got Paul Hill to fly in from London to guest-conduct a few of the pieces. About All Stars, Paul Hill had a lot to say during that tour of Toronto and in so doing helped to clarify to the public the kind of symphony orchestra the band had grown to become in the '80s under the guidance of Jerry Jemmott. He described the players as being "...so receptive, because they watch you all through and you communicate by being an energetic conductor which I've always been anyway. I don't know how to conduct any other way... they (All Stars) are far too extrovert and they need that extrovert conducting. That's part of the life there (T&T). Maybe that's why we get on so well these nine years..."[529]

Paul Hill indicated that he worked all over the world for the British Council and that he usually worked with amateur groups but didn't consider All Stars to be amateurish in their approach; and he went on to clarify what he meant: "...Of course we (i.e., himself and All Stars) were doing a fairly complicated program and it meant rehearsing and you need this kind of rehearsals constantly because of course the band plays largely by notations which are given to them by Jerry on the blackboard... I only know that working with amateurs... is an entirely different thing than working with what I call a professional group which the steelband is. When I say "professional" I mean professional in their outlook, highly disciplined, on time and they don't chatter and talk which amateur groups can do... However, unskilled, technically they (All Stars) may be or unskilled from the point of view of reading music, you raise your baton and bring it down and they'll come in on time with you. Well you generally don't get that with lots of other groups. It's really like conducting, I'm sure, a proper orchestra, except for the quality and tone, it's different, and it's a unique thing..."[530]

Sir Paul Hill conducting Trinidad All Stars: "They are not amateurs," he said.

Classical Jewels IV and V in 1983 and 1985 respectively were particularly sensational from all reports and in many ways verify what Paul Hill implied.

In one newspaper review of Jewel IV, the columnist said: "No record (digital or otherwise) or Dolby system cassette can reproduce the atmosphere of a concert hall, nor the response of musicians to listening audience and audience to musicians in performance... If only we could have concerts like Classical Jewels IV once every month..."[531]

The columnist described the visual impact of the orchestra on the audience as being a "perfect visual foil" for Lindy-Ann Bodden-Rich, the pianist, who accompanied the orchestra while performing Tchaikovsky's Piano Concerto No.1 in B Minor. "What an ambitious undertaking that was," she exclaimed, "and what a stunning performance from both orchestra and soloist! No wonder, Sir Paul Hill believes that All Stars should be seen and heard in concert halls in Europe and North America..."[532]

In regard to the other items on the program, the following is what the columnist had to say: "For this listener, the most interesting piece (and a new development in Pan) was Teleman's *Sonata in A Major* arranged for cello and tenor pans. Soloists, Anthony "Shortman" Guerra and Clive "Cokey" Telemaque delighted in this innovation. *Two Little Finches* by Kling, performed by Telemaque and Deryck Nurse, was great fun... Uncle Jem surprised not a few of the audience with his piccolo performance of *The Wren in the Poplars* by Adams. No pan concert, the columnist added, would be complete without a rousing finale... *Dance the Cachuca* from the Gondoliers by Sir Arthur Sullivan (brought) the audience on its feet cheering almost before the last note died away..."[533]

In conclusion, the reviewer praised the tuner of the Pans, Leo Coker, whom she confessed forced her "to restrain myself severely from the temptation to stand up to see where the French horns were; but of course, there weren't any; the skill and artistry of the tuner had deceived my ears..."[534]

Another fully committed attendant to all the Classical Jewels concerts exclaimed: "All Stars' Classical Jewels concerts are now an event that no one with any pretensions to an interest in "serious" music would willingly miss. No matter how famous the artists or how excellent the recording, there is no substitute for live music. And All Stars' live music sparkles with a special brilliance... Traditionally, for this reviewer, each new Classical Jewels is a voyage of discovery. What new music will All Stars tackle? What new instrument will the orchestra accompany? What new soloists will prove pan can complement the human voice?"[535]

And specifically describing what occurred at the Classical Jewels V concert, this is what the commentator said: "The high points were Mozart's *Concerto in A* for clarinet and orchestra and Telemann's *Sonata in B Minor*. Clive Telemaque and Leon Edwards (on tenor and tenor bass respectively) held this reviewer spellbound with their exciting, masterly interpretation of the Telemann Sonata; so much so that one wonders if the future for pan in serious music lies in duets, ensemble playing by three or four musicians (no, I won't call them "pannists", they are musicians who are great artists performing on new instruments) and as soloists in a concerto… when a composer of international repute finally gets around to composing for pan… The Prelude to Bizet's *L'Arlesienne Suite No.1* and the last Movement to Tchaikovsky's *Fourth Symphony* which began and ended the program demonstrated the great rapport between orchestra and musical director… When Paul Hill took over the baton for the Overture to Glinka's "*Ruslan and Lyudmila*" the orchestra pulled out almost all the stops; almost, because they reserved that last ounce of musical energy for a repeat (and repeated) performance of Sullivan's *La Cachuca*."[536]

Putting aside the commentator's obvious cultural need for foreign validation, she proved able to capture in words the spirit of the occasion and the power of the All Stars' aggregation. Also commenting on Classical Jewels V, another attendant, spot on in his description of the relationship between conductor and band, said: "The Catelli All Stars Steel Orchestra is a super, high powered tonal group: any conductor who would dare to whip it would be in precisely the same position of any violinist who would dare to dig his bow into a Stradivarius. Just as the strand demands that it be coaxed however firmly, so the steel orchestra makes identical demands."[537]

*1986—**The Hammer**—97.7 out of 100*

15,000 packed the North Stand and they went wild jumping up to the "Hammer" played by Trinidad All Stars. This was All Stars' fourth panorama victory. (Courtesy Trinidad Guardian, Monday, 27 January 1986.)

However, if for one moment anyone were to get the impression that because of all the accolades and encomiums bestowed on All Stars, obstacles were not simultaneously being deliberately placed in All Stars' path, that would be the furthest thing from the reality. If the treatment meted out to All Stars in 1982, going for a Panorama hat-trick of wins with the performance of **Heat**, could be deemed as unfair, there can be no words to describe the machination that was unearthed in 1986 to minimize or to "nip in the bud" the growing dominance of All Stars in the Music Festivals.

On Monday, 6 October 1986, the final stage of Pan Is Beautiful 4 was held and the results at the end of the show was as follows: Witco Desperadoes was placed 1st with 1125 points after having scored the best Test Piece while their other performances were *Rebecca* (Calypso) and *Polovtsian Dance* by Borodin in the category, Tune of Choice. Catelli Trinidad All Stars was placed second with 1120 points after winning in two categories; Best Tune of Choice, **Carnival Overture** and Best Calypso, **Unknown Band**, the latter of which they shared with Phase11.

According to popular sentiment, it was astonishing that All Stars could be "placed second although wining two of the three categories" and though having taken the Panorama crown earlier, it was felt that with such results at the Music Festival, the year "1986 was spoiled for All Stars."[538] Simply, it had never happened before. From the very first Music Festival in 1952, the tradition was that the winner of the Tune of Choice category was usually declared the winner and in reality had always been the best performing band on show. Suddenly, All Stars, having won the preceding Festival in 1984, could now win two of the three categories and yet not be declared the overall winner by as much as five points. Something had to be amiss.

Apparently, an incorrect version of the Test Piece, *Fire and Steel—Ode to Yo Yo*, composed by Winsford De Vignes was given to All Stars as early as July of 1986 and, according to Jerry Jemmott, that was the "version which the band practiced and played throughout the early part of the festival,"[539] but what triggered suspicion Jemmott pointed out was the repeated low scores the band was receiving in the preliminaries and the differences in interpretation that he was hearing from the other bands.[540] Jemmott said that it was then that he spoke to his assistant, Smooth Edwards, about this matter and it was Smooth who *jokingly said, be careful we don't have a different score from the adjudicators.*[541]

At that point, Jemmott indicated that *they agreed to get a new copy from Pan Trinbago and it was then they discovered the band was not playing what the adjudicators were seeing on their scores…* Jemmott said *there were several differences as most of the metronomes were left out of the first version, which meant that I interpreted "allegro" as I thought it to be... While this provided a minor problem*, he added, *it was the instructions on the 21st, 76th, 96th, and 98th bars which were not included in the original score that made all the difference in Catelli's performances...*[542]

Jemmott showed the reporter the two versions of the score and indicated that "the correct version was only handed to All Stars on the Wednesday before the finals."[543] The then PRO of All Stars, Eddie Hart, endorsed this when he told reporters after the Finals: "The band got the correct version of the Test Piece only two days before the finals, hence the low scores in the prelims and semis. It was not until when I asked for the correct version on Thursday (sic) that I was given the right version…"[544]

Despite all this, despite the fact that the matter of two versions of the score reeked of "irresponsibility" and could "only happen in Trinidad," Jemmott was of the view that even at that late stage All Stars would be able to "correct the mistakes for the final night," of course adamant that he would ensure that the band stick rigorously to the integrity of the correct score. He said: *I knew that the others had a chance to be judged on the correct version in the preliminaries so that they would know how effective their performances were… but we went into the final night without having that privilege.*[545]

In the end, Jemmott put forward the claim that *there was evidence to suggest that the bands paid no attention to percussions in the test piece… the bands did not stick to what was on the score sheets—and this includes the eventual winning band; this unfortunately was an oversight by the judges and this means that the bands were playing incorrectly…* In Jemmott's view, and he implied that it is a view that all knowledgeable musicians would support, **All Stars' performance on that night "surpassed all others."**

Finally, Jemmott queried *why it was necessary for a Pan Trinbago official to go into the booth where the adjudicators were summing up on the final night of competition*, and he declared that since the adjudicators did not need nor asked for any help, he found the intrusion very unusual. But the fact of the matter is that if any other band in Trinidad & Tobago had had such an experience in context of incorrect scores, the finals would not have been allowed to take place on the night of October 4, 1986; an injunction would have been filed.

Only All Stars would accept such treatment and walk away, pained and hurt but with heads held high. It is the culture of a band that has learnt throughout its history never to protest the decisions of judges and never to seek litigation in attempt to establish its worth and value. This band, because it is secured in the long history of its proven competencies, always walks away to come again and again.

Of course, Pan Trinbago tried to refute the charge in regard to the different versions of the test piece in the 1986 Festival, claiming that all the bands received the same score. All Stars deemed it silly to respond to the obvious but Uncle Jem sought to pinpoint the bigger picture in a letter to the President of Trinbago titled **Some Pointers to ensure that Pan stays Beautiful**, which in its entirety reads as follows:

While the tumult and the shouting still rage, it is important to shed some light and draw attention to the fact that all the evidence required to arrive at a just assessment of the performance of Catelli Trinidad All Stars Steel Orchestra of the test piece "Fire and Steel—Ode to Yo-Yo" on the night of the finals, October 4, 1986 resides in the recorded version. If these tapes are played back and compared with the official score, it can easily be established which band performed the work with the greatest fidelity to the score, particularly in relation to the parts for snare drum, cymbals and bass drum.

Special instructions were given concerning the drum parts. It is not a question of crying "sour grapes;" but of seeking to focus on one important aspect of performances—the faithful execution of a given score, i.e., playing what is written. No more needs to be said...

...I feel that it is in the interest of the Pan Festival for consideration to be given to the following areas:

1. ADJUDICATION: Pan Trinbago, as organizers of the Pan Festival, have the responsibility for providing the judges they employ with unequivocal guidelines for adjudication, to ensure uniformity of approach to marking in the interest of fair play toward the competitors. For example, why are no specifics included on the mark sheet under the headings "Rhythm—20 Marks" or "Interpretation and General Effect—50 Marks?" To ignore important elements of rhythm such as steadiness, spirit and variety is to fail to point the importance of these constituents to the judges, and thus deprive contestants of the opportunity to gain marks for observing elements of the rhythmic texture of the work performed.

In addition, to omit specifics from the headings "Interpretation and General Effect," even by failing to allocate points under each of the headings (say Interpretation 40 points, General Effect 10 points) is for the organizers to abdicate their responsibility to competitors, and to expose their performances, without direction, to the subjective judgment of the adjudicators to the extent of half of the available marks. Far be it from me to impugn either the competence or integrity of the judges of any Festival, but I feel most strongly that serious competitors deserve no less than to be assured of intelligent and informed adjudication based on acceptable criteria. There is a sufficient number of competent musicians available in the country to provide Pan Trinbago with advice on criteria for assessing Rhythm, Interpretation and General Effect. These musicians ought to be consulted on the matter.

2. SUGGESTIONS FOR THE FESTIVAL. It would seem desirable to reassess the rationale for the types of works comprising Festival music, especially in view of the criticism from some quarters about the amount of "classics" played. For instance: (a) CALYPSO. No one would argue that calypso should be eliminated as one of the offerings, for reasons which are well known and too numerous to be stated here. Suffice it to say that the traditionally close association between pan and calypso makes its inclusion essential. (b) TUNE OF CHOICE. The inclusion of this offering is necessary to provide stimulus to all competitors to exercise and extend their musicianship, and to enable competitors to select a work in which they feel they can excel—a showcase for their skill. (c) TEST PIECE. If there is to be a Test Piece at all, then it could well create a long-awaited opportunity for Pan Trinbago to commission works in the "Caribbean" musical idiom scored expressly for pan.

Over time, such commissions would contribute to a repertoire of Festival music specifically composed for pan, and thus satisfy a significant need in the **country which claims to be the "home" of the steelband, but somehow neglects to take the action required to establish and maintain its claim**. All that competitors require of the test piece is that accurate copies of the official score be made available to them, and we have the technology in Trinidad & Tobago to produce printed copies of the musical score… A Caribbean-style test piece would also be an answer to the public's criticism of the *predominance of classical music in the Festivals. I trust that the above comments will be taken in the spirit in which they are intended, namely as my contribution to ensuring that "Pan is Beautiful"...*[546]

Of course, there was never a response from Pan Trinbago to these salient issues raised by Uncle Jem and today there still remains a great need for a review and reformation of the approach to Pan Music Festivals. Given the response of the attentive sections of the general public, it is now certain that never again shall any band win two of the three categories in a Pan Music Festival and lose. That humiliation historically belongs to All Stars and All Stars alone. The only satisfaction that the Hell Yard people gained from the 1986 Festival lies in the acknowledgement that *Unknown Band* beat *Rebecca* into second place.

Nevertheless, when the year 1986 is taken into overall consideration, there were some treasured moments as All Stars was bestowed the Port-of-Spain City Council Award for its contribution to the culture of the Nation and also toured the United Kingdom during the course of the Commonwealth Games.

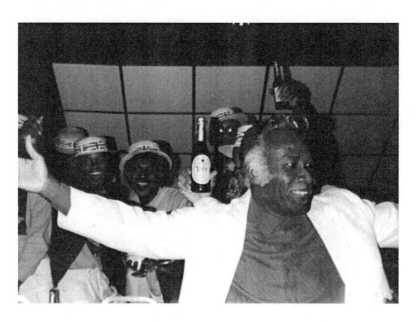

Uncle Jem in joyous celebration while on tour.

Fitzgerald "Uncle Jem" Jemmott, in his sartorial splendor, was the classical maestro under whose guidance All Stars was rarely ever defeated in the Music Festivals from 1968 to 1988. Now deceased, he would never be forgotten for his sterling contribution to the development of the institution and musical war-machine that is Trinidad All Stars Steel Orchestra.

Members on the 1986 Tour to the United Kingdom. This tour was planned as a result of the success of the 1985 Classical Jewels V Concert. Front Row (second from left) is "Africa" (dark glasses); Popwell is second to last in that row. Donny Andrews, Berry, Grip are in the second row, Sir Paul Hill stands above them, Fields and Muscles are at the end. At the end

of the third row is Tallist with Earl "Bunny" Wells above. Deryck Nurse and Dane Gulston are at the back. The ladies in the front row are from left, Gail "Red Lady" Clarke, Linda "After" Cudjoe and Rosalie "Cool Princess" John. Ulric "Bigs" James (deceased) stoops between "Africa" and Gail Clarke. This picture was taken at Wolverhampton on the way back from Scotland (courtesy All Stars' files). 35 members were supposed to be the full complement on this tour but in reality 45 persons participated.

Front row seated, second from left, Hayden Phillip ("Africa"), Sadist and Tambu. Standing, from the right, Fields, Big L, Donny, Biggs, Dane...(All Stars on tour to the United Kingdom (England and Scotland).

Pic 11: Yohan Popwell and Deryck Nurse: They, like so many others, virtually grew up in All Stars. In the recent past years, Popwell is the one noted for arranging most of All Stars' non-panorama repertoire, while Deryck, after graduating from UWI, has emerged as a classical music director and conductor.

The three Young Men who held Captaincy of Trinidad All Stars in the period 1971–1987. Errol "Reds" Collins, from left, Hamilton "Web" Alexander (center) and John "Poison" Douglas.

The 1988 Split

In 1988, misfortune struck hard and All Stars came face to face with its second major split in the ranks and the resulting loss of the Catelli/Hand Arnold sponsorship. Uncle Jem, Smooth Edwards, and others of the then executive walked away from the band leaving All Stars in the Panorama preliminaries 19 points ahead of its nearest rivals with the unfinished *Pan In Yuh Rookung-Ker-Tung-Kung*; there was no "introduction" up to that point. According to Errol "Reds" Collins there were four rounds of appearances involved in the staging of that Panorama and though Anthony "Shortman" Guerra did add an introduction, All Stars moved respectively from 1st, to 3rd to 5th and finally to 7th place on the final night.[547]

But the genesis to the 1988 split began with the remarkable achievements of All Stars in the very early years of the decade of the 1980s. The band had attained dizzying heights with successes at the 1980, '81 and '86 Panoramas as well as the Music Festivals, and the core leadership of the band began to seriously consider "more adequate compensation" for the work that had been accomplished.[548] The problem, according to Reds, arose because the sponsor, Hand Arnold, was a small management/marketing outfit with an agency-contract to manage and market Catelli and could in no way handle the level of expenditure on steelband sponsorship that had become the order of the day with the likes of the big companies like WITCO, NP and Petrotrin.

Obviously, given the huge success of the band, Uncle Jem, Smooth, Shorty, Tony, and Bunny were desirous of consideration in like manner as Bradley of Desperadoes and Boogsie of Phase 11, and more so as Insp. Prospect of Casablanca was obtaining from Iscott.[549] Reds indicated that the task fell to then, executive member, Ms. Barbara "UWI" Crichlow, to put together a proposal to the sponsors in which there was a demand for increased annual sums for Uncle Jem and for Smooth Edwards and his assistants.[550]

Barbara, who had joined All Stars in August 1981 on her return from attaining a Master's Degree in Planning from Howard University and by 1982 had replaced Clive Bernard as Secretary/Treasurer of the band, confirmed that she prepared a proposal to the sponsors but in her discourse there was no mention of the actual figures proposed for the Panorama and Music Festival arrangers.[551]

This is how she described the inputting of the data that underscored the proposal she crafted: *On New Year's Day, we usually would go down by Uncle*

Jem; Tony, Bunny, Smooth, Poison, and kind of have a brainstorm for what will be happening for the year… sometimes you don't know how the connection (comes), how we became such close friends, what drew us, but we became really close; and in talking, you know, hearing their dreams and their wishes and their history, and you hear them talking with this passion; it soon became my passion, and their dreams soon became my dreams… So I started putting down on paper their dreams, and decided that if this is what we wanted then we have to plan it and schedule things so that you achieve things over a period of time. And I did it basically in a spread-sheet format of the goals, the plans, the programs…[552]

Coming out of that, I got involved in implementing some of the ideas and trying to get the goals achieved, and that meant liaising with Catelli and Mr. Hale. We had a good, really good relationship, myself and Mr. Hale, but I know it had gotten strained with the production of that document, because what I had done for the band was a five-year development plan: instruments, music, the band room, physical, the whole thing and it was costing something like half a million dollars. (She laughed) *I'm laughing because I am remembering the interaction presenting the document, and Mr. Hale who had a really good rapport with me, suddenly went kinda cold…*

At the time the sponsors were giving probably about $50,000 so there was resistance to acknowledge the document calling for so much money. Reds was the captain at the time, and when I realized that he was not about to go that way, I said, listen we need to raise money, we have things to do, so let us find another way…[553]

Reds Collins, on the other hand, explained that he initially informed the core group that he could not go ahead with such a proposal because he knew it was not possible and more so because Hale and Company were just administrators who had to get approvals from shareholders, and the response from the core group was: "then, we have to get another sponsor." Reds informed that at that point he convened a meeting with the sponsors and "from the moment I hand the man the proposal, he take a look at it and immediately his countenance changed and Hale turned to Barbara and said, "I am sure you put this proposal together and she replied affirmatively."

According to Reds, Hale then said to them that he could never justify that kind of expenditure to his shareholders, furthermore that managers in their organization did not get that kind of money, and Reds concluded: "So it is there the whole thing start. They (Barbara and others) talked to Coco Cola, Roger Gibbon was the top man there, and talk got around, you know, these executive types meet and talk and exchange information so the relationship with Catelli/Hand Arnold became quite strained. That started since 1983 and that is the year I was voted out of the captaincy and Poison Douglas took over... Up to this day I cannot understand why I get voted out in 1983; the band was on a roll, going guns..."[554]

The reality was that the core leadership group comprised the key movers and shakers within the All Stars family and would have proven quite influential enough in lobbying for what they felt was required for further development. In regard to the 1983 elections, Smooth Edwards is of the view that Reds chose not to campaign, thinking that the band's records would hold sway in his favor, while Poison, who felt he could be captain of the band, campaigned.[555] The bigger view here however is that Reds' reluctance to press Hand/Arnold for greater financial returns made him unpopular among the influential people and this fact must have prompted Poison to make his move. But as happens in such cases, the results of people's actions tend to go way beyond what they originally intended and sets off other social and political currents and dimensions that could not then be perceived.

Although she did not specify Coco-Cola, nevertheless, Barbara Crichlow-Shaw did confirm that they began to solicit assistance from businesses around and in this context she mentioned the "bars" in the neighborhood that assisted with items such as jerseys, also the Co-operative Bank that was "right at the corner" of Charlotte and Duke, as well as the National Petroleum Company.[556] She indicated that once such approaches were made for alternative financing, Mr. Hale changed his attitude to the proposal and a general review was undertaken in the course of which there developed a mutual understanding on both sides that there would be an incremental approach toward meeting the goals set, and she admitted that though she did not put much emphasis on the construction of a building, Hale seemed to want to go that way, so the storeroom for the pans was fixed up and air-conditioned and additional monies were pumped from the sponsor "so we were able to do some of the other little things and move along."[557]

Reds insisted that, after he was out and Poison came in, he was no longer privy to negotiations with the sponsors, so he was unaware whether the Musical Director and Panorama arranger were ever successful in getting the level of compensation that had become the norm in the open market place.[558] Barbara Crichlow-Shaw, when asked if the band at that time proved able to get the sponsor to match the going market rates for musical directors and arrangers, replied in the negative but indicated that Uncle Jem and the arrangers were further supplemented from All Stars' earnings (e.g. pan-jams, classical concerts, winnings from Carnival parade, playing for functions and parties, etc.) and borrowings, i.e., overdraft facility at Co-operative Bank.[559]

Indeed, as indicated above, the subvention from Catelli/Hand-Arnold was only $50,000 annually but the expenditure indicated in the 1987 Budget documents submitted by Barbara Crichlow and found in the band files suggest a total expenditure of approximately $94,000 inclusive of payments to administrators and arrangers as well as tuners, blenders and chrome-furnishers.[560] So there was some additional compensation to members of the core group though, without fully audited accounts, it is impossible to identify source of funds, whether the additional monies came from the sponsor, from bank loans or through fund-raising activities and more so whether the general membership gained any increased payment.

The point to note is that just as the members of the core group were desirous of more adequate remuneration given the tremendous achievements of the band, so too were the average members desirous of returns for their output, and therefore, without any proper accounting and reporting to the general membership, a groundswell of discontentment became quite evident. Barbara, as the only woman on the then executive; the person with the best communication skills who was readily pushed by Poison and others to make public appearances to market All Stars, and who, being a young woman in the spotlight, much to the chagrin of some of the male membership, was particularly targeted by the groundswell so much so that, at one point, she indicated that Uncle Jem suggested that she be removed from public appearances in light of the building hostilities and in an attempt to quell the situation.[561]

"In as much as Anthony Guy, Bunny, Smooth and myself," she added, "were almost inseparable, they nicknamed us, "the gang of four" reflective of what had happened in China, and to some extent there was an element of petty jealousy based on what people thought executive members were getting… because I remember when Smooth got a 280C, a taxi, it caused big problems but Smooth was working as a Cultural Officer with the Ministry and was arranging, and he had asked for an advance from the band which he used, together with what he had otherwise, to purchase the car..."[562]

An altogether different take on the genesis of the 1988 split came from John "Poison" Douglas who, with the ouster of Reds Collins, held the Captaincy from 1983 until he lost to Beresford Hunte in the 1987 elections. Poison has a particular history which colors his perspective on that 1988 split and therefore it requires some examination. John Douglas said that he became attracted to All Stars first as part of a large mas'-playing contingent from his home community, Mt. Lambert, which was also the home community of deceased Junior "Peking" Jeffery, a teacher and one-time leader of the double-seconds section in All Stars and who then was by far the most influential and beloved elder in the area particularly in regard to musical orientation.[563]

After the first split in 1967, Douglas said it was painful for him playing mas' in the band that year and having to experience numerous abrupt stopping of the music—"every minute the band was cutting off and starting back" and there and then, with Peking as his official recommender, he joined the stage-side hoping that by so doing he could help "strengthen the band," much to the chagrin of his father, a Priest, who repeatedly locked him out of the house because of his involvement in steel-band affairs.[564]

Poison recalled that after two years, he was elected to the executive in the position of Assistant Secretary to Noel "Cin-Cin" Lorde who was Secretary and then to the Captaincy after Reds in 1983 lost the position.[565]

When asked to describe his relationship with Jerry Jemmott, he responded in this manner: *It was easy to build a relationship with someone like Uncle Jem who brought to the band such a wealth of musical knowledge; he was a father figure to us; as Musical Director, Uncle Jem took care of every single player; he knew the drawbacks of each and every one; he knew from what players were suffering and he was there for us at all times, working with each of us to build us into being better all-round persons and players...*[566]

Junior "Peking" Jeffery (deceased)

He was a primary school teacher and leader of the double-seconds section from the days of the Garret on Charlotte Street. Influential leader in the Mt. Lambert/Mt. Hope community and was responsible for introducing many of the then younger folk of that area to Trinidad All Stars such as John "Poison" Douglas, Terry Demas, etc.

John "Poison" Douglas took pains to reinforce the view that the Classical Jewels Concerts were the prime tool utilized by Uncle Jem to mold All Stars into a competent, professional musical aggregation to be respected by all and to be feared by all rival competitors. He further insisted that the Concerts triggered overseas tours; tours of Europe, the UK and the USA and in this way the band began to build an international reputation.[567] He also argued that the touring allowed for an "internal bonding" of the All Stars membership; and in this context he cited the question of "rooming" as being of the utmost significance making it an issue that management was forced to treat seriously.

"Before we left on tour," he said, "we used to sit down and make sure we had the rooming right, room-mates had to be members who were socially agreeable, if you got that right the bonding intensified, if you got it wrong, the entire tour could be a disaster despite economic success."[568]

He implied that these "tours" helped transform members: *When you play abroad and put down good music and you see people crying and rising to standing ovation, you get a sense of self-worth, you begin to measure your real worth when you begin to see things from an international point of view, when you see people treat you as they would any symphony orchestra. As a result, members began to strive further to be better players, better soloists and though it did not necessarily mean that pan people would rush to learn music formally, given the historic mental block, nevertheless it resulted in an easing of that block and some began to learn formal music and realized that it was not as difficult as expected and that in any case much of it they already knew.*[569]

When asked to indicate what he considered to be his most fulfilling experience during the period of his captaincy from 1983 to 1987, this was his response: *It came at the last Classical Jewels Concert under my captaincy (i.e., Classical Jewels V, 1985) when I and the executive promised that all participants in the Concert would go on a tour after the Concert; we did not know where we would be going but we made the promise. At that time there was evidence of growing disenchantment; members were saying the concerts were too much work…*

John "Poison" Douglas was the 10th captain of Trinidad All Stars (1983–1987).

It (the concert) was a major success. People saw the results. Paul Hill came and conducted and "brought down the house". So we decided on a tour of England. 35 people participated but we only had funding for 27 people; we were short by 8 tickets. I call the President, Sir Ellis Clarke, who used to attend all the Concerts and an audience was set up. Eddie Hart, Earl Wells, Telemaque and I went to the President's House and there and then Sir Ellis picked up the phone in front of us and began to call up Companies, he called 8 Companies and got the 8 tickets.

That was not because of me, it was because of the image that All Stars had built up over the years. It was one of the greatest successes and it pinpointed the results of all the hard-work and sacrifices that people had put into the development of the band. That is what All Stars meant to the world. I did not get those 8 tickets. It was All Stars that got them… I was pleased with the NAPA Concert held last year (2010). I was so pleased when I was invited to it. I had been trying for years to encourage the present leadership to reintroduce those Concerts and to recognize the importance of those Concerts… in fact, that was one of the underlying reasons for the split; the failure of those people to recognize that importance and significance.[570]

Douglas prefaced his analysis of the genesis of the 1988 split with the view that when an organization has a history of success, "when things are going good and smooth, there is a general tendency for people to feel and to give the impression that they could do things better, when in fact they are merely attracted to the power they sense they could possess if they take over."[571] Douglas, however, attributed what he described as a gradual build-up of indiscipline to certain elements, whom he chose not to mention by name, but whom he argued fostered the kind of atmosphere that led to members "feeling that they did not have to listen to instructions and that they could do anything they wanted," and that this situation continued to worsen until both himself and Barbara "UWI" Crichlow were voted out in 1987.[572]

Douglas, in regard to the actual confrontation between members and Smooth Edwards over his taking of some of All Stars' pans to the South, said: *When 1988 Carnival came, they (i.e., the new leaders) allowed members to play for any band they wanted so they could make their money—something that was totally against the culture and tradition of All Stars—ah mean in the past, yuh couldn't even go to listen to other bands, you would be fined. So Smooth say: "if members could play for other bands, then I could arrange for a next band." I not sure what answer he get.*[573]

Smooth did in fact take on an additional job but tension developed when he attempted to move pans, the property of All Stars, to the band in South. Interestingly, Reds Collins maintains that as Captain he did recommend Smooth to arrange for other bands but Smooth was never so inclined in those days and he recalled lending All Stars pans to Crescendos from Central Trinidad and that this was never a problem until the occasion when they pulled a number which required them to play just before All Stars on the same day and Reds said he had no choice but to blank Crescendos, however, if they were to perform after All Stars it would not have been a problem; in like manner he pointed out that it was sheer madness to even attempt to take pans, already blended for All Stars' performance at the North Panorama on the Sunday, down to South Panorama on the Saturday, that in Reds' book just was not on.[574]

Poison Douglas concluded: *As a result of confrontation over the pans, we felt that violence would take place, we could not allow All Stars to descend to such disrepute… we felt that if the new management saw us as a humbug to them and to the direction in which they wished to take the band, then we would prefer to leave and we left and formed FLABEJ.*[575] *A lot of people jumped on the bandwagon without understanding the issues, ignorant of the history of the band. They used to have a band outside the Yard and a band inside the Yard…*

We drew the conclusion that since All Stars was a democratic organization, people could make the decisions they want, so we let dem have the band to do what they wished with it… I always used to say I would be Captain of the band as long as the members would have me, I would never stay if not wanted. But as long as I was Captain, I would do as I see fit. I had to suspend a lot of people from the band because of their attitude… Imagine it was being said openly: "Who is Jemmott? Smooth ain't no big arranger, is Guerra who does give him the chords!"[576]

Clearly, such mouthing from elements of the general membership and from old members who were around the band could be deemed careless, thoughtless, and even probably malicious but must be taken in context of the breakdown of communication between leadership and membership and the resulting building hostility. Therefore it was not surprising that when the 1987 elections came the old leadership core group, it seemed, were no longer supportive of retaining Poison Douglas as captain. Barbara said that Poison sat back and allowed the groundswell to get the better of him; that when he was advised to address in direct terms the sentiments that were being expressed both within the band and around the band, as well as the elements of malicious propaganda that were being bandied about, his response was that it was all mere "election campaigning" and that people had their democratic rights, and as a result, she claimed, Uncle Jem was forced one night to sit the entire stage-side down and angrily lecture them about the propensity of "picky-head children" to destroy what had been built up painstakingly for their own good.[577]

Beresford Hunte confirms that members of the stage-side informed him that such a lecture did in fact take place but the gist of what those members took from all that was said, was that the core group was the driving force of the band and that All Stars would be nothing without that core, in other words it was an emotional appeal to the members to ensure that the core group remained intact and in charge.[578]

Once it became abundantly clear that the general membership was demanding change and that there was a particular person to whom they were looking to effect this change, members of the core group began seriously to court Beresford Hunte as the likely replacement for Poison Douglas and one can so deduce considering the fact that Berry, then a non-executive, non-committee, member of the band, found himself accompanying Barbara Crichlow on the last of the three trips she made to London as the advance party to fine-tune the logistics of the 1986 tour of Wales, Scotland and England that had been promised by the Poison Douglas-led executive as compensation for all the hard-work accomplished by all the participating 35 pannists involved in the 1985 Classical Jewels V Concert.

And whereas Poison highlighted the role played by the then President, Sir Ellis Clarke, in obtaining the sponsorship of the last 8 tickets, Barbara stressed the amount of work that had to be done to secure the initial 27 tickets; "we had to work our butts off, I know that I personally worked my butt off… "to make that tour a reality, and, in particular, she focused on the trips she made to London to hold meetings with all the agents and agencies involved such as Robert Hass and Company as well as officials of the Commonwealth Secretariat. In fact, she admitted that at one point, the tour "was blowing up so big", with even a proposed performance at the Royal Albert Hall, "that we couldn't get governmental support for it" and therefore, sights had to be lowered somewhat.[579]

Barbara "UWI" Crichlow was a livewire of the then Executive.

She confirmed that just around that time, Beresford Hunte "just kind of started coming around and hanging around the band, he was coming back in, he wasn't playing any instrument, he was just around," and when the issue arose in regard to finalizing the locations in London where the band was scheduled to perform, "nobody else could go and Berry was asked and he accompanied me and we stayed at my uncle's and she did indicate that after all the effort extended, "the tour was successful."[580]

Keith "Grip" Matthews, on the other hand, is adamant that the 1986 tour was "key" to "future developments within All Stars', firstly, he claims that "the turbulence within the then executive" was clearly exposed for all to see while on tour, and secondly that as a result of that exposure, "members openly began to refer to Berry as "Manage" during the latter part of the tour."[581]

Beresford Hunte admitted that, on return from the tour, members of the core group did sound him out on contesting the executive election but based on what they outlined he came to the clear conclusion that what they simply desired was a mere figurehead as Captain who would replace Poison within the core so they could continue to conduct business as usual.[582] Berry confessed that the "trump-card" he held when he consented to contest the Captaincy was the consensus on the ground that Grip Matthews, a committee-member since 1983, should also contest for the post of Secretary/Treasurer to replace Barbara Crichlow.[583]

Barbara herself confessed that a lot of what was happening on the ground at that point was "oblivious" to her "because her head was just into working for All Stars" and it was not until election time in 1987 that she was confronted with it all, but she did indicate that Ossie Hale was quite astonished when he heard that Grip Matthews, his driver, was contesting the secretary/treasurer post; in fact, she quoted Mr. Hale as having said to her: *Why is he (Matthews) doing that? He's not ready for that position. Why are they pushing him? You are doing a fantastic job.*[584]

There was also an implicit suggestion from Barbara that Grip was a member of the NAR (National Alliance for Reconstruction), the Political Party that was swept into governance in 1986 defeating the Peoples National Movement (PNM) (33-3), and therefore the developing upheaval in All Stars could be attributed to have been "a microcosmic reflection" of what was happening in the wider society.[585] What is difficult to reconcile here is Grip as "not ready" and Grip as influential political activist with an agenda. Nevertheless, Grip Matthews admitted that he, then 26 years old, was a member of the NAR Youth Group in St. Anns and had previously been a member of the PNM, but he rejected outright any notion that the national politics reflected on the developments within All Stars.[586]

And apparently, in an effort to underscore his capacity and "readiness" even then to shoulder responsibility, he intimated proudly: "I drove Ossie Hale until his death. Whenever the Hales went on vacation in those days, I used to stay and take charge of their home in Maraval until their return…"[587] Surely, it would have been a grave mistake to deduce that Grip Matthews "was not ready" to shoulder responsibility.

After the 1987 executive elections, Beresford Hunte and Keith "Grip" Matthews replaced John "Poison" Douglas and Barbara "UWI" Crichlow as

Leader and Secretary/Treasurer respectively. It meant that the two most important executive positions were no longer part of the old core-action group, largely influenced by Uncle Jem and which comprised persons such as "Smooth" Edwards, Anthony Guy and Bunny "Fancy Face" Wells. But with both Poison and Barbara out, there developed some tension at the level of the new executive that had to be resolved in one way or another.

However, the new Captain said that on assuming office in 1987, he was assured in no uncertain terms particularly by Uncle Jem that the affairs of the band were already in good hands and therefore all he needed to do was to allow matters to proceed as usual.[588] But Berry and Grip were already convinced that "business as usual" definitely could not be an option given their commitment to the general membership and what the members on the ground expected of them as the two new, key executive officers.

One of the immediate areas of tension was the then demand by Uncle Jem for payment from all band engagements and for any service he may have provided for the band despite the fact that he received a stipend; he was constantly grumbling that the new Executive seemed to have come to "cut his money".[589] It is said that on one occasion while Uncle Jem was rehearsing the Band, he stopped suddenly and loudly voiced the opinion that he was working so hard and his needs were not being met and it was then that he called on the players to "tell your Captain that I want to see him, now"; the message was conveyed to Berry who then went to Uncle Jem to ascertain what he required only to be told that the requirement was "water".[590]

Berry dutifully complied but later that night, at around 12pm, the new Captain said he telephoned Uncle Jem at home and expressed his displeasure with what had transpired earlier and demanded that he desist from any such effrontery in the future.[591]

Grip Matthews said that Uncle Jem's view of Berry then was quite unfortunate as in their first budget to the sponsors for the year 1987–1988, they requested that Uncle Jem's small stipend be raised but the sponsors refused to accede to this request.[592] According to Grip's recollection Uncle Jem as was the custom came on the Carnival Friday night of 1988 to clean up the Panorama tune, Duke's *Pan In Yuh Rookung-Ker-Tung-Kung*. In those days, Semis was on Thursday and Finals on the Saturday and the general idea was that the band would do in 1988 as they did in Panorama 1986 when they had practiced

Rudder's *Hammer* on the Friday Night with Uncle Jem until about 6.30 am the Saturday morning since Smooth had changed the entire arrangement.

Grip said, "when we ran the final take of *Hammer* on that Saturday morning, people on their way to work and others on the way to market, stood up and began to dance and when it was all over they all applauded spontaneously to such an extent that we knew in our hearts that once we played it as we did that early Saturday morning, the Panorama was ours for the taking."[593] Grip then pointed out that in the case of the 1988 situation, when Uncle Jem came that Carnival Friday night and said to the band: "Where is the Captain, ah hope he have enough refreshment for allyuh because we going whole night"; it was only mamaguy because nothing was changed or added to *Pan In Yuh Rookung-Ker-Tung-Kung* and the band went from 1st in the prelims, leading by 19 points, to 3rd, to 5th and eventually to 7th in the finals.[594]

It was then that Grip recalled that the incident that occurred with Uncle Jem summoning Berry and then demanding "water" did not happen during the 1988 Carnival season but during rehearsals for the 1987 Classical Jewels VI in November of 1987.[595] Smooth Edwards opines that Jemmott's apparent roughness was due to his military career: "he was a serviceman who rose to the rank of Sergeant, and it was his nature to talk down to people."[596]

However, the question remains why was nothing done to the 1988 Panorama presentation? The story is that Leon "Smooth" Edwards, unfortunately, was the one who felt most the brunt of the fury that was building up among the members of the band. In 1988 while arranging Duke's *Pan In Yuh Rookung-Ker-Tung-Kung*, Smooth Edwards also took on the job to arrange for T&TEC Motown of San Fernando. It is said that the new Captain declared an executive fiat that prohibited the lending of pans and Smooth in an attempt to load his vehicle with pans one night was prevented from doing so. Reds Collins' view, already outlined above, that the pans were already blended for All Stars' panorama performance on the Sunday may have caused members to be incensed that some of these very pans, already blended, were being taken for use by another band on the Saturday before the Sunday.

However, after Smooth was blocked from taking six tenors down to Motown, he ceased to work on the All Stars'1988 Panorama tune and, eventually, most of the old executive including Uncle Jem himself would walk away. Also, Catelli relinquished its sponsorship, thereby ending an era of relationship that had lasted some two decades, 1968–1988. The point is that there was never any clear policy in All Stars in regard to use of its instruments to boost other bands or even concerning its members playing elsewhere other than the accepted fierce tradition of the old days when members did not even dare visit another band. In 1988, the times had changed and it therefore required open and frank discussion, which sadly did not happen.

Performing on stage at the 1988 Panorama prelims. Courtesy Trinidad Guardian. All Stars took the lead by 19 points. On that Sunday, 31 January 1988, performing Duke's "Pan in Yuh Rookungkertungkung" that brought the house down, the band placed 1st with 260 points; Desperadoes, second, playing Rudder's Panama; Phase 2 and Starlift tied for third place playing respectively Woman is Boss and My Band; and Renegades, fifth, playing Pan In Me.

All Stars' Flagman (Michael "Fatman" Lucas) is embraced by Mighty Duke during the band's performance at the North Zone Finals. All Stars placed 3rd that night of Thursday, 4 February 1988.

Eleventh Captain

Beresford "Manage" Hunte was a long-standing member of All Stars and a tenor player since 1966 in the days of the Garret. After he stopped being an active pan-player in 1972, he continued his association with the

band as a usual mas-player particularly on Carnival Tuesdays. In the mid '80s, he, due to his popularity among many of the active old membership, found himself being constantly beseeched to take up an Executive position in the band. When tension began to mount between the leadership and the membership in the year 1986–1987, the promptings to contest for office intensified to the point at which he could no longer ignore the power of persuasion.

His first stint as Captain was from 1987 to 1989 at which point Reds Collins regained the Captaincy from late 1989 to 1995, only to be replaced by Berry in 1995 to 2016. After Berry fell ill on Carnival Tuesday 2016, he said, that he came to the conclusion that after 24 years (3 years in his first stint as Captain and 21 years in his second stint), it was time to step down and make way for a younger person.

At the 1962 Independence celebrations, Mr. Cecil Hunte, President of the Steelbandsmen Association and father of Beresford Hunte, meets and greets Princess Royal, representative of Queen Elizabeth during the State Ball held at the National Art Museum. Pix courtesy Beresford Hunte. Beresford's commitment to the steelband movement mirrored his father's legacy.

Smooth, however, in alluding to the development of hostilities within the band, cited 1986 as the year key to the genesis of the break-up and this is how he described the beginning of his alienation within All Stars: "Imagine," Smooth said, "we won Panorama with Hammer in 1986. We played last. When we reached by Renegades on the way back, the results come out, and you know, a guy who was giving a set a trouble, cussing me, dissing me, the arranger, and all kinda thing, lift me in the air, oh, God, we win, we win. And I say, nah, this is too much deceit. As he put me down I just went round Park Street, up Jackson Hill, went home and sleep. Everybody down in All Stars yard celebrating. The only man not there was me. I could not hang out with them..."[597]

There is the view expressed by Edric Straker and others that when that win was announced, members of the band lifted Anthony "Shortman" Guerra into the air because it was felt that the changes he recommended to the arrangement of Hammer were responsible for All Stars "making up some 19 marks from the semis" and grabbing the victory.[598] Nevertheless the above quotation from Smooth is quite telling; this was 1986, the old executive was still in place, the elections that brought Berry and Grip to office did not take place until 1987, yet Smooth was already expressing rancor in the band and deep-felt personal hurt. He even recalled that when Prime Minister Chambers came to visit the band that year, 1986, during Panorama practice, the "pavement fellahs" held up a placard showing Jemmott with a bag o'money to help their effort of spreading "wicked and vindictive" propaganda.[599]

When the elections came due, Berry intimated that what members of the previous executive desired was for him to become the Captain/Leader and for the rest of the Executive to remain as is, in which case he would be a mere figure-head and business would continue as usual, but what they did not anticipate was Grip Matthews contesting Barbara Crichlow for the Secretary-Treasurer position, and when faced with this turn of events, they approached Grip to step down but Grip refused. Berry concluded, "Grip is the person who upset the apple-cart."[600]

However, Barbara Crichlow-Shaw indicated that after the 1988 dispute, Uncle Jem was prepared to continue working with All Stars once certain elements were expelled from the band, in fact, she said his exact words were, "house cleaning had to take place" and she informed that there was a meeting between Mr. Hale and Berry, at which point certain conditions were outlined and it was left up to Berry to decide the way forward but he never took the required action and never got back to Mr. Hale, so as the saying goes, "that was it."[601] Smooth likewise insisted that according to All Stars' tradition "bad eggs are to be thrown out" in order to maintain the required discipline, but on this occasion he felt the leadership was not effective and refrained from doing what should have been done.[602]

Beresford Hunte acknowledged that a meeting with the entire All Stars executive was summoned by Ossie Hale, prompted, according to him, by the fact that Uncle Jem had chosen to inform the sponsors about "marijuana smoking and drugs" being rampant in All Stars leading to total indiscipline and disrespect to all authority and to him in particular.[603] Close examination of relevant newspaper reports of that period certainly indicate that Jemmott chose not to speak about "drugs" to the news media, stressing instead that he did not wish "to wash dirty linen in public" but lamented that there is "a general weakness in the leadership" as a result of which the younger players were being "influenced in the wrong direction" and he concluded that "after 20 years he sadly found he was no longer happy in the band."[604]

A few days later, Jemmott claimed that a "Pavement Council" infiltrated the band (*that was the very first reference to "pavement" people*) and that this led to indiscipline and a lack of respect for authority and he said that it was not something that happened just for the Carnival of that year, in fact he saw the problem as being much deeper than that, and he explained that "when a Musical Director goes in front of a band, he sees and feels everything… if a man winks, it comes out and somehow the body language was just not there; there was this "hate thing" coming out from among the membership; the atmosphere for Carnival was changed and the respect which was an integral part of the band was no longer there."[605]

And this general breakdown he attributed once again to "ineffective leadership" and he concluded: "The Captain of the band is a very nice person, a real gentleman, but when it comes to leading, he is not effective… I would hate to think that the band would simply disintegrate into nothing after all the years of work it took to build it. It would look like if all my efforts were selfish if this was to happen. All Stars need guidance; everything needs guidance, Government, homes, people. The band needs a level-headed person to take it through its present problems…"[606] And he surmised that the band could continue to be "a force in the steel-band world because it was an established institution."[607]

At the meetings with the sponsors, Jemmott's position, according to Berry, was that "a lot of the members had to go," whereas Earl Wells of the "core group" was adamant that All Stars could not exist without them, and Berry, being a long standing tenor pan player from since the days of the second Garret, responded, informing them that they all came and met All Stars and All Stars will continue to exist long after they were gone.[608] It was a tested truism reflected in the old Hell Yard and Garret adage already mentioned: *Stars pitch, they never fall*!

Berry spoke of the harsh response from Ossie Hale who after the second meeting mentioned above, proclaimed the following edict: the Sponsor could under no circumstances be associated with such turmoil and from henceforth the name "Catelli" is prohibited to be used in association with All Stars in any manner or form, and sometime after a cheque for $25,000 was given to the lawyer Theodore Guerra for him to disburse to All Stars "when and as he sees fit."[609] What a difference from that moment on the bull-track in 1968 when, without any formal engagement, Jules was asked to go on stage as Catelli Trinidad All Stars: what a difference, indeed. But by far the sharpest, clearest and most potent response to Jemmott on record was the response from Clive "Cokey" Telemaque.

Speaking to the news media, Telemaque, then vice-Captain, said: "I think things have gone too far. We didn't deserve to lose our sponsorship but the feeling among members of the band is that these people wanted out. It was they who wrote to the sponsors about problems within the band and after two meetings, one gets the impression that while the new management was all for reconciliation, the resigned six had already made their decision… I admit that there is a certain amount of indiscipline creeping into the band but it's not to the extent which people have been making it out to be. You can't blame any particular party for the problems. **I think it was a basic lack of communication** (my emphasis)."[610]

And in specific reference to problems in relation to that year's Panorama practice sessions, this is what Telemaque said: *If the arranger is unhappy with something it is only natural that you can't function at your best. The band's view was that nothing was wrong with the way we were playing but the arranger could have done a bit more with the tune. The arranger probably was not satisfied with the manner in which the band attempted to get this message across to him and it might have been seen as disrespect...*[611]

About the "drug charges", he said: *I have been here for 16 years and I can't point fingers at any one member who is on drugs. If you look at the panyard, you will see a wide open place where all kinds of people come. If we see someone going into the far corner we can't stop him, but we ensure that our members are told in no uncertain manner that they have a duty to the band and that drugs are out...*[612]

In regard to All Stars' continuity and longevity, Telemaque said: *I agree that the withdrawal of sponsorship is a big blow to the band but* **All Stars is not a fly-by-night operation**. *It is an institution and nothing can stop it from functioning. I think the general membership understands what has happened. We can't say for sure that no member would leave but the majority are behind the management and are all ready to put in whatever extra is necessary to maintain our standards. The band has already started negotiations with new arrangers but it is still premature to announce who these people are. The Festival is of vital importance to us. We have to put what happened behind us.* **The band is much bigger that any individuals**. *Some members of the band are in fact saying that the decision of the six resigned members is good for the band; they feel that for an organization to be good, there must be differences of opinion and one can't agree with what a minority says at all times; if criticism is constructive, then someone has to look at it...* and he concluded in this manner: *The next few months will be good, hard challenging ones for All Stars but we promise our supporters that like the Phoenix* rising out of the ashes, the band would continue to live on...*[613]

The mere mention of the word "Phoenix" proved to be quite an effective tongue-in-cheek message to the six ex-members that All Stars was informed of their intention to form a band with that very name, a fact that triggered the name change to FLABEJ.[614]

Interestingly, Desperadoes wrote a letter to All Stars, signed by their Secretary-Treasurer, Edison Holder, imploring All Stars not to go under despite the loss of sponsors and arrangers, saying such an eventuality would "weaken the steel-band movement" and dash the "hopes and aspirations of up and coming panmen."[615] Pan Trinbago, on the other hand, expressed disappointment with the actions of Hand Arnold, the Holding Company for Catelli, indicating that in exchange for the assistance to the band over the years, the band had provided "mileage and exposure to the company" and therefore they had treated All Stars unfairly which did not "augur well for good corporate image for the business community."[616]

Mr. Theodore Guerra, well-known, highly-reputed lawyer, long time All Stars masquerader and supporter and then Parliamentary Representative for Port-of-Spain South, called on Pan Trinbago, the "trade-union" of steel-bands, to guarantee that all sponsored steel-bands be given written contracts to prevent sponsors from "unilaterally terminating" contracts without adequate compensation, and he admonished the members of All Stars to take this development not as an end but just another beginning as he reminded them that the band had no sponsors in the '40s and '50s but was still one of the best.[617]

What undoubtedly cannot be missed in the entire 1988 fiasco is the typical elitist tone clearly depicted by the Musical Director, by some members of the core group and most certainly by Ossie Hale. It is the traditional view of middle-class professionals to see themselves as the divine leaders with THE PLAN and the mass membership as the unthinking horde to be led by their noses; they were the "picky-head children", to quote Uncle Jem, "who must learn to appreciate the good things being done **for** them" obviously by certain elite-types.

Barbara Crichlow-Shaw, in retrospect, admitted that she has thought about it (i.e., the 1988 blow-out) long and hard for years and the following is what she has concluded: "I think I understand the whole thing. I have come to terms with it. It was only because All Stars never thought that this was going to happen to them, that they would be asked **to share their arranger.** They thought somebody was coming to take their arranger. It was an emotional thing. It was like somebody **taking their heart** away. And they reacted. And when they rooted the pans away from Smooth, he likewise felt they **had pulled his heart out**. And that was it. And afterward, there was **this heaviness** in the band, which was unlike anything I had ever felt in the band before. But I never felt threatened." [618]

Beresford Hunte (center) addressing press conference at the Panyard on Tuesday March 29, 1988 at which he outlined the chain of events that led to the resignation of the six members and termination of the Catelli sponsorship. At left is Clive Telemaque, Vice-Captain, and on the right is Keith Matthews, Secretary-Treasurer.

Chris Haynes and Theodore Guerra (lawyer) were also present at the press conference.

In reality, one may surmise that she has yet to plumb the depths of the searing that visited All Stars in 1988; yet to fathom the intricacies of the socio-economic relationship that usually comes to exist between elite-type leadership and mass membership, and how in modern times there are very specific demands and responsibilities that are foisted on either side of such relationships. The tendency in today's world is for the masses to demand direct democracy; everyone must have a say, everyone must be made to feel they belong and be allowed to participate freely and fearlessly in the charting of future arrangements toward their common destiny. It is not about leadership working **for** but **with and alongside** membership. That is spinal in 21st century social relations.

Marcia Noel, interviewed Leon "Smooth" Edwards extensively on the 1988 split and based on information that she was able to cull from him, she said that when Smooth walked away from the band he had "no idea of the spiritual call upon his life" and it was not that he was "particularly religious" but All Stars was "his God" and All Stars was "his wife" as he "had no time for his (real) marriage" yet after leading the band into winners row in 1980, 1981 and 1986 and placing in the "first three for the six consecutive Panoramas, i.e., 1980–1986, Smooth left the band causing a part of nearly every All Stars pan player "to die" and that fact prompted Marcia Noel to ask: how could Smooth divorce his "wife"?"[619]

Leon "Smooth" Edwards in response to her questioning said: "My priorities were mixed up. I was practically worshipping All Stars. The band was first, second, third, even fourth. My wife and God were lower down the line… So God took it away."[620] He then referred to the incident that occurred during the 1988 Panorama season and he indicated that that incident made him feel that he had become the "target of bullets" that should have been aimed at the opponents and he clarified this by saying: "I always look at Panorama as a war. I always looked at the other bands as the enemy, and if I was supposed to be leading our team to this battle and my marshal is throwing bullets at me, I had no choice but to get out of the way."[621]

He also indicated that after he resigned because of the said incident the other "five key members" also walked away from the band and he listed these members as the treasurer, the secretary (*Barbara was the secretary/treasurer and Bunny Wells was her assistant*), the musical director, the main percussionist, and a former captain, all of whom he said formed the "core" whose influence in the band was so entrenched that their leaving at the same time with him "left All Stars with a hole in the middle" and he likened that to the "removal of a foundation stone."[622]

In conclusion, Smooth said that when Flabej, the band they formed, "failed to gain the recognition" in the time frame they expected, he and his family migrated to the US where he later "gave his life to God" and he added that "it was a time that helped me to repent and forgive those whom I thought of wrongly and started living my life the way I was supposed to."[623] He also told the reporter at that time that he was still an All Stars man, that he would always love All Stars and would never decry their name, and the reporter in turn concluded that Smooth was indeed grateful for the about-turn in his life, that he had now gotten his priorities right and his wife no longer had to compete with another "woman".[624]

Today, 2011, in retrospect, Smooth attributes the failure of FLABEJ to the power of All Stars as an institution and the fact that no one wanted to be seen to be assisting or to be associated with a bunch of people who rebelled and broke away from All Stars, and this was so despite the fact that Jemmott was then the leading Classical Arranger; he, Smooth, was the leading Panorama Arranger and Barbara was a live-wire as a skilled communications person who had contacts among all the leading Corporations in the country; yet none of the promises to FLABEJ ever materialized.[625]

In response to the query whether there were any attempts in 1988 to bring the two factions of All Stars together to have an open airing of the contentious issues, John "Poison" Douglas said: *Of course, they brought back Jules, even Prince Batson at one time. Eddie Hart tried his best. There were several meetings. Nothing was resolved. Our position was that nothing would work, as long as there were threats… So Uncle Jem, Smooth, Barbara, Tony, Bunny and I left. And Catelli also left when nothing was resolved. After that split, the quality of management needed to run that band as before, just was not available. The band suffered tremendously as a result. We did not want to ever leave All Stars.*[626]

When it was suggested that the lack of financial compensation for the membership seemed to be a burning issue and the question was asked pointedly whether member-players were compensated adequately and equitably from the proceeds of events such as the Classical Jewels concerts, Douglas declared: "*Catelli had a management team in place that would handle the finances, and* *in my time there would be **a financial report presented to the band after each concert**. I do not know what happened after my time. What we learnt from Ossie Hale and others in terms of modern management is priceless. If there was any issue of finances, it was never raised. Everybody used to get paid...*

There was a system of payment, a standard thing, starting with the Musical Director and down to the various players. They used to get good pay. I used to insist on that. I also set up a system for work in the Yard during Carnival whereby players would be paid the same rate as government workers to do the painting, wielding and so on. My position was that All Stars was based on team effort and just as the arranger would be paid everybody was important and had to be paid."[627]

In regard to the organization of the Classical Jewel Concerts, there is evidence to support John Douglas' statement about the involvement of Hand Arnold's management expertise. Dalton Narine, after discussions with Ossie Hale himself, was noted to have said: "When a concert is planned there are regular meetings, chaired by Hale, to work out who does what. Meetings are very informal but there's nothing amateurish about the way the concerts are organized. Orchestra and sponsor, with friends and relatives of both, work in harness to produce the finished product—the music, backed up by promotions, ticket sales, front-of-house, program design, printing, costumes. Over the years of planning and organizing concerts, tours, festivals—not to mention Panorama—sponsors and orchestra have built up real personal relationships in a team effort to produce beautiful, exciting sound on Trinidad's own musical instrument that will, God willing, find a respected, honorable place in the international world of music."[628]

Web, the captain who preceded Reds Collins and John Douglas, also confirmed that in his period of captaincy, a similar work relationship between the sponsor and the All Stars executive existed.

However, attempts were made to locate at least one of the financial reports mentioned by Douglas from the band's files but all attempts were unsuccessful. It seemed rather strange that none of such reports was found in the band's files especially given the joint management relationship that was ongoing. However Keith "Grip" Matthews, who then still worked at Hand Arnold, is a long standing member of the band for some 30 years, played in all Classical Jewels Concerts from 1981 to 1991, was a Committee Member from 1983 to 1987 when he won the post of Secretary/Treasurer, a post he held until 1992,[629] made the point that those **financial reports were kept at Executive level of the band and were never disclosed to the membership**.[630]

In stark contrast to the position that everyone received "good pay" and all the rest that John "Poison" Douglas implied and disclosed above, are the utterances over the years of members of the band, and, as an example, the words of the first person to be noted are those of **Joseph "Joe" Long:** He started playing double seconds with All Stars in 1968. He was a member of the band for some **49** years, touring extensively; visiting places as far flung as China, India, Ghana, Nigeria, Canada, the UK and the US, Jamaica, Barbados, Puerto Rico and St. Maarten. The 2004 Newsletter indicates that Joe Long "played in all Classical Jewels and all Pan Festivals from 1973 to 1996 and has held the post of Section Leader for the double-seconds section."[631]

Joe Long said: *After playing in the last three Classical Jewels (i.e., Classical Jewels 111, IV and V) before Berry became Captain (i.e., 1987) I could tell you the pay I get. For Classical Jewels IV, ah get $150; for Classical Jewels V, ah get nothing, dey say the show bust. Then Berry became Captain. After Classical Jewels VI, Uncle Jem ask for (sum mentioned); Anthony Guy, (sum mentioned); Bunny Wells (sum mentioned) and so on. And Berry ask them "what about dem fellahs?" Then the new Captain declare that the money will share up among everybody. When I went to sign to receive pay, mih hand shaking; $900. "Yuh know how much I do with dat money. I tell them fellahs, ah say, yuh see Berry, dat fellah is we Captain fuh life…"*[632] *"…Sometime after dat, Uncle Jem stand up in the Yard and call me, "Joe, tell dat fellah allyuh call Captain, I calling him!" I tell him, "Uncle Jem, if yuh want respect, then yuh must respect everybody, especially we Captain"*.[633] The point made by Joe Long has to be noted. Joe Long died 21 October 2017.

The second person's utterances to be noted are those of **Peterson "Carenage" Simon:** He, now also deceased, joined All Stars as a percussionist in 1992 playing congas and drums. The 2003 Newsletter establishes that **Caro**, as he was commonly called, played in the Steelband Panoramas and Music Festivals from 1994, toured Australia, Ghana, Barbados and Jamaica; he also held the position of Section Leader.[634]

Caro spoke as follows: *When Berry take over the last time (i.e.1995), dis band had nothing, only Pan and $7,000 in the bank. From the time we win the On-The-Road competition and get the first $100,000 prize, Berry say we not spending dat and he invest in units in the Unit Trust. Now the executive saying* is Units for all the stage-side players; now they talking about organizing Pension for us and Insurance. What more a member could want? Yet some of them does want pay for any little thing they do in the Yard.[635]

Joe Long: *...When I and (name mentioned) had the wrangle, Berry call me and say "Joe, I will have to apply discipline measures to you because you are a senior player." He give me a letter banning me for six months. Boy, it hurt but I was humble and accept the discipline. I used to come in the Yard and sit down and watch on. One day I come in the Yard and Straker was fabricating pan stands and I take off mih shirt and start to help him. Reds come and tell me dat I on ban and I should not be doing dat. I tell him that the ban is in regard to playing pan and not about doing odd jobs in the yard. Dis is my Yard I could do any work I feel to do. The very Reds, the vice-Captain, had recommended a one year ban fuh me.*

After a while Berry come to me and he say, "Joe, yuh hurting," and ah say, "yes". He say, "okay!" And he organize my reinstatement. The administration people give me a one line letter saying: "welcome back!" When Berry see dat letter, he chew them out, tear up the letter and make dem do over a proper letter to me. Yuh see we Captain; he is a fair man...[636]

What is made abundantly clear by the direct words of members like Joe Long and Peterson Simon quoted above is the nature of the relationship between leadership and membership that is now demanded. However, the entire 1988 fiasco was, to some extent, put to rest, on either side of the fence, when in 1998 Nelson Villafana, the then Musical Director, brought Uncle Jem back to All Stars yard to tour his old stomping ground and witness a practice session, and on meeting Beresford Hunte face to face for the very last time, Uncle Jem shook Berry's hand and the following dialogue ensued:

Uncle Jem: "You are doing a fantastic job. I am really impressed."

"I am trying, just trying..." replied Berry.

Unfortunately, Uncle Jem died long before this document was conceptualized and researched, so there could be no opportunity for him to respond to the issues raised by the 1988 split. However his role in the development of Trinidad All Stars can never be overstated. Efforts made to peruse his personal papers were unsuccessful.

Left, Leon "Smooth" Edwards as a young pan-player in Trinidad All Stars. While at QRC College, he joined the band and quickly, under the guidance of Uncle Jem, began to reveal his musical capabilities and his passion and unique gift for arranging music.

There developed a divergence of views on how to proceed after members of the old executive walked away in 1988 and Catelli relinquished the sponsorship. One tendency suggested that a new sponsor be found, whereas those, who were in opposition to sponsorship from Corporate citizens, suggested that the extensive support-base enjoyed by All Stars (i.e., from as far off as Tobago and Point Fortin) be utilized to raise funds by way of weekly or monthly contributions; that contribution cards be issued and that the trusted and loyal Street Captains in the various localities be given the responsibility to collect and transmit the contributions to 46/48 Duke Street.[637] The executive began considering the pros and cons of the options.

Berry Hunte indicated that the moment Catelli relinquished their sponsorship, the Neal and Massy Holdings Group began propositioning All Stars and had taken the initiative to present to the band the Company's prospectus as well as a proposal for sponsorship,[638] however, what is not common knowledge is that from since 1978 a number of All Stars members such as Smooth Edwards, Anthony Guerra, Anthony Guy, Ian "Stumbo" Greaves and Cecil Lynch had been employed at Neal Massy, largely due to the initiative of Mr. Roy Regis, then a Director at N&M and a passionate All Stars supporter. Later, deceased Franklyn Olliverre, formerly of High-Landers and an executive member and frontline player of Phase 11, who at the time worked in the Production Department of Neal and Massy was instrumental in getting employment for Glen Sandy (still there as an upholsterer on contract).

So, there was already some aspect of a long-standing relationship existing between band members and the Company. As a result of the initial reluctance to consider the N&M proposal, the new All Stars executive began to pursue the option of total self-reliance, and to launch this process a Concert at Spectacular Forum was organized at which a number of calypsonians such as Cro-Cro and Tambu offered to perform gratis as a contribution to All Stars, and it was there that a professional like Gillian Balintulo gave freely of her time and energy while doing her first performance with All Stars—*Somewhere Out There*.[639] Despite the involvement of artistes of such a caliber, the show was not a financial success.[640]

The failure of that Show at Spectacular Forum led the band to seriously consider the Neal and Massy option. Roy Regis however provided the story behind the story when he indicated that he was summoned to the office of Sidney Knox, Chairman of the Neal and Massy Holdings, who raised the issue of All Stars' need for sponsorship after having lost Catelli. Mr. Knox apparently was being encouraged by person or persons unknown to take up sponsorship of All Stars but was likewise cautious about proceeding to commit "shareholders money in any organization" that was beset with "strife and confusion." Roy Regis explained to Mr. Knox that following the recent elections of officers of All Stars there were significant changes; new persons came in and "key members who possessed the musical expertise" had resigned.

Mr. Regis requested two weeks' time to investigate the situation and to report on the current state of affairs within Trinidad All Stars. Roy's report clearly indicated that despite some evidence of an "unsettled atmosphere," the band was "a very solid and responsible organization in existence for over 50 plus years" and therefore "N&M should be recommended to get involved with a highly organized and admirable group."[641] Roy was thanked by Mr. Knox who in turn suggested that "the rest be left to him." Roy Regis also assures that he was aware that Mr. Knox was also consulting Mr. Michael Arneaud himself a fellow Director of Neal and Massy and likewise an ardent supporter of All Stars.[642]

By the end of August 1988, the official signing of the sponsorship agreement between the two entities was finally accomplished giving birth to the new configuration: Neal and Massy Trinidad All Stars.[643] At that time Mr. Gaston Aguilera, then Neal and Massy's Finance Director, declared that the "full sponsorship would cover management support and expertise, assistance with advertising and promotion and financial support," and though he did not quantify the budgeted sum, he assured the public that the figure was arrived at after discussions held between the two parties, i.e., an organizing committee of N&M and All Stars officials.[644]

Beresford Hunte, the Captain, advanced the view that with such a full sponsorship in train, All Stars would participate in the Pan Is Beautiful V World Steelband Festival competition due to be held then from October 20th to November 6th 1988 and he dared to suggest that All Stars would win that festival "not only for All Stars but also for Neal and Massy." [645] This could not be considered wishful thinking given the band's record in Festivals since 1968, i.e., 1968—1st; 1972—1st; 1980—1st; 1982—2nd; 1984—1st; and in 1986—2nd, despite winning the categories of Best Tune of Choice and Best Calypso; but the band flattered to deceive in that 1988 competition placing 3rd with its performances of Tchaikovsky's *Cappriccio Italien*, the test piece, *Pan Waves* by Earl Caruth, both of which were conducted by Gillian Nathaniel Balintulo and for the calypso category the band performed the Smooth Edwards' 1987 arrangement of *Curry Tabanca* by the Mighty Trini.

According to Berry, Gillian Balintulo and All Stars at least had the honor of being placed higher than Solo Harmonites whose pieces were arranged and conducted by Jerry Jemmott.[646]

Rudy Wells came back in 1989 in yet another attempt to rescue the situation but then many were of the view that he was quite out of touch with the Panorama scenario more so as the band's performance of his arrangement of Kitchener's *Two To Go* did not meet with the judges' approval. Many may wish to point finger at Wells' arrangement but true to say the 1988 split had taken significant toll on the morale of the band and the usual glamour and panache of All Stars were not evident. Smooth Edwards who had done them proud in the Panoramas from 1980 to 1988 was no longer present and there was a "Smooth Tabanca" that permeated the entire band.

All Stars, then quite plainly a much demoralized unit, ended up in a "b-class" competition organized by Pan Trinbago to accommodate the "best of the rest", i.e., the best of the lot who did not make the finals, only to be beaten there into second-place by the medium-band Simple Song.

The 1988 signing of the agreement that formalized the Neal and Massy sponsorship of Trinidad All Stars. Beresford Hunte (Captain) signed on behalf of the Band and Gaston Aguilera, Neal and Massy's Finance Director on behalf of the Company. (Courtesy Trinidad Guardian)

In 1990, All Stars, fighting to regain its Panorama prominence chose to allow one of Smooth's assistants Anthony "Shortman" Guerra to arrange the music and All Stars chose to go with Tambu's *Let's Do It* but the band proved unable to get beyond the preliminaries. With the band battling to regain its premier status, the internal elections came up in 1989 and Reds Collins, a former Captain, 1977–1983, campaigning on the promise "to bring back Smooth Edwards" defeated Beresford Hunte who understandably was the Captain associated most with the departure of Smooth, the loss of the previous sponsor and the fall of the band into the category "Best of the Rest", and therefore he, Berry, paid the ultimate price.

Keith "Grip" Matthews has another view in regard to Berry's loss at the polls: "In early 1988," Grip contends, "Berry had gotten transferred in his job from WASA North to WASA South and as a result was seldom in the pan-yard; I can't recall Berry even seeking to campaign in that election, worse yet, Berry's Vice-Captain, Cokey Telemaque was then even more absent than Berry, in fact Cokey was so distant that as official Vice-Captain of All Stars, he moved on to play with Renegades for Panorama for three years... the point is that neither Berry nor Cokey involved themselves in that election."[647]

Clive "Cokey" Telemaque informed that he had in fact started with Renegades before he joined All Stars in 1972, that he was elected Vice-Captain of All Stars on three occasions, that he did at some point resign from the Vice-Captaincy and went and played with Renegades for three years, 1990—*Iron-Man*; 1991—*Rant and Rave*; 1992—*Bees' Melody*, that he never had problems with Berry's Captaincy but he distrusted other persons who came to office.[648] There is a view expressed by some that the band did not play a composition by Cokey and his reaction was to go to Renegades for three years. Cokey informed that he did in fact compose *Is Pan* in 1989, sung by Protector who tied in first place with Tambu in the Young Kings competition that year but intimated that there were other factors that triggered his leaving.[649]

Berry's long-standing friendship with the elder Wells, since the Garret days, and his respect for this gentleman who was then doing his second music degree abroad, must have also served to cost Berry the captaincy since it was widely known that he, Berry, was prepared to accommodate Wells whenever available to arrange for All Stars, and, as mentioned above, Wells' arrangements had sent the band to the "Best of the Rest" category and there was mounting resentment about this.[650]

Another factor that militated against the 1987–1989 Executive, also mentioned above, would have been All Stars' unusual 3rd place position in the 1988 Music Festival, playing *Cappriccio Italien*, tune of choice, *Pan Waves*, test piece, and calypso, *Curry Tabanca*, despite, the fact, according to Grip, that the band was thrown off in the opening bars of *Cappriccio Italien* by the vibrating of Andy Cupid's tenor pan hooks that were not properly attached.[651] Reds Collins, however, gained much leverage from these happenings; he had no such affinity to Wells as Berry did, and once he, Reds, was back in control, he informed Wells that he was neither impressed nor happy with the quality of his Panorama work, and as a result sought to go back with Shortman Guerra aided by Deryck Nurse and Yohan Popwell.[652]

In 1991, All Stars got into the finals with *Get Something and Wave* arranged by Anthony Guerra but could only muster ninth place.[653] From 1992 to 1997, All Stars proved fortunate, through both Eddie Hart's and Cecil "Jimo" James' influence, to have Eddie Quarless join the ranks and his first offering was a sublime arrangement of Duke's *The Phung-Ug-Nung Sweet*, with which All Stars was able to reach as far as the semis.[654] There is, however, one staunch supporter of Desperadoes who swears to this day that that *Phung-Ugh-Nung* was really sugar sweet and rates it as one of the best offerings from All Stars bar none."[655]

And although a few All Stars players may be inclined to agree with that opinion, though not to the same degree, nevertheless, there are many who are left to wonder if someone can rate *Phung-Uh-Nung* this highly what would be that person's ratings for Eddie Quarless' subsequent three arrangements: 1993—*Dus In Dey Face*; 1994—*Pan Earthquake*; and 1995—*The Heavy Roller*.

The All Stars Newsletter describes this resurgence as follows: *…Tribute must be paid to Eddie Quarless for keeping the Trinidad All Stars* **peton** *alive… By our diligence and dedication, we returned to Panorama acclaim during the 1993 Carnival season. Our arrangement of David Rudder's* **Dus' in Dey Face** *received a standing ovation from both North Stand and Grand Stand at the Queen's Park Savannah, creating Panorama history unsurpassed! Even though we were awarded only third place. The crowd at the Savannah rose spontaneously, unhesitatingly, in acknowledgement of our virtuoso performance, chanting:* "**We want more! We want more**!"[656]

Reds Collins insist to this day that Eddie Quarless was at first adverse to the "Shot Call" rant that Guerra, Popwell and others wished to add to the arrangement,[657] however, Richard "Fats" Quarless, Eddie's elder brother, recalled that Eddie while at his home asked one of Fats' daughters what particularly the youths of the day loved about General Grant's rant "Shot Call!" which was then extremely popular and from the ensuing discussion Eddie included in the arrangement of *Dus in Dey Face* bits of the "Shot Call" motif inclusive of the "booyakaa, booyakaa" sound of heavy artillery employed by General Grant precisely because *Dus in Dey face* was about war, musical war… "it was that enhancement of the arrangement," Fats concluded, "that caused the Savannah to erupt."[658]

Smooth's view, supported strongly by Barbara Crichlow-Shaw, is vastly different to that of Reds and Fats Quarless, he insists that it was the intervention and input in the arrangement of *Dus* by Tony Guy, whose return from Japan for the Carnival was sponsored by the band, that made the difference.[659] When contacted Tony Guy, who now lives in Japan, said: *In '92, Eddie Hart asked me what I thought about the music that was being done by Eddie Quarless who was the arranger for panorama. Anthony "Shortman" Guerra and myself had worked with Smoothman from the early days doing in-house music for the band until Web and Uncle Jem handed the panorama mantle to Smoothman and the rest is history. I'd have to say that that was Eddie Hart's reason for asking my opinion. I told him what I thought and also pointed out what could be done to enhance the music. He asked me to meet with Quarless but I was reluctant to do so because of all that had happened in All Stars (1988).*

However, Eddie Hart convinced me to meet Quarless privately which I did and offered some pointers which were accepted by Quarless… he and I clicked from that meeting. In 1993, Quarless was again the arranger for All Stars and I was asked officially by the management to assist Quarless. However, in addition I received a call on the same issue from Roy Regis, who works quietly behind the scenes, doing so much for the welfare of the band. It was that call from Roy Regis, someone for whom I have great respect and admiration, which prompted me spiritually to make the decision to do it…

Tony Guy then explained his approach to working with Eddie Quarless: *I looked at Quarless as an investor with lots of resources (musical ideas) to invest and I was going to use my experience in the market-place (panorama) pointing out where, when and how much to invest. Of course it was no easy task as the members were not yet into his style of music and at times he wanted to emulate Smoothman's style. I told him that he should not do so. I also told the members that Quarless is NOT Smoothman and therefore his style and contribution will be different and it was time for them to get behind him and the music and play their asses off like they did back in the '80s.*

*Then it was coming down to the wire when the music needed to "**get down n' dirty**" and Quarless was open and ready to let me tweak it and do with it what my "rama" experience thought me over the years; most of all it is about including the people and all the elements that are synonymous with "de* rama"... *de panorama jumbie as we call it and of course it had to be done musically... de things that make people go crazy; and that final night rendition/performance was the result of that doing...*[660]

Tony Guy: he helped spice up "Dus in Dey Face" in 1993.

Considering the three views, it would seem that Eddie, though reluctant at first, may have finally become convinced of the inputs of others. But David Fraser of the Weekend Heat Newspaper looked deeper and said, *It was more than Dust in Dey face*, and he described the performance as follows: *Neal and Massy Trinidad All Stars last week turned on a "magic" not heard during their recent performances. Their mystical performance hypnotized the crowd from the beginning. When one thought at the middle passage of their tune that the arrangement would have been a repetition of what had passed in pieces played before, more came, one after the other, with hurricane force. If Pat Bishop was here she would have definitely remarked, despite how biased it may have been, of the performance's greatness.*

All Stars gave a rendition similar to the Fifth Movement of Mozart in F Major 7th. It was not Dust in Dey Face. It was golden; it was enlightening to each ear. Their runs were not singular, but backed up by well-arranged pieces played simultaneously by the double seconds and guitar pans, while leaving the tenor to create its spooky magic in the lead. The night, cloudy and damp, came to a luminous glow to the many thousands who helplessly allowed themselves to be entrapped in musical delusions of grandeur. Like a tribal pilgrimage to Africa, the crowd raised their hands as if they were responding to a call from Road March King, Superblue, or giving praise to their witch doctor. Testimony to this was the euphoric emanations of the mystified crowd enshrined in the beauty of musical harmony and the creativity and greatness of the men who discovered steel...

...Last year, the BOMB's Editor, Kit Roxburgh, now hospitalized, wrote of All Stars, and his piece reminded one of the pictures he recreated of the musical transcendence All Stars had thrown into the space-less sky over the Queen's Park Savannah. Life temporarily halted for a moment as sugar became sour, in the taste buds of many. "The ear is greater than any other sense God has given man", a middle-aged, half-white, semi-literate secretary shouted, when her body became possessed with the demon of Pan. "It is a serious instrument," said Peter Aleong, adding the PAN is not something to be played with. "It is a spiritual instrument, and only it can do this to people anywhere in the world," Peter said. As the atmosphere changed, it appeared as though musical notes were travelling through the grand stands in translucent form reminding the soul of who is in control of the power of "PAN". All Stars' musical wonder of "Dust in Yuh Face" left the Savannah mesmerized for the evening, and the world, for a lifetime...[661]

"...In 1994, Eddie Quarless" interpretation of Lord Kitchener's Pan Earthquake—another outstanding jewel among acclaimed Panorama gems, earned us second place..."[662] If, in reality, *Dus In Dey Face* brought "encore" demands from the crowd who were only appeased when they recalled that "encores" are facilitated in live concerts but are never allowed in such competitions, then, the rumblings of the musical earthquake simulated by Eddie Quarless' arrangement during that 1994 performance of Kitchener's masterpiece must have seemed so real that people were left literally "quaking" in their boots.

Eddie Quarless an excellent jazz musician, exponent of numerous instruments including, saxophone, flute and piano, also an ex-member of the police band, arranged Panorama selections for Trinidad All Stars from 1992 to 1997. His arrangement of David Rudder's "Dus in Dey Face" has gone down in Panorama history as the only occasion when the audience demanded an "encore".

Pic (Eddie in his younger years) courtesy the Quarless family. He died in 2014 at the age of 62.

Reds Collins informed that "Splav" Waddell from "Starlift" and "Third World" who was commentating that night came to All Stars and said that the band's performance of "Earthquake" was unbeatable and that up to that moment he was still feeling the tremors, and furthermore Reds intimated that the info from inside sources was that All Stars was first on the score-sheets of all the Judges until the last band, Desperadoes, played "Fire Coming Down".[663]

One newspaper commentator was so moved by the positions to which All Stars had been regulated in this period (1982–1995) that he coined a piece of satire in a letter to the editor titled "All Stars' Treasury of Losses". The following is what that person had to say: "…I would like to suggest to Pan Trinbago and the people who give national awards on Independence Day, a special award for Neal and Massy Trinidad All Stars as follows: "Greatest Collection of Pan Losses. " The honor roll to be read as follows: PANORAMA—1982—*"Heat"* 2nd placed (nearly achieved Panorama Hattrick); 1984—*"Doh Back Back"* 2nd place (had the crowd screaming); 1985—*"Soucouyant"* 3rd place (lost by one point!); 1987—*"Curry Tabanca"* 4th place (??); 1993—*"Dus" in Dey Face'* 3rd place (first and only ever (*calls for)* encore at Panorama); 1994: *"Pan Earthquake"*, 2nd Place (nearly got there); 1995—*"Heavy Roller"* 4th Place (that 4th place again!).

MUSIC FESTIVAL—1986: 2nd (won two out of three categories and somehow placed 2nd overall); 1992—2nd (lost because of one judge marking them 21 points behind (*the winner*). As anyone can see, All Stars' record is hard to beat and will not be equaled in the near future (Pamberi is a distant second!). That is why Trinidad All Stars is my pick for this special award…" That letter to the editor was signed: **LOVER OF "LOSING" PAN MUSIC— Diego Martin**. And the person ended the letter with the following "PS: *Congratulations to Eddie Quarless on a remarkable Panorama Hattrick— keep on jammin' dem!*"[664]

Despite the fiasco of the 1992 Music Festivals, wherein it was discovered that the aforementioned foreign judge who scored the winner 21 points ahead of All Stars was a personal and dear friend of the conductor of the said winning band, All Stars chose neither to file legal action nor complain and eventually was placed second losing by five points. However, undaunted, All Stars went on to top both the 1994 and 1996 Music Festivals, winning in each case two out of the three categories, i.e., Best Test Pieces and Best Calypsos, the respective calypso pieces being *Dus' in Dey Face* and *Earthquake* which must have made Eddie Quarless feel fully vindicated.[665]

Nelson Villafana

Then once again going for a hat-trick of Music Festivals in 1998, having won in both 1994 and 1996, under the musical directorship of Nelson Villafana, All Stars was once again made to feel the wrath of the Establishment. All Stars' Tune of Choice was *The Moldau,*[666] and their Caribbean Piece was *Excerpts from Shades of Port-of-Spain* by Rudy Wells. There was no Test Piece in 1998. **The Moldau,** described as a "symphonic musical poem" by composer Bedrich Smetana, assimilates the flow of a river from its mountainous sources, through the forest and the countryside, unto the City.[667]

It is played largely by flute and clarinet representing two different "spring sources utilizing the interplay of rapid, rippling notes" back and forth until the flow merges into a full-fledged river. It was described as a most enthralling and mind-blogging piece of music probably the most difficult ever attempted by a steel orchestra at the Music Festival. All Stars was thrown out of the Prelims by **one point** on the grounds that the band supposedly left out a section of the score.

Musicologist Dr. Jeanine Remy of Invaders openly denounced the fact that the best performance of the night was treated with such disdain and Pat Bishop lamented that the country as a whole would lose and be poorer for not hearing All Stars' *The Moldau* again in the semis and finals. All Stars were stunned that they, the band with the most outstanding music festival record were casually simply thrown out by the stroke of a conspiratorial pen for of all things *misreading the score*.

In 1996 and 1997, the panorama arranger, Eddie Quarless, stuck to arrangements of Kitchener's *Power of Music* and *Guitar Pan* placing 5th and 6th respectively.[668] Interestingly, a new feature was introduced in the Carnival proceedings of 1996. In an effort to encourage and enhance the presence of steelbands in the now much heavily commercialized, middle-class controlled Carnival, a "Pan and Mas Competition" was introduced with a first prize of $100,000 to the best steelband parading with costumed masqueraders at all four competition venues in Port-of-Spain.

Terry Joseph, cultural guru, now deceased, described what happened in this manner: *Neal and Massy Trinidad All Stars won the inaugural Pan and Mas Competition and has gone home with the whopping $100,000 first prize—three times as much as Amoco Renegades won for being adjudged the best band at the Panorama, just 72 hours before (Renegades won $32,000). But there is no argument from any quarter as everyone agreed that the All Stars were at their finest on Carnival Monday and Tuesday...*

...Each band in the contest was supposed to play a different tune at each of the four competition venues in Port-of-Spain and to present costumed masqueraders. All Stars did even better, by playing a medley of pop classics (including "Stardust", "Impossible Dream" and "Can't Live Without You") at Victoria Square, their Panorama selection ("The Power of Music") at the Savannah, "Pan in Ah Rage" at Adam Smith Square and the "Barber of Seville Overture" at South Quay. Their mas, Fleet's In (in Hawaii) featuring sailors in uniform as well as Hawaiian "hot shirts", was also well received by the crowd at the Savannah, where the band was accorded lusty applause. To win

the biggest prize ever in the history of steelband competitions is a status befitting the Neal and Massy Trinidad All Stars...[669]

According to Captain Beresford Hunte, All Stars won the "Pan and Mas Competition" which was the brain-child of the Minister of Finance in the then UNC Government, Senator Brian Kuei Tung, collecting thereby $100,000, half of which ($50,000) was deposited as savings at the Unit Trust, a matter that did cause some dissatisfaction among certain elements in All Stars, one of whom even went as far as to seek legal advice on whether the band as an entity possessed the legal ambit to invest such monies.[670] Some of that prize-money was also utilized as collateral to finance a loan from Pan Vesco to purchase a much needed Panel Van.[671]

There is no record of any such competition having been staged in 1997, but in 1998 a scaled down version "Pan On The Move" was held and All Stars won again playing *Me and Mih Lady* and another Neville Jules' medley—*At Last*, *Lady In Red* and *Try A Little Tenderness* but thereafter due to an injunction filed by Sagicor Exodus and the fact that the resulting litigation was never resolved, this particular competition was abandoned.[672]

The Panorama prize-money in those days were quite minimal, however the lesson to be learnt is that Panorama should not be the "be-all and end-all" for steelbands that are serious about the Carnival tradition and their institutional presence therein; furthermore, that the commitment to this tradition and to such a presence during Carnival pays off at the end of the day. All Stars has gained tremendously from such a commitment; every year collecting prize-monies both for playing music and masquerading at the various judging points while other steelbands simply fold up after Panorama and J'ouvert until the following year; All Stars has over the years reaped a financial bonanza as a result and has been placed on a sound financial footing that is unmatched by any other steelband, furthermore the actual level of payments pan players receive now from All Stars after each Carnival remains the best kept secret in T&T.

Nevertheless, by 1997, it seemed that the frustration of not officially having won Panorama with any of his six offerings began to affect Eddie Quarless negatively and the relationship between himself and All Stars began to deteriorate rapidly, to the extent that after Carnival 1997 the two parties came to the conclusion that a parting of ways was the only logical recourse. That opened the floodgates for the simmering groundswell that had been seething below for quite a while demanding the return of the Smooth-Man; it was a deep seated "tabanca" (melancholic yearning) that pervaded 46–48 Duke Street.

By 1995, Beresford Hunte who had lost to Red Collins in the previous elections was returned to the captaincy and realized at that point that no leader of the All Stars could have continued to ignore the groundswell demand for the return of Smooth Edwards, particularly after Eddie Quarless' departure. If Smooth's first sojourn in USA, Fort Lauderdale, to be exact, was short-lived, 1980 to 1983, his second sojourn in Washington, DC, was a full twenty years, 1988 to 2008; however, after 10 years, he began in 1998 to return at Carnival time merely to arrange for Panorama and only decided to move back fully to T&T in 2008.[673]

Smooth Edwards confessed that he experienced a spiritual awakening in Washington DC; "I was saved," he proclaimed, and that made him turn away from his former lifestyle and vowed from then on to engage the Pan instrument only in the service of the Church to which he became attached.[674] He said: "When I left All Stars all kind of bands approached me. After about two weeks in the US and by then being saved, I remember Ainsworth of Exodus calling and I said to him, boy I lost that desire. I was on a different head. And that was the end of the conversation with Exodus. When All Stars get lick up (i.e., Best of the Rest Category in 1989), they call me back the year after. I say I ain't have no zeal. Every year All Stars calling and ah saying I ain't feeling for pan. And then one night, about ten years later, I suddenly begin dreaming, just dreaming; this voice telling me: *if you don't use it, you go lose it*; *if you don't use it, you go lose it*; and I say, what is this, boy?"

"The only thing I could lose is the arranging, and that very week them fellahs from New York contact me and say, aye Smooth, we want you to go back and do arrangements. I say, all right, cool. But they did not believe; I had blank them for the past ten years. They say they coming down by me and they really come, Neville Jules, Banga (i.e., deceased Earl Lewis) and the Nelson boys, Sydney and Lennox, the four of them came, they brought a set of tapes from the band to try to convince me, and I say but ah already tell allyuh "yes" and that is how I began to arrange again. The committee then contacted me and we settle on the terms. That is the first time I give them fellahs a figure. I never give them a figure before. It was then whatever they give me."[675]

In reality, in 1998, it was the first time that Smooth chose to hammer out a purely professional contract from All Stars, the band in which he grew up as it had grown up so many others: Popwell, Deryck Nurse, Terry Demas, Cokey Telemaque, etc. In a later discussion, Smooth recalled that "Charlo", the then deceased flagman, used to call him constantly over the years begging him to return to arranging for All Stars.[676] In fact, while "Banga" (Earl Lewis), Sydney and Lennox Nelson and others in New York were considering the trip down to Washington to meet with Smooth, there were people at home engaged in discussion with the same objective of getting Smooth back. Once such session was held at the home of the lawyer, Kwasi Bekoe.

This meeting was held on July 14th 1997 at the home of the lawyer, Kwasi Bekoe, in Trincity. The major issue was the question of a formal approach to Smooth to return. From left, Jason "Stumps" Lewis, Denise Riley, Big L, Nelson Villafana (Musical Director), Steve Gomez, and Neville Jules. In the background, Bukka Rennie and Beresford Hunte (Captain).

Big L (Anthony John) addressing the meeting at Kwasi Bekoe's home in July 1997.

Eddie Hart was also present for that crucial meeting at Kwasi Bekoe's home in July 1997.

"In 1998, Smooth stepped back into the fray as if he had left only the day before.[677] Everyone took stock of his return. The PRO of Renegades, Steve Grant, sent a message to All Stars indicating that they intended to make the 1998 Panorama win their 10th and their fourth in a row playing Shanaqua's *Pan for Carnival*.[678] After the Prelims, Clive Bradley, then with Nutones of Arima for the then past three years, was ahead by 11 points and he said that he found it strange that Renegades, the three-time defending champs, was sending out threats to All Stars, that it was "the first time in history the champions were sending threats to anyone" and he confirmed that he had visited All Stars and found them to be "very good, they are the closest to me" then he concluded that Smooth is the only man with a chance to beat him: "I see Smooth and myself taking the Panorama," Bradley admitted.[679] One member of Nutones intoned: "We are moving with our little magician, Bradley... but we know Smooth is a dangerous man in a pan final. Do not trust him, he (Smooth) is one of the most dangerous arrangers ever..."[680]

After the North Zone Finals, Renegades were ahead of All Stars by two points. At the National Finals, Bradley's Nutones of the East Zone, playing Rudder's High Mas' won the Panorama just as he predicted and All Stars came third but as usual All Stars won the Peoples' Choice at that Panorama, and the Pan On De Road competition during the Carnival, as well as the Sunshine Award for the Best Steelband Recording for 1998.

Here then with the return of Smooth is the Panorama track record of Neal and Massy Trinidad All Stars up to 2006: 1998, *Me And Mih Lady*, placed **third** (Sunshine Award for best arranged Panorama recording, best On De Road and People's Choice); 1999, *Having a Ball*, placed **sixth**; 2000, *Jump For Joy*, **seventh**; 2001, *Rain Melody*, **second**; 2002, *Firestorm*, **first**; 2003, *Pandora*, **second**; 2004, *Ah Pay Mih Dues*, **second**; 2005, *Free Up, Free Up!*, **seventh**; and 2006, *Soca Warriors*, **second**.[681] Interestingly, there is a noted story about the choice of *Free Up, Free Up* for the 2005 Panorama. All Stars made the cardinal mistake of taking up the option offered by Pan Trinbago that year for competing large bands to do any of the past calypsos that were not done previously by the said band for a Panorama competition, despite the warning from many that that Pan Trinbago option was a recipe for disaster and a trap that would lead to nothing but failure. So said, so done.

Just as it was suggested, the recollection is that no band in the large-band category made any headway in that competition with a calypso of yesteryear, hence the seventh place allotted to All Stars. However, out of nine Panorama presentations since Smooth's return, All Stars, with his arrangements, gained one First place, four Second places, and one Third place. Mighty going for a supposed 'gatherer of notes'..."[682] "Smooth is not an arranger," said Pelham Goddard, "he is a gatherer of notes." Well, what a phenomenal gatherer of notes, for if one were to extend the above count to the year, 2007, when All Stars won its 6th Panorama with Smooth's arrangement of De Fosto's *Pan Lamentation*, then the first Million Dollar prize-winning band, the count for the 10 Panoramas, 1998 to 2007, would indicate 2 Firsts, 4 Seconds, and 1 Third, i.e., 7 top places out of a possible 10. How can anyone dare to suggest or to imply that such a level of success is the result of a hit or miss musical rambler?[683]

It was the hope and dream of All Stars people to win the 2006 Panorama with their choice, *Soca Warriors*, and be sent to Germany to play this music and stun the football world, but it was not to be; Phase 11 with "*This one is for you, Bradley*" won and went to Germany. It is all that which Tinika Davis had in mind when she felt moved to pen the following Facebook post:

...2006, I would have been 20 years old at that time. It was the most exciting Panorama ever. Was sure to win with this arrangement of Soca Warriors from de genius himself, Leon Edwards, Smooth man. We won people's choice but didn't win Panorama. This was the year I fell out of love with pan. Thinking about it now I probably fell outa love with Panorama and dem judges. LoL. I was heartbroken. Like devastated. Like mih own mother and father died. At 20 years old after results I jumped between my moms and pops on their bed musbe after 3 or 4 de morning and cry like ah baby.

Is when ah made up mih mind to jus do it, duh the hustle and de fun cus you sacrifice life, limb, family time, relationship time, friendship time. Loss wuk kinda sacrifice cus you could either dead driving to wuk cus yuh sleeping on yuself or sleeping on de job so no wuk happening. On top ah dat, de arrangement, execution, delivery and response from audience couldn't be disputed and WE STILL DIDN'T WIN! So da was dat wid de passion I had for pan and panorama. Lost de zeal to commit after dat. Just went on de hustle cus de money done small and de judging was shit, and being a pannist at dat time was my occupation. So, eh heh, good.

But other than dem sour vibes, I enjoyed playing on the stage side. Played percussion for this on Timbales and Bongos. Love double-seconds but this song... especially de jam... oui pa! Ah used to feel de pores on de back ah mih neck raising as we transitioning to it and as we left de 4 to start de WAR... like ah gun shot went off in my head and is shots firing on dem skins. Musbe was one pack ah shit ah playing but de feeling ah was reeling ah couldna care less. Just felt an intense focus but still light and free to fire. Smooth got de magic yo! I'll forever have a love/hate relationship with that song and panorama final. Lol! Learned a lot as a player and performer from this band. Need to get back some of dat discipline and dedication and commitment to TEAM. Big up Smooth and de Trinidad All Stars Family.[684]

Smooth's success with All Stars is the result of phenomenal talent, and so, in discussing his ability virtually to "make the dead stand up and dance," particularly when in his arrangements he launches into what is now regarded as re-harmonization of the melodic lines and chord structure of the original work, this is what this author had to say: "Listen, I am neither professional musician nor musicologist, whatever the hell that is, but I can say the following. When Smooth leaves, the verse and chorus of the original piece of music, and, as is the Panorama requirement, begins to develop the melodic theme or melodic lines, his strong point or forte is not so much the rephrasing of the lines, for which Bradley was the noted genius, but rather the mastery of creating fresh, new melodies that harmonize with the original theme and provide a coherent framework…"

"Most times these new melodies of Smooth prove to be even sweeter than the original work. In other words, there is a certain power and beauty that result from his changes based on the supportive pattern of chords which give the impression of a new melody though the original melody is ever present in sound that can be heard throughout the performance moving from one section of the band to another and back and forth. The audiences scream, shout and dance because he connects. And he is never afraid to repeat so as to sustain rhythmic appeal…"[685]

"Sometimes in the course of his harmonizing he proves able to create a classical-type ambiance and mood as in *Rain Melody*; a jazzy-jam effect as in *Fire-Storm*; even a melancholic, almost cathartic feel as in *Pay Mih Dues* (the best comparison would be Bradley's Pan In Danger for Carib Tokyo); or a straight, constant, celebratory calypso breakaway which he must have deemed essential to the theme of *Soca Warriors*, a jovial jam-song comprising a string of simple musical hooks… The point is that it is all Smooth's way, it is never borrowed, and it is his own way of doing and interpreting. In the end, all arrangers use certain time-worn musical tools and devices to create the effect they desire. There is no rocket science to it. When all the ingredients in the mix are there in the right measure and in the right order, the totality of the product provides aesthetic pleasure…"

"…Those who sit in the Yard, night after night, listening attentively to Smooth building his musical craft, will tell you that there comes a specific moment, THE MOMENT, when all the intrinsic parts of the piece of work suddenly gel together and breathes itself to birth; no one wishes to miss that trilling moment. In the end, it is all subjective. It either moves you or not; there is either connection or disconnection. When for instance, an arranger from the West walked into his band yard and told all the players to each hold and roll any note of their choice at a particular point in the arrangement, that was described to us by many from the West as sheer genius but to the same people Smooth's creative splurges in the arrangement of *Soca Warriors* is musical trash. The proof of the pudding is in the eating."

"Smooth moves more people than most of the other arrangers, and that is probably why, under his guidance, All Stars continued to monopolize the sporadic People's Choice category over the years, just as they had done before his time. The category of People's Choice was abandoned largely because of this fact. When the People's Choice category was reintroduced in 2006, Arnim Smith, then a top Pan Trinbago official, remarked: 'like allyuh want to give All Stars money again'."[686]

At the same time, all this was happening and Smooth was continuing to work his magic in 2007 winning the Panorama with *Pan Lamentation*, which was the year when All Stars took away Boogsie's proverbial whip,[687] Neville Jules, then 80 years old, was also continuing from afar to add to his contribution to the All Stars musical war machine.

The Smooth-Man now in his adult years. Having returned to the All Stars fold in 1998, he has been able with his arrangements to keep All Stars in winners' row almost as a matter of course. He, more than all other arrangers, connects with the listening public and makes them dance. Pan Trinbago had acclaimed him "Best Arranger for the Eighties," but since his 1998 return he has proven even more successful.

In an article titled "Who is Neville Jules?" the following was said: *In 2007, Neville Jules was enjoying his 80th year and the man was still wining "Pan in the 21st Century" and "Bomb" competitions with his arrangements of pieces such as "Mas Que Nada", "Mood Indigo", "Green, Green Grass of Home". "How Great Thou Art", "The Good, the Bad and the Ugly", etc. arrangements that he sends down annually from New York for his beloved Trinidad All Stars to rule the roost come Carnival. In fact both in 2006 and 2007 All Stars won all the Bomb Competitions, at four out of four judging locations, with Jules' arrangements. Interestingly, after Bradley, the eminent steelband music-arranger, died, the world famous pan virtuoso, Andy Narell, was asked by When Steel Talks (WST) if he could identify anyone to take up the mantle, and Andy Narell said: "There's a 79 year old guy called Neville Jules who is the elder Statesman of arrangers as far as I'm concerned. His Bomb Tunes are some of the sweetest steelband music ever created..."*[688]

Raf Robertson, the local jazz pianist, recently added to this view of Neville Jules when he said: *I judged a J'ouvert pan contest (Bomb competition) a few years ago and All Stars came up... Neville Jules brought the band up and they played his arrangement of "Theme from The Good, The Bad and The Ugly" (which Jules arranged when he was 78) and I'm in awe of a guy who has never been to music school, but adheres to all the principles of arranging. Arranging period. Like art, it needs balance. And I'm hearing all the harmonies, all the lines... I say but this guy is a genius, though they may call him an icon...*[689]

When Jules turned 70, another commentator said: "To reach the 70-year milestone in life is a great achievement. To reach it on a wave of gentility, respect, adoration and acknowledgement and acceptance of one's lifetime endeavors as a positive contribution to the development and enrichment of one's community is an extraordinary accomplishment..."[690] That commentator concluded that "as much as he (Jules) was enmeshed in music and the instruments, Neville was forever concerned with the bringing together of the Community. He never denied the nurturing and blooming of talent. As the most illustrious leader of Trinidad All Stars, he was always eager to pass on his unique God-given talent. He never indulged in "dotish" recrimination and undue defamation of fellow All Stars.

Jules was the supreme leader. It is acknowledged that he never got his full due as a supreme panman—as instrument-maker, tuner, arranger and deft pan-player. We thank Pan Trinbago and the corporate community, therefore, for having brought some joy to Jules by highlighting his unique pan innovation, the Bomb, as one of the main competitions come Carnival time…"[691] It is on that legacy of Jules that All Stars, the social institution, by dint of history is commanded at all times to seek to build and to measure itself in the journey to fulfill its destiny. There are many who are yet to comprehend the true nature of All Stars, this steelband that transforms itself, come every Carnival, into a most devastating musical war machine.

In 2010, Trinidad All Stars went to the Panorama a deeply divided organization. The underlying factor was that Smooth Edwards decided to take the Band into the competition with his own composition "Large is Large" which, unlike his 2008 composition "Pan Rivalry", did not meet with the approval of the majority of the pan-playing members and supporters; the melody just did not resonate with the people. With "Pan Rivalry" it was a case of instant "love" from 100% of the players and supporters, so Smooth did not have to lobby for that choice. On the other hand, De Fosto's "Smooth Sailing" described by many as a Panorama gift to the band had all the hallmarks of an All Stars "winner", and people were convinced that Smooth's insistence on "Large is Large" was tantamount to throwing away a Seventh Panorama for the band.

A small but influential group of the older players stood firm with Smooth and were demanding that the arranger must be allowed to have his way regardless of tradition; while the majority which comprised the younger players, a large chunk of whom were young women, objected strenuously to the virility of the attempt to impose. In regard to the Sixth Panorama win in 2007, that made All Stars the first "million-dollar" prized band, Smooth himself admitted in an interview that the choice of De Fosto's "Pan Lamentation" came as a result of "discussion",[692] however on this occasion he seemed not interested in such an engagement.

There developed a stand-off when Smooth told the Management team to find another arranger if they were not prepared to go with "Large is Large" and that he would have to be compensated for the cost he accrued in hiring a singer and musicians to produce a recording of "Large is Large".[693] Management found themselves with their hands tied when it was discovered that Smooth had already collected an advance from the sponsors, Neal and Massy, for arranging the Panorama tune, so at the end of day, it was a done deal, All Stars was forced to go with "Large is Large".[694] Practice sessions throughout that Carnival season were quite lukewarm; in fact Smooth himself was absent from most of the sessions.

All Stars went through the motion without its usual panache and gusto and was placed third on the final night. The proof of the pudding is the eating; whenever All Stars played the verse and chorus of "Smooth Sailing" on the road Carnival Monday and Tuesday, the reaction of the crowds told the whole truth and nothing but the truth. People became more convinced that a Panorama winner had been thrown away. Regardless of the methodology utilized to select the Panorama tune, what is key to the success of All Stars is that synergy between players and arranger. This has been proven time and time again.

JUBILATION in the Neal and Massy All Stars camp after Panorama finals

The 2007 "Pan Lamentation" victory: Terry Demas raised the trophy high in salute of the first million dollar winning band.

Some months after that Carnival, an article appeared in one of the weekly newspapers condemning the Management Team for being "apathetic" and "indifferent", for "not knowing that time does not change; it is the essence of life," blaming them for "a more than 50% drop in its ability and capacity to attract revenue through performances et al;" for not recognizing that "there is an utter need for a shake-up of the administering body of the organization" and most interestingly the article concluded that "time is overly against the present "moribund" administration; but it's on the side of the complainants/ innovators."[695]

So, the logic therein is that "the present management does not know that time, the essence of life, does not change; yet time is overly against the present management." To put such logic into any coherent framework, one would have to be completely irrational, particularly given the fact that the present management of All Stars has generated the greatest level of income and assets in the history of the entire steelband movement and has attained an economic growth path unsurpassed by any other period in the band's history. Interestingly some of the people the article indirectly quoted and mentioned were some of the very people who were belligerently insisting on "Large is Large". Was the Panorama-choice issue the salient factor underlying this rather mysterious but critical newspaper article? Only time will tell!

Come July 2011, Smooth indicated the following: "There are people making much more money than me outside here. *I still have the All Stars thing for the band*. If I really go to charge them what other bands paying; in that case, All Stars owe me money. *A prophet has no honor in his own home*. I'll be honest, this year a medium band approached me and they send me a contract and I send a copy to All Stars, if that is what a medium band offering me, then All Stars have to get their act together. I ain't know what I will say when it is time again to sit down…"[696] Later on, references were made by Smooth to what Professor was getting from Courts Sound Specialists and what Ray Holman was demanding and getting despite not winning Panorama.[697]

Interestingly, it has been established that on his return to arranging in 1998, the terms of his service were hammered out with the executive committee and there was contractual consensus; Smooth was paid all that he requested each year for the ten years (1998–2008) that he returned for Carnival and payment included his air-plane tickets. Now Smooth gets the figure that All Stars can afford comfortably plus an ex-gratia bonus if the result is a Panorama win. The All Stars management, however, remains adamant that the players must also be compensated fully for their output precisely because no victory is possible without their commitment to the Panorama effort.

However, because of the peculiar history, one sometimes senses from Smooth a rather complex mix of a strained, emotional attachment to the band coupled with an underlying, cerebral requirement for a stark, objective professional relationship; in other words, on the one hand he seems to want a strictly professional arrangement with All Stars, while, on the other hand, there is this old emotional connection that desires more out of the relationship, and that the key issue is not money. However, when asked about this, Smooth's definite response was that he desires today only a straight forward professional relationship with the band but as the arranger he feels that "some room should be left to him in deciding the choice of tune..."[698]

One is then left to wonder about the great possibilities that would most certainly emanate from any mutual healing between this genius panorama arranger and this band that expresses his music as no other can. This is a band which, the elders past insisted, was a "family" whose greatest leader and steel-pan music inventor, Neville Jules, has never been fully acknowledged by society, just as it is widely accepted today that its greatest panorama arranger, Leon "Smooth" Edwards, is likewise consistently spurned by certain elitist elements. Today, the time demands a closing and a tightening of the ranks within Trinidad All Stars.

The question that the then management team had to consider is whether the newspaper article mentioned above signaled a new level of monetary and emotional demands from the general membership and whether this news report in anyway reflected any genuine smoldering of antagonism against their administration, and, if this was in fact so, what were the issues and policies that had to be addressed immediately. But even if it was all a matter of some person or persons merely playing politics or harboring a political agenda vis a vis the next band elections, it never hurts for an Executive to be introspective and to constantly review administrative policies, plans and overall vision. The lessons learnt from 1967 and 1988 ought to be chilling reminders.

In both of these cases, remuneration and recognition for function was the underlying issue that was left unaddressed and eventually fed emotional outbursts that led to the splits. Was the then Management team been fully modern, democratic and transparent in its operations? Had the membership been presented with all the details of how the band's largesse is being invested and/or distributed? Had the vision of the then executive been fully ventilated to the satisfaction of all and sundry, and if not, why not?

For example, at that very moment, there was a burning need to expand the number of players on the stage-side. The stage-side had over time become almost a closed-shop with new, able members desiring to get in but seemingly knocking on an apparently closed door. It is said that a few of the stage-side members earned so much playing out almost every weekend in the year that they did not have to spend salaries that they earn from their regular 8 to 4 employment. The fact that some of the new members were unemployed did make the issue a pressing one. A rather simple but effective solution emerged logically as a result of an interesting development that took place in 2008.

It was the year that All Stars placed second in the Panorama playing Chucky's *Thunder Coming* but having won in 2007 and being the very first million dollar prized band, it proved enough for All Stars to be provided with a most lucrative contract to perform in Spain for 4 months.

The following extract describes that 4-month extravaganza: *Expo Zaragoza 2008 held in Spain is an international Exposition consisting of over 100 participating countries of which 14 are from the Caribbean Community and the Trinidad All Stars Steel Orchestra was contracted to provide steelband music daily (approximately 440 performances) at the Caribbean Pavilion from June 9 to September 14, 2008. One local newspaper reported that at one of the forty-five minutes performances, the fourteen pan musicians of the Trinidad All Stars steel orchestra had over 800 patrons who were not familiar with its sounds swaying their hips and tapping their feet to the infectious music. The orchestra received a standing ovation and continued playing after receiving numerous encores. Their music and the trimmings in the Caribbean Pavilion certainly transformed it into a Caribbean atmosphere enjoyed by all in attendance...*

Owing to its unique sound and being the only new acoustic musical instrument invented in the last century, the steelpan, which can play all types of music, continues to fascinate patrons who have neither seen nor heard this instrument before. The dexterity of its players and the versatility of the instrument are main contributors to its success... The Caribbean Pavilion (there were also performers from Barbados, Bahamas, Antigua and Barbuda as well as St. Lucia) continues to attract thousands of visitors daily and is rated in the first 5 of all the pavilions at the Expo and has been earmarked as the venue for the closing Party hosted by the Commissioner of the Exposition. Congratulations to the Caribbean Community...[699]

It was described by Berry as a most grueling tour; the band had to learn new music unique to Spain and on some days they did provide as much as 4–5 performances but at the end of the tour each member returned with significant financial returns, and even those members of the stage-side who practiced but were not chosen to go on that tour were also paid out of the returns.[700] That special provision has exposed to Management a methodology that can in future be utilized to remunerate all concerned for their consistent involvement in the affairs of the band, in fact Web Alexander, No. 8 Captain, indicated that this measure of paying those who practiced but were not chosen to go on tour, was first introduced during his captaincy.[701] Whether or not such remuneration had occurred in the past, it certainly had not yet been made a policy imperative.

But that was not the only solution to the administrative problems of the stage-side that was posed in 2008. The tour was for such a long duration that something had to be done to cover the demands for appearances and performances by All Stars on the local scene. Normally with all steelbands the approach would be to forego taking on jobs locally because; "the band on tour". Smooth having returned to T&T permanently in 2008 was present and made a sterling contribution in keeping the rest of the stage-side, inclusive of a few new people, practicing and up to mark with the repertoire so much so that after some time there was the expected banter and brag that the "B" side at home better than the "A" side in Spain.

The talk in fact took on added dimension when Smooth took the then local-based stage-side to the first "Eight of Hearts" concert put on by "Vice" Cudjoe and his team at the Angostura Compound and there All Stars virtually mopped up the place against all contenders including Phase 11 and Desperadoes with tonal quality and a repertoire that was beyond compare. The dominance of All Stars' so-called "B"—Side was so devastating and complete that silence reigned thereafter; not one single report of All Stars' supremacy on that night has ever been published. Town, simply dumbfounded, refused to talk. The solution posed was that the stage-side could readily be divided into two complete self-contained units, thereby opening up the room to include new members who are desirous of playing professionally as the main source of their daily upkeep.

But at the second "Eight of Hearts" in 2010, there was no such silence afterwards. In a piece titled: "Eight of Hearts Concert—All Trumphs", the following is what was said about All Stars: *In my opinion, many of the steelbands in Trinidad have a tremendous amount to learn from All Stars in terms of performance protocol. Jerry Jemmott left an indelible mark on All Stars in terms of performance, and when you couple that with the repertoire in their arsenal, it is a difficult act to beat. Earlier on I used the metaphor of an All Fours game to talk about the concert and referred to each band's performance as high, low, jack and game. Well, as far as All Stars was concerned, you have to add a hang-jack to the mix—in spite of the fact that eight of hearts is high. Virtually impossible—but I think you know what I mean. All Stars played two medleys—one which had vocalist Sheldon Reid mixing it up with the patrons.*

In addition to having an excellent voice, Sheldon really knows how to interact with patrons. He diplomatically found the most beautiful women in the audience to croon songs like Help Me Make It Through The Night, Can't Live Without You and Let It Be Me and before that, the band played J.S. Bach's Air On A G-String. This particular piece had all the nuances that All Stars is famous for, and on this night, the band did not disappoint. While I am sure that most people were tapping their feet while they sat and listened to all the bands before All Stars, it would be fair to say that it took this long for people to actually leave their seats and form a bit of a dance floor in front of the band as they played what may be termed the anthem of calypso arrangements in Trinidad—Woman On The Bass. For me, it does not matter how many times I have heard this arrangement or rendition of Woman On The Bass, it sounds fresh every time...[702]

Another outstanding issue was summarily addressed objectively later in 2010 when Management decided to go forward with the Classical Jewels NAPA Project. Since Classical Jewels V111 in 1991 under the musical directorship of Nelson Villafana, All Stars had ceased to continue with the two-year concert program for 19 years. Furthermore, Nelson Villafana died in October 2002 and likewise the Band had chosen not to appoint a classical musical director to replace him. There is an aspect of this issue that was raised by Smooth Edwards and which probably needs to be debated: Smooth Edwards was of the view that what is required now is not a Musical Director but a Classical Music Arranger,[703] in other words, Smooth did not say it, but the implied logic would seem to suggest that there be a Panorama/Calypso Arranger and a Classical Music Arranger, two separate and distinct positions of equal rank.

During the Jemmott Years, Uncle Jem as Musical Director was such an imposing influence that he naturally took responsibility to "clean up" the Panorama tune, and it was not unusual at Classical Jewels Concerts for Leon "Smooth" Edwards to be listed as the Assistant Musical Director. But much has flowed under the bridge since those halcyon days.

So, come November 2010, someone had to rise to the challenge of the occasion and Deryck Nurse, another product of All Stars and a recent music postgraduate from the University of the West Indies, rose to fill the breech to the max. Initially, there were some doubting-Thomases who were not convinced that Classical Jewels 1X could possibly be accomplished, but, as rehearsals began, Deryck Nurse's true reading of the authentic classical music scores was way beyond all expectations and his mind-boggling competence served quickly to push all doubts aside as everyone banded together in a united effort that was glorious to behold.[704]

The richness of the program raised "goose-pimples" on the arms and skins of the audiences and the accolades and encomiums flowed: "Last Sunday's staging of Classical Jewels 1X was another clear reminder of why Neal and Massy Trinidad All Stars is reputed to be **the finest steel orchestra in the world**… And while there was no panel of adjudicators to give this verdict, that did not diminish the fact that the celebrated steel orchestra delivered a high-energy, scintillating performance, that repositioned it to the pinnacle of pan. Under the musical direction of principal conductor Deryck Nurse, the production was arguably the best of its kind in years… Classical Jewels was a divine opportunity for Trinidad All Stars to show off not just its music making magic, but the home-grown talent of its sons and daughters…"[705]

This band has never in its long history had to import talent from outside, all the other bands have had to do so at some point. This is why we describe All Stars as an institution as well as a nurturing family, because children virtually grow up here and become accomplished adults in the musical as well as other fields, just consider the likes of people like Deryck Nurse, Dane Gulston, Clive Telemaque, Yohan Popwell, Terry Demas, Mia Gormandy, Jacqueline Smith, etc. and as Roy Regis points out no other band in history has had "more brothers", actual siblings, than All Stars and that list is quite extensive, starting from the 1930s to the present: the Drayton brothers (5); the Olliverres (5); the Mitchells (3), the Alexanders (5) (Ellis, Hugh, Oscar, etc.), the Stowes (3); the Longs; the Grants; the Nurses; the Wells'; the Haynes's; the Andrews's of Mt. Hope (6)—Mervyn, Donny, Kurt, Alvin, Michelle and Kijana. Quite notably children and grand-children followed parents and grand-parents into the social institution that is All Stars; signaling thereby a bonding that is stronger than the norm. That was the sense one got while seated in NAPA experiencing Classical Jewels 1X.

Another report read as follows: "*On Saturday evening the music was sweet but the show was just too short... The audience rewarded the musicians with a standing ovation at the end of what must be hailed as a magnificent performance on the night... Under the direction of Deryck Nurse, the All Stars opened with the rousing "Fanfare For The Common Man", a piece composed by Aaron Copeland in 1942 originally for brass and percussion. The bright tones of the steelpans brought new life to the music... The band followed that piece up with "Air On A G-String" from Johann Sebastian Bach's Orchestral Suite No.3 in D Major and "Shades of Port of Spain" by Rudy Wells (also home-grown). Long-standing All Stars member, Clive Telemaque then took center stage to perform "Helter-Skelter" and would return later in the evening to perform "Czardas" alongside fellow seasoned pannists, Dane Gulston, Yohan Popwell and Terry Demas... June Nathaniel sat in to direct the All Stars as they performed "Finlandia" and later on, "Barber of Seville".*

Another guest conductor was Jessel Murray who took over the baton when the band played "In A Monastery Garden" and "Chorus Of The Hebrew Slaves"... Mia Gormandy performed "El Rio" on tenor receiving cheers and whistles as she exited the stage following her rendition that saw the pannist moving as fast as lightening around the steelpan then at the drop of a hat delicately brushing the notes slowly almost like a gushing river of water becoming calm and settled..."[706] The other daughter of All Stars featured at the concert was Jacqueline Smith of Marionettes Chorale fame, who played bass pan in All Stars for three Panorama performances, and who on the night "*filled the hearts of the masses with a touching performance of Ave Maria.*"[707]

In the end, it was all summed up in this way: *After 19 years in stasis, Trinidad All Stars wiped the dust from the legendary music brand, Classical Jewels, under its banner, only to discover that the trademark is just as pristine as the day it was put into the time capsule. To the absolute delight of music* lovers... the superb steel orchestra reminded patrons of the wealth of talent that abounds within... As fate would have it however, the band staged the event this year to toast its 75th anniversary and (to) declare that Classical Jewels—the Millennium Series—would begin in 2012...[708]

Then, it was onto Panorama 2011. If All Stars in 2010 was divided, drooping, flaccid and lukewarm, in 2011 they were united in effort, focused, hot and vamping. The entire production process of Classical Jewels 1X had welded the musical war machine back to normalcy, with its historic panache and gusto. Moreover the choice of "Showtime" as the panorama tune was greeted with a collective vibe, everybody was in synch. With All Stars in such a state of oneness and readiness, it may have been a cardinal mistake for Alvin Daniell to suggest that "All Stars was the show band of the '80s and imply that Silver Stars, (hoping not merely for a hat-trick but also for a beaver trick), was the show band of the present day."

That statement when reported brought smiles to the faces in Hell Yard. And the smiles became chuckles of amusement when, according to the report, it was further suggested by Alvin Daniell that Silver Stars were going "to have to finish (their) tune with a flourish that is going to make Bravo (Donell Thomas) flip this time on stage."[709] And therein lies another story.

When Yohan Popwell and Barry Bartholomew desired to take a section of All Stars players which included, Yakeem, Coombs, Dane, Nigel Williams, etc. into the second Pan Ramajay Competition, they ended up using both Eastside Potential Symphony's pan yard and pans and went into that competition registered as Potential Symphony and won, and then as Panazz Players at which point they won three consecutive Pan Ramajay competitions. They contend to this day that the then Captain, Reds Collins, blanked them outright from going to the Ramajay using All Stars' instruments and name on the grounds that that form of jazz ensemble music was not All Stars' forte and therefore not in All Stars' interest, punto finale.[710] Yohan Popwell insists that they would have gladly used All Stars' name if they were allowed.[711]

As a result, the ensemble from All Stars resorted initially to utilizing Potential Symphony's facilities and began highlighting on the bass a seven-year old boy they met at Potential's yard and who as a result became widely known in pan circles; his name, Donell Thomas aka "Bravo". On that final night of Panorama 2011, "Bravo" could have flipped over on stage any amount of times, it would have meant little; the fate of Sliver Stars had been sealed, they had come face to face finally with the real musical juggernaut, the All Stars musical war machine and the authentic show-band of all time bar none, ready, united and focused. Indeed, after all the rehearsing and drilling had been accomplished and everyone was well-oiled, primed and chumping at the bait as they waited to go on stage, Reds Collins, when he was captain, was wont to say at such crucial moments: "All Stars, tonight is de Bongo Night!"[712]

They performed "Festive Overture" under the guidance of the principal conductor for Classical Jewels 1X, Mr. Deryck Nurse.

Mia Gormandy performing "El Rio". She was a frontline tenor player in All Stars before going abroad to pursue her studies and development as a professional pannist and musicologist. Congrats to Mia—the 2014–15 recipient of the Howard Mayer Brown Fellowship for promising minority graduate students pursuing a doctoral degree in music. This Fellowship was presented to her by the American Musicological Society for research on her dissertation, "Pan in Japan".

Smooth welcomes the President of the Republic of Trinidad & Tobago to Classical Jewels 1X, while Berry looks on.

June Nathaniel conducted "Finlandia" and "Barber of Seville".

Gervase Warner, the CEO of Neal and Massy Holdings, expressed what he experienced with All Stars at Panorama 2011. He said: *Final night, we (on) the track. Another band was playing where they should not have been playing along the track, so we couldn't stop where we would normally stop to practice. The organizers say come forward, come forward, and just before the stage, they say, alright, alright, you could stop here and take your last practice if you* like. Some people were pushing forward, some people stopping and telling Berry, you could practice here.

But Berry said, "We don't need to practice, It's Showtime!"[713] And playing first posed no terror for All Stars—the band had played at the No. 1 position in 1973 and won its 1st Panorama, and would you believe on the same day in March 2011 as in March 1973, i.e., March 5th. The older folks of Hell Yard who hold institutional memory kept harping on such a fall of fate and the fact that unknown to most people, All Stars in the middle of the Year 2010 held a review session and decided then that the Mas for Carnival Monday 2011 will be called "SHOWTIME", and that was long before there was any calypso composition called, Showtime. "All Stars cyar lorse dis Panorama," the old folks kept harping, too many coincidences were in the band's favor.

But with this musical war machine nothing was left to the mere fall of fate. The Smooth-Man's arrangement of Edwin Pouchet's Showtime was devastating. This is what one commentator said of the performance: "What can I say? Like the adjudicators, I, too, was star-struck when Neal and Massy Trinidad All Stars put down an explosive showtime, taking the fight to champion band PCS Silver Stars. Right in their backyard, All Stars delivered the death-blow, denying the Silver Stars a hat-trick of wins. It was a master stroke by Leon Edwards (Smooth) who shelved his own tune this year, plucking Showtime from a bag of some 58 pan songs (at last count). I've always said that Smooth has this uncanny knack of selecting a song to stir the savannah crowd..."[714]

Another commentator who interviewed Smooth had this to say: "...Leon "Smooth" Edwards, arranger for Trinidad All Stars, just might be a prize fighter the way he used the knockout to punch the lights out of his adversaries at the Queen's Park Savannah... Last Saturday night, Edwards proved that he could tear out the guts of a watch and make it whole again, but in his own image. You could tell how, in the panyard, he had sauntered into his own head as composer and sprang back out having remade the work more personal. And that's how Trinidad All Stars won the Panorama..."[715]

And the commentator went on to quote Smooth saying: "**It's showtime and All Stars is about show**," Edwards said. *People are saying we have the strongest frontline pans, but we also have the strongest bass players. It was a conversation in pan. We brought out the middles, too. Serious conversation about Show-Time. It's in the same line as all the classics I've done, including*

Woman on the Bass, which still rules after 31 years. The commentator then said that Edwards wasn't just mouthing off. His victory left Exodus, Phase 11 Pan Groove and Silver Stars watching from the canvas as every Duke Street star pranced around in celebration, and he concluded by describing the Panorama as a true "slugfest".[716]

And it was once again a clean sweep for All Stars for in conjunction with the Panorama win, the band, playing Terry Demas' arrangement of *You Are My Special Angel*, won all but one of the Bomb Competitions organized at the various judging points throughout the city.[717]

At the victory party organized by the Neal and Massy Holdings Group held at the Belmont Salon of the Hilton Hotel on May 20, 2011, the CEO of the Group, Mr. Gervase Warner admitted that the conglomerate he leads "can learn from the band's unique approach to teamwork." He is reported to have said that Trinidad All Stars is a specialized institution to which the business community should pay close attention, that in the corporate environment of Neal and Massy "we are always trying to get hundreds of people to work together, to work as a whole, to look out for one another and play their part in harmony and synchronous melody. The hard work, the dedication, the drills and the enjoyment that you'll see to get out of it; it is like you were born to play pan. I think that there is something fantastic about that, that we as a corporation can take away from what you'll have done… This year, when I came down to the panyard, the thing that struck me the most was a unique energy from the band. It was like a different kind of togetherness. It was like one force. I knew something was up this year. You all could have felt it, too. I think that is a big part of what the Trinidad All Stars has always been about. Quite frankly, it is what we at Neal and Massy are about…"[718]

Little did Mr. Warner know that he was in fact reiterating what Andy Narell said after having worked on a concert at Queen's Hall with All Stars in 2007: "I can't say enough about the dedication and work ethic of Trinidad All Stars, a truly world class orchestra… Over the course of six months they put in more than 100 rehearsals to learn the music and prepare for the concert and they taught me a lot about togetherness and unity of purpose…"[719]

In conclusion, Mr. Gervase Warner was reported to have saluted the All Stars management under the guidance of its then captain and general manager, Beresford Hunte, for their foresight, and he advanced the view that the blessings bestowed unto Trinidad All Stars was underpinned by its unswerving commitment to fostering and maintaining well-knit community relations in East Port-of-Spain, and that the opportunities All Stars provides for youth in that caption area to come in and be part of something that is successful, be part of a team that wins, is really tremendous, and as a result of all this he surmised that Neal and Massy Trinidad All Stars "**are a force for good**."[720]

The idea of All Stars being a "force for good" was also reinforced by Dalton Narine, a Vietnam veteran and a one time All Stars player who admitted the role played by All Stars and Neville Jules in his rehabilitation and recuperation from the psychological effects of that war through his "*re-introduction to All Stars music and extreme regimen*" which "*saved his life.*"[721] What a testimony.

On Friday, 16 September 2011, Neal and Massy Trinidad All Stars left on a thirteen day tour to Singapore where they performed at the Singapore Grand Prix Formula 1 event together with some 300 world famous artistes including Shaggy, Mariah Carey and Shakira.[722] The tour was done on the invitation of a Trinidad-born entrepreneur who resides there. "We made our mark in Singapore and made T&T proud," said Beresford Hunte. However, Berry took time to point out that having won the 2011 Panorama, which guaranteed All Stars the first prize award of a lofty $2 million, brought to the band a new stress level.

Berry explained: "This may surprise you, but winning the 2011 Panorama was like a two-edged sword. Folks found us and poured out their hearts and soul, outlining their respective needs before the band settled and worked out a plan of how to properly invest. It seems as if winning turned losing… suddenly, the band owed any and everyone, even some promoters, when we quoted our price to perform, suddenly found we were charging too much to perform, also, neither government, private sector nor anyone else so much as hired the band to do an overseas tour, though one band that was not even in the Panorama was given an overseas contract…"[723]

In the meantime, Berry said that All Stars will continue to "make a difference in our community, and, among other things, the band has engaged some 18 socially displaced youth residents of the Credo House Foundation, from Upper Duke Street, in learning to play the instrument as a means of utilizing their time wisely and expand their marketability; All Stars will continue to use its panyard as a recreational and/or educational facility for the external community…"[724]

Then it was on to even greater successes, when Carnival 2012 came around. From the word "go", the band's own Cokey Telemaque presented the Smooth-man with a winner that was irresistible. And even if the moniker "Smooth" may have initially come about due to his propensity to respond with the single word, "smooth" when anyone enquired of him, "how yuh going? "; today, it addresses the sweet agility of the transition of the musical passages so evident in his reharmonization, for that is where the man's genius lies. Five points clear on a final night, in this here time, is like supremacy over-qualified. It was a stunner. All Stars' 8th Panorama victory was probably its sweetest ever.

This is how one commentator described the band's performance of Cokey's *Play Yuh Self* on that eventful night: *Panorama was cooking around the clock, as it were, and Trinidad All Stars made no bones that they had come to play themselves. The band rolled in 25 canopies or so, each sporting a goal decorative trim, and on the roof a humongous star that supported six smaller ones. Conspiracy theories might not abound in pan but interpretation with little or no evidence suffices in the steel band world. Was All Stars sending a message that with six victories in the bag for arranger Leon "Smooth" Edwards, a seventh was imminent? (Rudy Wells arranged Rainorama for the band's first Panorama title in 1973.) What gall! Then again, what foreshadowing!*

…Most of the players seemed to be on a galactic ride. They wore gizmos on their hats that flashed red, blue or green. A showy, show band for real. All Stars showed that they could sardine their formidable frontline four-deep so judges could catch the bird whistles warbling off those chromed pans. One time, they employed a frangipani line that explains our culture… this time the tenors screamed back a riff on Play Yuh Self, the four-pans and basses in on the interplay. The song transmitted to the audience. You could tell.

To hear arranger Smooth, the players were having a ball, literally: "Everything's not on the frontline pans. It's a conversation about what's about to happen in the various sections. They let you know what each family of instruments has in mind." Edwards said, "It's sharing the load. The instrumentation is like that of a symphony orchestra. Melody is not limited to the violins alone. Each instrument in a fine orchestra has a lead. Cellos, oboe, whatever. The technique was deliberate. Teamwork featured the dexterity of the players. For example, the basses are energetic, playing themselves and passing the ball around. Why play defense when you can take shots at the goalkeeper. While the opposition is marking the tenors, the cellos gone running with the ball. Then the basses end it all, enhancing it. The coda is the death knell. Closing of the gates. Not a man would remain standing!"

You could hear the smile in his voice. Smooth doesn't yap a lot. Except for calling out notes, he is a man of reticence, not a man would remain standing? Ha! It was as if his music sounded so deep it might have been from the bottom of the ocean. Smooth was on the money, though… Tied with Phase 11 in the semifinals, Trinidad All Stars clearly won the Panorama, judging by the ovation… Such as it is, five points would be difficult to swallow for the Woodbrook band. Half a point might have been easier to take…[725]

That night, the Pan-Yard howled until the morning sunlight burnt its way into the consciousness of the celebrants. Throughout the earlier ensuing hours bits of folklore had flowed consistently like the ebb of tides, and many had pronounced on the power of the Orisha man's bell, still there to summons All Stars on stage in order to gird their loins to embrace dizzying heights of super excellence, yes, they all agreed Prince's bell is like no other bell, but it was Mae Mae, made famous by Sparrow's calypso, who had the audacity to point to the spot where she said the ghost of a one-time Bookman, Jim Bill Sobers, usually stood, alert in his ever present protection of this locality.

2012 turned out to be a most successful year for the band: Panorama Winners once again; sixth placed in the George Bailey Band of the Year Competition for its *Fleets In* presentation on Carnival Tuesday, ahead of big mas' bands such as Trini Revelers; Large Band of the Day for its Monday presentation, *Music Let's Dance*; Best Costumed Steelband on Carnival Tuesday. Finally on December 2nd the National Carnival Bands Association (NCBA) in celebrating their 50th Independence Anniversary presented Trinidad All Stars Steel Orchestra with a national award "in recognition" of the band's "commitment, dedication and service to the Carnival Art Form of Trinidad & Tobago."

Then it was on to 2013. A hat-trick of Panoramas beckoned. Smooth said: "Hopefully I will be in Trinidad this year for the finals, so it will be a different result (to that of 1982), a different scenario…"[726] And the then Captain, Beresford Hunte, admonished: "Trinidad All Stars is an institution, not just a steelband. We're in the heart of the thing. So much so that we close rehearsals with the National Anthem and then form a circle around the band to say a prayer. Every night. Each section a different night (meaning that the various sections of the band rotate the prayer-lead)."[727] "...We are not in charge of results, but we are in charge of our performance... whatever happens during 2013 National Panorama Competition, All Stars music must resonate positively in the heart and minds of music lovers everywhere..."[728] At this point, surely, there is little left to be said about this institution born and nurtured in this, the Yard of Hell. Indeed the wonders shall never cease...

2011 Panorama Victory: The youths of All Stars celebrate.

From the left, Jason "Stumps" Lewis, Asst-Manager Operations; Leon "Smooth" Edwards, arranger, Gervase Warner, CEO, N&M; and Beresford Hunte, Captain and Manager, Trinidad All Stars, at the presentation of the collage at the Belmont Salon of the Hilton at the victory celebration on May, 20, 2011. Pix courtesy the Business Guardian.

The young pannists of All Stars celebrate victory at the Hilton. From left; Nikisha Patrick, Onika Baird, Dwayne Ifill, Lisa Nichols and Cassie Figaro (the daughter of Selris Figaro ex-National Footballer and ardent All Stars supporter who was also a member of the Jacksonville Youth Club that played a key role in sustaining All Stars after the 1967 split).

Youngsters of All Stars share photo-op with the arranger. From left; Shaquille Noel, Brittany Garcia, Leon "Smooth" Edwards, Anissa Boyce and Obadele "Supreme" Allick (this youngster out of St. Margaret's RC is being cited as a future master of the double-tenors, also of interest is the fact that he is the son of our new found female flag waver. Pic courtesy the Business Guardian.

From left: Staci-Ann Patrick, triple-guitar player, then; Nigel Williams, Finance Manager of All Stars then, the man noted for this strict adherence to transparency and accountability, and Amanda McMillan, N&M employee benefits manager. Pix courtesy Business Guardian.

Beresford Hunte, then Captain and Manager of Trinidad All Stars enjoys the company of Candace Ali, N&M Corporate Communications Officer at 2011 celebrations.

All Stars Performing in Singapore at the 2011 Formula 1 Grand Prix.

Members of All Stars were enthralled by the "Sky Park", located at a height of 200 meters on top of three skyscrapers, as if on three pillars. The Sky Park includes casinos, bars, restaurants, the largest outdoor swimming pool (150 meters long) and a Museum of Modern Art.

All Stars during the 2011 Singapore tour performing while on a specially designed float.

2012—SteelfestTT: N&M Trinidad All Stars and Shenzhen

Deryck Nurse conducts All Stars and musicians of the Shenzhen Aihua Arts Troupe of China.

The National Gas Company of T&T in conjunction with Pan Trinbago gave the Nation a 50th Anniversary gift in the form of a Festival titled "SteelfestTT", the theme of which was "Steelpan—Uniting the Sounds of the World" and the crowning glory of the program was the joint performances of the double Panorama Champions, N&M Trinidad All Stars, and the Shenzhen Aihua Arts Troupe of China that comprised dancers, vocalists and musicians utilizing traditional Chinese instruments such as the Erhu, a pole with only two fine metal strings, millimeters apart; the Yangqin, a metal string instrument played with two hammers; the Pipa, a Spanish styled guitar; a Ruan, a Chinese guitar; an accordion, as well as a bamboo flute. These instruments blended well with the pans and underscored the theme of "Uniting the Sounds of the World".

All Stars exhibited their professional competence in their handling of the five Chinese original pieces, e.g., "Joy", "Rosy Clouds Chasing the Moon", and "Up and Up", conducted by the Chinese musical arranger, Huang. The Chinese instrumentalists likewise competently handled the Classical pieces they played alongside All Stars, e.g., "Air from Suite #3" by JS Bach, however they all confessed experiencing great difficulty handling the calypso rhythms.

The leader of the Chinese group, Huang, also conducted the combination of All Stars and Shenzhen.

2011 Performance for Heather Headley

Trinidad All Stars, on Saturday Dec 17, 2011, opened the Heather Headley Show at NAPA *performing a mix of musical genres*, according to Leiselle Maraj of the Newsday.

In a letter to the Captain of All Stars, Heather Headley said:

"Mr. Hunte, I wanted to take a moment to thank you and the Trinidad All Stars for playing such a beautiful role in my "Home" concert. It was so much fun to perform with the members of the orchestra; I wish we could have done more together. Before we left America, I told the band that they would hear steel pans sing, and your orchestra did more than that. They are amazing. Please thank them all for me. Enjoy the New Year… and Carnival. God bless…"

2007—T&T Steelpan and Jazz Festival

Performances of Andy Narell and Trinidad All Stars.

Andy Narell brought a film crew to Trinidad in 2007 to film a project that he had undertaken with Trinidad All Stars and which involved his composition of original music. He said that he insisted on this filming in T&T in order to provide "a sense of the place that gave birth to the steelpan," and so "learn the story of its source." (*extract from ANDY NARELL Alive—featuring five films and 2 DVDs*).

Andy also outlined his view of All Stars after his involvement with the band at the 2007 Queens Hall Concert which was a segment of that year's Trinidad & Tobago Steelpan and Jazz festival. He said: "I can't say enough about the dedication and work ethic of Trinidad All Stars, a truly world class orchestra. Over the course of six months they put in more than 100 rehearsals to learn the music and prepare for the concert, and they taught me a lot about togetherness and unity of purpose."

"Thanks to Neville Jules, Berry Hunte, Nigel Williams, and all the supporters of Trinidad All Stars. Special thanks to Deryck Nurse, who undertook the job of studying my scores and teaching the music to the band by rote, for a job truly well done. Finally, thanks to Patrick Raymond for the idea, and Ainsley Mark, the director of the Trinidad and Tobago Steelpan and Jazz Festival, who believed in all of us and took a flying leap to make this project happen…" (*extract from ANDY NARELL Alive*).

The highlight of the Queens Hall Concert was the collaboration of Andy Narell and All Stars on pieces such as "The Passage", "Song for Mia", "Tatoom", "Moment's Notice', "Baby Steps", and "Izo's Mood".

In Memoriam

(Those stalwarts who transited while this document was being prepared)

Oswald "Cherrie" Eligon, the last of the great bassmen nurtured in the Charlotte Street Garret at the top of Maple Leaf Club—truly one of the finest in his day.

In Memoriam

Caro in his usual glee!

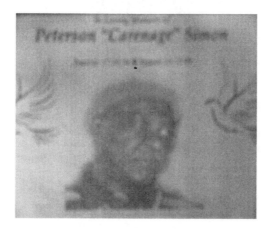

Peterson "Caro" Simon, All Stars' percussionist, has gone but will never be forgotten. He was the person whom anyone entering the Pan-Yard in bye-gone days would have most likely encountered. Hard-working, jovial and loyal to the max, he touched everyone with that mystique which was his very own. His funeral was massive; the crowds filled the church and spilled over into the street causing traffic jams at the corner of Park and Henry. Many in wonderment stopped to ask "who died?" And the response always was simply: "Carenage or Caro from All Stars." The above picture depicts exactly how we all would love to remember him.

In Memoriam

Gideon Harris

A Trinidad All Stars stalwart. No contribution to the band was ever deemed too much for him to handle even singlehandedly. The noblest and kindest of hearts. RIP Gideon!

In Memoriam

Roy Gibbs

Roy was a Jack of All Trades; handled design of pan racks and all the early electrical and welding requirements. Probably the longest serving secretary of the band. There from since the days in the George Street Coal shop, the first Garret in Bully's club, the second Garret at Maple Leaf and only stopped playing pan in 1980, by which time age had caught up with him and as he said he "could not even whistle the double-second runs in Woman on the Bass, far less to play them" and so he quietly laid his pair of sticks in the middle of the pan and simply walked away... Roy died in 2012.

In Memoriam

Courtney Vincent Charles—"Charlo"

Charlo was the flagman for Trinidad All Stars from 1958 to 1968. He was anointed by the great and legendary flagmaster, Samuel "Jitterbug" Peters, to be the successor. Like many of the old stalwarts of All Stars, Charlo was a raconteur or master of the oral history of All Stars. He passed away in New York in 2012. RIP Charlo.

In Memoriam

10 March 1935–21 January 2015

Aldwyn "Audra" Preddie, the man for whom Neville Jules invented the Trombone Pan in the early 1950s. Neville insisted that had Audra stayed with the Pan Movement he would probably have been one of the greatest virtuoso players. It was deemed a pity that Audra switched to conventional instruments. Early All Stars members say Audra had "perfect pitch" and an uncanny musical hearing.

In Memoriam

Double-Seconds: 1968–2017: 49 years of devoted and committed service to Trinidad All Stars: Gone; never to be forgotten.

In Memoriam

Hugh Alexander: "Joe Bell"
Sunrise 1932–Sunset 2017

At the 1954 Music Festival. Joe Bell walked on stage, knocked the skirt of a pan and All Stars bowed to the audience. It was the first time this was done. The British Adjudicator referred to him as "Sir Edward Beecham", an internationally known conductor of classical music. Sparrow sang about Joe-Bell, a consummate saga-boy and member of the famous "Janet's Gang" of Charlotte Street. Outstanding frontline tenor-pan player from the days of the Garret. Gone but never to be forgotten.

Sule, from the left, Natasha, Brenton, Shaoubaca, Nalo, Dane and Cokey—a frontline, unmatched.

The Stars radiated again in 2012. All Stars' 8th Panorama Win!

2012 Bomb Competition Winners—"What a Wonderful World" arranged by Terry Demas, a protégé of Neville Jules.

Since the conception of the Bomb Competitions All Stars has won over 26 such competitions, most times doing a clean sweep throughout the City. Most of these winners were arranged by Neville Jules. In recent times, from 2001, All Stars had two hattricks of winning bombs:

2001—Precious Lord (arr. Smooth Edwards)
2002—Green, Green Grass of Home (Jules)
2003—How Great Thou Art (Jules)
2006—Mood Indigo (Jules)
2007—The Good, the Bad, the Ugly (Jules)
2008—I Believe (Jules)

All Stars also won the $10,000 People's Choice—making the band triple winners in 2012. What a remarkable year. It is also interesting to note that All Stars on Carnival Tuesday with "Fleets In" won the 6th prize in the large band category.

Sixth Place in 2012 Band of the Year

Pic courtesy Caribbean Beat and Abigail Hadeed

As has been the tradition from since 1935, All Stars has maintained its presence as the largest and most popular steelband on the road during the Carnival. The flagwaver here, Ms. Rhonda Allick, has taken over the reins in the vein of the great ones such as Jitterbug, Jim Bill, Charlo, etc. Her popularity like her flag-waving ability has been growing steadily over the past few years. She had been dubbed "the Energizer Bunny".

Courtesy—The Guardian

2012—Victory Performance of "Play Yuself"!

In 2013: All Stars, as many had predicted, were not awarded the Panorama three-peat for the second time; similarly on two occasions the band was denied Music Festival three-peats in the course of its glorious history. Cokey Telemaque motivated by the words of an on-looker who, after listening to All Stars' performance of his 2012 composition "Play Yuself", said, "it hard to beat All Stars, is the **bounce and drive** they always have." Cokey heard those words, went home and in half an hour composed his 2013 panorama tune. It was the very same thing back in the 1930s and 1940s when the people on hearing the band coming in the distance used to say "bet that is Hell Yard." The bounce and drive was always there, the hall mark of the band since the days of Sagiator and, the first ironman, Lulie.

The members reported that after their performance of Smooth's earth-shaking arrangement of Cokey Telemaque's *Bounce and Drive* at position No.7 on the final night in 2013, the members of all six bands that preceded All Stars, stood up and applauded as All Stars exited the stage and moved their pans out of the Savannah and down Charlotte Street. **It was a salient honor from their peers**. Then it mattered not what the judges said. However, the people spoke and once again in 2013, All Stars was declared winner of the People's Choice Award by the masses who attended the 2013 Panorama. And for yet another year All Stars made their presence felt in the Carnival. In 2012 the band was 6th placed in the Band of the Year Competition, however on Carnival Tuesday in 2013, All Stars moved up to 3rd place.

On Carnival Monday 2013, the band was declared Band OF THE DAY for its portrayal of Fashion Extravaganza and won yet again the Pan Trinbago's J'ouvert morning Bomb Competition. But once again the vile detractors were to show their true colors and their noted historic malevolence in dealing with the band from Hell Yard. Apparently, it was decided early in the year by the organizers of the Champs in Concert on the Saturday after Carnival that the winner of the Panorama 2013 People's Choice Award will also be invited to perform alongside the other winners but once Trinidad All Stars was declared the People's Choice it seemed as though some wished to reverse this decision.

In the end, Trinidad All Stars was not informed of this requirement to perform at the Champs in Steel Plus Show until the very day of the Show and this is despite the fact that two members involved in the organization of this Show played mas with Trinidad All Stars during the course of Carnival Monday and Tuesday and never saw it fit to mention to any official of the band this requirement to perform at the Champs in Concert Show. On March 14, 2013 Trinidad All Stars received a letter of apology which read as follows: "Please accept sincere congratulations on your Steel Orchestra's performance that resulted in your band being chosen by the public to be the **People's Choice in Panorama Finals 2013**. The opportunity is taken here to offer profound apologies for the circumstances which saw the Neal and Massy Trinidad All Stars, not taking part in the **Champs In Steel Plus Show**. The Central Executive by this letter registers regrets and gives assurance of our continued high opinion of the Trinidad All Stars Steel Orchestra..." And Hell Yard's tongue-in-cheek response to this apology was, "yeah, right," mindful that this band from the Yard of Hell, regardless of ill-treatment, shall never desist from its usual sterling commitment to the Pan, Mas, and Calypso tradition.

In 2014, this commitment, after four generations, brought the crowning glory, *Sailors Ashore in a Tropical Fiesta*, band of the year... The Mas fraternity was stunned. They fumed and they cussed but the rules of the game could not be defied. Once Trinidad All Stars stuck to the letter of law: register and portray one masquerade band on Carnival Monday and Tuesday and the Band of the Year will be the one that gained the most points when the marks for both days were added. True to say, it was a rule geared to force the big mas' bands to portray something on the Monday which over the years had degenerated significantly with all of them just donning simple T-shirts and shorts, saving the costumes for Tuesday.

All Stars read the rules carefully and immediately ceased to portray "Festivals" on Monday and "Fleets-In" on Tuesday and instead merged the two into one band: ***Sailors Ashore in a Tropical Fiesta***. Berry concluded: "Once we do that, they can't beat we at all…" So said, so done.

However, later in the year 2014, yet another bit of malfeasance, whether geared deliberately to deflate the historic significance of the band from Hell Yard or inadvertently so, reared its head. The plot had been conceptualized and brewed since 2013 but only came to the light of day in June of 2014. It was described as a creative, mythical exposition on the history of Pan titled, "Pan! Our Music Odyssey" put together by a local Pan professional historian and his French producer. This is the storyline in a nutshell that this docudrama projects: a young man leaves West Port-of-Spain after some association with rioting and the stabbing of an individual on the Gaza Strip (i.e., string of nightclubs on Wrightson Road), during some altercation supposedly over a woman.

The storyline then places this young man at an Orisha Yard in Tacarigua with a burning desire to tune a 45 gallon drum or big pan which he finally tunes and launches at a competition at the Palladium Theatre in Tunapuna much to the accolades and acknowledgement from all and sundry.

Of course, the Big Pan first appeared at a competition at the Monarch cinema in Tunapuna and was played by Cyril "Snatcher" Guy of Boom-Town, a band located in Mother Gerald's Orisha Yard. It was tuned by the Orisha master-drummer Andrew "Run-In" Beddoe who was Mother Gerald's paramour. Snatcher was laughed off the stage. All the leading soloists at that competition played 8-note small paint pans, including Ellie Mannette and Neville Jules. Yes, we acknowledge the freedom of creative rights, but what could be the purpose of such a creative splurge? The promoters of the docudrama will have to answer one day.

But there is more insult to injury. Throughout the entire docudrama, Boogsie Sharpe is given ample time to explain his 2013 Panorama piece; how *he add a piece of Latin that nobody ever do*, while Smooth Edwards who was contesting then for a hat-trick with Telemaque's *Bounce and Drive* is never interviewed. Imagine that! But more than that, every moment that the band All

Stars appears in the docudrama, the background music being played is the music of Phase 11, Boogsie's music. Oversight, you say! Hardly likely! All Stars is featured only as an institution praying and seeking motivation as well as divine assistance and intervention.

As a matter of fact, the only other arranger featured extensively along with his music is Andy Narell. Anyone, ignorant of our history, viewing this docudrama is left with the impression that the two premier Panorama arrangers and Panorama bands are Boogsie and Phase II and Andy Narell and Birdsong who both reflect the future. However, Narell raises an interesting viewpoint when he wonders aloud about the radicalism and revolutionary spirit of the early pan pioneers as opposed to what he sees as the "conservatism" of the musical presentation of panmen today. Narell simply refuses to accept that "panorama music" is T&T's carnival music, that is its purpose. The response of the old folks of Hell Yard to all this is: "So what is new?" Are we being asked once again to accept foreign validation and interpretation of our own indigenous product?

Tony Guy, left, and Leon "Smooth" Edwards at Panorama 2014.

Tony said: "I had exiled myself out in Asia for many years, not communicating with anyone but my family. However a few years ago I was inspired to reconnect with Smoothman and this year, 2014, we talked about me coming back to T&T to work with him again and I did, plus, of course, I seized the opportunity to deal with other personal matters."

Then, as if to say the successes of 2014 were not enough, All Stars in its 80th year, 2015, rose to its 9th Panorama victory with the fantastic performance of "Unquestionable' composed by Clive Telemaque, arranged by Smooth Edwards. It took the total devastation of the Panorama field by All Stars' performance of "Unquestionable", Smooth's 8th victory, for someone such as Alvin Daniell to proclaim openly for the first time that *Smooth is an accomplished arranger. He selects his tune very carefully, and uses chromatics that are relevant to the tune of choice. They are designed to give a nice range of melody and as theme with which to work. I like his thematic arranging style. He knows music very well, everything he does fits well... He painstakingly goes through a tune at a slow pace to make certain that it is being played accurately. As a result, practice is demanding and time-consuming...*[729]

Then, to crown it off, All Stars also won People's Choice and, for the second time, the Band of the Year titled with its mas presentation **Ships Ahoy in a French Festival**. No band in the history of Carnival has ever won both the Panorama and band of the year titles in the same year. What a way to celebrate and signify 80 years of commitment to pan, calypso, and mas!

But as usual, some critics came bustling out the woodwork. How a Sailor Band could win Band of the Year for two straight years? They playing the same thing for the masquerade, just like they play the same thing every year and winning Panorama! Such puerile nonsense had to be answered and the appropriate answer came in an article titled: ***Trinidad All Stars versus Two Piece and Fries:***

...Why is Trinidad All Stars so successful?

This band has been the most successful in every existing competitive format be it the music festivals, bomb competitions, best-beating on the road, people's choice, and even the much touted annual Panorama competition; in the 51 years of Panorama, actually 50 since there was none in 1979, All Stars have been in winner's row (1, 2, 3) more times than any other band, All Stars: 9 Firsts, 10 Seconds and 6 Thirds, **25** times. How come? That's the question many people have been asking since the 9th Panorama victory and successive Band of the Year acclaims in 2014 and 2015.

Commentators have noted the attributes of disciplined, intelligent, collective functioning, and leadership with vision, as the hallmarks of such consistent achievement. And, yes, All Stars as an institution has displayed all those characteristics. **But All Stars is successful in competitions precisely**

because it is not only about competitions. Above all else there is this **underlying, salient commitment to the Hell Yard legacy**. Hell Yard is the birth place of All Stars. Furthermore, it is also the locus of the first, conscious, organized defense of the people's Carnival Art-Forms. After the 1880 defeat of the people's mas by the constabulary led by the infamous Captain Baker, some people, resolute that there be no repeat, organized themselves, and posters appeared around POS preparing the citizens mentally for the battle that was to come in 1881, telling the people boldly that Governor Freeling was in support of the People's Carnival but Baker was against it.

Hell Yard is also the birth place of PAN, not the usage of discarded implements for percussion, but the steel orchestra voicing not merely rhythm but as well melody and harmony. For these two reasons, All Stars is of the firm belief that Hell Yard should be declared an International Heritage Site in accordance with UNESCO's imperatives and criteria…

…The then Leader of Trinidad All Stars, Beresford Hunte, repeats ad infinitum that All Stars is not a Panorama band, it is much more, competitions are engaged as a means of sharpening proficiency, but the commitment is to the Hell Yard legacy which is a much bigger picture, it is about the development of the Steelband Movement and the Carnival Art-forms. To that end, All Stars' involvement is full-time all year round; community thanksgivings, community socials and religious services, children's Christmas celebrations, daily parking facility, etc. From 1935 to the present, All Stars has never shirked its commitment to the People's Carnival and its handmaidens of calypso, mas and pan.

In February 1940, the third and fourth Captains of Hell Yard, Eric Stowe and Big Head Hamil, made the first recording of Pan using "three-note kettles" backing up Roaring Lion in a lavway titled "Leggo de Lion". In 1945 the seventh Captain, Neville Jules made the first melody pan, the four-note ping-pong, and began the development of a "family of pans", the steel orchestra. From then on, with the change of name from Hell Yard Boys to Cross of Lorraine to Trinidad All Stars, the band has remained consistently the largest masquerade steelband on show during Carnival, from USS Bad Behavior to USS Fleets-In, although there were moments in the glorious '60s when Synco, Tokyo, Desperadoes, Invaders, Silver Stars, Dem Fortunates and others rose to the occasion and eclipsed the All Stars efforts in the carnival arts…

...But there were always two Carnivals contesting for space; the Carnival of the "creole" elites (The Mardi Gras) and the People's Carnival that was referred as the Jamette or low-class Carnival. As time went by the commercialization of Carnival gave pride of place to the Mardi Gras at the expense of the People's Carnival, and concomitantly there developed a tendency toward pushing the steelband movement out of the Monday and Tuesday parade. That tendency coincided with the demise of portrayal at the altar of female narcissism. Decorated panties and bras; "two-piece and fries" according to an All Stars person.

There was talk about allowing steelbands to parade only on the Sunday in order to avoid the congestion and to remove Piccadilly as a judging point. The idea of the East Dry River bands (i.e., All Stars, Renegades and Radoes) parading together was floated as a measure to ensure the continued presence of steelbands and portrayal mas in the Carnival but that bigger picture was dashed as the desire to defeat each other at Panorama subverted the ideal. Starlift and All Stars kept the ball rolling on Monday with All Stars registering as a medium band in order to ensure that Starlift won the big band category until the "authorities" refused to accept All Stars' classification as "medium". Again co-operation was always and continues to be the key to how All Stars functions...

...Eventually, given the marked absence of steelbands in Carnival, everything went westward. Today Carnival has been removed effectively from the inner city of Port-of-Spain, no spectators, Frederick Street like a ghost town, Woodford Square empty. Grand Stand, North Stand, empty. Only South Quay remains as an inner-city judging point where people gather but once the Socadrome becomes established, South Quay shall also become a ghost town. All the little people of East POS who for decades made some money through vending downtown on Carnival Days to help with the needs of their families have been pushed aside. Vending is now largely the exercise of the middle-class property owners on the Avenue who either do the vending for themselves or rent space to those interested in so doing. What a pity. No wonder they shall be forced to opt to barricade themselves even more behind wrought-iron gates and grills.

In the meantime, Trinidad All Stars will remain true to its legacy. The band shall continue to ensure that when Monday mas points are added to Tuesday points the result will surmount that of the bikini and beads mas bands until they get the authorities to change the rules as All Stars expects them to do in due time. But nevertheless this band shall continue as always to push on down George Street into the inner city much to the delight of all those who are sick, or bed-ridden shut-ins, who only have to open their windows to see the splendor of this their band that has emerged in such glory from the very bowels of their city. And do not be surprised if next year, 2016, going for a hat-trick, All Stars turns up with a big king and queen. Talk done!"[730]

On Monday, 9 March 2015, a Panyard Crusade was held at All Stars yard. "Honorary member" status was conferred on Archbishop Harris and Fr. Clyde Harvey. Archbishop Harris in his address noted the "positive impact that steelbands have had on their members and their communities" and expressed the strong belief that panyards can provide "the spark for societal change."[731] He congratulated the band for its double, i.e., winning both 2015 Panorama competition as well as 2015 Band of the Year in the parade of mas' bands, the latter feat being even more amazing given the fact that it was also accomplished in 2014 making it consecutive victories.

He deduced that this happened because All Stars was "the only band that was playing mas, not bikini and beads and nakedness," and he wondered aloud whether All Stars' success in this regard could probably cause a "fading away" of bikini and beads and signal a "revolution that brings societal change not only in Carnival."[732] Archbishop Harris confided that this was his first panyard visit and assured that he planned to visit again next Carnival along with Father Harvey.[733] The young members of the band rendered two pieces "All of Me" and "Take My Hand Precious Lord" much to the appreciation of the clerics.

Beresford Hunte in response informed the Archbishop and Father Harvey that "All Stars was not just a steel orchestra but an institution which has been around before all political parties. Things are not happening by guess and by mistake. We normally have two thanksgivings every year, one at Holy Rosary and another at the panyard… these are things that we have been doing over the period of our longevity for our successes… Our watchwords are Discipline, Dedication and Magnificence and the band strives to be the best it could be. Our habit is to perform to please the people, the judges and ourselves. The only way you can do that is through hard work and dedication; it does not come any other way and this is something we try to instill in the young people."[734]

The claim that All Stars is not just a steel-orchestra resonated later that year, early July of 2015, when All Stars purchased the property, next door, at

42-44 Duke Street. The announcement came at the celebrations held "Under the Trees" at Normandie, St. Ann's where the 9th Panorama victory and as well as the band's 80th Anniversary were commemorated. Beresford Hunte indicated that the purchase was "a financial investment for the band as they work toward becoming financially self-sufficient… We cannot solely depend on contributions and earnings from Panorama performances and other small ventures. **This is critical for our growth and development as a social and cultural institution.**"[735] In regard to this purchase of the property listed as 42-44 Duke Street, Nigel Williams said: "This is in keeping with our long-term vision to grow not just as a steel orchestra but as a business institution. We have been looking out for things in which to invest and went after this property vigorously."[736]

Beresford Hunte took the opportunity to thank the management team for their hard work keeping the band at the top; also Mr. Gervase Warner CEO of Massy Holdings for his "passion and interest in the band", for "his willingness to help whenever needed;" and he paid special homage to the arranger, Leon "Smooth" Edwards, 8 times Panorama winner; Clive Telemaque composer of panorama music for the last four years, first on two occasions, i.e., *Play yuh Self and Unquestionable,* and second also on two occasions, i.e., *Bounce and Drive* and *Excitement*; and as well Terry Demas for arranging Bomb tunes and Road music.[737] So, in addition to having already purchased outright No. 48 Duke Street and thereby extending the yard to the West, the band now has purchased also the property to the East, No.42-44 Duke Street. The band therefore now owns 42-44 Duke Street, 46 Duke Street, 46 A Duke Street as well as 48 Duke Street. Trinidad All Stars Steel Orchestra is now a multi-million dollar business conglomeration,

However, the band was not yet done with its feats for 2015. On Sunday, 9 August 2015, All Stars were to face the world at the International panorama Competition, 12 foreign bands and 12 local bands for a first prize of $250,000 (US) or approximately $1.65 million (TT). The Smooth-man went to work with the choice of "Curry Tabanca", 60 players had to be chosen, the music compressed to not more than 8 minutes. Hell yard came alive. This is what one commentator had to say about that performance: *Not even the stoutest opponents of Massy Trinidad All Stars could argue that the band doesn't deserve first place and the more than one million dollars TT first prize. When the band appeared on stage, its musicians appropriately dressed in East Indian wear, one could actually cut the confidence oozing out of the Duke Street orchestra. For Sunday, arranger Leon "Smooth" Edwards removed two minutes from the band's 1987 arrangement of the Mighty Trini's Curry Tabanca to bring the piece within the required eight minutes playing-time…*

…From the first note, All Stars sounded like a winner and the best steel orchestra thus far on the day, with eight more still to perform in the competition. Musically, All Stars was perfect and visually it was intoxicating, its music embellished by a large troupe of East Indian dancers, perfectly choreographed for some rhythmic and percussive interpretations in the final third of the selection…

…All Stars' superiority over all rivals could be appreciated when one looks at the 78-point disparity between the winning score of 476 and the 24th placed Gunslingers. All Stars scored 12 points more than second placed Supernovas…[738]

When it was suggested by a Newsday Journalist that it was the "dougla music created in the engine room of Massy Trinidad All Stars" that earned the band its victory in the International Panorama, this is how Clive Telemaque responded: "…We had no problem getting it together this time around, compared with 28 years earlier when Smooth first introduced the tassa drums for Panorama 1987… We utilized two drum sets, two African drums, Bongo and Cymbalta, two tassa drums, one scratcher, a cowbell and two pieces of iron… they (the drummers) knew the song and could play the phrase in order to get the compactness in the percussion… the tassa high cutter, we needed that. You could hear that sound for miles away and the dholak came as the supporting drum to the high cutter."

"In fact, during practice, we found the dholak drum was distinct; it was singing out more because the player had two different sounds, playing one side with the palm of his hand and the other with a stick. The African drum played the same beat as the dholak… It was different to the normal kind of panorama arrangement… Smooth captured the mood well," and Telemaque concluded that the 2015 version was "Curry Tabanca, Slight Pepper…"[739]

Smooth Edwards offered a similar explanation: "It was a challenge to bring the tassa as there are different variations and if they play the wrong variations with calypso, it won't mesh… In 1987 we were trying to force the wrong version but we got it to work after a lot of prodding. Now I realize what took place back then and would apologize for the way I thought (then). I found out this time around that the tassa drums had more than one beat, in 1987 we had them under strict manners to get them to play what we wanted… this time around the tassa players are younger but more musically mature. The son of the guy who played in 1987 was here this time around, saying he was five years old at that time…"[740]

In other words, this time around, there was no need for the strict "mannersing" as in 1987, this time the tassa players were mature enough musically to "play with the phrasing" of the music as Telemaque indicated above. Given this International Panorama victory 28 years after, Smooth feels fully vindicated in his belief that back in 1987 All Stars was dealt a deliberate blow.

One outspoken Independent Senator said in her column: "All Stars rapturously bounces off music that could turn a casual music lover into a whore for steel music that sweetens the air… According to its website, the band has a vision to be the world's premier steel orchestra and universally acclaimed for musical superiority in pan music—**already mostly achieved.** They have spun their objectives to not only pursue excellence but also to create an economically viable organization, develop members' skills, and perpetuate social and community improvement as a means of uplifting society… It has been a long journey since 1935—**80 years of steelpan heroism**. All Stars is the champion and *sine qua non* of the indigenous artform…"[741] In other words All Stars is indispensable to the historic nurturing of steel band supremacy. A truer statement on steelband musical development has never been made.

Trinidad All Stars at the International Panorama performing Smooth's masterpiece "Curry Tabanca".

"All Stars—We Rule De World". *This Black and Gold T-Shirt was especially printed by supporters to celebrate winning the International Panorama.*

Shortly after the International Panorama victory, the band election of officers became due and Mr. Beresford Hunte began to signal his intentions to step aside in 2016 and allow new blood to take the reins; he had served for 23 years; 1987–1989 and from 1995 to 2016. Whether it was because of increased "politicking" arising from Berry's intended departure, or news of Neville Jules's fall in New York to full Alzheimer's disease or the much expressed view that since winning the Band of the Year consecutively 2014 and 2015) followed by both national and international Panorama 2015, All Stars will not be allowed to win anything in 2016, the band suddenly entered a period of listlessness.

An offer from Pan Trinbago's Northern Region to utilize its annual "1, 2, 3 Celebratory Program" to honor All Stars for its Three Winnings in 2015 at a function to be held at All Stars yard was politely turned down, at the same time, between August 16 and the start of 2016 Panorama practice, nothing was happening at the Yard, even the stage side seemed to go into a comatose position. Things changed somewhat when the liveliness and vitality of 2016 panorama practice began but listlessness was to take over again when nothing was done to the Panorama tune, *Leave We Alone*, between semi-finals and finals. Nothing, despite sitting down in third place and picked to play last on final night.

It was very uncharacteristic for the musical war-machine from Hell Yard. What was the cause for this apparent temporary paralysis? It was so unlike All Stars! Only an in-depth psychological examination will tell the story behind the story. Certainly the 6th placed position at the 2016 finals surprised no true member and supporter of the band. Likewise the sudden decision not to add Monday marks to Tuesday's to declare the 2016 Band of the Year was also no surprise. For the first time in the last decade, since 2006, All Stars was placed outside winners' row in Panorama. It took the Point Fortin Borough day celebrations to awake the band out of its apparent listlessness. Thanks indeed to the Point Fortin supporters of All Stars, the Mayors included, who over the years have never once flinched in their show of appreciation.

One journalist described it as he saw it: *Massy Trinidad All Stars put a different spin on things and brought a tsunami of people with them—their supporters were dressed in black T-shirts in front of the band while their fans and well-wishers moved alongside the truck. All Stars had people dancing cheek-to-cheek with songs like KC and the Sunshine Band's "How about a Little Love", "Help me make it through the Night", "Doh Stop the Party", and Nelson's "Disco Daddy".*[742]

One Pan-Culture enthusiast pointed out that All Stars was one of the bands that attracted a large crowd and created the most excitement at Borough day.

He identified All Stars as one of the bands that performed "concerts on the move" with "repertoires of more than 30 selections".[743] That was nothing new or exceptional for All Stars on Borough Day; for the past ten years All Stars repertoire in Point Fortin has been in the vicinity of 25–35 tunes, hence their popularity among pan supporters who go to Borough Day religiously. The report concluded that All Stars "had a very large following jumping to selections like I'll Always Be There For You; Soca Junkie; Curry Tabanca; Is Carnival time Again; What A Feeling; Raze; Woman On The Bass; Unknown Band; Sugar Rush; Different Me; GBM Nutron's Scene; Disco Daddy; Adrenalin City; You Gotta Be Careful; Total Disorder and KC and The Sunshine Band's How About A Little Love...[744]

But come what may, there is always a ray of goodwill that pops up out of the blue, most times when least expected. This occasion it came from a pan enthusiast who posted a compliment to All Stars on social media. This is what was said:

...Thank you, Trinidad All Stars. This is a very special thank you to the Trinidad All Stars organization. I have always maintained that the true purpose of the steelband, the reason it was created was to provide music for the (mostly poor) masses at Carnival time.

We should not forget that prior to the advent of steelband, Carnival was mostly a middle class affair, sometimes even on trucks, and we were basically at the sidelines with our tamboo bamboo and bits of metal. After WW11, the steelbands brought us to the streets, where we took over the Carnival, until we gave it up as the Panorama became our main focus at Carnival.

As I watched my favorite steelband crossing the stage on Carnival days, it occurred to me that Trinidad All Stars have never forgotten their roots, and their continued impressive presence on the streets at Carnival show us their belief that, yes, we do Panorama, and we do it very well, thank you; but on Carnival days we belong on the streets with our fans and supporters...

...I would insist that part of the struggles that many steelbands face is because of the unconscious neglect of their communities, most noticeable by their lack of participation in the nation's premier festival. The continued success of All Stars shows that this organization does not suffer from such lack of insight. Thank you, Trinidad All Stars, from a fan and a supporter, and a lover of Trinidad's culture. Thank you, and may you have continued successes as a steelband organization that realizes that it is about more than steelband competitions (even though you excel at them). It is about our people and our culture. Let's keep our culture alive!⁷⁴⁵

Clearly, he understands the "rootedness" of All Stars and the synergies that have worked over the past 80 plus years for this band from the Yard of Hell.

2017 Trinidad All Stars Won Its 10th Panorama

Full extreme blew the competition away.

Both the North Stand and the Grand Stand rose up and saluted the band with a standing ovation.

Classical Jewels X1—From Jules to Jemmott—Nov 2017

Sule Sampson conducting his own work: GLORY. This piece was written 14 years ago in celebration of his late father's life.

Deryck Nurse (below) conducting violinist, Eleanor Ryan, and the band.

Mia Gormandy conducting her arrangement of the "Theme from Magnificent Seven".

June Nathaniel conducting two pieces "Quando me'n vo" and "Jupiter"

Praises must be bestowed on Deryck Nurse who ably put the Classical Jewels X1 program together. He personally conducted a number of pieces: 21st

Century Fox Fanfare; Main Theme from Star Wars; The Four Seasons and Morning, Noon and Night in Vienna.

The band's executive explained the purpose of the title of Jewels X1:

"From Jules to Jemmott" in the following manner: "Neville Jules and Jerry Jemmott are icons of the steelband movement and pillars of Trinidad All Stars. Jules, the innovator and disciplinarian, would pave the way for Jemmott, the master musician; under their guidance, calypso met classics, passion married technique, and All Stars developed the musical lexicon that defined our sound and repertoire…"

Peter Ray Blood wrote: "Perfection. That's the most apt description one could affix to Classical Jewels X1…"

Chapter Five
Building the Physical Assets and Reforming the Administrative Structure

While the musical products of All Stars were being competently addressed over the years by a number of individual arrangers or "voices" (nine, to be exact), the members at the same time were engaging themselves in the ongoing evolution of a new Constitution for the Band and likewise were involved in developing the physical assets and landscape at 46/48 Duke Street. This process of landscape development all began with the asserted campaign to move the band back to its place of birth, i.e., Hell Yard.

Hamilton "Web" Alexander described what happened in this manner: "In the 1970s, the Pan Yard was situated in the old bus terminal on St. Vincent and Independence Square. We got news that we had to move because of the construction of the two tall buildings (i.e., Twin Towers). We were told that we should seek a new pan yard. The education I received from Prince Batson and Neville Jules about Hell Yard convinced me that the place for our Pan Yard had to be back home, Hell Yard. At one point the authorities offered the band a place in Duke Street Quarry. I turned it down because that was the home of City Syncopators. My determination to acquire Hell Yard led us to convene an all-day seminar entitled "Back to Hell Yard". This seminar was attended by people from our then Sponsor, Catelli/Hand Arnold, Ossie Hale and Frank Kirkley, also present were people like Pete Simon and Peter Pitts, as well as Kelvin Scoon, who was our PRO at the time…"

"…Access to Hell Yard posed a small problem because there was no clear entrance… I thought of building a bridge across the river from Piccadilly Street down to Hell Yard but this initiative to acquire an entrance never came to fruition under my stewardship. Reds Collins who took over from me in 1977 made sure the dream materialized. My understanding is that the idea was taken to Dr. Eric Williams. He, being a historian and knowing the significance of Hell Yard, it was just a matter of time before the band acquired Hell Yard..."[746]

Reds Collins took the story further indicating that it took a lot of negotiating and audiences with almost all the various government ministries to seal the deal and acquire 46 Duke Street which was state land,[747] in fact 46 was bought by the State from private owners, the Charbonne family, and passed over to All Stars in 1980,[748] and, though Reds Collins did not pinpoint this, the acquisition of the clearly defined Lot 46 nevertheless solved the problem that Web indicated in relation to a clear and proper entrance to Hell-Yard, i.e., the River Reserve—"the Big Sink".

Reds said: "We moved back but we had no legal documentation and I felt we could readily be evicted at any time, so I raised these concerns with the Sponsors and they suggested that there were two options before the band; either to form and register a Limited Liability Company or a Co-operative in which all assets, land, etc., could be entrusted. We opted for a Co-operative, and for the teething processes we got help from the Co-operative Division of the Ministry of Labor. Poison came in as Captain after the 1983 elections, but he never pursued the full implementation in regard to the functioning of a genuine Co-operative..."[749]

In reality, nothing, fundamental, was accomplished for quite a while until the registration of the Trinidad All Stars Steel Orchestra Co-operative Society Ltd in 1989, during Reds' second stint as captain; then another quantum leap came when Nigel Williams as Finance Manager of All Stars presented his prescriptions for financial controls to the Trinidad All Stars Co-operative Society Ltd in 2003.[750] But it is not that efforts were not made; in the three year development proposals submitted by the John "Poison" Douglas executive for 1985–1987, it was clearly stated that legalization of the organization was on the agenda as a necessity to deal "with our commercial enterprises" and to engage the "international marketing" of the band.[751]

However, during the Carnival season of 1987, this executive committee was able to "pave approximately 1600 sq. ft of the yard (i.e., 46 Duke Street), thus providing more rehearsal space" and allowing for "replacement of the termite ridden structure," that served as the pan house.[752] They nevertheless regretted that they were unsuccessful in registering the band as a Co-operative; in acquiring Group Insurance for the membership and in determining the ownership of the lands to the rear of the Panyard or north-west of 46 Duke Street.[753]

The short-term, medium-term, and long-term proposals outlined by Beresford Hunte and Keith Matthews in the document titled "Projections 1988–1993—An Insight" continued more or less along the same vein as that of the previous executives in terms of proposed group insurance, establishing the cooperative, adopting a constitution, filling up, paving and landscaping the yard with a proposed phased development of a Pan Theatre, etc.[754] but their major areas of departure were a commitment to annual audited financial statements; and the designing of a manual accounting system for the band;[755] and to fulfill these obligations (MCT) Mark Castillo Toney & Co—Chartered Accountants of 245 Belmont Circular Road were the ones charged with the responsibility.

Mr. Ainsley Mark of MCT was quite generous in his words of praise for Keith Matthews and the yeoman job he did from 1988 to 1992 to keep the management of the band's finances on a good footing.[756] In addition, the All Stars management team led by Berry and Grip guaranteed that 25% of all Band earnings from engagements would be retained by the steelband, while 75% would be disbursed amongst the membership; furthermore there was to be an organized, concerted effort toward acquiring a mobile trailer for transporting players and instruments on Carnival days as well as the outright acquisition of additional land at 48 Duke Street.[757]

However, the determination of the ownership of that said portion of land, No. 48 Duke Street, i.e., west and north-west of No.46, proved to be the biggest challenge to the complete re-settling of All Stars in their old home and the development of the vision for this home shared by so many people. The problem was largely as a result of a most troubling dispute with a neighbor. The genesis of the dispute is as follows. In February of 1980, All Stars got the official permission from the State not only to occupy the premises identified as 46 Duke Street but also the parcel of State Land, North of 46 Duke Street referred to as Hell Yard (i.e. The River Reserve and identified on the Cadastral Sheet as 46-A) bounded to the North by the Dry River and to the West by the properties listed as 90-98 Charlotte Street.[758] On September 14, 1989, nine years after, the Trinidad All Stars Steel Orchestra Co-operative Society Ltd was formerly registered in accordance with Section 17 of the Co-operative

Societies Act, Chapter 81:03 with its official addressed given as No. 46 Duke Street, Port-of-Spain.[759]

What is clear from documentation held in All Stars' files is that the neighboring occupant of 90-98 Charlotte Street at the time Leonard S. Browne and Co. Ltd whose Principal Officer then was one Andrew Atherton, seized the opportunity after fire destroyed an old building at the back of Lot 92 Charlotte Street, bordering Hell Yard, to construct a new rectangular structure with a new perimeter wall that encroached upon Hell Yard "by some 20 feet in that it had (been) extended some 20 feet East of and beyond their original boundary."[760]

In fact, this new perimeter wall was erected after Andrew Atherton requested that the band remove a number of pan racks that were lodged on that portion of Hell Yard, east of his original wall and boundary, and All Stars had complied only because the reason given suggested that it was a temporary measure to allow "his builder to construct a work bench." All in all, in retrospect, it became clear that this attempt to defraud All Stars of a portion of Hell-Yard was well-timed and quite opportunistic as matters were pushed to a head just as the band was experiencing the effects of the 1988 split when the sponsors had abandoned ship. Apparently the officials of Leonard S. Browne & Co. Ltd interpreted the "split" in All Stars to be synonymous with a weakening of spirit.

The claim by Andrew Atherton, principal officer of the Company, that they owned the land in question turned out to be false; checks with City Hall revealed that they held a "Curtilage Agreement", dated then as recent as November 10, 1988, which provided them with a "monthly tenancy" on the land East of No.92 Charlotte Street.[761] However, once All Stars, registered as a bona-fide Co-operative Society, made formal presentation to the Government in 1989 to acquire Hell-Yard to establish its Cultural Centre, the temporary Curtilage Agreement with L.A. Browne & Co. Ltd was terminated by notice of November 7, 1990 and government officials instructed the Company to "among other things, demolish the wall," but the Company would not budge despite numerous instructions from the said government officials, including the Director of Surveys, and even after officials of the new sponsors of All Stars, Neal and Massy, intervened on behalf of the band and pleaded with them to comply in the interest of steelband development.[762]

With construction of the Cultural Centre having begun in June of 1993, not on the Western side of Hell Yard as originally intended, but on the Eastern side due to the intransigence of the Company, All Stars found itself in a situation whereby Carnival 1994 was fast approaching and there was no place to rehearse a band of 120 plus members nor any place to stack pan-racks, and so, left with no other alternative, band members in November of 1993 demolished the Company's illegal perimeter wall and utilized the space afforded thereby on the Western side of Hell-Yard.[763]

The Company in response filed an injunction against Errol Collins, Captain, and Denise Riley, Secretary, of All Stars in an attempt to restrain the band from use of the said piece of land but all their legal shenanigans proved futile in the long run and Hell-Yard in its entirety remains to date the home of All Stars.[764] "When I came back to the Captaincy in 1989," says Reds Collins unapologetically, "I met this big, long wall… there was no space to stack the pan racks… we break down the wall, and that was that…"[765]

From that moment, the onus fell on the members of All Stars themselves to take responsibility into their own hands for the development of their yard. The first big challenge, according to "Grip" Matthews, was the question of what should be done with the huge depression, "the big sink", that largely defined the topography of the piece of State land, along the River bank, north-east of 46 Duke Street.[766] Grip indicated that it had been the intention of the John Douglas executive, and of that group he singled out Barbara Crichlow in particular as the one who spearheaded the idea, to transform the "big sink" into a type of sunken amphitheater, and for quite some time everyone seemed quite enamored of that idea and were quite ready to go along with this intention until one Sunday in 1987 while rehearsing for the Classical Jewels concert, it rained quite heavily, the Dry River over-flowed its banks, filled up the "big sink" to capacity, and as he said, "water went flowing all the way down George Street" and that brought an end to the amphitheater idea; from then on the resolve was to fill up the depression (i.e., 46-A) and level it off with 46 Duke Street.[767]

During the years 1987 and 1988, there had been numerous fires in the capital City and at that very moment, Don Ramdeen, who provided trucking service to All Stars for quite some time, held a contract to demolish the burnt out buildings, and, as All Stars yard was closer by, it wasn't a difficult proposition to get Don Ramdeen to deviate from dumping all the rubble in the Beetham landfill and, at no cost to All Stars, to fill up the "big sink".[768] "Grip"

Matthews, then Secretary-Treasurer of the band, recalls the many hours, even on Sundays, that he and people such as "Chappie" (Michael Chapman) and "Stumbo" (Ian Greaves) spent awaiting the dump trucks to help spread the rubble.[769]

Reds Collins, who was returned to the Captaincy in 1989, concurs with Matthews, and indicated that once the depression was filled up, the next step was the paving of that portion of No. 46 plus the reclaimed section, and he cites, in addition to the two persons already mentioned, individuals such as Deryck Nurse, Chris Haynes and Hayden Phillip ("Africa") who all worked tirelessly, "cement-truck after cement-truck", until the yard as we know it today was produced.[770]

Both "Grip" and "Reds" confirmed that they received assistance in the reconstruction of the yard from the then Mayor of Port-of-Spain, Mr. Augustus Williams, as well as from Mrs. Sharon Alfonso of Trinidad & Tobago Regiment. They also indicated that their audience with Mr. Carson Charles, then Minister of Works in the NAR Government, who was given the responsibility to manage the Cottage Industry development, brought funding to erect the steel frame for the existing building.[771] Whereas Reds pointed out that they had to fight against the "octagon-shaped, type of structure designed for selling knick-knacks to tourists that the NAR Government seemed hell-bent on putting up all over the country," he acknowledged Grip as the one who was able to come up with the technical drawings for the kind of structure All Stars desired.[772] Grip on the other hand made it known that it was "an architect friend of Barbara Crichlow" whose resources he tapped to obtain designs for what was originally supposed to be a "three-story" building.[773]

However, from 1993, Colin Bishop replaced Keith "Grip" Matthews as the Secretary-Treasurer of Trinidad All Stars, and therefore, he, Colin, now had the responsibility according to the Leader, Reds Collins, to make the necessary contacts in furtherance of the completion of the panyard projects as directed by the Management team.[774] In that very year, 1993, there was a need still to complete the foundation of the building and to block up and cover the steel frame. Reds Collins informed that in 1993 there was supposed to be another Classical Jewels Concert but he advised Hugh Henderson and Sydney Knox to forego any financial contribution to the Concert in preference to funding the building and he said this was done and all the band members who worked on the building then were paid by the sponsors, Neal and Massy Holdings.[775]

Grip Matthews, though at that point no longer a member of the executive, countered that all the Classical Jewels Concerts were self-financing and therefore did not require funds from the sponsors to be realized.[776] In fact there is evidence to support this as the financial statements for the year June 1987 to July 1988 indicate that receipts from the Classical Jewels Concert was $73,800.54, while the expenditure was $51,926.05 reflecting a gross profit of $21, 874.49[777] which was quite in line with what obtained then for such Concerts at Queen's Hall.

On the other hand, Colin Bishop argued that he was informed by representatives of the sponsors, i.e., Hugh Henderson, Maria Macmillan and Eunice Alleyne, that panyard capital development would be funded that year from the Classical Jewels Budget and he expressed great disappointment that the rest of the executive saw nothing wrong with this suggestion which in his opinion resulted in "the band's only performing fund raiser at that time being silenced till 2010."[778] In reality the quantum required for the completion of the Panyard could in no way be fulfilled via the Classical Jewels budget.

However, the panyard building development continued and the All Stars' executive proved able through the influence of Linton Browne and Jean Elder of the Unemployment Relief Program (URP) to base a work gang and materials in the panyard; 50% of the work gang was provided by URP and 50% comprised unemployed members of the band.[779] As a matter of fact Douglas claimed to be the first to have successfully made it possible for band members to work in the Panyard as a URP gang, welding racks and painting pans at Carnival time, and being paid URP rates.[780]

This arrangement continued even after the NAR government came to power in 1986 and changed the URP to LID; in fact at that point according to Grip Matthews, LID also paid members of the band working on the building and he, Matthews, admitted that he was charged with the responsibility of taking the labor-force work sheet to Diego Martin to ensure that the payroll was organized on a timely basis.[781] So there was much precedence since the mid-1980s for what the executive led by Reds Collins was able to accomplish in the early to mid-1990s.

The final thrust, however, to complete the panyard structure was given added impetus when Winston Ross of the Self Help Commission made the commitment to Colin Bishop to deliver $70,000 in materials to All Stars yard, with the "option to consider further amounts on the condition that the resources

were not wasted," and when this commitment was formally announced before an audience that included top Neal and Massy communications personnel, Mr. Hugh Henderson expressed "no difficulty in matching the amount of $70,000."
[782]

So, what exists today as the Trinidad All Stars Pan-yard, replete with paved grounds as well as a two-story Administrative Centre outfitted with office space, storage space, practice area and merchandise shop, took the energies and efforts of all the executive committees from the early 1970s to the present as well as the input of the active sections of the broad membership; and therefore to move on from there onto even greater heights inclusive of a modern, transformational facility shall demand even more sterling efforts.

Constitutional Reform

As indicated in the previous sections, Trinidad All Stars Steel Orchestra has always been imbibed with a certain focus and purpose. Over time, this organization, notwithstanding the numerous trials and tribulations it has had to face, has never once shirked its responsibility to itself, to its founders, to the wider surrounding community from which it derived its birth, and, more so, to this nation of Trinidad & Tobago.

Nigel Williams, probably to date, the band's longest serving Treasurer or Finance Manager, expressed this ongoing commitment best in his introduction to his presentation to the band titled "Internal Controls for Co-operatives": *Trinidad All Stars Steel Orchestra has embarked upon a journey that should result in a more effective and efficient modus operandi. A complete restructuring of the management structure and style should lead to a self-sufficient institution with a more commercial view to this business of Steel Pan. This vision to some might seem new, but it is in fact a continuation of something that started over seventy (70) years ago. The steelband movement has been plagued with a dependency syndrome on corporate sponsorship. Whilst it is a fact that having the financial resources makes life easier, what does not make sense economically is that some of these sponsors give a little but expect a lot. To some steelbands, sponsors are Gods.*

To Trinidad All Stars, sponsorship is of mutual benefit. Trinidad All Stars has value; this steelband can demand that they be treated as a valuable entity. This steelband has contributed significantly to the community, the country, its members and to the steelband movement. Due to the nature of a steelband and the fact that it is not viewed as a legal entity, All Stars decided to form a Co-operative Society that can handle all legal transactions and can benefit the institution and its members. With this in mind, it is of paramount importance that the persons charged with the responsibility of running this Co-operative understand their role and function.[783]

As already indicated, the Trinidad All Stars Steel Orchestra Co-operative Society Limited was registered as No. C/229/89 on September 14, 1989 and according to the memorandum from the Director of Surveys to the Director, Town and Country Planning dated Feb. 2, 1990, Cabinet had agreed that *No. 46 Duke Street comprising 4025 sq. ft be leased to Catelli Trinidad All Stars Steel Orchestra. The lease to be granted in favor of the Co-operative to be established by Catelli Trinidad All Stars.*[784] However, in regard to all the lands that comprise the Hell Yard home of Trinidad All Stars there needs to be clarity: No. 46 Duke Street, the paved area where the Bar was originally located, was acquired in 1980 by the Government for the Trinidad All Stars Steel Orchestra Co-operative Society from the Charbonne Family who were the private owners, and with that acquisition of No. 46 the band gained access to the River Reserve, (i.e., 46-A), the "Big Sink" that was eventually filled up after 900 plus loads of fill provided by Don Ramdeen Trucking Service, following which this area was paved to facilitate the erection of the present building.[785]

No. 48 comprises the lot that was purchased outright by Trinidad All Stars from its earnings as a Steel Orchestra without the financial involvement of any sponsor, and this is the area to the west where the barrack lodging was once located and which now borders the wall that encloses the property of one Mr. William Munroe, moreover it was the north-western section of No.48 which had become the subject of contention and litigation with the neighboring company, Leonard S. Browne & Co. Ltd.[786] So given legal formality, it can be argued that No. 46 plus the reclaimed River Reserve, is technically owned by the Co-operative Society, while No. 48 was bought outright and is owned by the Steel Orchestra; so three once distinct portions of land have now been made into one single, geographic and topographic continuum, but in legal terms, the Cooperative Society and the Steel Orchestra are not synonymous.

Apparently, the approach to dealing with this contradiction or anomaly was to make sure that the key officers of the Band were also the key officers of the Co-operative Society, so in the period 1989–1991 for instance Red Collins was both the Captain of the Band as well as President of the Co-operative Society, and likewise Chris Haynes was the Treasurer of both.[787] Glenda Esdelle the Secretary of the Co-operative in her very first report stated the following: "Your Board met at the Executive level on ten (10) occasions. The decision to hold monthly meetings was not strictly adhered to because of foreign commitment of the Band and involvement in national competitions, the World Steelband Music Festival and Classical Jewels."[788] Then in 1990, Glenda Esdelle also said: "There was a problem with members serving on (the) Executive of the Band and (the) Co-operative. It was exacting as one infringes and impinges on the other. The curfew also curtailed ability to hold one Board meeting per month..."[789]

So, from the onset, there were problems. The principal activity of the Co-operative was to manage a Consumer Shop and to purchase and sell to members, goods, stores and consumable articles,[790] while the main activity of the Steel Orchestra was the performances and engagements utilizing their musical product. How these two distinct and apart purposes could ever be harmonized and managed expediently especially when the managers are one and the same people, was the big question. It simply did not work. Furthermore in the reports on file, there was constant lamentation that the required work of the Co-operative Society was not being fulfilled despite all the training seminars and consultations organized by the Co-operative Division of the Ministry which were attended by key people such as Glenda Esdelle, herself, and Keith Matthews.[791]

In addition to this, all efforts to push a membership drive for the Co-operative that would take the count from 65 to 100 members was never realized,[792] despite the plea from the President Reds Collins for "management expertise" so that the deficiencies could be addressed and the training as well as the membership drive could be intensified resulting in the shares being increased to the extent that the Co-operative could "accumulate funds and have a continuous supply of money."[793]

After taking all the above into consideration there could be no surprise that Members' Equity in the Co-operative only raised from $3,295.00 according to the balance sheet as at June 30th 1990 to $4,395.00 as at November 30, 1992.[794] The solution had to be the removal of the management of the Co-operative far away from the hands of the executive officers of the Steel Orchestra who would then stick to their professionalism as creators of the musical product, and thereby open up the way for the subsequent hiring of the management expertise required to handle competently the administration and marketing of a Co-operative. This was never done and for all practical purposes the Trinidad All Stars Steel Orchestra Co-operative Society Ltd was just thrust aside.

If indeed, the situation is as described, and so far there is no evidence to suggest otherwise, the big question that arises, is whether this Co-operative that legally "owns" sections of Hell Yard can be simply abandoned? The Bye-Laws (nos. 1–52) of the Trinidad All Stars Orchestra Co-operative Society Ltd registered and approved on September 14, 1989 by Arnim Greaves, then Act. Commissioner for Co-operative Development, are totally silent on the issue of any procedure for the winding up of a Co-operative Society.[795] Is it then simply a matter of the membership, or a quorum thereof, meeting and passing a resolution to either go out of existence or to revitalize the Co-operative Society?

It would appear that all the above stated questions were left in abeyance after 1992. Sad that this had to be the outcome of the grand effort despite the early warnings that "a Co-operative is a user-owned and controlled business from which benefits are derived and distributed equitably on the basis of use…" and that precisely because of the above maxim "…Co-operatives have to adhere to their fundamental principles to distinguish them from other types of business organizations" and that the professional maintenance of such an intrinsic nature had to be the major key to the ladder of success.[796]

In the future, All Stars as an institution will have no choice but to re-assess this matter. If the Co-operative remains an objective then the structural relationship of the two entities, i.e., Band and Co-operative, will have to be worked out, professionals will have to be employed to manage the affairs and some precise percentage of the earnings of members will have to be set aside to build consistently the shareholding assets and mutual funds as well as its required investment portfolio.

If, however, the interest of the members in a truly functional Co-operative Society waned significantly, then the very opposite was the case in regard to the issue of Administrative reform with the view to strengthen the operational capacity of the Steel Orchestra per se. Between the last quarter of 2003 to July 2004, a cross-section of players and even former executive officials such as Noel "Cin-Cin" Lord and Reds Collins with assistance from a random group of professionals chosen from the All Stars' support-base led by Mrs. Lenore

Superville, Mrs. Joan Gower de Chabert, Gideon Harris (now deceased), Darryl Joseph, etc. began an in-depth engagement in dialoguing and workshopping the issues surrounding constitutional reform for Trinidad All Stars Steel Orchestra with special regard to organizational structure and the operational policies essential to nurture and support it.

In the course of extensive debate, the vision for the Band was reaffirmed as follows: "To be the world's premier, professional Steel Orchestra, financially independent and universally acclaimed for the highest level of musical excellence."[797] Categories of membership were established. Regular Membership, i.e., any playing or non-playing individual accepted by the Management Team to either "participate in continuous structured rehearsals for performances" or "one interested in the welfare of and active in the undertakings of the Organization."[798] Furthermore, honorary membership or Life membership could be conferred on any individual "on the recommendation of the Management Team for significant and sterling contribution to the welfare of the Organization."[799]

It was proposed that the Management Team be comprised of the following: Manager, i.e., formerly Leader or Captain; Assistant Manager (Operations); Assistant Manager (Administration); Finance Manager; Human Resources Manager; Musical Director; Marketing Manager and Community Relations Manager.[800] The Manager and his two Assistants were to be elected positions, while all the others were to be appointed positions in accordance with the traditional guidelines, but the Manager, the chairperson of the Management Team, had to be "the motivator, thought-leader and innovator"; "the chief servant of the Organization elected by the membership to provide sound leadership on their behalf." [801]

As regard to whom would be deemed eligible to be elected to the three management positions for a period of three years by secret ballot at least 14 days after the Triennial General Meeting, the following was outlined: any regular member who is financial and has served the Organization for "at least five immediately prior (preceding) and consecutive years, subject to screening by an electoral committee duly appointed by the Management Committee."[802] And finally the appointed officers were to be chosen by consensual agreement of the three elected managers plus "one performing regular member and three non-performing regular members" convened no later than one month after the election of the three elected managers.[803]

The code of ethics or code of conduct, deemed as the expected mode of behavior that would nurture the kind of internal relationships to make the new organizational structure work, was outlined in a Statement of Purpose which read inter-alia: "Managers (who) hold positions of trust and respect within the Organization (must) assume fiduciary, legal and moral responsibilities to conduct the affairs of the Band in the best interest of the members at large, and seek to protect the image and integrity of the Band in the eyes of its members and the public..."[804]

The officers of All Stars therefore had to swear and sign a declaration of acceptance of the code of conduct in which it was outlined that "integrity took precedence over all other principles," and that integrity meant and required that they "guard jealously the reputation of the Band by maintaining constant vigilance over all phases of operations and by quickly, tactfully and judiciously adjusting or correcting any grievance or complaint found to have substance" and without in anyway using their positions to "further personal interests or to secure special privileges."[805]

And though there was to be strict adherence to the rule of confidentiality in regard to the handling of private information and the transactions of internal, discreet affairs, nevertheless there had likewise to be a firm commitment of the managers to "convey understanding" and allow for widespread membership expression at "well attended annual membership meetings" where "accurate account information will be available at all times" and where there would be a "constant effort to keep members properly informed" in order to "maintain their confidence" in those managing the affairs of the Band on a day to day basis.[806]

Interestingly, as a result of the workshops which were organized to assess the opinions of the membership and to allow the membership to exercise their own interventions in the process of formulating policy, one particular section of the membership boldly set parameters to their own actions and involvement as well as that of the leadership personalities. They advocated the following:

1. Members should not be disrespectful to those in authority; in case of any dispute arising out of instructions from any person in authority, one should comply, and then complain.

2. Respect must be given not only to the personality but more importantly to the office. Comply with the directives of section leaders as well as any director of rehearsals.
3. Members should be able to complain on those in authority and have it addressed promptly. If there is a complaint, the situation should not be aggravated by excuses.
4. Criteria for selection for engagements should be clearly outlined to all players, and section leaders should have a key role in the selection process.
5. The musical selections that comprised the band's repertoire should be scored in order to make them more readily available to players, and each player on the stage-side should have an understudy, so that there is no dependency on any one person, and no one person could ever hold the entire band to ransom.
6. Players must be made quite aware of what and for what they are being paid, and players who practice regularly and are not selected for any specific engagement should be given a stipend in appreciation for their efforts when payments are being made for the said engagement.
7. In regard to practice sessions, members involved must be consistently present and punctual.
8. There should be a permanent dress-code for engagements. Players need more appropriate and stylish uniforms instead of the normal, ordinary T-shirts.
9. Practice should be structured so as to ensure that the Band is fully and adequately represented on all engagements.
10. Each playing member must take full responsibility for his or her instrument, i.e., cleaning and securing instrument before, during and after all engagements.[807]

The Workshop Group that advanced this 10-point program was comprised of the following people whose names appeared at the bottom of the document: Ren Hamlet; Shaoubaca Elie; Shareen Walcott; Jackie McKell; Petal Joseph; Darrel Joseph; Monica Roach and Ogbon Mikre. It was quite noteworthy that these members, understanding the significance and importance of their involvement in an Organization such as Trinidad All Stars Steel Orchestra, had come to see disciplined functioning not as an imposition from leadership above but as a form of self-actualization and self-determination.

Nevertheless, there is the view that despite the fact that this 10 point code of conduct was adopted wholesale by both the leadership and membership of the band, there is a widening "gap" in the sense that rules and regulations listed on paper or mouthed can in some instances be a far cry from the actual practice that obtains.[808] The conclusion is that this matter must be addressed in the course of any review of the new structure; such a review to date has never been done despite the mutual understanding that it would be done after the very first six months of operating under the rubric of the new structure. Ex-Captain, Web Alexander is of the further view that the code of ethics and conduct should be enforced fully at all times and that copies of it be strategically placed at key areas of the panyard to be read and be inculcated by all members.[809]

The first election under the new constitution was held on Tuesday 24 August 2004. It was supervised by the electoral team which was comprised of Mrs. Lenore Superville, Mrs. Joan Gower de Chabert and Mr. Bukka Rennie. All the prospective candidates were screened by the electoral team. At the night of the elections, all the candidates were required to make a short presentation to the eligible voting membership elucidating their vision for the band and the program of activity that they intended to implement. Before the voting began, each member of the electoral team gave a short address on the importance of the process and reinforced what was expected of both the elected managers as well as the role of the membership in keeping democracy alive and vibrant in the Organization.

The results were as follows: Mr. Beresford Hunte was elected Manager, unopposed; Assistant Manager—Administration was Mr. Darryl Joseph, also unopposed; and Assistant Manager—Operations was won by Mr. Jason Lewis by a wide margin against the opposing candidate, Errol "Reds" Collins.[810] Within one month of the elections, the Management Team of Beresford Hunte, Jason Lewis and Darrel Joseph, in accordance with the new constitution, met with one floor representative from the stage-side, Mr. Cleve Leonard, and three (3) other members, Ms. Stacy-Ann Patrick, Mrs. Lenore Superville and Ms. Jennifer Selby, to appoint the non-elected members of the Management Team as follows: Nigel Williams—Finance Manager; Clarence Payne—Human Resource Manager; and Franklyn Lewis—Community Relations Manager.

The other positions, i.e., Marketing Manager and Musical Director were left to be settled at a later date.[811]

It was this executive who in the process of seeking to re-brand the band and augment its marketing thrust that took the decision in 2006 to re-format its web-site and launch a new Logo. It was explained that the Logo "represented the many facets of the institution:

1. **Black Background**—the black background represents the rich fertile earth from which the Trinidad All Stars was born…
2. **One Gold Star**—the single Gold Star represents the fact that many individual stars come together to form one great Star; its juxtaposition against the black background forms the image of notes on a pan symbolizing the inseparability of pan and All Stars; All Stars is pan, pan is All Stars…
3. **Dancing Sailor**—the sailor is a tribute to the sailor heritage of All Stars. Note the sailor is dancing to the music of the band…
4. **Musical Banner**—the musical banner being waved by the sailor and wrapped around the star is filled with musical notes, symbolizing the rich musicality of the band in everything it does.
5. **Spotlight**—the spotlight under the sailor symbolizes the showmanship of All Stars; whenever All Stars plays, they play in the spotlight…"

Logo

Both Kenneth Scott (artist/designer) and Darryl Joseph, then assistant manager-administration, have indicated that the new Logo was the result of their collaboration. Mr. Scott was precise in his description that the "sailor with flag banner on a circular spotlight" was his major input, while the "notes on the banner" and the "backdrop of the huge star" was Darryl's.[812] Darryl Joseph who provided the literary background explanation to the various parts of the logo also indicated that his wife assisted in the entire process.[813]

At the second election, under the ambit of the new constitution held in 2008, Beresford Hunte was returned as Manager, unopposed, while Darryl Joseph did not contest the post of Assistant Manager-Administration, leaving that post open to a grueling stand-off between Keith "Grip" Matthews and Ms. Denise Riley, two long-standing members of past executives, with Denise Riley being successful in the final analysis. On the other hand, Jason "Stumps" Lewis gained the upper hand against Cleve Leonard for the post of Assistant Manager-Operations.

In the course of the 2008 elections the Electoral Team comprising Mrs. Lenore Superville, Ms. Joan Gower de Chabert and Bukka Rennie was joined by Leon "Smooth" Edwards who assisted in the screening process and at the night of the elections also addressed the eligible voters outlining his own view of what was required of each member in the exercise. It was in the course of discussion with the Electoral Team during the 2008 elections that the view, already mentioned, was raised by Smooth Edwards about the need for a Classical Music Arranger rather than a Musical Director per se. However, outside of the Finance Manager, who has been Nigel Williams for the past decade, the appointment of the other Managers has not been given much consideration since 2004.

The third election within the ambit of the new constitution became due in October-November of 2011 but was postponed to early 2012. The results of the 2012 elections were as follows: Beresford Hunte, once again unopposed, Manager; Jason "Stumps" Lewis defeated Reds Collins for the post of Manager-Operations; and Denise Riley defeated Denise Hernandez for the post of Manager-Administration.

Mr. Chris Haynes was appointed the Community Relations Manager with responsibility for community outreach programs and carnival masquerade, thereby taking over from Mr. Superville, who for many years took up the responsibility of a "Jack of All Trades", handling management of the Pan Yard per se, the Bar, the carnival masquerade, etc. at times at the expense of his own family business. Beside Beresford Hunte, Jason Lewis since 2004 and Denise Riley since 2008 have consistently been elected to office by the membership. Both these officers have expressed their personal views on matters relative to the ongoing welfare of Trinidad All Stars.

Jason "Stumps" Lewis

In 1991, he composed "J'ouvert in ah Band" in honor of the legendary Neville Jules. It was played at the Classical Jewels X1 concert.

"Stumps" joined All Stars in 1983 at the age of 13. At that time he was a student at the POS South East Secondary School and played with the school band. From 1983 to the present, a period of 35 years, Stumps has been a member of the All Stars Stage-side, 15 years on the tenor-pan, and 20 years on the drums. He was first elected as a Trustee in 1989, then just 19 years of age, and he indicated that when he joined in 1983, he underwent a brief indoctrination wherein it was outlined what being a member of All Stars meant and what was expected of him.

It may have been as a result of such briefing that led to his enrolment in a Steelband Management Course at UWI in 1991. Subsequently he went on to hold in sequence a number of executive positions in All Stars, i.e., treasurer, vice-captain, public relations officer and, since the structural reform in 2004, he has won the post of Asst. Manager—Operations consistently up to recent times; interestingly "Stumps" after describing his post as "Operations

Manager" in accordance with the new constitution, maintained that though the structural reform has *made a difference*, some aspects of it *are not working* and therefore need to be reviewed *with a fine-teeth comb*.

The relationship between members of past and present executive bodies, he regards as basically good because, in his view, the *key members* over time, have, to a large extent, been the *same people*. Stumps insists that his most significant contribution to All Stars has been the *consistency of his dedication* plus his *musical tribute to Neville Jules*, the greatest leader produced by All Stars and the father of the modern steel orchestra. In response to the criticism that the present Stage-side has been negligent in regard to performing regularly all the band's winning Bomb-tunes which are always in demand by audiences throughout the country, Stumps as the then person responsible for the repertoire over the past years, argues that to resolve this dilemma, *a proper rehearsal structure* must be established.

Nevertheless when asked about his vision for the band, then 83 years old and which would be 100 years old in 2035, he advocates strongly for the nurturing of an All Stars Youth Band that would be a home source for succession planning as well as the institutionalization of an Academy of Music Literacy at the Pan-Yard.

Denise "Dimples" Riley: Denise joined the band in the Carnival season of 1985 but confesses that she initially came to the band "as a chaperone" to her youngest sister, Marcia, and after trying the double-seconds she moved to the six-bass, the sound of which enthralled her. She indicated that on joining she was interviewed by Ms. Barbara Crichlow and though she was never made to undergo any process of indoctrination or presented with a code of conduct to which she must adhere, nevertheless she functioned in a manner that "quickly earned respect among (her) new found peers."[814]

In 1996, after eleven years, she was nominated unopposed to replace Mr. Colin Bishop as secretary/treasurer and found herself having to deal with both administrative as well as financial duties, an experience that led her to support the decision to eventually separate the said duties. Over the years since then, Denise has served as secretary, treasurer, assistant-manager—administration and finally manager-administration.[815] Denise has enjoyed over the years preparing budgets for the sponsor as well as procuring and even designing uniforms and special kits for the band. In fact she designs all the panorama final night kits.

She considers the work she did with the special committee set up to build back the band after the 1988–1989 split to be her most significant contribution to All Stars. She plans in future to work toward establishing a "pension fund and burial plan" for elders of the band to assist them with their needs, hoping thereby to build a "closer relationship between the band and the elders' association." When asked whether she, as a prominent female executive member, viewed herself as a role model for the young female members who comprise over 50% of the membership, this was her response:

...I have never agreed with putting myself up on a pinnacle to be a role model. Role models often disappoint and I believe that one should not idolize another, but should learn from the failures and successes of a person...[816]

Denise Riley on the Six-Bass.

In summation, it is important to note that there is a general feeling in the band presently that though the new structure is a reflection of the most modern forms of democratic functioning, some officers operate as if they are unaware of the full nature of their roles and there is a tendency to vacillate between extremely opposite poles. Either they assume or abrogate unto themselves untold powers that suggest that they are not accountable to anyone, in which case they choose to act and refuse to report or account to the overall Leader or

Manager who holds the responsibility for the "overall cohesiveness and effectiveness of the entire Management Team."

Or, on the other hand, they choose to leave everything up to the overall Leader or Manager on whose shoulder everything falls and as a result the pressure becomes so great that eventually it has a debilitating effect and stymies the development and progress of the band as a whole. Again and again the membership was forewarned during the election process about the great difficulty of operating and managing modern democratic structures whereby all and sundry must assume the obligation and responsibility for the welfare of the whole organism or fall back to the easiness and lazy comfort-zone of allowing one-man dictatorial rule for which steelbands have been so greatly noted in the early history.

But that is not the nature of Trinidad All Stars, an organization which from its inception, and by its very name, has always sought to recognize, acknowledge, and nurture the talents of all its members. Yes, there were always strong leaders in the past, but the tradition and culture of All Stars never allowed the emergence of any form of totalitarianism as was typical of other bands.

The 2016 elections brought a new executive to chart the years ahead. Beresford Hunte decided to step down to make way for younger folk. Nigel Williams was elected unopposed as the 12th Manager of the Trinidad All Stars Steel Orchestra. Jason "Stumps" Lewis was elected once again to the post of Manager-Operations and Nicole Belgrave won the post of Manager-Administration. The subsequent official appointees were as follows: Keith Matthews—marketing; Staci-Ann Patrick—human resource; Darryl Joseph—public relations; Nelca Licorish—finance manager and Christopher Haynes—community relations.

In 2019, as was constitutionally due, the election was held on August 19th and the following were the results: Nigel Williams was elected Manager, unopposed; Nicole Belgrave, was elected Asst Manager Administration as Denise Riley declined. Keith "Grip" Matthews was elected Asst. Manager Operations defeating both Jason "Stumps" Lewis and Christopher Haynes by a close margin. The appointed officers are as follows: Nicholette Hannaway—Finance Manager; Karlene Lewis—Human Resource Manager; Community Relations Manager—Dane Gulston; and Public Relations Officer—Staci-Ann Patrick.

A Collective Management Vision has been issued:

Interestingly, what has become pellucidly clear is that the band continues slowly gravitating toward encapsulating concepts of both a modern Public Corporation and that of a Cooperative Society whereby the group, whose core activity involves entertainment and the creation of cultural products, can be authorized to act as a single entity with a growing asset base and an investment portfolio that in the immediate future shall serve to satisfy the needs of the entire membership. Already there have been proposals for the establishment of a pension scheme and a type of provident mutual funds for the cover of medical and other such requirements.

Some may wish to describe such considerations as "pie-in-the-sky" idealism but in reality members of Trinidad All Stars for quite some time now have been enjoying benefits from tours, trips abroad and local performances even if they were not selected to be part of the actual engagements but were consistently present at the required practice sessions. This is indeed a novelty in the history of the steelband movement and it reveals much more about the nature of the institution that is All Stars. **The band traditionally has always sought to nurture and extend its democratic instinctiveness.**

That is why when, in the course of searching for a "name" for the band in 1946, it was suggested that the band, because of Jules's presence, be called "Black God and Kings", Jules rejected that idea on the grounds that he "did not want to be any God"[817] and settled for "All Stars', which implied that everybody be deemed a STAR in his or her own right. In this band's functioning, everyone has to glitter and shine forth while remembering at all times that, as the old Hell Yard maxim reassures, ***Stars pitch, they never fall!***

Chapter Six
The Epilogue

The Case: Hell-Yard Must Be Declared an International Heritage Site

Based on all that has been established above in Chapters 1–3, the following acknowledgments are evident:

1. Neville Jules of All Stars is the inventor of the family of pans that by and large comprise the Steel Orchestra, starting with:
   a. The *4-Note Ping-Pong* or melody-pan utilizing small paint-pans which led to the explosion of the search for notes, five, six, eight, nine, and then onto thirteen and fourteen notes using the special KMR pans Jules obtained from the POS slaughter-house. Eventually after 1947 there emerged throughout the country the 45-gallon oil-drum tenor pan with additional notes.
   b. The *Bele or Belleh* pan which became quickly outdated. It was called "the Belly" by Patrick Leigh Fermor and he described it as one that "seconded" the tenor pan or "Tock-Tock" and was "divided into seven deeper notes". Oliver Joseph, an early player of the Bele, indicated that it was "strapped around the shoulder and played with two sticks, the stick in the left hand was held downwards, and the one in the right hand was held upwards."[818] OJ vividly recalls playing the Bele on a Carnival Day "till the skin on his shoulder peeled off and he was bleeding."[819]
   There is also the indication according to John Edward Slater that around this time Jules created an improvement on the traditional military-styled kettle beat as well as the beat of the du-dup or bass-

kettle, obviously the Bele was the instrument used to affect the cross-over from the traditional military beat. It is quite evident in the picture of Red Army (see Pic 2); note well how the sticks are held by the Bele players in the center and foreground of the picture.

c. The ***Five Note Tune-Boom***, an early form of bass that was particularly developed by Jules to carry the bass-lines to his arrangement of Lord Melody's *Georgie Porgie* in the Christmas of 1947 as they prepared for 1948 Carnival. It was described by Patrick Leigh Fermor as the "Base-Bum, a vast biscuit container from a local factory." It quickly gave way to Jules' Two-Bass and Three-Bass utilizing the whole special caustic-soda drum without cutting.

d. ***Alto Pan***—While the big tenor originally carried 18-notes, the Alto Pan was deeper, with wider skirt and carried 14 notes according to Oliver Joseph; two notes in the center and twelve around. TASPO went to England with two Altos played by Belgrave Bonaparte and Sterling Betancourt. According to Mannette, Lieutenant Griffith made him and Tony Williams tune 14-Note Alto Pans for TASPO (**i.e., 1951**). See pics 4 and 5 of bands with Alto pans in 1947 and 1949, the latter ironically being Mannette's Invaders, while Lieutenant Griffith was still working in St. Lucia.

e. ***Cuatro/Guitar Pan***—"Guitar Pan" was the name given to Jules' Cuatro Pan by Boots Davidson and that name stuck. The first musical arrangement by Jules that brought this Pan into special focus in 1950 was the song "Three Little Japanese"[820] from the 1885 Gilbert and Sullivan Opera, "The Mikado" which became quite popular in the USA in the 1930s and onward. TASPO did not have Guitar-Pans.

f. ***Two-Bass and Three-Bass*** which led shortly to *Five-Bass and Six-Bass and High and Low Basses.*

g. ***Grundig Pan*** (also quickly outdated)—forerunner to the modern Cello range of Pans. Neville explained that he created the *Grundig* because he wished it to be played somewhat like the *tenor-kettle*, playing riffs "but on the chords".[821]

h. ***Trombone Pan***—This was the special Pan "made for Audra" (i.e., Audra Preddie) who did not stay in the Pan movement as he moved on to play traditional instruments first with Aubrey Adams and later the Marionettes.[822] Jules maintained consistently that if Audra had stayed with Pan he would have become one of the great virtuoso-players or masters. It is a view supported by Julien Darius (JD).

i. ***Tenor-Bass***—Invented and introduced by Jules for the performance of Claude Debussy's "La Mer" at the 1954 Music Festival. The 1951 TASPO pictures clearly show that the instruments used were single tenors, single altos, double-cellos and a three-bass. Therefore all claims to the contrary have to be debunked. The members of TASPO reached England in 1951 playing single pans except for the two double-cellos played by Tony Williams and Dudley Smith and one three-bass played by Boots Davidson.

Outside of Neville Jules's personal creations and contribution to the development of the steel-pan music chronicled above in No.1 (a–i), the following should be noted as being generally accepted and promoted as common knowledge.

2. **Ellie Mannette** of Invaders was responsible for introducing the combining of both the concave and convex method of tuning which became the standard principle throughout the Nation and were applied to all Jules' pan inventions starting from the 8-Note Ping-Pongs and Five-Not Tune-Booms.[823] He was reputed to be the sweetest and most exacting tuner in the early period.

3. **Lt. Griffith** further enhanced the chromatic methodology of tuning, i.e., ascending or descending in semitones or tones according to the said scale which became the accepted norm throughout, and, in the course of preparation for the TASPO tour, the notes on the Tenor as directed by Griffith was increased to 23 notes and the Double-Cello was created.

4. **The Single-Second Pan:** This Pan was deeper than the Altos and carried less notes. Slater declared Jules as the inventor. See Slater's

diagram of Jules' second pan (sic) in **Pic 1**. Jules has never claimed to be the inventor of this Pan. As a matter of fact he indicated that the first one he saw was made by Sonny Roach of Sun Valley.[824] TASPO did not have single second-pans. Any claim that TASPO had "second-pans" are misconceptions.

5. **Boom-Town** of Tacarigua presented the first ***45-gallon drum tenor pan***. It was played by Cyril "Snatcher" Guy, tuned by Ladd Wiltshire under the guidance of Andrew Beddoe. After this the 45-Gallon drum became the chosen ideal with which to build the pan instruments. The initial public reaction to this size of pan when it was introduced at Monarch Cinema in Tunapuna is ample evidence that it was the first of its kind.

6. **Belgrave Bonaparte** of Southern Symphony was the inventor of the ***Double-Seconds***. There are many eye-witnesses to him playing it at the 1954 Music Festival. Also this band was the first to attempt to put a Steel-Band on wheels on Carnival Day, using the format of a box-cart/ platform with wheel-bearings which failed miserably.[825] The following Carnival, 1956, North Stars of St. James perfected this development with the use of bicycle wheels.

7. The ***(Fourths and Fifths) Tenor Pan*** is alleged to be the result of collaboration between Philmore "Boots" Davidson and Anthony "Muffman" Williams who became very close friends in Britain and worked together after TASPO returned home in 1951. There is no evidence besides the words of Noel "Ginghee" Davidson, elder brother of Boots, to support this contention. What we know is that Boots was the most accomplished, formal and advanced musician of the TASPO lot and could read and score music.

Ginghee died in 2018 and as well Tony Williams died in December 2021 so there is no one around to concur that the 4ths and 5ths Tenor: 16 notes around the circumference and 12 in the center was the result of the collaboration between Boots and Muffman. The 4ths move clockwise from the top around the pan and the 5ths move anti-clockwise. Tony Williams, however, was the one who placed the notes in a "spider-web" design, a design which never caught on and was never utilized by other bands while the "fourths and fifths" notation did. So we are left with the following (a) it was the result of a collaboration between Boots and Muffman;(b) it was the result of a Tony Williams' copy of a pan sold to him by the lawyer, Lennox Pierre; and (c) it was all the work of Anthony Williams, a carpenter by trade, given his penchant for astrology, numerology, religion and science and his use of the Bible for inspiration in developing his pan skills.

Recently, since Muffman's death, there appeared an article in When Steel Talks (22 December 2021) titled "The Prometheus of Pan—Dr. Anthony Williams" by Garvin Blake, who played with Pan-Am North Stars, in which the following statement is made: *It would be years before I realized I was playing an instrument laid out in the cycle of fifths, a scientific organization of pitches dating back to the sixth century BC that's fundamental to western tonal music. Tony didn't read about this harmonic relationship in a music theory book. He used his own ingenious mathematical method to arrive at the cycle.* The point is: who and what are we to believe?

8. **Double High-Tenors** was invented by Bertie Marshall and this is widely known and accepted by all and sundry.
9. **Quadrophonic Seconds** was the result of collaboration between Rudolph Charles, Bertie Marshall, and Wallace Austin. This is also accepted, common knowledge in today's world.

The reality is that everything else, all other additions or variations to the Steel-Pan Orchestra beyond what is listed above, may be considered "bells and whistles" or merely the addition of depth and color.

From the very beginning, the spinal importance of Pan to the general well-being of citizens of T&T was duly recognized. Slater talked about the mysterious and spiritual effect that the Belleh, the Grundig and such pans had on the people. Jules said that he only knew that a Pan was good when it was tried out on the streets and the people responded with body and soul.

Albert Jones, described as a "foremost authority" on Pan Development explored the connection between Pan and the culture of the people in the following manner: "...*The beauty of Pan is that it can play all music. However, it's best suited for Calypso. You see it originated from calypso music, with the people who were developing an instrument to go with the calypso tradition. So, Pan evolved in the Calypso tradition. You can feel most comfortable playing calypso on pan. A guy in England will play his type of music on pan and feel comfortable doing that... But Trinidadians feel most comfortable playing calypso... A culture is something. Our culture is Calypso and Steelpan. The piano was made for the European classics and that is their culture.*

Drums and jumping and dancing go together, as you can see among some Africans and Native Americans. That is how culture evolves, with one activity complementing another. For us, it's Steelpan and Calypso. That's our culture... If anyone knows the history and background of Pan and Calypso, he will know that they originated simultaneously out of colonial efforts to suppress African culture... If you study the places where Pan first came from, you'll find it came from those places where there was Shango, an African presence... Every single band was either in front or behind or next to or near a Shango yard..."[826] And it was Othello Molineaux who dared to sum it all up so sweetly and succinctly when he said: **Pan is the spirit of Trinidad! It is the heartbeat of the Nation...**[827]

A Pan-Man's Contribution to Jamaican Music

It was that very "heartbeat" of Pan that Nearlin "Lynn" Taitt, double-second pan-player, arranger and tuner of Seabees from San Fernando took with him to Jamaica in July of 1962 and created history as a studio guitarist. While attending "Rock-Steady and Reggae Night" at the Montreal Jazz Program in 2009, I was stunned when Marcia Griffiths, an original member of the "I-Threes" called Nearlin Taitt, who lived then in Montreal, onto the stage and declared to the world that Lynn Taitt was the mainstay behind the development of Jamaican Music; what, however, was not said is that Nearlin Taitt, now deceased, was a Trinidadian "double-second" pan player from San Fernando who settled in Jamaica and the folklore in T&T has it that it was his efforts to transpose the "strum of the second-pan" onto the guitar that gave birth to the Rock-Steady Beat and the rest, as they say, is now history.

Lynn Taitt himself did indicate that just as there are "fast and slow calypsos", it was in his desire to "slow down the Ska beat" that led to the development of Rock-Steady and Reggae.[828] Taitt, much like Audra Preddie of All Stars, was a steel-pan prodigy, a man with perfect-pitch, who switched to the traditional musical instruments, and he played several of them, the guitar being his main preference, and supportive of T&T's folklore, his guitar style was described as "inventive and unconventional with a sharp percussive sound,"[829] in other words his pan strumming influenced his guitar licks. Lynn Taitt therefore is the connection between Pan-creativity of T&T and Rock-Steady/Reggae of Jamaica both of which together have signified more than anything else the Caribbean personality and identity.

It is of interest to record what Lynn Taitt said of his work in Jamaica, and what Jamaicans, themselves, said of him as they lamented his passing. Lynn Taitt said: "I was always trying new things with my guitar… Is my experience from playing Calypso on guitar that I use to help shape sounds in Jamaica…"[830] When questioned whether his guitar licks or "bubbling notes style" echoed the inflection of the steel-pan, Lynn Taitt responded in this manner: "Yes, that's a part of it; it's playing the bass line and other things too."

Taitt then asked the interviewer: "Have you ever heard of the Trinidadian musicians Joey Lewis and Clarence Curvan? They led groups in Trinidad in the '50s that played Reggae bass lines, but didn't realize it at the time…"[831] Lynn Taitt was diagnosed with cancer in early April of 2008 and by March 2009 was given two weeks to live, so when he was being lionized on stage at the Montreal Jazz "Rock-Steady-Reggae Night" in the summer of 2009, he knew that he was in his last days.

Lynn Taitt

Lynn on the left

On Sunday, 30 August 2009, Lynn Taitt made the following announcement to the world: "Even though I record so many songs on guitar and I love to play guitar, I love steel-pan most of all. It's not even close really, I love steel-pan…"[832] In 2005, Mikey Chung of Jamaica speaking about Rock-Steady and Reggae said: "Lynn Taitt, he's the father. Lynn Taitt was a steel-pan player. Yeah, and when he came to Jamaica, he said he was emulating the steel-pan with his guitar…"[833] Lynn Taitt was cremated and his ashes returned to Trinidad.[834] We are yet as a Nation to honor fully this man for his contribution to the music that T&T and Jamaica has given to the world.

Today, the very heartbeat of Pan, just as Reggae, has influenced much and continues to engulf the entire world. This spark of creative ingenuity that emanated from Hell Yard has now captivated the imaginations of everyone from New York to Tokyo, and it is not merely about providing that joie de vivre, that joyous rapture that is so essential to a meaningful and balanced life in today's stressful world, but more so the fact that it has now been realized universally that the community of a Pan ensemble is by nature transformational; i.e., *pan have a jumbie,* as we in T&T have come to know since the very early days; meaning that Pan possesses a bewitching power that calms even the most restless soul and transforms the most instinctive delinquent into being the most sociable and well-adjusted human being.

Furthermore, according to Philbert Solomon of the Solomon Steelpan Company based in Pennsylvania... *the Pan does not need anything to play: no batteries, no electricity, nothing... only human energy,*[835] which is an advantage in regard to attracting people at all levels of social standing, but Philbert Solomon also makes the point that, whereas today in the USA and throughout the world interest in the traditional classical symphony orchestras is dying as the young people shy away, the very opposite is the case in regard to Pan; that the attraction to the versatility of Pan is powerful and Pan "is taking over", and he argues forcefully that Pan is the future and "will eventually keep all music alive," in other words that Pan will serve to bridge the Cultures and be the key also in preserving classical European music.[836]

Solomon, a Guyanese now operating a quite successful family Pan tuning and distribution business in the US, is probably well-placed from experience to plumb the depths of this bewitching power of Pan for as he pointed out: *Guyana got involved seriously in Steelband after Jules and his boys visited Guyana... when Jules and his group visited and performed in Market Square, people heard what this thing could do.* **It took them by storm**. *It was the first time they heard a bunch of guys play these things at one time. After Jules left, within a year we had three or four bands. Guyana got very serious into Pan in the '60s.*[837]

In fact, All Stars was first taken to Guyana in 1952 by a Guyanese impresario, Cyril Shaw, to participate in what was termed the "first ever International Steelband Competition" involving a band from Barbados and one from Guyana.[838] All Stars won that competition and it was reported that All Stars "had the capacity audience at the famous Georgetown Cricket Ground swarming and breaking down the stage in jubilation and appreciation of the orchestra's performance of a truly break-down rendition of *Bless This House.*"[839]

In fact, "Bless This House" had by then become quite popular internationally since it was a favorite song of Vera Lynn, the sweetheart of the Allied Armed Forces during World War 2. Today that incident in Guyana is a noted item in the history of All Stars and has become deeply embedded in its folklore. The second visit of All Stars to Guyana came in 1972 as part of the T&T's contingent to Carifesta 1. So Solomon had to be referencing the 1952 visit and since he was born in 1946, it means that he was at that time only six

(6) years old and therefore what he described about All Stars' visit in 1952 is really what he probably was told by older folk.

Nevertheless, as evidenced by other reports, All Stars really took Guyana "by storm" and today the same can be said about other parts of the modern world when first visited with the spirit of Pan that we call the "Pan Jumbie". According to Leroy Ali Williams, another one of those modern tuners who live in the USA and whose life has been transformed by engagement with Pan, it is not merely "the instrument of the twentieth century… it's the instrument of civilization… It is not an ordinary instrument; it's a medium that can accomplish any number of ends…"[840]

In fact, the very word "PAN" means "all-embracing", "universal", relating to the whole of any kind, genus, or type. And fortuitously, the instrument so named reflects, by its very shape and function, that very meaning of the word. The reality is that this musical phenomenon called Pan which had its birth in Hell Yard out of the imagination, intelligence and ingenuity of Neville Jules is today our "gift that has been bestowed unto the world."[841]

In commemoration of all that has been advanced above, it is time that both the inventor and the place of invention be duly honored in value and consideration commensurate with the level of importance and significance of this wonder of the world. To this end it is proposed that Hell Yard, All Stars' Pan Yard, prime downtown property, portions of which were purchased outright utilizing funds from winnings over the years, be transformed into the **Neville Jules Centre For Social Change** and that this Pan Yard be declared an **International Heritage Site**.

There are six (6) basic criteria outlined by UNESCO that form the basis for the declaration of heritage sites: "…(i) the site being considered must represent or reflect a masterpiece of human creative genius; (ii) the site must exhibit an important interchange of human values, over a span of time, or within a cultural area of the world; (iii) the site must bear a unique or exceptional testimony to a cultural tradition or to a civilization which is living or has disappeared; (iv) the site must by its history illustrate a significant stage in human history; (v) the site must be an outstanding example of human interaction with the environment especially when the site is vulnerable to irreversible change; (vi) the site must be directly associated with events or living traditions, with ideas, beliefs, and with artistic and literary works of outstanding universal significance…"[842]

The narrative of Hell Yard fits the criteria outlined above. From the latest data (1997) on poverty prepared by the Central Statistical Office of Trinidad & Tobago, 65% of the households of East Port-of-Spain exist below the poverty level. The unemployment rate therein was put at 31%. Given that the subsequent national economic recovery of the mid 1980s was largely generated in the energy sector which is high-skill intensive, suggest that this recovery would have had little impact on the socio-economic realities of East Port-of-Spain. The fact that the level of crime, the level of economic despair, and the extent of single female-headed households continue to rise in East Port-of-Spain is testimony that the situation needs to be addressed urgently and directly and not merely by state welfarism.

The Neville Jules Centre for Social Change has been conceptualized in all its component parts to be a self-sustaining center for the development and social transformation of East Port-of-Spain and environs from where the large majority of All Stars' members, supporters and well-wishers emanate. Already the people of the area utilize the All Stars Yard in a crude and rudimentary way to satisfy their needs, whether it is sport, musical pleasure, music-tutoring, remedial reading, computer training and welding, also for social engagements such as weddings and funerals. The aim is to have full Community participation as the key critical underpinning for the transformation of the community into a sustainable one.

Already too, All Stars has included a Community Relations Officer within its present Executive structure whose portfolio is geared to maintain the active participation of the community in all the activities of the Band. In addition since September 14, 1989, the Trinidad All Stars Steel Orchestra Co-operative Society Ltd was duly registered and approved by the then Commissioner for Co-operative Development with the stated main objective being "to encourage the spirit and practice of thrift, self-help and economic co-operation among members and to promote the development of co-operative ideas by educating members in co-operative principles and practice and by affiliating or collaborating with any other co-operative societies or organizations."

Though the Co-operative Society Ltd was dormant for quite some time, it was rekindled recently as the necessity to purchase nearby properties demanded. In this regard the original individuals who championed the cause of the All Stars Co-operative Society must be identified: Reds Collins, Chris Haynes, Glenda Esdelle, Keith "Grip" Matthews, Beresford Hunte and Nigel

Williams. On the overall, the collective assets of both the Trinidad All Stars Steel Orchestra and the Trinidad All Stars Co-operative Society Limited per se total well over 35 million (TT) and the growth is quite steady.

Standing: From left to right—Kenny Waldron (the tailor who designed the flag), Granville Roberts, Oliver "OJ" Joseph and Edward Shurland. Stooping: Neville Jules and Mano Charles. (Courtesy Jerry Serrant)

These six comprised the section of Trinidad All Stars that toured Guyana in 1952 and brought the house down with their performance of "Bless This House". The crowd swarmed and broke down the stage "in jubilation and appreciation" of what they heard.

All Stars today is therefore economically healthy and ready to take its membership onto another level and in so doing continue to be the guiding light for the Pan fraternity in T&T. Beresford Hunte was always anxious to underscore the outreach impact that All Stars as an institution has on the further development of the steelband movement, and to concretize this view, Berry explained that it was the nurturing work accomplished by Jules and Jemmott which brought the growth of people like Smooth Edwards who won his first Panorama at the age of 28 and has now over 35 years' experience arranging Panorama music; Tony Guy, percussionist, who now works professionally in Japan, Bunny Wells in the USA, and Anthony "Shortman" Guerra (deceased), described by many as a "chord specialist".

Berry indicated that All Stars has continued that trend and since then has also nurtured many young gifted players who have grown to be arrangers for other bands and he names Yohan Popwell who led the famed Panazz outfit that won the Pan-Ramajay Competition on four consecutive occasions, has already won Panorama in New York, and successfully arranged for medium bands such as Sforza, Scherzando and Harmonites; Cokey Telemaque who worked with Gonzales Sheikers and is developing as a composer of music for Pan, his *Play Yuh Self* for 2012, *Bounce and Drive* for 2013, *Excitement* for 2014, and *Unquestionable* for 2015, and *Leave We Alone* for 2016, were outstanding; as well as Shenelle Abraham who for 2012 took up arranging duties for Skiffle Bunch of San Fernando and has been doing so successfully for St. Margaret's Boys of Belmont since 2003.

Interestingly, Dane Gulston has now also begun to arrange music, and Sule Sampson's classical composition "Glory", was already performed at "A Pan in the 21st Century" competition and was performed once again at the classical Jewels X1 concert. Berry summed up his thoughts in this manner: "When All Stars presents a repertoire on any given day, what people do not realize is that what we present usually expresses over **seven (7) individual voices.** Our repertoire usually reflect the voicing of Jules, Jemmott, Wells, Smooth, Popwell, Glen Sween (Yakeem), Terry Demas, Telemaque, Andre Boucaud, Deryck Nurse, and in a lot of instances, the majority of the repertoire comes from Popwell's efforts. This is so unlike other bands whose repertoire usually expresses the arrangements of **only one or, at most, two individuals**, but not All Stars, that's our salient difference..."[843]

Having been a nurturing crucible for so long, it is therefore the intention now of the Trinidad All Stars Steel Orchestra to make the case and to lobby for their home, Hell Yard, where the family of Melody-Pans was conceptualized, i.e., where Pan as a crafted musical instrument was given its first breath of life; where as well the Carnival Arts was fought for and defended against the colonial onslaught in 1881 during the Canboulay Riots, and where for over 80 plus years All Stars has maintained a firm commitment to Pan and Mas; to be declared an International Heritage Site in the course of a proposed phased development of the pan-yard into the **Neville Jules Centre for Social Change**.

Trinidad All Stars therefore calls on the powers that be to join this noble and most defining effort, in particular All Stars calls on the East Port-of-Spain Development Company Ltd, an Agency of Government, which in a recent advertisement advised the population of its intentions to articulate "…a strategy for sustainable development which proposes actions to develop and promote historic and cultural attractions, including exploring opportunities for heritage tourism and establishing heritage districts in Belmont and Port-of-Spain…"[844] **Our world, fresh out of the dependency and strictures of colonization, has only now begun to awake to the reality of the power of cultural products and their importance to the re-defining of ourselves. It is therefore timely that the Trinidad All Stars story be told at this very moment as the society of T&T grapples with the demands of the future.**

Only recently the country was informed that the Ministry of Planning and the Economy in the then PPP Government had set up a 16-member High Level Panel of Experts and directed that panel to "focus its work on advancing arts and cultural projects, encouraging investments in cultural heritage with the aim of developing culture-based industries for the local and global markets."[845] The report from this Panel apparently was submitted to the Minister on August 17, 2011 and to date the recommendations have yet to be revealed, however it is said that, given the involvement of members of the Artist Coalition of Trinidad and Tobago on the Panel, would suggest that the citizenry can expect to see a welcomed push for the development of *long overdue projects such as the Carnival Museum,* "*the establishment and upgrade of national heritage sites,*" *and* "*the creation of business incubators in East Port-of-Spain to transform it to a heritage city…*"[846]

Furthermore, when Pat Bishop, one of the leading lights involved in the Panel, died on the job, Mr. Rubadiri Victor, President of the Artist Coalition of Trinidad and Tobago, in honor of Pat Bishop, appealed to the nation to seize hold of its courage to dream. This, in part, is what he said: "Imagine this: the whole of George and Nelson Streets is a great heritage arcade of restored turn-of-the-century buildings on the outside—but inside are concert halls, restaurants, recreated barrack yards and a sprawling modern multi-media museum called the House of Music. It is based around the restored Christopher Brothers Recording Studio at 7 Nelson Street—one of the oldest recording studios in the world… Trinidad has the second oldest recording industry in the world, it is only fitting. The House of Music is a magnificent facility and Port-of-Spain's main tourist attraction—a place where great concerts of all types are held…"

"…The project to build it and restore these buildings was one of the major projects in the rehabilitation of East Port-of-Spain and the resurrection of Laventille and environs. The East Port-of-Spain Heritage City project had finally honored these great communities that are the **mothers of pan, mas and calypso**. Beautiful schools, community centers, **redesigned panyards**… all kinds of industry had sprung up overnight… master artisans of all sorts had become global brands. A cable car system now connects the Hill to the City… Magnificent stylish buildings—combination museums, concert halls and Internet cafes—have been built all over the hill as rewards to communities which had eradicated crime. But it was the people that had finally been given the resources to fly."

"In fact, the cultural renaissance in T&T was being led by Laventille—just as it was before. Laventille's pan and mas factories pour out hundreds of millions of dollars in goods every year to service the 300 Trinidad-style carnivals worldwide (i.e., *Carnivals that generate an annual worth of over $15 billion US according to the Henry/Nurse Study—BR)* Our students are known as the most creative on the planet—proficient in the skills of five civilizations… All over the phenomenal island—magic, beauty, truth and industry. **Industry emerging from native genius. We have found ourselves in ourselves**… This is what Pat was fighting for. Let us make this dream manifest."[847]

On the other hand, in regard to an overall view of Port-of-Spain as a modern metropolis and what is required culturally and economically to further develop it as a particular brand in context of global demands, the following is what has been expounded by one local visionary: "Port-of-Spain can become the creative city of the English-speaking Caribbean and such a transformation has already begun with areas such as Ariapita Avenue evolving into a commercial and social hot-spot... It is a small representation of how other cities have evolved and it should be welcomed... Creative cities are a magnet for this new entrepreneur who has moved beyond the bricks and mortar type of establishment... We are now attracting people whose incomes are generally generated from intellectual property and services, and these include everything from media, advertising and software engineering to restaurants and culinary services... The quality of entertainment services is an important factor in this creative style of development... Conducting business and meetings no longer occurs in offices, it's in places like coffee bars and restaurants, so the concept of the office is a virtual one... It's the **lime** factor that gives T&T its competitive advantage."

"The global middle-class chooses places like the Avenue to lime (i.e., *to hang out*—BR) and work, but Trinbagonians wrongly perceive liming as unproductive... Contrary, it's the most productive thing we do: it breaks barriers, creates trust and generates creativity and that is what we need to be emphasizing... We need to introduce new ways of thinking rather than holding fast to the old concept of trying to attract direct foreign investment. Once a holistic framework and strategy is implemented and sustained in transforming Port-of-Spain as a creative capital of the Caribbean, we can easily sell that to the rest of the world..."[848]

Forty years ago, a tiled plaque was placed on the wall of the structure in Hell Yard that then housed the bar and storeroom. That commemorative tablet reads: "This stone was laid by Senator Muriel Donawa-McDavidson on Saturday April 19th 1980 for Pan Theatre Museum and Cultural Centre of Trinidad All Stars Steel Orchestra." Today, we of Trinidad All Stars say to all those of like mind and to this Nation, now experiencing its 61th year of Independence, that this, the oldest steelband in the land, has already committed itself philosophically and practically to all that has been advocated above, and now in documenting our history we hereby boldly and proudly reveal what we have dared to bring to the national agenda.

The Proposed "Neville Jules Centre for Social Change"

Rebuilding Hell-Yard

Demolition of the old yard

Administration Building: "I Love Trinidad All Stars"—Dedication

The Pathway to the Proposed Neville Jules Centre for Social Change

The ground floor level is supposed to accommodate the following: (i) a Pan Promenade, (ii) Information and Archival Room, (iii) Audio-Visual/Multi-Media Centre, (iv) Public Washrooms, (v) Bar/Cafeteria, (vi) Practice Yard /Entertainment area/Pan Rack location.

First and Second Floors—500 seat auditorium, performing arts center, Computer Room, Admin Offices and Recording Facilities.

The following poem written in 1972 was awarded 1st Prize for Poetry in the UNESCO Sponsored National Cultural Council Literary Competition. It captures the powerful effect that Pan has on people and the cultural uplifting that comes from engagement with this phenomenon.

All Stars

(for Neville—the Moustache Man)
By A. Bukka Rennie

Give me
Give me the Carnival mentality
Any day,
For otherwise the norm of life
Says follow the crowd,
Go no further than the mob
Pigeon-holed by social convention
And the might of powers that be,
Where the biggest crime is to shine,
But not with Carnival,
Its mentality is to walk alone,
In quiet isolation,
If needs be
Away from the contemptuous noise
To go where none has gone before
To achieve what no one has even dreamed.
Give me that Carnival mentality
Any day
With its glowing triumph
And unrecognized breakaway…
High up in de garret
At de top o' de stairway
O'Maple Leaf Club
Night and day,
Day and night,
Man practicing "BOMB"
In to-tal secret.
Dey playing dem pans
Wid dey bare fingers
So de notes cyar escape
To anxious ears

Of de gamblers and de jametes below
Or float thru' de window
Down to passing folks in de streets
Where guards patrol
Discouraging all rival,
All stranger,
Looking up, as if dey want to know
De garret affairs.
Only one from each section, the garret had space to start; so a tenor, a seconds,
A guitar, a grundig, one bass and rhythm
practice apart.
No one know how de entire band go sound
Excepting de Mouche Man
Dis selfless, faceless wanderer
Of steelband creation
Who have it all in he head.
De only time de players
Hear de entire band
Is when de "bombs" drop
At early dawn
When dey play with sticks
Before de big, big crowd
In de makeshift theatre
Dey calling Nagib yard…
Give me,
Give me the Carnival mentality
Any day.
Is divergent thinking
Is divergent acting
Is carrying on
Like you want to
Like you like to
Like you must.
It is not the sickening sameness
And the death
Of prearranged routine,

The suicides of conservative cowardice.
It is reaching for the sky,
Aiming for the raging colors
That bend to glitter
That extend and push and stretch
Human endeavor
Despite the pain and bleeding
Onto Olympian realms…
At half-past four
De Mouche-Man come,
Pick up de iron and knock
Three times, enough.
And silence prevail
Over de five thousand
Dusky excited figures
Huddle-up together
Jam-pack like sardine
Shivering from de chill
Of sleepless night
And daybreak yet without de sun…
At dat moment
Every year, de same cry,
De same scream:
"whey Rupert? Whey Rupert?
Allyuh find Rupert!"
And a search begin…
Den outa de shadows
A figure come
Drunk with de anxiety
Of de moment of decision
Borne by ten/twelve sturdy arms
And dress up in a black university
Graduation gown, with de flat, square head-gear,
They call the mortar-board
And dey drop he lightly,
Carefully,

Between de six bass drum
In time to begin de count-down…
NUMBER ONE!
De fust bomb drop
Wid ah precision,
It stun de bleary-eye thousand…
NUMBER TWO!
De crowd come alive
Dey cheering wild
NUMBER THREE!
Pandemonium in de place,
Mankind crying
Nobody cyar hold back feeling
Nobody care who call who "ooman",
Is tears and hand-shake,
Loving embrace,
Supporters and players
Touching each other
In acceptance
Dey lift de Mouche-Man in de air
Oh God, oh God. All Star go kill dem dead
Again dis year!
Start up de riddim, Shurlan,
To hit de road,
We go shatter Salvatori to bits
With dem allegros and chromatic bricks…
Give me,
Give me that Romance any day,
That reaching for rainbows
Beyond the plebeian plateaux
Beyond the chatter
Of riffraff on the ground,
The multitudes of mere mediocrity,
Chasing not the supposed impossibility
Of the variegated bend
But limiting self to the fixed dimension

Of exchange-value and GREEN
Never to see, never to behold,
Never to smell the true pot
Of Apollonian gold…
And Jitterbug,
Jitterbug, de garret cleaner,
De master flag-waver
Wave flag like he insane.
He pass de flag thru he legs
And behind he back,
He thro' it way up
Into de semi-darkness o' de early morn
Till like it touch de stars
In a kinda salute to de universe
And to this unwavering band.
De flag twirl, it spin, it turn
And come down to rest
Back in Jitter hand
Like if it move to de command
Of remote control…
And Jitterbug dance,
Dance with he eyes closed
Leading dis band
With he radar instinct
Taking position from de breeze
That blow de tears
Away from he unnecessary eyes…
Give me that Carnival mentality
Any day,
That struggle for commitment,
That pain to make, to come good,
To excel beyond and above
The prison walls,
That jumping up… and up… and up
Till exhaustion blind the eyes
And sight shifts to the mind

Trained on the light of street lamps
And the flittering flies
That rise above the shadowy gloom
Contending to get closer
Living only to become ONE
With the yellow gleam…
Mayfield, Janet and Ruby Rab keeping order,
Nobody dare
Skylark with dis Band
Else is butt and baton
Fierce buttocks and bosom,
Who go want dat humiliation?
On de road, Bumpy Nose Wells,
Put in de introduction
To a fresh road tune
While de Band moving;
Talk about spontaneous accolade
From a genius performer,
Even de Prime Minister
Get up and wine
To All Stars music
But dat ent all,
De same Bumpy Nose, earlier dat morning
Lean over he freshly bu'n tenor
Dat just b'un and tune dat morning,
Still black with soot from de fire
And he, leaning over it,
But away from it,
Like he 'fraid it,
But the sticks touching notes, lightly
With each flick o' he wrist
And de Pan talking murder,
Echoing like a voice in de wilderness
Of pain and glory,
De master's voice like de peals
Of ah pumping organ:

PRELUDE/ IN/ C/ SHARP/ MINOR!
Dey make a circle "round him dat morning,
Dey set him apart
He stood alone
And touch notes in sequence
He could never feel again…
Rupert and Gordon
On six bass apiece,
Cyar play near each other
Because dey never do de same thing twice,
Dey leave de basic chords,
Dey improvise, dey fill de spaces
And each time de tune go down
Dey coming different, better each time
Trying to outdo each other…
Rupert play he falling down
And touch six notes in ah run dat almost didn't sound
And Gordon laugh…
Keep dem apart, keep dem apart
Or dey go do and do
And cause chaos in de land…
But Innapo stay on five tangerine and black
With his flasked back-pocket,
A real picture of creative consistency
Like gravy linking de meat with de finer points
Stopping only to wet he throat
And stimulate he magic hands
Humming and damping bass…
Give me that Carnival mentality
Any day.
It is total involvement,
Total participation,
It is about focusing YOU
When to exist is to contend
For sheer strength of beauty,
Imagination and portrayal of the closest Truth.

Where to be equal
Is to be just another reveler
And difference is not about race and class
But performance,
As if to agree
God did not make the mass of men
Equal performers
Held at bay on common course
But Samuel Colt did…
Panorama night Eddie Hart pelt "way he sticks
And swear never to play again.
And he walk down town like a zombie
As though he suffering
From a mental stroke
Like if ah blood vessel
Capside in he brain…
De judges say too much arrangement,
De tune beat too slow…
Rupert cry long tears, heart-broken, torn apart
Like ah deep-wounded animal
For All Star play it, like dey had to play it
Like only dem could feel it
Like dey all will do again next year
When de mouche-man choose
De most open tune
So he could do
What he want with bare fingers
Back in de garret…
Give me,
Give me that Carnival mentality
Any day,
Give me that strength
To reach for the sky,
Allow me to clutch
The raging colors
That bend to glitter

Like flies that flitter
Living only to become
ONE
With the neon gleam...

    Young women have virtually taken over the panyards... Throughout the developing world, women have been spearheading all progressive activity.

Nicole Belgrave: Young six-bass player, came fresh out of South East Secondary, a long time nursery from where many All Stars members came. Certainly she did not see Shurland, Rupert, Gordon, Cherrie nor Innapo, but she's got the All Stars touch, as though somehow their spirits have been reawakened in her being. Nicole is now assistant manager—administration.

They, Smitten by the Pan Jumbie, Come from the Other End of the World to Involve Themselves...

Koruri Hanatu. She comes every year from Japan to play Double-Seconds in All Stars for Panorama and on the road Carnival Monday and Tuesday. A most disciplined person, during practice she would remain behind her Pan dutifully until the session is over. She is also a music arranger back home.

Kenzo Aoki: A Japanese school-teacher who came and played for the Carnival, but was threatened by Japanese authorities and almost lost his job. He said that All Stars' "Woman on the Bass" is still the most played pan-music in Japan.

Jim Bill Sobers takes command of the Flag. (Prince Batson and Jim Bill, both deceased, were Orisha grandmasters of All Stars and the folklore indicates that they are still the spiritual guardians of the Yard.)

(Picture courtesy Harold Moylan) Neville Jules (left) greets Sterling Betancourt (right) in Woodford Square. On this occasion, Sterling, one of the TASPO players, was on a visit to T&T.

From left, Roy Gibbs (deceased), Cin-Cin (deceased), Baptiste (deceased), Edward King, Leon Noel (deceased), and Teach (deceased).

Smooth Edwards with "The Bell"

(This bell given to All Stars by Prince Batson, our most high Orisha-Man, summons all to attention. It is heard from all points even though amidst the loudest noises. Dey say: it mount!)

A. Bukka Rennie

This book, "Mettle & Metal—The Birth of Steel-Pan Music and the Story of Trinidad All Stars Steel Orchestra", is dedicated to Neville Jules and to the hope that never again in the history of T&T will any creative genius be ever treated with the disdain and utter disregard as has been done to this son of the soil who gave to the world the melody-pan and the steel orchestra.

Modern Africa—Presentation by Trinidad All Stars on 18 February 1969, one year before the Black Power social explosion of 1970, now termed the 1970 Social Revolution. It is because All Stars is so deeply rooted amongst the people that the band could have foretold by its presentation the necessities of what was about to come.

Rudy Wells

Rudy Wells' Profile

Rudy Wells was a long-standing member of the Trinidad All Stars Steel Orchestra from since the days of the Garret. He developed as an arranger in the mid '60s and was a key protégé of Neville Jules. Bukka Rennie in his poem "All Stars" highlights Wells as the person who developed the introduction for one of the road tunes while the band was moving during the J'ouvert Morning of 1966, and also described Wells' outstanding performance later that very morning as a double-tenor player during the band's presentation of its Bomb-tune "Prelude in C-Sharp Minor." Wells left T&T in 1969 to teach pan and music in the Virgin Islands. He became the musical director for a steel orchestra he initiated there. He returned home for Carnival 1973 and arranged Kitchener's "Rainorama" which became Trinidad All Stars' very first Panorama winning presentation.

In 1974, Wells went on to the Berklee College of Music in Massachusetts, USA and did both a Bachelor's Degree and a Master's Degree in Music and Educational Management with the aid of sponsorship from the Rockefeller

Foundation and his Virgin Islands benefactors. Rudy Wells, now deceased, was a retired Educator who over the years nurtured numerous students who are today both entertainers and teachers themselves throughout the Virgin Islands and the USA.

He was honored to be the composer of ***Dawn of the Millennium*** which was the Test Piece for the First World Steelband Music Festival held in T&T in 2000. He also composed ***Shades of Port-of-Spain***, which has since become a favored number in the classical repertoire of the Trinidad All Stars Steel Orchestra.

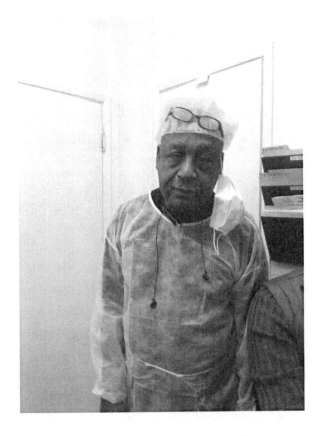

Dr. Leroi Boldon, now a Vet in Los Angeles, USA.

Dr. Leroi Boldon's Profile

Leroi Boldon born in 1936 joined Trinidad All Stars at the tender age of 12 in 1948. The first instrument he played was Jules' "Five-Note" bass or "tune-boom" as it was then called and finally settled on the "Cuatro-Pan" that was eventually renamed "Guitar-Pan". Leroi says without any hesitancy: *I became a man in the band. I grew up in that band. I mean, I have been in the Army, the United States Army, I was an officer. I was a Captain in the US Army, and I have never seen—and I have been around Generals—but I have never seen a stronger disciplinarian than Neville Jules. I mean he had a way. There was a guy in the band called "Bully", a tough customer, always walked with a dagger, and Neville made Bully cry one night just by looking at him. Up to now when I see Jules I get nervous...*

Leroi became Secretary of Trinidad All Stars in 1952 at the age of 16. Jules recognized Leroy's potential for leadership given his academic development and training as a member of the Cadet Force at St. Mary's College and urged Leroi to take up an executive position in the band. "*I was a little boy, fining big men, it didn't go well with them at all,*" Boldon says. *Imagine Bully and Mano fall out over some woman, and Jules asking me, 16 years old, when will I be talking to those two gentlemen, he didn't say "bad-johns", yuh know, he say "gentlemen"...*

Leroi Boldon speaks proudly about his decision as the Secretary to invite representatives from other bands to Maple Leaf Club after the Carnival of 1958 to socialize and to bond as brethren of the steelband fraternity. Boldon indicated that Jules himself though at first doubtful was eventually most gratified with the response of the invitees. They all came, said Boldon, and he recalled Ellie telling Jules jovially at that function, "if is Classics, yuh want, then is Classics yuh go get" in reference to the All Stars' Bomb of 1958. Boldon left T&T in 1959 at the age of 23.

Today, Dr. Leroi Boldon is a veterinary surgeon operating on the west-coast of America. For some time he continued to play pan with his own band in and around Sans Francisco and still maintains that the greatest player of the tenor pan he has ever heard was Neville Jules in his prime.

Winston Gordon (died June 2023)

Winston Gordon was one of the long line of supreme bass-players in the All Stars pantheon. In the mid '60s, himself and Rupert Alexander comprised the then dynamic-duo of the Six-Bass section. Gordon and Rupert were competent musicians quite capable of adding their own notes to Jules' bass-lines as they would in jest compete against each other and later see which of the two got more money placed on their bass by overjoyed well-wishers and pan-pushers "Dey never do the same thing twice," said Bukka Rennie in his poem.

Gordon was the one earmarked by Jules as his protégé to take over and Jules began to allow him to do arrangements, to find his own voice. In 1966, Gordon arranged "Stella by Starlight" and set that J'ouvert morning afire. Gordon said: "Rupert Alexander, myself and a few other guys spent our spare time in a club opposite Maple Leaf Recreation Club on Charlotte Street. We enjoyed punching and listening to tunes on the Juke Box there. We all loved Jackie Gleason's "Again" but I had a penchant for "Stella by Starlight." I listened to it until I had it internalized and so I was inspired to give it a try on pan. It was my personal choice for a bomb tune.

"It was the Sunday of Panorama Prelims that year and when the Band had completed our performance on stage and left the Savannah, I reassembled the band at the corner of Keate and Frederick Streets and gave the count to start Stella by Starlight. I was elated beyond belief and unable to contain myself until ten minutes later, we were stopped by the Police for playing music on the streets without permission. Nonetheless, I was on top of the world. I was not sure that my harmonies were correct but the music sounded good."

"I was not musically schooled but thanks to Neville Jules from whom I learnt so much in the music center, known as the Garret, the home of Trinidad All Stars…"

In 1967, there was a split in All Stars and Gordon and others left to form Boston Symphony which only lasted for two years. He then played with Starlift for a while and probably kept a low profile there as he concentrated on his professional career.

Gordon began working at Nova Scotia Bank as a messenger and proved to be such a diamond-asset to that bank that he was able to work his way up the corporate banking structure to becoming eventually a Bank Manager. He is now retired, lives in Tobago and, for quite a number of years, has been the manager and arranger for RBTT Redemption Sounds of Tobago.

Dane Gulston

Dane Colin Troy Gulston began hanging around All Stars when they were down on St. Vincent Street. In fact, he was one of the people who assisted in the task of moving the band back home to Hell Yard in 1980. As a youngster he faced some problems with his parents for this seeming attraction to the steelband movement. But that did not deter him officially joining All Stars in 1982 as a tenor player. Dane indicated that it was the "style", "fashion" and "flair" that were synonymous with the name "Trinidad All Stars", the way they presented their music, which drew him to the orchestra. He also said that this affinity to "style" and "show" must have resonated with him as he grew up in a family in which every member, including mother and father, loved likewise to dress up and be stylish.

Dane said that Lennox "Sonny Tool" Alleyne was the elder member who took the foremost responsibility for his molding. He also recognized others such as Earl "Bandit" Brooks, Tedd Willis and Deryck Nurse as having played a role in cementing his membership in the band but stressed the mentoring that "Sonny Tool" provided. "Sonny Tool", having been groomed so to be by the likes of Neville Jules and Jerry Jemmott, reinforced all the characteristics that had become overtime the hallmark of a Trinidad All Stars player: the discipline, the constant strive for excellence; the professional approach to "knowing" the instrument, the way in which the instrument was to be treated, and most of all when "you come to practice, practice is seriousness, not play."

"All Stars made me who I am today," Dane exclaimed. "All that I have actually achieved in my career today, including winning Scouting for Talent in 1996, is owed to All Stars." He said as a "soloist", and an "arranger" and all that it takes to be a "total performer" he has learnt from some of the greatest people who touched his life through All Stars; people like Jemmott, Sir Paul Hill, Gillian Balintulo and Rudy Wells. He assured that other outstanding All Stars players such as Clive Telemaque and Yohan Popwell will also say the same thing and "this reflects on the kind of institution that All Stars is."

"Wherever we go, people see us as products of All Stars." He is grateful that a Youth Band has recently been formed and he assures that these youths will follow likewise as long as the All Stars discipline is maintained and reinforced. All Stars today is showing the rest of the pan fraternity that "steelband is a business. Playing that instrument is a full time job like any other serious job from which hopefully in the future we can all derive a pension."

Dane closed by saying that he is thankful to the past and present management of Trinidad All Stars for the *"opportunity; all I came with was my sticks, no instrument, the band provided the instrument and molded my thinking for the future. I say thanks to all…"* He was appointed Community Relations Manager in 2019.

Yohan Popwell

Yohan joined Trinidad All Stars Steel Orchestra in 1981, immediately after the Carnival of that year. "I wanted to be close to my best buddy, Deryck Nurse," he says in giving his reason for the choice he made then. Pic 13 of Yohan and Deryck shows how young they both were when they came to All Stars. Yohan Popwell has since emerged as a double-second virtuoso player and a master arranger. He was one of the youths who took seriously to his personal development as a professional musician under the guidance of people like Jerry Jemmott, the first musical director, and others like the Nathaniel Sisters, Gillian and June and Nelson Villafana.

Yohan indicates that when he joined the band he was "not indoctrinated as such" but he simply found himself having "to follow what he saw around him" and the rules and regulations, though clearly posted and handed around for all to read and comprehend, became concretized by the way things were done, the way people operated and behaved generally.

In today's times, "given the changes in which we live," Yohan recommends a "strong code of conduct for the membership." He said pointedly: "I will like to see things that the band had in the past like strong discipline and respect for time be returned to the band, it will make All Stars a better organization. In addition he feels that since the band now owns its property, the aim should be "self-sustainability", "new legal businesses should be opened up", and there should be "more shows in the yard to earn increased income." In regard to the Panazz ensemble, he pointed out that himself and Barry Bartholomew "hand-picked the All Stars members" because they desired to put together "the best ten member group" possible for the ramajay competition. He lamented that they were not allowed to go as an "All Stars" ensemble, so the accolades of **Four-Wins** had to go to Potential Symphony (1) and to Panazz Players (3 consecutively). What a pity!

Since Yohan has moved on to arranging professionally he has to date chalked up **SEVEN** Panorama winnings in T&T and abroad: In T&T, with Medium Band, Sforzata, 2005, 2006 and 2009. In New York with Big Band, Sonatas, 2004, 2007, 2009, 2010. When it was pointed out that today whenever Trinidad All Stars performs anywhere, if the repertoire is comprised of a list of ten, most times he would most likely have arranged almost 50–60% of the music presented, he responded gleefully: "I feel honored to hear that the band plays a significant amount of songs I did for them. **It is not about the money I am paid**. It is always nice to get returns for your hard work. **But I actually like seeing the members' faces light up when they begin to do a new song; that gives me joy**."

Massy Trinidad All Stars—Netsa Nathan, Cassie Figaro, and Shaoubaca Elie. The very first engagement after the Massy Re-branding.

On stage final night at the 2015 Panorama: "Unquestionable" (composed by Clive Telemaque on the right, forefront) proved truly unbeatable. 9th Panorama victory for Massy Trinidad All Stars.

Tinika Davis (center with sticks); a crack-shot on the double-seconds, began her career in All Stars. Now that she has graduated as a master percussionist from the UWI School of the Arts, she decided in 2015 to end her pan-playing days with the band in which she began. Pix courtesy David Wears.

The Trophy Page

A smattering of the trophies won by Trinidad All Stars over the years. No other band has amassed such quantity. The trophy for winning Band of the Year 2014 is center, first row.

Nigel Williams: The 12th captain of Trinidad All Stars Steel Orchestra. The chosen one to lead the band from Hell Yard into its next realm of existence.

Having been the band's successful accountant for many years, they say he is their corporation soul.

Nigel took over from Beresford Hunte in 2016. Gervase Warner, CEO of the Massy Group of Companies, speaking at the 9 June 2012 ceremony to mark All Stars' 8th Panorama victory at Pier 1 in Chaguaramas, lauded the financial prudence practiced by the band's executive which he said placed the band "ahead of many well-established companies."[849] And he concluded by paying special tribute to Nigel Williams: "Words cannot describe the contribution that this man has made to this band. As the band's treasurer he has ensured the financial affairs of the band are always above board and transparent and we value his integrity. At no time under his watch has this band ever been accused of misuse of funds. He also lives by the credo "eat little and live long" and it is because of his hard-nosed approach to saving that you, the members, will reap the long-term benefit…"[850]

The Twelfth Captain with The Bell. He is also the driller of the Band for Panorama. They call him "Kilimanjaro". Other bands try to employ his skills as drill-master, but All Stars will never agree to such a possibility.

Terrence "Terry" Demas

Terry has been a member of All Stars for 47 years. Started playing bass in 1973 and has played in all Music Festivals from 1980 and all Classical Jewels from 1978. He has been the leader of the Bass Section from 1977 until he took up arranging duties.

Terry has remarkable talent and skill. He is All Stars' human musical encyclopedia. He arranges all the music for the road on Carnival days and keeps the band in vogue with all the popular melodies. He was the one who for many years took the "Bomb" arrangements from Neville Jules in New York and returned home at Carnival, without any score, to transpose the music to the players of the various sections all from memory. When Jules, due to his health, could no longer arrange the music, Terry took over. Here is a list of his work to date:

2011—*You are my special angel (1st)*
2012—*What a wonderful world*

2013—*Close to you*
2014—*I swear*
2015—*You are always on my mind*
2016—*Lay back in the arms of someone you love*
2017—*I don't know how to love him*
2018—*Theme from the Magnificent Seven—(1st) (Elmer Bernstein)*
2019—*Can't Take My Eyes Off of You (Frankie Valli)*
2020—*Sing Out My Soul*

Terry Demas

Terry's Vision for All Stars:

1. People who have made a contribution in the past in whatever way to the band should be recognized and commended for their service and this should be an ongoing thing.
2. Discipline must always be an integral part of the organization.
3. The band must always strive for excellence in whatever venture they may undertake.
4. The band has to tap into the international market with strong marketing strategies. They have been doing very well locally but other bands seem to be focused on tapping the international market and All Stars is being left behind.
5. There could be a mini stage side playing music with other musical instruments but the pan must be the main focus. This will give the band the capacity to play in any musical scenario.
6. The band should consider a music school so that children as well as adults can come to learn music. This will help the community of East Dry River.

Master Composer of Panorama Music

Clive "Cokey" Telemaque

2012—Play Yuh Self—Panorama winning tune
2013—Bounce And Drive—Second Place
2014—Excitement—Second Place
2015—Unquestionable—Panorama winning tune
2016—Leave We Alone—Sixth Place

In five panorama compositions: 2 Firsts, 2 Seconds and one Sixth place. What a record!

Clive's most potent statement about the band: "All Stars is not a fly-by-night operation. It is an institution and nothing can stop it from functioning. The band is much bigger that any set of individuals..." Clive is also the President of the TASSF—The Trinidad All Stars Seniors' Foundation.

2017 Carnival Tuesday: This is a picture of historical significance:

Eddie Hart (left) who joined All Stars in the days of the Garret on Charlotte Street. He played double-seconds.

Martin Albino (second from left) of the Albino family from Success Village Laventille, younger brother of Merle Albino DeCouteau and Alwin Albino. Martin was leader of the double-second section in days of the Garret. He played tenor on the road for Carnival 2017 and Carnival 2018, just to experience once again the vibes.

Beckett (right) was one of the four men who played the famous "Grundig" pan in the days of the Charlotte Street Garret. Other Grundig players were Junior "Peking" Jeffery(dec); Fitzroy (Po Po) and Granville (dec), the tailor who designed the flag.

Akende Rudder (second from right), is the daughter of Edgrell "Vats" Rudder who gave the band the name "All Stars" in 1949.

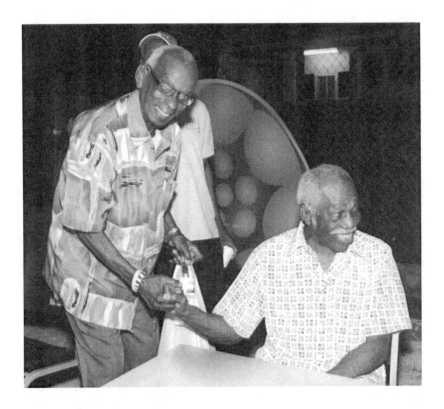

Neville Jules (seated) greets St. Clair Plowden, the man who for many years recorded the particulars of all members of All Stars including the fines with which they were penalized for breaking the rules and regulations and for other forms of misconduct. Plowden was known as "the Bookman".

Neville and wife accompanied by other senior members; Oliver "OJ" Joseph (deceased) is third from left.

A reunion of elders: Plowden (second from left); Neville Jules (center) and Fisheye Olliverre (right)

A Star of All Stars

Mia Gormandy

Mia, according to the records and the Trinidad All Stars Newsletter (2003), joined All Stars in 1998 playing the tenor pan. It is reported therein that Mia's musical gift "prompted her keen interest in pan and piano" and led to her formal music training at the tender age of 6. "In 2001, she toured Australia with All Stars and won both Junior Festival competitions that year. In 2002, she captured the **Champ of the Champs** title and was awarded the **Dennis**

Kerr Cup for the most outstanding instrumental performance at the National Music Festival. In December 2002, she was awarded **The Myrna Huggins Wood House Memorial Trophy** for excellence in music—pan and piano—at her school, St. Joseph's Convent. In May 2003, Mia won the local leg of the **Hal Jackson Talented Teen** competition and in July represented Trinidad in the International Competition held in St. Thomas. Mia competed among 29 contestants from different states of America and countries of the world and **placed second**, playing on tenor pan **The Flight of the Bumble Bee** by Rimsky Korsakoff. (Trinidad All Stars Newsletter, August 2003)."

Pursuing her studies and development as a professional pannist and musicologist in the USA, Mia was the 2014–2015 recipient of the **Howard Mayer Brown Fellowship** for promising minority graduate students pursuing a doctoral degree in music. This fellowship was presented to her by the **American Musicological Society** for research on her dissertation "Pan in Japan". Now married, she is Dr. Mia Gormandy-Benjamin, wife of Mr. Kygel Benjamin, arranger of the Trinidad All Stars Youth Steel Orchestra. Mia has now been appointed the official Musical Director of Trinidad All Stars Steel Orchestra. A lot is being expected in the future from this lady.

Glen Sween, now Yakeem Abdullah. The records indicate that he first played tenor bass when he joined All Stars in 1972 and then switched to bass. He has played in most Classical Jewels and Music Festivals since then and was the first bassman to play a Nine-Bass in a Music festival. He has toured extensively with the band, visiting countries such as Canada, China, India, the USA and Bermuda. He is also an arranger. The first tune he arranged for All Stars was "Sylab Coming Down" by Roots, also "In D Centre" by Duke, as well as "Carnival Time Again" by Brother Marvin for which he has received tremendous accolades, and it's a favored road-tune with which the band pulls off on J'ouvert mornings and most certainly during Point Fortin Borough Day.

Keith Fields on six-bass. Note the stance and posture, typical of the All Stars tradition.

The Garret Boys: 60th Bomb Anniversary

This group of past Trinidad All Stars players, bonded by the shared experiences of a dynamic, historic legacy, and triggered by the initiative of Martin Albino,(front row, seated, third from the left) took time on Tuesday 5th February 2018, to celebrate the 60th Anniversary of the creation of the BOMB, the "calypsorization" of European Classical Music in 1958 when the band swept the city with the explosion that was Neville Jules' interpretation of Ludwig Van Beethoven's Minuet in G Major, rehearsed with bare fingers in total secret. Neville Jules was then 30 years of age. They each in turn shared golden memories of their days as a family of musical troubadours housed up in the Garret of Maple Leaf Club on Charlotte Street.

Interestingly, Brinsley Johnson, told the gathering of his experience when he attempted to join the US Army. He was asked if he was ever a member of any organization and when he answered in the affirmative, he was asked to name the organization. He told the interviewer "Trinidad All Stars Steel Orchestra" and his application was put on hold pending investigation. What the US Army found out about All Stars opened the door for him and cleared the way for his military career. In All Stars' DNA has been the austere, disciplined functioning nurtured by the legendary Neville Jules. When the steelband movement joined the march of workers and their Trade Unions in commemoration and celebration on May Day of 1959, George Goddard leader of the Steelbands' Association was disturbed that the Police wished to stop Trinidad All Stars from playing.

He said: "At the time, police wanted to stop Trinidad All Stars, the most disciplined and law abiding of the steelbands, who was playing Schubert's 'Intermezzo' in chipping tempo."

Leon Long on nine-bass.

He joined Trinidad All Stars in 1968. He has been playing bass for the past 53 years. The band's records and Newsletter indicate that he has toured extensively with the band to far-flung countries such as Australia, China, India, UK, USA, Spain, etc. He has played in all the Classical Jewels Concerts except in 1978 and all the Music Festivals from 1973 to the present. He held the position of Section Leader of the Bass Section in the 1980s. Uncle Jem dubbed him "Don Giovani".

Franklyn "Deek" Mayhew—The Ten-Bass Master. He is also the Secretary of the TASSF—The Trinidad All Stars Seniors' Foundation.

Burial of Neville Jules

On Friday, 20 March 2020, the funeral rites for Neville Jules who died in New York, was held at the Trinity Cathedral in Port-of-Spain. Due to covid-19 protocols, only 10 persons were allowed into the church to witness the funeral rites of this great man; the father of the steel orchestra. He was buried at the Lapeyrouse cemetery.

Ingrid Jules stands before her husband's casket as the last rites are bestowed.

The Neville Jules Junction

On Saturday, 13 February 2021, the Mayor of Port-of-Spain, Joel Mr. Joel Martinez, officially declared the corner of George and Duke Streets, The

Neville Jules Junction, in honor of the celebrated cultural icon and pan pioneer, Neville Jules. The Mayor said: *Mr. Neville "Cap" Jules' love for Trinidad All Stars led him to create certain traditions within the band which I have heard still exist to this day. There is no dispute over the pride that he has brought to the capital city and especially to this area and to Trinidad All Stars.*

From left, Dane Gulston, Gervasse Warner, Mayor Joel Martinez, St. Clair Plowden, Eddie Hart, and Nalo Elie, captain of the All Stars Junior Band.

The Administrative Office of the Trinidad All Stars' Seniors Foundation was officially established in December 2021. In the above picture, Clyde Telemaque, President of the TASSF, opens the door to the Office. This augurs well for the further and future cementing of the relationship between TASSO and TASSF.

End Notes

[1] Michael Anthony: The Making of Port-of-Spain, Vol. 1, p.54.

[2] Ibid.

[3] Michael Anthony: op.cit. p.49.

[4] CO 884/4, CON:40, R.G.C. Hamilton's Report on Disturbances in Trinidad Carnival. Public Records Office, Kew Gardens, London.

[5] Ibid.

[6] Stephen Stuempfle, "The Steelband Movement in T&T", PHD Thesis, University of Pennsylvania, 1990.

[7] Michael Anthony: The Making of Port-of-Spain, Vol. 1, p.58.

[8] Hamilton Reports, op. cit.

[9] Ibid.

[10] Ibid.

[11] Hamilton Thomas: Interview at 93 Pelham Street, Belmont, Sunday, 24 March 2002.

[12] Ibid.

[13] Ibid. Big Head Hamil also indicated that the Penny Bank was moved from the other side of Port-of-Spain to East Port-of-Spain. Obviously, this had to be a strategic business move for the Bank.

[14] Jerry Serrant: "The Trinidad All Stars Saga, From Hell Yard An' Back", pp 5-6.

[15] Trinidad Royal Gazette, Vol. 107, No.7, February 10, 1938—A.W. Seymour, Colonial Secretary by Command of His Excellency, Sir Mark Aitchison Young, KCMG.

[16] See Bukka Rennie's "History of the Working-Class of T&T 1919-1956", Majority Press, 2nd Edition, pp. 44-45.

[17] Stephen Stuempfle, op. cit. cites Andrew Pearse, 1956, p. 184.

[18] Stephen Stuempfle, op.cit.

[19] George "Sonny" Goddard: Forty Years in the Steelbands 1939-1979—cf. Wellington Yearwood's and Anthony Rouff's stories, pp. 22-24, published 1991, Karia Press.

[20] Ibid, pp. 29-32.

[21] Ibid.

[22] George "Sonny" Goddard, "Forty Years in the Steelbands, 1939-1979", p. 20.

[23] "When Steel Talks" Oscar Pile Speaks, posted by Glenroy Joseph, Feb, 8, 2010.

[24] Prince Batson: Interview at Eligon Ave., Diego Martin, 01/02/2002.

[25] George "Sonny" Goddard: op.cit. pp. 25-26.

[26] Prince Batson; op.cit.TI.

[27] See Michael Anthony's The Making of Port-of-Spain op.cit. pp. 51-55 for a view of the tension that existed between Catholics and Anglicans in the early period of British Colonialism.

[28] Stephen Steumpfle, op.cit.

[29] Jerry Serrant: From Hell Yard an' Back—The Trinidad All Stars Steelband Saga—The Bobolee Beat.

[30] Hamil and Jules: op.cit. 24/03/02 at Pelham Street, Belmont.

[31] Ibid.

[32] Andre McEachine: "From Oval Boys to Invaders—1939-2008—Anecdotes of the Invaders Steelband A Branckas Publication, 2008, p. 31.

[33] Big Head Hamil, Prince Batson and Neville Jules made the point in their discourse. Prince and Neville in particular as young members of "Second Fiddle" talked about how protective of their bamboo implements the older folk were. Hamil and Jules at 93 Pelham St, Belmont 24/03/02 and Prince and Jules at 17 Eligon Ave., Diego Martin, 01/02/02.

[34] Those were the words of Ellie Mannette quoted by George "Sonny" Goddard op.cit. p. 28 and also by Andre McEachine: "From Oval Boys to Invaders" 1939-2008, A Branckas Publication,2008, p. 72.

[35] George "Sonny" Goddard: op.cit p.19; quoting Oscaret Claude's 1946 article in the Trinidad Guardian: Evolution, History and Future of the Steelband.

[36] Jerry Serrant: From Hell Yard and Back, op.cit. p. 12. They merged in 1935.

[37] Big Head Hamil's interview; op.cit.

[38] Vincent De Souza and Bernard Lange: The Earliest Beginnings of the Steelband", published by NEM Insurance Limited, 1989.

[39] Sonny Jones therefore supports the position expressed earlier by Jerry Serrant.

[40] Sonny Jones: Sunday Express, December 22, 1996—Pan Pioneers by Kim Johnson.

[41] Elmo "Bully" Alleyne, Thursday November 10, 2005 at Diego Martin.

[42] Sonny Jones: Sunday Express, 22 December 1996 and Pan Pioneers by Kim Johnson, p. 108.

[43] Noel "Ginghee" Davidson: Interview at Cipriani Extension, Morvant, Tuesday, August 19, 2008.

[44] Jerry Serrant, op.cit.

[45] Hamil and Jules op.cit. It was said that Hamil once cuffed a man on Charlotte and Duke and the man fell down on Park Street Corner or that he struck a fellah at 9pm one night and the individual did not get up until 2am the following morning, or that Hamil by himself stopped Bar 20 members from walking down Charlotte Street, all of which indicates the might of the man and how much he was held in awe.

[46] Kim Johnson: Pan Pioneers—Sonny—A Man of all Bands; Sunday Express, 22/12/96.

[47] Kim Johnson: Hell Yard—A Place of Rhythm and Riot, Hamilton "Hamil" Thomas, 11 January 1998 The Early History of Steelpan in Trinidad & Tobago.

[48] Ibid.

[49] Hamil and Jules op.cit.

[50] Ibid.

[51] Ibid.

[52] Stephen Steumpfle: The Steelband Movement in T&T, University of Pennsylvania, 1990, p. 16.

[53] Discourse with Hamil and Jules on Sunday, March 24, 2002 at 93 Pelham Street, Belmont.

[54] Ibid.

[55] Jerry Serrant, op.cit. p. 19.

[56] See Anthony Mark Jones: Steelband—The Winston "Spree" Simon Story, p. 19.
[57] Discourse with Hamil and Jules, op.cit. 24 March 2002.
[58] Elmo "Bully" Alleyne: Interview Friday, 17 May 2002. "Police" is Estein Small (See Goddard).
[59] George "Sonny" Goddard: op.cit. p. 38.
[60] Sterling Betancourt indicated that "holes created that resonating sound" Brent Magazine, Sterling Stuff, August 2010.
[61] Noel "Ginghee" Davidson; Interview at Cipriani Extension, Morvant, Tuesday August 19, 2008.
[62] Hamil and Jules, op.cit.
[63] Hamil identifies this iron-man as Andre "Loolee" Abbott.
[64] Ibid.
[65] Jerry Serrant, op.cit, pp. 17-19.
[66] Elmo "Bully" Alleyne, op.cit.
[67] Oliver "OJ" Joseph: op.cit.
[68] George "Sonny" Goddard, op.cit. p. 38.
[69] See *The Advent of the Steel-band and My Life and Times with It* by John Edward Slater p. 11 and *Unheard Voices- The Rise of Steelband and Calypso in the Caribbean and North America* by A. *Myrna* Nurse, iUniverse, Inc. New York, 2007, p. 62.
[70] Helene Bellour, Jeffrey Chock, Kim Johnson and Milla Riggio—The History of Renegades Steel Orchestra of Trinidad & Tobago, Macmillan Caribbean, 2002, p. 31.
[71] George "Sonny" Goddard, op.cit. p. 10.
[72] Norman Darway Adams: Stories in Steel, 2005, pp. 13-14.
[73] Website: When Steel Talks, Days of the Steelband Wars, posted on Inter-Net February 8, 2010.
[74] Jules, op.cit. 25/01/02. Also A. Myrna Nurse, op.cit. p. 25.
[75] George "Sonny" Goddard, op.cit, p. 39.
[76] Jerry Serrant in his work already quoted says Jules went in "around 1941". Jules, himself, is quoted in A *Myrna* Nurse's "Unheard Voices" as indicating that he went into Hell Yard in 1939 which puts his age then as 12 years.
[77] Neville Jules: Interview at 17 Eligon Ave., Friday, 25 January 2002.

[78] A. *Myrna* Nurse: op.cit. p.32.

[79] Oliver Joseph: Interview, Thursday, 22 October 2009, at 2211 Trogon Terrace, Maloney Gardens.

[80] A. Myrna Nurse op.cit. p. 62 quotes Albert Jones as identifying Zigilee with the "chu-fac" while John Edward Slater in his book The Advent of the Steelband and My Life and Times with it—cites Jules as the maker of the "chu-fak".

[81] John E. Slater, op.cit. p. 11.

[82] Neville Jules: 25/01/02, op.cit.

[83] Ibid.

[84] Joe-Bell (Hugh Alexander) while listening to All Stars rehearse their Panorama tune in 2003, related stories and described such scenarios of the old days.

[85] John E. Slater, op.cit. p. 11.

[86] Marcia Henville, "Memories of Old Man Zig", Sunday Express, January 4, 1988.

[87] Jerry Serrant: op.cit. When Oliver Joseph was interviewed by BR in October 2009, this quotation was read to him and he was asked if he still stood by what was related there and he acknowledged the sentiments of the quote in its entirety.

[88] Oliver Joseph: Interview at 2211 Trogon Terrace, Maloney Gardens, Thursday, 22 October 2009.

[89] Ibid.

[90] Oliver Joseph: Interview at 2211 Trogon Terrace, Maloney Gardens, Thursday, 22 October 2009.

[91] Elmo "Bully" Alleyne, op.cit.

[92] Trinidad Guardian: Empire Day Message from the Secretary of State for the Colonies, Sunday, 23 May 1943.

[93] A. Myrna Nurse, op.cit. pp. 25-26.

[94] Ibid.

[95] A. Myrna Nurse, op.cit. p. 20.

[96] Evening News, Friday, 17 August 1945, p. 7.

[97] Trinidad Guardian, Wednesday, 15 August 1945.

[98] Sunday Guardian, Sunday, 19 August 1945—"Behind the Curtain" by Ubiquitous.
[99] Evening News, Saturday, 18 August 1945, Front Page.
[100] Evening News, Thursday, 23 August 1945—Letter to Editor by San Fernando reader.
[101] Sunday Guardian, Sunday, 4 November 1945, "Behind the Curtain" by Ubiquitous.
[102] 1947 Political Reports, Secret Dispatch No.15, CO 537/2255, 3 November 1947, Governor J.V.W. Shaw to Arthur Creech-Jones.
[103] Trinidad Guardian, Tuesday, 11 December 1945—"Revive String Bands" by Burgess (POS).
[104] Ibid.
[105] Trinidad Guardian, Saturday, 16 December 1945, "Ban on Bands Praised" by F.M. Campbell-Bryce—Pastor, Holy Apostolic Tabernacle, Couva.
[106] Trinidad Guardian, Friday, 21 December 1945.
[107] Trinidad Guardian, Thursday, 20 December 1945, "Music Without Strings" by Phil Madison.
[108] Jules at Eligon Ave op.cit.
[109] John Edward Slater, op.cit. p. 11.
[110] TNT Mirror Newspaper: Friday, 6 March 1987—A Special Mirror Investigation by Harold Ramoutar—The Birth of the Steelband.
[111] Norman "Darway' Adams: op. cit. pp. 11-12.
[112] Jerry Serrant, op.cit. p. 26—"In the Beginning—Jules tells it himself."
[113] Trinbagopan.com—"Neville Jules Speaks on Pan" posted 11 June 2007, pp. 1-2.
[114] A. Myrna Nurse, op.cit. p.25. Also Interview with Jules, op.cit. 25/01/02
[115] Trinidad Guardian, Tuesday, 5 March 1946.
[116] Trinidad Guardian: "Before They Were All Stars" by Robert Clarke, Tuesday, 19 February 2002.
[117] Ibid.
[118] West Indian Rhythm: Bear Family Records—P.O. Box 1154, D-27727 Hambergen, Germany. Email: bear@bear-family.de N.B. The Bear Family Records acquired all the DECCA Masters of recordings done in Trinidad. The author is grateful to Mr. Harold Moylan who provided this information as well

as a CD with "Lion Oh" that also included two virtuous solo performances by the legendary Neville Jules on a big tenor, i.e., 45 gallon oil drum.

[119] Ibid.

[120] Dr. Oswin Rose: Telephone discussion on Thursday, 15 September 2011.

[121] See the Decca Record Card of "Lion Oh"—West Indian Rhythm—Bear Family Records.

[122] Port-of-Spain Gazette, 15 February 1940, p. 7.

[123] George "Sonny' Goddard, op.cit. p. 26. N.B. The Hell Yard Band did not take the name "All Stars' until late 1940s. In 1940 the name used was "Hell Yard Second Fiddle."

[124] Darway, op. cit, p 13 and Fedo Blake's History and Evolution of the Steelband, pp. 144 and 145.

[125] Charles Edward Smith—"A New Trinidadian Music", Disc Album 719; 2 ten-inch records. 1948 Disc Company of New York, 117 W. 46 St. Asch Recording Studios, New York, 19, N.Y.

[126] Sunday Guardian, 2 February 2003—"First Pan Record Recovered."

[127] Oliver Joseph: op.cit. p. 9

[128] Ibid.

[129] John Edward Slater, op.cit. p. 15.

[130] Jerry Serrant, op.cit. p. 38.

[131] William Dalrymple: "PLF: The Man Who Walked" published on BST, September 6, 2008, Cf Telegraph.co.uk.

[132] That factory was the Sunrise Biscuit Company that was located on Prince Street.

[133] Patrick Leigh Fermor: Traveler's Tree—A Journey through the Caribbean Islands, London, John Murray, December 1950, Fisheyes Rudolf Olivier's Steelband, pp. 170-172.

[134] Neville Jules: Telephone conversation between BR and Jules on Thursday November 12, 2009 wherein Jules explained how his "bass-boom" worked and how the pan that Fisheye played then was not the 45 Gallon Drum but a much smaller drum, no more than 12-20 inches in circumference, with the initials KMR stamped at the bottom, which they bought from a factory near the then slaughter-house in Port-of-Spain. The metal of this particular pan was of good

quality, it accommodated more notes, as much as 10-14, and was played off the shoulder with one stick.

[135] Oliver Joseph op.cit. p. 10.

[136] Patrick Leigh Fermor, op.cit. The Traveler's Tree.

[137] Stephen Stuempfle; op.cit.

[138] Jerry Serrant, op.cit. p.51 and Prince Batson: Interview at Eligon Ave.

[139] Jerry Serrant, op.cit. p.51.

[140] Trinbagopan.com- Neville Jules Speaks on Pan, posted June11, 2007.

[141] Jerry Serrant, op.cit. and Trinidad Guardian, Tuesday March 5 and Wednesday March 6, 1946.

[142] Jerry Serrant, op. cit. pp.45-46.

[143] Ibid.

[144] Jules at Eligon Ave., op.cit.

[145] Trinbagopan.com, op. cit. Jules identified the Magazine as LOOK.

[146] A.*Myrna* Nurse, op.cit, p.349. Ellie told the story about seeing Sonny Roach and another panman named Granville playing 4-note ping-pongs in 1939 early 1940, and on another occasion Ellie claimed that one Eddie Myers made the first ping-pong; see A. *Myrna* Nurse op.cit. p. 351.

[147] Jules at Eligon Ave., op.cit.

[148] Trinbagopan.com, op.cit.

[149] A. Myrna Nurse op.cit. p. 13.

[150] Ibid., p.355. Ellie claims here that the tune-boom was invented by Fisheye who left Red Army and joined Invaders bringing his tune-boom with him and he, Ellie, copied it.

[151] Ibid, p. 15.

[152] Trinbagopan.com, op. cit.

[153] Jerry Serrant, op.cit, p. 53.

[154] Kim Johnson: Pan Pioneers—If Yuh Iron Good You Is King, p. 209.

[155] Oliver Joseph: Telephone discussion, Monday, 16 November 2009.

[156] Jerry Serrant, op.cit. p. 127.

[157] A.Myrna Nurse, op.cit. p. 12.

[158] Ibid, p. 14.

[159] Ibid, p. 12.

[160] Leroi Boldon: Interview email dated Wednesday, 18 November 2009.

[161] Ibid. The pan made for Audra was the "trombone pan" which was only used for about one year, according to Neville Jules—Telephone Discussion, Friday, 20 November 2009.

[162] Audra Preddie: Telephone discussion, Thursday, 9 June 2011.

[163] Ibid.

[164] Leroi Boldon, email, op.cit.

[165] Leroi Boldon, Interview Sunday, 1 March 2009.

[166] Ibid. "Man" is McDonald Olliverre.

[167] Oliver Joseph, op.cit.

[168] Ibid.

[169] Ibid.

[170] Ibid.

[171] Ibid.

[172] Oliver Joseph, op.cit.

[173] Shannon Dudley: Music From Behind The Bridge—Steelband Spirit and Politics in T&T, Oxford University Press, 2008, p. 278.

[174] John Edward Slater, op.cit., p. 23.

[175] A. Myrna Nurse, op.cit. p. 62—Albert Jones' Story.

[176] A. Myrna Nurse: Albert Jones' Story—"Ingenuity in Steelband's Social and Political Organization", op.cit, pp. 62 and 82.

[177] A. *Myrna* Nurse, Rudolph V. King's Story, op.cit. pp. 96–98.

[178] A. *Myrna* Nurse, A Vignette by Vincent Hernandez, op.cit. p. 152.

[179] Ibid, pp. 152 and 157.

[180] A. *Myrna* Nurse, "Leroy Ali Williams's Story" op.cit. p. 274.

[181] Bukka Rennie Column: "Pan Development Controversy," Trinidad Guardian, 29 December 1999.

[182] There are several references in the story of Pan to Baptist Sankee Songs, in fact these songs were the compositions of an American Gospel singer, Ira David Sankey (1840-1908) and his hymnal was widely used in T&T. He did 1200 songs. Two other Baptist Songs named by OJ were "A Little More Oil in the Lamp" and "Adam in the Garden hiding, hiding from the Lord."

[183] A *Myrna* Nurse, op.cit. pp. 62-63.

[184] Trinidad Guardian: Tuesday, 17 September 1946.

[185] A. *Myrna* Nurse, op.cit. p. 152.

[186] Neville Jules: Telephone conversation, 20 November 2009.

[187] Kim Johnson: Pan Pioneers—"If Yuh Iron Good You Is King" pp. 208-209.

[188] Jeffery Ross Thomas: A History of Pan and the Evolution of the Steelband in T&T, MA Thesis, Wesleyan University, USA, p. 121.

[189] Noel "Ginghee" Davidson: Interview at Cipriani Extension, Morvant, Tuesday, August 19, 2008.

[190] Stephen Stuempfle: The Steelband Movement in T&T, PHD Thesis, University of Pennsylvania 1990, p. 51.

[191] Evening News, Tuesday, 10 July 1956; "Past and the Future guide the Craftsmen who work in Stone and Metal"—This is Your City by J. Grimes.

[192] Christy Eversley: Conversation at his home in London, August 2005. He also said in that interview that he heard *"George Porgie"* being played by the band in the Dry River.

[193] Ibid.

[194] Ibid. Also see Evening News, Tuesday, 10 July 1956.

[195] Sunday Mirror, Sunday, 3 July 2005, "Pan was born in St. James" by Joeline Thomas.

[196] Ibid.

[197] Julien "JD' Darius interview, April 2011.

[198] Jules at Eligon Ave., op.cit. Also A. Myrna Nurse op.cit. pp. 13-14.

[199] Neville Jules indicated to Kim Johnson that it "was around 1947". See Kim Johnson's work, p. 171

[200] A.Myrna Nurse, op. cit. p. 13.

[201] Kenrick P. Thomas: PANRIGA—Tacarigua's Contribution to the Evolution of the Steelband Phenomenon in Trinidad & Tobago, Original World Press, Washington, D.C. and 55 Edward Street, Port-of-Spain, 1999, pp. 44-45.

[202] Randolph "Ladd" Wiltshire: Telephone discussion with BR in November 2000.

[203] Cyril "Snatcher" Guy: Conversation at Arima with Clive Timothy—November 2000.

[204] Bukka Rennie: "Pan Debate Must Be Opened UP", Trinidad Guardian, 13 November 2000.

[205] Discussion with Kenrick Thomas at Eddie Hart Grounds, Sunday, December 20, 2009.

[206] Cyril "Crapaud" Scanterbury, at Sammy's Bar, St. Vincent Street, Tunapuna, Friday 18/12/2009.

[207] Kim Johnson: op.cit. p. 171.

[208] Ken Duval: Telephone conversation, January 4, 2010.

[209] Ibid.

[210] Angela Pidduck: White Boys Playing Pan, Newsday Saturday, 10 January 2009.

[211] Ibid.

[212] Roy Regis: telephone discussion, 29/12/10.

[213] Kim Johnson—Pan Pioneers; "If Yuh Iron Good, You Is King", 2006 Pan Trinbago pub. p. 102.

[214] Prince Batson: Interview at 17 Eligon Ave, Diego Martin, Friday, 1 February 2002.

[215] Elmo "Bully" Alleyne, op.cit.

[216] Discussion with Ms. Akende Rudder, daughter of Vats Rudder, Monday, 2 December 2013.

[217] Jerry Serrant, op.cit.

[218] Neville Jules, op.cit.

[219] Ibid.

[220] Ibid and Leroi Boldon's interview at the Old Boys' and Girls' Association Headquarters at the corner of George and Duke Streets, Sunday, 3 March 2009.

[221] Prince Batson, op.cit.

[222] Harold Moylan: "A Study of a Group: The Trinidad All Stars Steel Orchestra"—An Undergraduate Paper presented 4 December 1961—Sociology Dept., University of Toronto, Canada.

[223] Ibid.

[224] Ibid.

[225] Prince Batson, op.cit.

[226] Leroi Boldon, op.cit. p. 5.

[227] Prince Batson, op.cit.

[228] Ibid.

²²⁹ Noel Carry: Discussion in All Stars Pan Yard, Tuesday, 8 June 2010, between 10pm-12pm.

²³⁰ Sonny Blacks: Facebook Posting, 6 November 2020, 9:55 am.

²³¹ Jerry Serrant, op.cit. pgs. 40 and 41.

²³² Shannon Dudley: op. cit p. 60.

²³³ See Norman "Darway' Adams, op.cit. for documented details.

²³⁴ Harold Moylan: op. cit.

²³⁵ Neville Jules: Interview at 17 Eligon Ave., Diego Martin.

²³⁶ St. Clair Plowden: Discussion at All Stars 2010 Mas Launch, Friday, November 20, 2009. Also interview at All Stars Pan Yard in 2006.

²³⁷ Ibid.

²³⁸ Neville Jules, op.cit.

²³⁹ Jerry Serrant, op.cit.

²⁴⁰ When Steel Talks: Interview with Neville Jules, 2003.

²⁴¹ John Edward Slater, op.cit. p. 8.

²⁴² Jerry Serrant, op.cit. p. 30.

²⁴³ Guy Boldon: The Great Neville Jules Escape.

²⁴⁴ Prince Batson, op. cit.

²⁴⁵ A. Myrna Nurse, op.cit. p. 24.

²⁴⁶ Ibid.

²⁴⁷ Neville Jules at Eligon Ave., op.cit.

²⁴⁸ A. Myrna Nurse, op.cit. Chapter 4, p.83—The Albert Jones's Story.

²⁴⁹ John Edward Slater, op. cit. p.15—The Pulsating Beat.

²⁵⁰ Leroi Boldon, op.cit.

²⁵¹ Ibid.

²⁵² George "Sonny' Goddard, op.cit. p. 53.

²⁵³ Jeffery Ross Thomas, op.cit. p. 178.

²⁵⁴ Ibid, p. 179.

²⁵⁵ George "Sonny" Goddard, op.cit. p. 61.

²⁵⁶ Ibid, pp. 61-62.

²⁵⁷ Jeffery Ross Thomas, op.cit. p. 180.

²⁵⁸ Jules and Batson at Eligon Ave, Diego Martin, op.cit.

²⁵⁹ Ibid.

²⁶⁰ George Goddard, op.cit. p. 61.

[261] A. *Myrna* Nurse, op.cit. p. 31.

[262] Prince Batson at Eligon Ave., op.cit.

[263] Prince Batson at Eligon Ave. op.cit.

[264] Ibid.

[265] Kim Johnson: "If Yuh Iron Good You Is King" p. 153.

[266] Jeffery Ross Thomas, op.cit. p. 180.

[267] Oliver "OJ" Joseph, telephone conversation on Tuesday, 24 November 2009.

[268] A. *Myrna* Nurse, op.cit. p. 363.

[269] Sunday Express: Ellie Mannette—Journey to Roots, by Terry Joseph, 29 October 2000.

[270] Neville Jules at Eligon Ave., op.cit.

[271] Lennox Pierre—Conversation at Jean Pierre Complex—"Pan is Beautiful' Festival.

[272] Anthony Mark Jones, op.cit. p. 28.

[273] Norman "Darway' Adams, Reply to Bukka Rennie, 8 March 2004.

[274] Bukka Rennie, Pan History 211: Good-day and Good-bye, Mr. Darway, Trinidad Guardian, 17 March 2004.

[275] Leroi Boldon, Interview at All Stars Old Boys Association HQ, 1 March 2009.

[276] George Goddard, op.cit. p.70 cf Trinidad Guardian, June 17, 1951 p. 7.

[277] Roy Regis: a critique of an early draft of this work. Also telephone discussion on 29/12/10.

[278] Les Slater: Sixty Years after TASPO—Ellie's First-Hand Reply, posted on WST, 24 January 2012.

[279] Ibid.

[280] See A Myrna Nurse's Unheard Voices, p. 356.

[281] Les Slater, op. cit WST, posted 24 January 2012.

[282] Leroi Boldon, op.cit.

[283] Neville Jules: Telephone conversation, 20 November 2009.

[284] Leroi Boldon, op.cit.

[285] A. *Myrna* Nurse, op.cit. pp. 34-35.

[286] Oliver Joseph, Interview at Maloney, op.cit.

[287] Jerry Serrant, The Maestro Neville Jules, op.cit.

288 John Edward Slater, op.cit. p. 23.

289 Prince Batson: "The Steelband that grew from Hell yard"—Sunday Guardian, 13 October 1985.

290 Courtney Vincent Charles: Interview at the Pan-Yard, Tuesday, 29 March 2011.

291 Harold Moylan: op. cit.

292 Oliver Joseph: op.cit.

293 St. Clair Plowden, op.cit.

294 Jerry Serrant, op.cit. p. 63.

295 Jerry Serrant, op.cit. p.63.

296 This 1957 LP was recorded at Dial Records and later Kay Records on Nelson Street.

297 Stephen Stuempfle, op.cit. pp. 40-43.

298 Jerry Serrant, op.cit.

299 Ibid.

300 Roy Regis in his critique as an early reader of this work.

301 Lennox Pierre, Discussion at Jean Pierre Complex, Pan is Beautiful Festival (1980).

302 Ibid.

303 Hugh Clarke: At his Green Street home in 1982.

304 Kenrick P. Thomas, PANRIGA, op.cit. pp. 79-82.

305 Ibid.

306 Teddy Pinheiro: Discussion after the funeral of Carlyle "Mackie" McIntosh, 1 September 2010.

307 Kenrick Thomas, op.cit. pp. 95-97.

308 Sunday Guardian, August 10, 2003, Sunday Vibe, p. 61.

309 Roy Regis: Telephone discussion, December 5th, 2012.

310 Noel "Ginghee' Davidson; Interview at Cipriani Extension, Morvant, Tuesday August, 19, 2009.

311 Ibid.

312 Ibid.

313 Ibid.

314 Ibid.

315 Norman "Darway' Adams, Stories in Steel, op.cit. p. 5.

316 Noel "Ginghee' Davidson, op.cit.

317 Ibid.

318 Ibid.

319 Carlyle McIntosh, op. cit.

320 Oliver Joseph: Discussion at Pan-Yard, Monday, 11 July 2011.

321 George "Sonny' Goddard, op. cit. p.72.

322 Noel "Ginghee" Davidson, op. cit.

323 Cyril S. Matthew, The Story of Pan Am North Stars, printed by ScripJ Ltd, 2017, Trinidad & Tobago. pp. 86-87.

324 Esther Oxford, "Farewell to the Man of Steel", October 1994.

325 London Weekly TIMES, "Carnival Champion Boots" laid to rest among friends"—Fond Farewell for Drum-Man loved by all, October 1994.

326 Noel "Ginghee" Davidson, Interview, 19 August 2008.

327 Jerry Serrant, op.cit. pp. 57-58.

328 Noel "Ginghee" Davidson, op.cit.

329 Patrick Leigh Fermor, op.cit. p. 170.

330 Norman "Darway' Adams, op.cit. p. 28.

331 Jerry Serrant, op.cit, pp. 72-73.

332 This subject is explored fully in "History of the Working-Class in T&T, 1919-1956" by Bukka Rennie. The new edition of this book, published by Majority Press in 2011 is now available.

333 Jerry Serrant, op.cit, p. 74.

334 Ibid.

335 Trinidad Guardian: Wednesday October 31, 1984—Prince Baston interviewed by Dalton Narine—"Adjudicators Confused Panmen".

336 Ibid.

337 Ibid.

338 Errol Hill: The Ping-Pong: Caribbean Plays, One-Act Play 21, UWI Extra-Mural Dept, T&T. PR 9360, T89 H6 P5/A.

339 Ibid, p. 13.

340 A. *Myrna* Nurse, op.cit, pp. 169-170.

341 Ibid.

342 Ibid, p. 385.

[343] Response to The Bukka Rennie Column: *Lies and Distortions of Pan*, Trinidad Guardian, Nov 1, 1999 The unnamed author of this response cited The *Nation*, Friday May 27, 1960 as his source.

[344] The Nation: Friday, 27 May 1960.

[345] Ibid.

[346] Ibid.

[347] A. *Myrna* Nurse, op.cit. pp.173-176

[348] Teddy Pinheiro: Discussion after the funeral of Carlyle "Mackie" McIntosh, September 1, 2010

[349] A *Myrna* Nurse: op. cit. Clifford Alexis's Story, pp 200-201

[350] See Goddard's Forty Years in the Steelbands, 1939-1979, p. 155.

[351] Ibid. p. 156.

[352] Cecil Paul: Pan discussion with Bukka Rennie. May 2018.

[353] Ibid.

[354] Goddard, op. cit. p. 101.

[355] Neville Jules, op.cit. at Eligon Ave.

[356] Newsday Section B, Monday, 31 January 2005, pg. 15, Schools Broadcasting Unit, Morning: 10.15am and Afternoon: 2.15pm.

[357] Anthony Mark Jones, STEELBAND, Winston "Spree" Simon's Story, the Introduction.

[358] Ibid. pp. 13-14.

[359] Trinidad Guardian: "The Return of Mr. Steelband" by Eric Roach, 13 January 1967.

[360] George Goddard, op. cit. p. 78.

[361] Jerry Serrant, op. cit, p. 71.

[362] Ibid. p. 72.

[363] Lennox Brown: "Pan Power in Classics and Jazz", 1987 PAN SPECIAL, pp. 12-13.

[364] Ibid.

[365] Leroi Boldon interview, op.cit.

[366] Jerry Serrant, op.cit p.40. Serrant quotes Francis Diaz popular barber and well-known singer.

[367] Discussion with Winston Rennie who was tutored by Denner in the early to mid-1960s.

[368] Austin: Discussion at the Pan-Yard, Carnival 2011.

[369] Prince Batson: The Band which Grew From Hell-Yard, op.cit.

[370] Trinbagopan.com: Neville Jules Speaks on Pan, posted 11 June 2007.

[371] A. *Myrna* Nurse, op. cit. pp. 33-34.

[372] Trinbagopan.com "Neville Jules speaks on Pan", posted 11 June 2007.

[373] Ibid.

[374] Glenroy Joseph: Blog as told by Dawad Philip, FB Post, Saturday, 31 October 2020.

[375] Trinidad Guardian: Wednesday, 31 October 1984—Dalton Narine interviews Prince Batson in Santa Cruz—"Adjudicators Confuse Panmen."

[376] Pan-Yard discussion with Kenneth Palmer, KP, All Stars' then bartender, who grew up in Point Cumana and was an original member of Boys Town; Wednesday, 21 March 2012.

[377] Courtney Vincent Charles: Interview, op.cit.

[378] Ibid.

[379] Julien Darius (JD) interview: 26/04/11. JD confirmed that Paulie of Commandoes was Popo's brother.

[380] Kim Johnson—Pan Pioneers, op.cit. p.169; Jerry Serrant, op.cit. p. 46; Darway Adams, op. cit. p. 31.

[381] Neville Jules: Telephone conversation, Friday, 20 November 2009.

[382] Prince Batson, op.cit. Invaders' *Birdie's Mambo* came after, i.e., 1952 when they came 2nd to All Stars in the J'ouvert Morning Best Steelband Competition; Serrant p. 68.

[383] Jerry Serrant, op. cit. p. 48.

[384] See the Decca Master of the 11 February 1940 recording of *Lion Oh*.

[385] Jerry Serrant, op.cit. pp. 6-8.

[386] Ibid.

[387] Courtney Vincent Charles: Interview at Pan Yard, Tuesday March 29, 2011.

[388] A. *Myrna* Nurse, op. cit. p. 28.

[389] Jerry Serrant, op.cit. p. 6.

[390] A. *Myrna* Nurse, op. cit. p. 28.

[391] Prince Batson: The Band which grew from Hell Yard, Sunday Guardian, Oct 13, 1985.

[392] Jerry Serrant, op.cit., pp. 6-8.

[393] Winston Gordon: Tribute to Jules; note delivered at Clyde McColin's funeral.

[394] Courtney Vincent Charles: Interview at the Pan Yard, Tuesday, 29 March 2011.

[395] Jerry Serrant, op. cit. p. 125.

[396] Pan Jumbie: "Oh, for those good Old Days"- Sunday Express, Section 2, 24 January 1988.

[397] Jerry Serrant, op. cit. p. 127.

[398] Courtney Vincent Charles: Interview, op.cit.

[399] This obviously was about musical warfare because San Juan All Stars that year had an impressive bomb—"Till The End of a Rainbow" arranged by Aldwyn "Madman" Jordan of Tunapuna. Members who played pan with the San Juan band in that period indicate that Madman also tuned the pans and the previous year had arranged the popular song "Tammy" which had a great impact in Port-of-Spain.

[400] Courtney Vincent Charles: Interview op.cit.

[401] Prince Batson, Sunday Guardian, 13 October 1985.

[402] Leroi Boldon: Interview at All Stars Old Boys Association Headquarters, 1 March 2009.

[403] Courtney Charles, op.cit.

[404] A. *Myrna* Nurse, op.cit. pp. 38-39.

[405] Jerry Serrant, op.cit. p. 127.

[406] Bukka Rennie: Pan—The Road Ahead—Is It In Danger? Pan Special, February 1987, p. 16.

[407] Trinidad Guardian: Tuesday, 19 February 2002.

[408] Note from Winston Gordon provided at Clyde McColin's funeral, 24 November 2017.

[409] Jerry Serrant, op.cit., p. 19.

[410] Ibid. p.44.

[411] Courtney Vincent Charles: Interview op.cit.

[412] When Steel Talks: 1 March 2013, posted by Ian Franklin.

[413] CLR James: Party Politics in the West Indies, Imprint, p. 153 and The Bukka Rennie Column: Lessons from Chaguaramas, Monday, 9 July 2001.

[414] CLR James: Party Politics in the West Indies, op. cit. p. 22 and B. Rennie op.cit.

[415] Bukka Rennie Column, op.cit.

[416] Ibid.

[417] People's National Movement: 5th Annual Convention, Report of the General Council, Appendix 3, Report on April 22 Independence Demonstration, pp. 16-17.

[418] Trinbagopan.com: Neville Jules Speaks on Pan, posted 11 June 2007.

[419] Beresford Hunte: 2010 panyard discussion.

[420] Winston Gordon; e-mail, posted 02/09/2020.

[421] Ibid.

[422] A. *Myrna* Nurse, op.cit. pp 29-30. Also see Trinbagopan.com—Neville Jules Speaks on Pan, op.cit. Jules spoke to Nurse in 2002 and five years after, 2007, to Trinbagopan.com yet the consistency of his interpretation of events in regard to this split is remarkably outstanding for a person of his age.

[423] Trinidad Guardian: "Hilton All Stars Clear Air", Thursday, 30 March 1967.

[424] Jules said "they talked amongst themselves and they decided how (they) were going to split and keep the job." Cf. Trinbagopan.com—Neville Jules Speaks on Pan, op. cit.

[425] Winston Gordon; From Messenger to Manager, Sunday Business Guardian, 25 March 2001, p. 4.

[426] Ibid.

[427] Ibid.

[428] Ibid.

[429] Ibid.

[430] Noel Lorde (Cin-Cin) one of the new members said that Jules drummed this into their heads at every opportunity he got. Interview with Cin-Cin.

[431] Ibid.

[432] Telephone discussion with Noel "Cin-Cin' Lorde on Thursday, 9 December 2010.

[433] Courtney Vincent Charles: Interview, op.cit.

[434] Trinbagopan.com—Neville Jules Speaks on Pan, op.cit.

[435] Prince Batson: The Band which Grew From Hell Yard, op.cit.

[436] Hamilton "Web' Alexander: written submission—March 2018.

[437] Hamilton "Web' Alexander, "Part of the History of Trinidad All Stars"—a written submission.

[438] Telephone discussion with Noel "Cin-Cin' Lorde, Thursday, 9 December 2010.

[439] Hamilton "Web' Alexander, written submission, op.cit.

[440] Trinibagopan.com—Neville Jules Speaks on Pan, op.cit.

[441] Lincoln "Abbos' Aberdeen said: "Bukka, ah hear yuh writing All Stars history, doh forget dat is I who get a report to the newspapers and dat report prompt Catelli to sponsor the band!"

[442] Trinbagopan.com—op.cit.

[443] A. *Myrna* Nurse, op.cit. p. 30.

[444] Oliver Joseph: HELLYARD.

[445] A. *Myrna* Nurse, op.cit. p. 30.

[446] Sunday Guardian, 19 February 1984, "Masters Of The Classics" by Dalton Narine.

[447] Ibid.

[448] Ibid.

[449] Ibid.

[450] Trinbagopan.com, op.cit.

[451] Roy Gibbs: Interview at the Old Boys Association HQ, George Street, 7 March 2009.

[452] Trinbagopan.com, Neville Jules, op.cit.

[453] Sunday Guardian, 19 February 1984—"Masters Of The Classics" by Dalton Narine.

[454] Roy Gibbs, Interview op.cit.

[455] Noel "Cin-Cin' Lorde: Panyard discussion on Uncle Gem's approach to musical development.

[456] Leon "Smooth' Edwards: Interview at East Grove, Wednesday, 20 July 2011.

[457] John "Poison' Douglas: Interview at COPOS HQ. Pembroke Street, Tuesday, 1 February 2011.

[458] Ibid.

[459] Ibid.

[460] Ibid.

[461] Ibid.

[462] Fitzgerald Jemmott: "Arrangement for Steelbands—Some Hints" Steelband in Perspective, Pan Trinbago Magazine, Government Printery, Trinidad & Tobago, 1973, p. 10.

[463] Ibid.

[464] Ibid.

[465] Ibid.

[466] Prince Batson: The Band Which Grew From Hell Yard, op.cit.

[467] Roy Gibbs: Interview, op.cit.

[468] Trinidad Guardian: Wednesday, 2 October 1968.

[469] Ibid.

[470] Ibid.

[471] Ibid.

[472] Hamilton "Web' Alexander: op.cit.

[473] Hamilton "Web' Alexander: written submission, March 2018.

[474] Leon "Smooth" Edwards: op. cit. Web Alexander said Jules also helped with pp. 99.

[475] Hamilton "Web' Alexander: op.cit.

[476] Pan Trinbago: Steelband In Perspective, compiled by Dennis LeGendre, 1973, p. 33.

[477] Sunday Express, 4 March 1973.

[478] Ibid.

[479] Edric Straker: Conversation outside "Serviceman's Bar" on Marriott Street, San Fernando, 2 November 2013.

[480] Alfred Aguiton: Author of Liner Notes to the album "Inside Out."

[481] Leon "Smooth' Edwards, op.cit.

[482] Ken Toppin: Evening News, Thursday, 7 November 1974.

[483] Brian Dockray: Trinidad Guardian—Friday, 13 November 1974.

[484] Osmond C. Hale: Foreword to Classical Jewels magazine.

[485] Bertie Fraser: Tribute to Classical Jewels, Message from the President of Pan Trinbago.

[486] Hamilton "Web' Alexander: Discussion at the Panyard, Friday, 21 January 2011.

[487] Hamilton "Web' Alexander; op.cit.

[488] Web Alexander says that it was Michael Andrews, not to be mistaken for Mervyn Andrews, a cousin who died.
[489] Hamilton "Web' Alexander, op.cit.
[490] Ibid.
[491] Leon "Smooth' Edwards, op. cit.
[492] Ibid.
[493] Ibid.
[494] Sunday Guardian: Sunday, 6 February 1977.
[495] Leon "Smooth' Edwards, op.cit.
[496] Ibid.
[497] Ibid.
[498] Ibid.
[499] Cecil Lynch: Discussion at the Pan Yard, September 2012.
[500] Pan Special '87: Of Champ and Challengers…THE BIG "C', p. 8.
[501] Leon "Smooth' Edwards: Interview at East Grove, 20 July 2011.
[502] Ibid.
[503] Ibid.
[504] Ibid.
[505] Errol "Reds' Collins: Telephone discussion, Saturday, 13 August 2011.
[506] Jerry Serrant: Trinidad All Stars Newsletter, Issue No. 8, December 2003.
[507] Reds Collins: PanYard discussion.
[508] Sunday Guardian, 6 January 2013—"All Stars out to hold on to title" by Sean Nero.
[509] Jerry Serrant: TAS Newsletter, Issue No.8, Dec 2003.
[510] When Steel Talks: "Cool Hand Smooth, All Stars Arranger, Bounce and Drive, on Hat-trick Hunt by D.Narine.
[511] Jerry Serrant: TAS Newsletter, Issue No.8, Dec 2003.
[512] Trinidad Guardian: Monday, 5 March 1984.
[513] All Stars Newsletter, Issue No.8, 2003.
[514] Trinidad Guardian: Monday, 18 February 1985.
[515] All Stars Newsletter, Issue No. 8, 2003.
[516] Pan Special '87—One Point Heart-Break, op.cit. p. 4.
[517] Ibid.
[518] All Stars Newsletter, Issue No.8, 2003.

519 Ibid.

520 Leon "Smooth' Edwards: Interview at East Grove, 20 July 2011.

521 Pan Special '87, op.cit.p. 9.

522 Trinidad Express, 18 August 1980—"All Stars A-Twinkle".

523 Sunday Guardian: 23 November 1980.

524 Ibid.

525 Ibid.

526 Trinidad Guardian: Tuesday, 6 November 1984—"Suite Pan at Complex sets Stage for Pan is Beautiful 4" by Dalton Narine.

527 Trinidad Guardian: Tuesday, 6 November 1984—"All Stars…Our very own Symphony Orchestra".

528 Sunday Guardian, 12 October 1986—Steelband Music Festival Post Mortem—2, p 10, by Valentino Singh.

529 Trinidad Guardian: Wednesday, 11 July 1984—William Doyle-Marshall interviews Paul Hill.

530 Ibid.

531 Sunday Guardian, 27 November 1983—"Great Classical Jewels IV from All Stars" by Ellen Drew.

532 Ibid.

533 Ibid.

534 Ibid.

535 Trinidad Guardian, Saturday, 16 November 1985—All Stars Sparkle—A Result of Hard Work by Anne Hilton.

536 Ibid.

537 Trinidad Guardian, 16 November 1985—A Violinist Looks at All Stars in Concert, by McDonnel Carpenter.

538 Pan Special '87, op. cit. "Of Champ and Challengers—The Big C".

539 Sunday Guardian, 12 October 1986—Steelband Music Festival Post Mortem-2 by Valentino Singh.

540 Ibid.

541 Ibid.

542 Ibid.

543 Ibid.

[544] Trinidad Guardian, Monday, 6 October 1986—"Despers Won" by Francis Joseph.
[545] Sunday Guardian, 12 October 1986, Steelband Music Festival Post Mortem, op.cit.
[546] Sunday Guardian, 9 November 1986—Open Letter to Arnim Smith, President of Pan Trinbago.
[547] Errol "Reds' Collins: Interview at Pan Yard, Friday, 13 May 2011.
[548] Ibid.
[549] Ibid.
[550] Ibid. Reds did in fact present the sums proposed.
[551] Barbara Crichlow-Shaw: Interview at Diego Martin, 3 April 2011.
[552] Ibid.
[553] Ibid.
[554] Reds Collins: Interview, op.cit.
[555] Leon "Smooth' Edwards: Interview at East Grove, 20 July 2011.
[556] Barbara Crichlow-Shaw, op.cit.
[557] Ibid.
[558] Reds Collins: op.cit.
[559] Barbara Crichlow-Shaw: Telephone discussion, Friday, 20 May 2011.
[560] 1987 Budget Breakdown submitted by Barbara Crichlow.
[561] Barbara Crichlow-Shaw at Diego Martin, op.cit.
[562] Ibid.
[563] John "Poison' Douglas: Interview at COPOS, Pembroke St. Tuesday, 1 February 2011.
[564] Ibid.
[565] Ibid.
[566] Ibid.
[567] Ibid.
[568] Ibid.
[569] Ibid.
[570] Ibid.
[571] Ibid.
[572] John "Poison' Douglas—Interview at COPOS, op.cit.
[573] Ibid.

[574] Reds Collins, op.cit.

[575] "F" is for Fitzgerald, "L" for Leon, "A" for Anthony Guy, "B" for Barbara, "E" for Earl Wells and "J" for John Douglas.

[576] John "Poison' Douglas, op.cit.

[577] Barbara Crichlow-Shaw, op.cit.

[578] Beresford Hunte: Telephone discussion, Friday, 20 May 2011.

[579] Barbara Crichlow-Shaw: Interview, op.cit.

[580] Ibid. Barbara's uncle was Frank Crichlow, the owner of then famous Mangrove Pub that housed the Mangrove Steelband.

[581] Keith "Grip' Matthews: Telephone discussion, Wednesday, 13 April 2011.

[582] Beresford Hunte, op.cit. Berry indicated that it was Smooth himself who first approached him.

[583] Ibid.

[584] Barbara Crichlow-Shaw, op.cit.

[585] Ibid.

[586] Keith "Grip' Matthews: Telephone discussion, Wednesday, 13 April 2011.

[587] Ibid.

[588] Beresford Hunte, op.cit.

[589] Ibid.

[590] Ibid.

[591] Ibid.

[592] Keith "Grip' Matthews: Pan-Yard discussion, 9 July 2011.

[593] Ibid.

[594] Ibid.

[595] Ibid.

[596] Discussion with Leon Edwards at Pinehaven Gardens, 12 June 2014.

[597] Leon "Smooth' Edwards, op.cit.

[598] Edric Straker: PanYard Discussion, Friday, 1 February 2013.

[599] Leon "Smooth' Edwards, op. cit.

[600] Ibid.

[601] Barbara Crichlow-Shaw, op.cit.

[602] Leon "Smooth' Edwards, op.cit.

[603] Beresford Hunte: Telephone discussion, Sunday, 22 May 2011.

604 Trinidad Guardian, Tuesday, 22 March 1988—"All Stars Loses Catelli Sponsor" by Valentino Singh.
605 Sunday Guardian, 27 March 1988—"The All Stars—Catelli Break Up" by Valentino Singh.
606 Ibid.
607 Ibid.
608 Beresford Hunte: Telephone discussion, Sunday, 22 May 2011.
609 Ibid.
610 Sunday Guardian, March 27, 1988—"The All Stars—Catelli Break Up" by Valentino Singh.
611 Ibid.
612 Ibid.
613 Ibid.
614 Leon "Smooth' Edwards: Interview 20 July 2011. He indicated that the name was changed because they became aware that "the whole of All Stars know we going and call the band, "Phoenix".
615 Trinidad Guardian: Saturday, 26 March 1998—"Despers gives support to All Stars Steelband".
616 Ibid.
617 Trinidad Guardian, Wednesday, 30 March 1988—"MP calls for Written Contracts for Bands."
618 Barbara Crichlow-Shaw, op.cit.
619 Express: Monday, 5 February 1996 "The Smooth Operator" by Marcia Noel.
620 Ibid.
621 Ibid.
622 Ibid.
623 Ibid.
624 Ibid.
625 Leon "Smooth' Edwards: Interview at East Grove, 20 July 2011.
626 John "Poison' Douglas, op, cit. 1 February 2011.
627 Ibid.
628 Dalton Narine, "Masters Of The Classics", Sunday Guardian, 19 February 1984.

629 All Stars Newsletter, Issue No.4, August 2003.
630 Keith "Grip' Matthews: Telephone discussion on Tuesday, 8 February 2011.
631 All Stars Newsletter, Issue No.11, March 2004.
632 Pan Yard Discussion in 2003.
633 Ibid.
634 All Stars Newsletter, Issue No.6, October 2003.
635 Pan Yard Discussion, 2003.
636 Ibid.
637 This strategy was first articulated by Bukka Rennie at his Printery in Tunapuna in the course of discussion with Beresford Hunte, Willis and Sandy.
638 Discussion with Beresford Hunte, op.cit.
639 Ibid.
640 Ibid.
641 Note from Roy Regis, 23 November 2017.
642 Ibid.
643 Trinidad Guardian: Wednesday, 31 August 1988.
644 Ibid.
645 Ibid.
646 Beresford Hunte: Discussion at the panyard.
647 Keith "Grip' Matthews: Discussion at Pan-Yard, Saturday, 9 July 2011.
648 Clive Telemaque: Telephone discussion, 26 July 2011.
649 Clive Telemaque: Telephone discussion, 1 March 2015.
650 My personal reading of Berry's position at that point.
651 Keith "Grip' Matthews: Discussion at Pan-Yard, 9 July 2011.
652 Reds Collins: Interview at Pan Yard, op.cit.
653 All Stars Newsletter, Issue No.9, January 2004.
654 Ibid.
655 That is a stated opinion of one Calvin "Sticko' Lewis, ex-national football player
656 All Stars Newsletter, Issue No.9, January 2004.
657 Red Collins: Pan Yard discussion.
658 Discussion with Richard "Fats' Quarless at Sammy's Bar, Tunapuna, August 2010.

[659] Discussion with Smooth Edwards: June 2014 at Pinehaven Gardens.
[660] Tony Guy: Explanation of his input to 1993 Panorama performance.
[661] "MAGIC' FROM ALL STARS: Weekend Heat, Saturday, 27 February 1993, by David Fraser.
[662] All Stars Newsletter, Issue No.9, January 2004.
[663] Reds Collins: Pan Yard Discussion—Feb 2012.
[664] Trinidad Guardian: "All Stars' treasury of losses", 8 March 1995.
[665] All Stars Newsletter, Issue No.16, August 2004.
[666] Ibid.
[667] Beresford Hunte: Panyard discussion.
[668] All Stars Newsletter; Issue No.9, January 2004.
[669] Express: Saturday March 2, 1996—"All Stars: Fit to be Winners" by Terry Joseph.
[670] Discussion with Beresford Hunte, 23 March 2011.
[671] Ibid.
[672] Discussion with Beresford Hunte, 2010.
[673] Leon "Smooth' Edwards: Interview at East Grove, 20 July 2011.
[674] Ibid.
[675] Ibid.
[676] Discussion at Pinehaven Gardens, June 2014
[677] All Stars: The History Speaks, Trinidad Guardian, G-Life, Part 1, Thursday, 4 May 2006 by B. Rennie.
[678] T&T Mirror: "Bradley—I'll take Panorama" by Marilyn Joseph, Friday, 20 February 1998.
[679] Ibid.
[680] Ibid.
[681] All Stars: The History Speaks, Trinidad Guardian, G-Life, Part 11, Friday, 5 May 2006 by B. Rennie.
[682] All Stars: The History Speaks, Trinidad Guardian, G-Life, Part 11 Friday, 5 May 2006 by B. Rennie.
[683] Ibid.
[684] Tinika Davis, Facebook Posting, 6 August 2020.
[685] Bukka Rennie, All Stars—The History Speaks, Part 1, Thursday, 4 May 2006.

[686] Ibid. Arnim Smith it is reported made that statement.

[687] In 2007 "Banga" (i.e. deceased Black Earl) produced Jerseys that said : Smooth Take Away the Whip and Shared Licks. Boogsie's tune was titled "Sharing Licks."

[688] "Who is Neville Jules?" by Bukka Rennie.

[689] "Panorama Murdering Silence", Dalton Narine's interview of Raf Robertson, Trinidad Guardian Saturday, 5 March 2011.

[690] Express: Wednesday, 21 May 1997—" A Trinidad All Stars Tribute to Neville Jules—Man of Steel turns 70" by McDonald "Jerry' Serrant.

[691] Ibid.

[692] Newsday: Sunday February 25, 2007 Section A, p. 7.

[693] Discussion with Beresford Hunte.

[694] Ibid.

[695] The Bomb News: "Trinidad All Stars in need of New Management" by Selwyn Carr, Wednesday, September 22, 2010, p. 6.

[696] Leon "Smooth' Edwards: Interview at East Grove, July 20, 2011.

[697] Leon "Smooth' Edwards: Discussion at Pinehaven Gardens, June 2014.

[698] Leon "Smooth' Edwards: Discussion at Pinehaven Gardens, June 2014.

[699] WHO'S **WHO:** Trinidad All Stars at EXPO ZARAGOZA 2008.

[700] Beresford Hunte: Discussion at the Pan Yard.

[701] Web Alexander: 2018 discussion re: his contribution.

[702] T&T Review: Eight of Hearts Concert—All Trumps—7 June 2010, by Orville Wright.

[703] Smooth Edwards: View expressed to Bukka Rennie during the band elections of 2004.

[704] Beresford Hunte: Discussion at the Pan Yard.

[705] Guardian: All Stars performs musical magic at Classical Jewels by Sean Nero, Saturday, November 13, 2010.

[706] Daily Express: All Stars offers Sweet Music by Wayne Bowman, Wednesday, November 10, 2010.

[707] Guardian: All Stars performs Musical Magic, op.cit.

[708] Guardian: All Stars Toasts to Classical Jewels for 2012, by Sean Nero, Friday, November 12, 2010.

[709] Sunday Guardian: Panorama 2011: Sliver Stars Goes For Hat-Trick by Sean Nero, January 16, 2011.

[710] Nigel Williams: Telephone discussion, Wednesday, 8 June 2011.

[711] Yohan Popwell: Telephone discussion, Monday, 23 May 2016.

[712] Barbara Crichlow-Shaw: Interview, op.cit.—She said she admired Reds for those words at the crucial moments. Reds said he took the phrase from a calypso and used it because it worked.

[713] Newsday Section B: "All Stars takes Victory Lap" by Joan Rampersad, Tuesday, 24 May 2011.

[714] Guardian: All Stars Leaves 'em Star-Struck by Pan Buzz, Friday, 11 March 2011.

[715] Guardian: Carnival 2011 Souvenir Edition—"The Return of All Stars."

[716] Ibid.

[717] Trinidad Guardian: "Another Bomb Victory for All Stars", Tuesday, 15 March 2011.

[718] Business Guardian: "Corporate T&T can learn from Trinidad All Stars" Thursday, 2 June 2011.

[719] Sunday Express. Mix. DVD Set details Narell's Work, 11 December 2011, p. 3.

[720] Business Guardian: "Corporate T&T can learn from Trinidad All Stars", op. cit.

[721] When Steel Talks: submission by Dalton Narine: "How Pan (and Neville Jules) saved my Life."

[722] Sunday Guardian: 18 September 2011.

[723] Guardian: All Stars Radiates, Monday, February 13, 2012, Sandra L. Blood.

[724] Ibid.

[725] Dalton Narine: All Stars beats Phase11 by five points—Panorama's Politics of Music—Carnival 2012—Trinidad Guardian, Souvenir Edition.

[726] Sunday Guardian: 6 January 2013, "All Stars out to hold on to Title" by Sean Nero.

[727] When Steel Talk: "Cool Hand Smooth, All Stars Arranger, Bounce and Drive, on Hat-Trick Hunt" by Dalton Narine.

[728] Sunday Guardian: 6 January 2013—"All Stars aiming for hat-trick" by Sean Nero.

[729] "The Making of a Smooth Arranger" by Lynette M. Lashley, Ph.D., Sunday Express, 5 April 2015.

[730] Bukka Rennie: Express newspaper column.

[731] Catholic News: Sunday March 15, 2015, published by Catholic Media Services Ltd, printed Trinidad Express Newspaper Ltd.

[732] Ibid.

[733] Ibid.

[734] Ibid.

[735] Daily Express; Current Affairs, LIFESTYLE, Wednesday, 8 July 2015, p. 1.

[736] Ibid.

[737] Ibid.

[738] Trinidad Guardian: Pan Rises in Trinidad, Friday, 14 August 2015, Life, B9, Pulse by Peter Ray Blood.

[739] Newsday: Taking All Stars to the Top; Section A, Sunday August 16, 2015, by Sharmain Baboolal.

[740] Ibid.

[741] Sunday Guardian: All Stars Leave You with Tabanca; Commentary, 16 August 2015 by Helen Drayton.

[742] Newsday: Thousands hit streets for Pan—Friday, 13 May 2016, by Gary Cardinez.

[743] Trinidad Guardian: Pan Conquers Point—Friday, 13 May 2016, by Peter Ray Blood.

[744] Ibid.

[745] Glenroy Joseph: "Thank you, Trinidad All Stars"- Facebook Post, 14 September 2016, 11:54 am.

[746] Hamilton "Web' Alexander, op.cit.

[747] Reds Collins: Interview, op.cit.

[748] This was clarified by Beresford Hunte. The plaque on the wall of the Bar supports this.

[749] Reds Collins: Interview, op.cit.

[750] See "Internal Controls for Co-operatives" by Nigel Williams ACCA.

[751] Catelli Trinidad All Stars: Proposals 1985-1987—Rejuvenation—Ain't No Stoppin' Us Now!

[752] Ibid.

[753] Ibid.

[754] Projections 88-93, An Insight—developed by Beresford Hunte and Keith Matthews.

[755] Keith Matthews: Panyard discussion, op.cit.

[756] Ainsley Mark; Telephone discussion: August 2011.

[757] Projections 88-93, An Insight, op.cit.

[758] See Affidavit registered by Errol Collins before Leopold McLean, Commissioner of Affidavits, and filed in the Supreme Court of Port-of-Spain on 8 February 1994.

[759] See Certificate of Registration No. C/229/89 signed by Arnim Greaves, Act. Commissioner of for Co-operative Development.

[760] Errol Collins Affidavit, op.cit.

[761] Ibid.

[762] Ibid.

[763] Ibid.

[764] See Private Action—Trespass; Civil Appeal No. 27 of 1994 and High Court Action No. 401 of 1994.

[765] Errol "Reds' Collins: Interview, op.cit.

[766] Keith "Grip' Matthews: Interview at the Panyard, Saturday, 9 July 2011.

[767] Ibid.

[768] Ibid.

[769] Ibid.

[770] Errol "Reds' Collins, op.cit.

[771] Keith "Grip' Matthews op. cit and Errol "Reds' Collins, op.cit.

[772] Errol "Reds' Collins, op.cit.

[773] Keith "Grip' Matthews: op.cit.

[774] Errol Collins: Panyard Interview, op.cit.

[775] Ibid.

[776] Keith "Grip' Matthews: Panyard Interview, op.cit.

[777] Trinidad All Stars Steel Orchestra: Source and Application of Funds, June '87-July '88.

[778] Colin Bishop: Written Submission, op.cit.

[779] Colin Bishop, op.cit.

[780] John Douglas: interview at COPOS, op.cit.

[781] Keith "Grip' Matthews: Interview at Panyard, op.cit.

[782] Colin Bishop: Written Submission, op.cit.

[783] Nigel Williams, ACCA: Statement of Project, Internal Controls for Cooperatives.

[784] Director of Surveys: Memo to Director, Town and Country Planning, dated Feb. 2, 1990.

[785] Beresford Hunte: Telephone discussion, Wednesday, 24 August 2011.

[786] Ibid.

[787] Trinidad All Stars Steel Orchestra Co-operative Society: Report of Board of Directors, Nov 1989-April 1991.

[788] Ibid.

[789] Neal and Massy Trinidad All Stars Steel Orchestra Co-operative Society Ltd: Report of the Second Annual General Meeting.

[790] Ministry of Industry, Enterprise and Tourism, Co-operative Development Division, Audit Section; Audited Accounts of Trinidad All Stars Steel Orchestra Co-operative Society Ltd 1989-1990.

[791] TASSO Co-operative Society Ltd—Report of Board of Directors—Nov 1989–April 1991.

[792] Report of 2nd Annual General Meeting, 23 May 1991.

[793] Ibid.

[794] Audited Accounts Sept. 1989 to June 30, 1990 and Unaudited Balance Sheet as at Nov. 30, 1992.

[795] Trinidad All Stars Steel Orchestra Co-operative Society Ltd: Bye Laws, Item 10 of Application for Registration, approved by Commissioner for Co-operative Development.

[796] Nigel Williams: Notes: Internal Controls for Co-operatives, op.cit.

[797] Trinidad All Stars Steel Orchestra: Draft Constitution, July 2004.

[798] Ibid.

[799] Ibid.

[800] Ibid.

[801] Ibid.

[802] Ibid.

[803] Ibid.

[804] Trinidad All Stars Steel Orchestra: "Proposals for a Code of Ethics for Officers".
[805] Ibid.
[806] Ibid.
[807] Workshop Group: Code of Ethics, Rights and Responsibilities of Members.
[808] Jackie McKell: Telephone discussion—Thursday, 8 September 2011.
[809] Web Alexander: Discussion after his reading of the manuscript—March 2018.
[810] Trinidad All Stars Newsletter, Issue No.17, September 2004.
[811] Trinidad All Stars Newsletter, Issue No.18, October 2004.
[812] Telephone discussion with Kenneth Scoot of Diego Martin.
[813] Telephone discussion with Darryl Joseph.
[814] Denise Riley: Written submission, ob.Cit.
[815] Ibid.
[816] Ibid.
[817] Trinibagopan.com—Neville Jules Speaks on Pan—26 May 2007, posted June11, 2007
[818] Oliver Joseph: Discussion at Panyard, Monday, 11 July 2011.
[819] Ibid.
[820] Discussion with Jules at Diego Martin, op.cit.
[821] When Steel Talks: Interview with Neville Jules, 2003.
[822] Audra Preddie: Telephone discussion.
[823] A. *Myrna* Nurse, op.cit. Albert Jones Story, p. 63. Jones indicates that Ellie had more ideas than other tuners about handling metal since he was a machinist, but that Ellie got involved **long after** others had started the process.
[824] Shannon Dudley: Music From Behind The Bridge; Oxford University Press, 2008, p. 278.
[825] William King indicated that while playing mas with St. James Sufferers he observed Southern—Symphony in the vicinity of the POS Railway fighting to push the platform that had broken down.
[826] A. *Myrna* Nurse, op. cit.—Albert Jones Story, p. 83.
[827] Ibid, Othello Molineaux's Story, p. 262.
[828] See Howard Campbell's "Remembering Lynn Taitt' pub. Jan 27, 2010 and Jim Dooley's "Crossing Boundaries and Borders—A Lifetime in Music'.

829 http://en.wikipedia.org/wiki/Lynn_Taitt; Biography.
830 www.Tallawah.com/articles-reviews/lynn-taitt/ A tribute to Nearlin "Lynn' Taitt.
831 Ibid.
832 Ibid.
833 Ibid. Interview with Kenneth Bilby.
834 Ibid.
835 A. *Myrna* Nurse, op.cit. Philbert Solomon Story, p. 249.
836 Ibid, 251.
837 Ibid, 233.
838 Jerry Serrant, op.cit. p. 81.
839 Ibid. Jerry Serrant, p. 81.
840 Ibid, Leroy Ali Williams's Story, pp. 275 and 280.
841 A. *Myrna* Nurse, op.cit. Philbert Solomon Story, p. 247.
842 UNESCO: Heritage Sites, Cultural Criteria—http//en.wikipedia.org/wiki/World Heritage.
843 Beresford Hunte: Panyard discussion.
844 Newsday Section C, Monday, 20 September 2010, p. 7.
845 Newsday's BUSINESS DAY—Thursday, 25 August 2011—"Developing a Cultural Industry" by Miranda La Rose.
846 Ibid.
847 Rubadiri Victor—"Battle for Soul of the Republic"—Daily Express—Friday, 26 August 2011.
848 Dr. Keith Nurse: "Cutting-Edge Entrepreneurship"—Guardian Business Supplement, Thursday, 5 May 2011.
849 Business Guardian: An All Stars Affair, June 2012. Week Two, p. 37.
850 Ibid.